Spes Scotorum: Hope of Scots

Spes Scotorum
Hope of Scots

Saint Columba, Iona and Scotland

Edited by
DAUVIT BROUN
and
THOMAS OWEN CLANCY

T&T CLARK
EDINBURGH

T&T CLARK LTD
59 GEORGE STREET
EDINBURGH EH2 2LQ
SCOTLAND

www.tandtclark.co.uk

First published 1999

ISBN 0 567 08682 8

British Library Cataloguing-in-Publication Data
A catalogue record for this book is available from the British Library

Typeset by Waverley Typesetters, Galashiels
Printed and bound in Great Britain by MPG Books Ltd, Bodmin

Os mutorum,
lux cecorum,
pes clausorum,
porrige
lapsis manum.
Firma vanum
et insanum
corrige.
O Columba spes Scotorum
nos tuorum meritorum
interventu beatorum
fac consortes angelorum.
Alleluia.

Mouth of the dumb,
light of the blind,
foot of the lame,
to the fallen
stretch out your hand.
Strengthen the senseless,
restore the mad.
O Columba, hope of Scots,
by your merits' mediation,
make us companions
of the blessed angels.
Alleluia.

from the *Inchcolm Antiphoner*

Contents

Part III. The Columban legacy

List of Illustrations

Preface

THE year 1997 was a hectic one for church groups, councils, local history societies, the media – and also scholars in various fields – as they celebrated in diverse fashions important religious centenaries. The fact that it was the 800th anniversary of the Glasgow Fair seems to have passed without a party, but key dates in the careers of saints did receive more attention. St Martin of Tours, one of the fathers of western monasticism, died 11 November 397, though his celebrations were rather more subdued in Scotland than those of St Ninian, whose foundation of Whithorn is linked in tradition (alas, a late and unlikely tradition) to the death of Martin. St Augustine of Canterbury, who arrived in Kent bringing Pope Gregory the Great's mission of conversion to the Anglo-Saxons in 597 was celebrated more in England than north of the border. Without doubt, the saint most widely and perhaps on occasion garishly celebrated in 1997 was Columba, Colm Cille, Calum Cille, whose death on the 9th of June in 597 was marked, we are told, by great storms which kept visitors away from his island monastery on Iona, allowing his monastic family to mourn him in quiet and on their own. June 1997, described by Mairi MacArthur in one of the essays in this collection, was an altogether more fraught occasion, complete with dignitaries arriving by helicopter and live televised religious services on the island. The year as a whole included the naming of stamps, tartans and locomotives after the saint, as well as pageants and documentaries.

It was always going to be a busy year for scholarship as well. Several major conferences were held to mark the Columban year, some of them deliberately on non-Columban themes. Academics who normally skulk in obscurity were in heavy demand at parish study groups and on radio talk-shows; for some, the round of talks began in early January and ended in mid-December. Amongst all this, the Scottish Catholic Historical Association played its part, and this volume represents the fruit of their year's labour in Columba's overflowing vineyard.

The Scottish Catholic Historical Association has always been dedicated to sound scholarship made accessible to the general public, since the launch of its journal, *The Innes Review*, in 1950. The SCHA marked the 1400th anniversary of one of the 'apostles of Scotland' in print and in open forum. A series of articles were commissioned on Columban themes, and these appeared in the two issues of *The Innes Review* during the year. In June, two days before the actual feast of St Columba, a conference was held by them in St George's School for Girls: a well-attended, leisurely day, which left the audience filled with high-class scholarship and strawberry tarts.

From that original diptych of journal and conference, we have fashioned this volume of essays to commemorate the 1400th feast of St Columba. Five of these essays appeared earlier in *The Innes Review*, although most of these have been substantially revised. Two essays are versions of papers given at the 7th June conference. Two are new essays, specially written for this volume by speakers at that conference, and one is a newly commissioned piece.

The study of St Columba, of his monastery on Iona and its artistic and literary productions, of the later history of his monastic family, and the influence of Iona on the religious and secular history of Scotland takes in many disciplines, many perspectives. In the talks during the year and in this volume, we have tried to be representative of at least some of these different fields.

The book is divided into three sections. In the first, historical aspects of Columba and Iona are explored, utilising the tools of several specialisms: those of the documentary historian (Bannerman and Broun), the literary and religious historian (Clancy), and the onomastician (Taylor). These four studies reveal the far-reaching influence of Columba and his foundations on Scotland's history, shaping its religious attitudes, providing emblems of battle and patrons in the midst of war and disease, helping to lay the foundations of its political structures and its own written self-identity, and shaping the landscape we walk and drive through, with its legacy written on maps and road signs.

The second section explores the written world of Adomnán, the biographer of Columba, and his successor as abbot of Iona and head of Columba's monastic family. Although we have only two long Latin prose works from his hand, Adomnán's deep learning and attractive voice make these works ones on which much labour could be expended. Here, essays try to understand the varying techniques of his exegetical method and his subtle, layered narratives (O'Loughlin and O'Reilly), and study his mental maps of Scotland, encoded in his *Life of Columba*, and his views on religious structure, exploring furth of these to examine the mix of monastic and pastoral in the Columban familia in Scotland (Márkus).

The final section deals with the Columban legacy in the modern world. That legacy consists of the tangible and the intangible, and all three writers are interested in how people over the past century have related to that legacy, what they have chosen to do with it, how they have chosen to interpret and celebrate it. O'Sullivan surveys over a century of archaeology on Iona, and its results, asking some critical questions in the meantime about how we have approached the finite resource of the monastery's concrete remains, and how we should address their future. MacArthur casts a quizzical eye over the two centenary celebrations in 1897 and in 1997, and considers how the local community on Iona did, or did not, feature in them. And finally, Meek looks at the use and abuse of saints, and especially of St Columba, in the late twentieth century.

There are several other aspects of the Columban legacy we would like to have had represented, but circumstances left it otherwise: legal, artistic and musical aspects. The last demands some comment. Although we know comparatively little about music on early Iona, Scotland is fortunate to possess an important manuscript of the fourteenth century from the island of Inchcolm, dedicated to Columba, in the Firth of Forth. This manuscript preserves offices for the feast of St Columba, and the music has recently been recorded and received several performances, to justified acclaim. One of the scholars who was foremost in the rediscovery of and interpretation of this manuscript, the *Inchcolm Antiphoner*, was Dr Isobel Preece, née Woods, a musicologist in the University of Newcastle. She was to have addressed the SCHA conference, and contributed to the volume. She died, suddenly and still young, in January 1997. The words which introduce this volume, from the Inchcolm Antiphoner, are printed here in her memory.

If one feature of the year's scholarship stands out in the mind, it is the way in which, over and again, scholars returned to the fact that, though we were celebrating Columba, it was always and first to the other abbot of Iona, to Adomnán, that we had to turn. He is the first lens through which we usually view the saint, and the best and most eloquent. He is a constantly surprising and endlessly rewarding writer, a historian, exegete and a storyteller. But he was also the pivotal figure in Iona's revival of importance in the late seventh century, through his writing, his diplomacy and his legal and religious zeal. To him belongs one of the most important anniversaries celebrated in 1997: the 1300th anniversary of the enactment of his Law of the Innocents, a law guaranteed by over ninety churchmen and kings throughout Ireland and Scotland. The law protected non-combatants from violence, and provided special care for women: perhaps the first law to legislate against violence towards women, ranging from the verbal to the brutally physical, from domestic fights to battlefield injuries and workplace accidents. It was a comprehensive, religiously inspired, and international law. Adomnán combined his scholarship with a zeal for justice, and a flair for administration and diplomacy.

And so, although these essays represent a celebration of the legacy of Columba in Scotland, they also represent the latest stage in a process to which Adomnán, as his biographer and successor, was the most notable and most approachable early contributor: the unfolding legend of the saint, Columba. Under Adomnán's patronage, this volume is dedicated to the memory of another scholar and religious man, who balanced Dominican administrative duties with kick-starting the scholarly and public enterprise which is the Scottish Catholic Historical Association and *The Innes Review*. He was its first editor, and contributed numerous important articles. Alongside this he worked for and with the poor, with prisoners and addicts, with the outcast.

The editors of this book, who are also the present and future editors of *The Innes Review* and in that very small sense (and, we confess, in that alone) his *comarbai*, dedicate this volume to the memory of Antony Ross OP, an echo of St Adomnán in our time.

THOMAS OWEN CLANCY
DAUVIT BROUN

23 September 1998
The Feast of St Adomnán

PART I

Columba, Iona and the making of Scotland

1

Columba, Adomnán and the cult of saints in Scotland

Thomas Owen Clancy

THE cult of the saints is one of the defining attributes of the Middle Ages. The ancient world had only foreshadowings, at the most, of the perception of the blessed dead which would lead to those images we associate with the medieval world: shrines, relics, and pilgrimages. Peter Brown has vibrantly demonstrated the cultural wrench that the cult of saints presented for the ancient world, as it grew into a strange and personal relationship between the living and the previously shunned dead.[1] Likewise, one can begin to sense the end of the medieval world in the increasingly humanist approach to saints and saints' Lives during the fourteenth and fifteenth centuries, an attitude which would develop in the Reformation into outright hostility towards all aspects of the cult of saints.[2] Our own relationship with saints is almost certainly marked by this humanist distrust of the miraculous and otherworldly. Saints now are, by and large, holy – sometimes even nice – predecessors to be emulated; they are the stuff of morally uplifting anecdotes, rather than bedside companions, friends in need, or powerful patrons in the kingdom of heaven.[3]

[1] Peter Brown, *The Cult of the Saints*; for a recent survey of work on early medieval saints' cults, see Geary, *Living with the Dead in the Middle Ages*, 9–29.

[2] See Vitz, 'From the oral to the written in medieval and renaissance saints' Lives'.

[3] One can sense the shift from intercessor to tourist attraction in the reaction of the Anglican Bishop of St Davids to the news that the presumed bones of David embedded in the cathedral's walls were 600 years too recent: 'We are not interested in the cult of relics in the Church of Wales. What is

In the festal year of 1997, I wonder just how much of the celebration invoked Columba, rather than patting him, historically, on the back as being a good Christian or Scot or Irishman; or how many that year prayed, as they did sometime in the early fourteenth century on the island of Inchcolm:

> Mouth of the dumb,
> light of the blind,
> foot of the lame,
> to the fallen stretch out your hand.
> Strengthen the senseless,
> restore the mad.
> O Columba, hope of Scots,
> by your merits' mediation,
> make us companions
> of the blessed angels.[4]

The exploration of the cult of saints in its many facets has, in recent years, contributed significantly to our understanding of the thought-world of the Middle Ages. Scholars such as Peter Brown, Caroline Walker Bynum and Patrick Geary have opened an often alien but always fascinating world for us in their sympathetic studies of the relationship between living and dead in the Middle Ages, of the presence of the holy dead, and the medieval understanding of the body.[5] In Scotland we do not have

important is that St Davids is still a place of pilgrimage in the 20th century.' Rt Revd Huw Jones, quoted in *The Scotsman*, 1 March 1997, p. 3. On these matters, see further Meek and MacArthur below.

[4] *Os mutorum, lux cecorum, pes clausorum, porrige lapsis manum. Firma vanum et insanum corrige. O Columba spes Scotorum nos tuorum meritorum interventu beatorum fac consortes angelorum. Alleluia.* From the 'Inchcolm Antiphoner', Edinburgh University Library MS 211.iv; translation by Gilbert Márkus in Clancy, *The Triumph Tree*, 317–19. On the Antiphoner, see McRoberts, 'A catalogue of Scottish medieval liturgical books and fragments', 51. For a partial edition (and performance) of the Columban material, and discussion of the provenance, see the late Isobel Preece's programme notes to the Capella Nova CD, *Columba, Most Holy of Saints*, and for discussion, Purser, *Scotland's Music*, 39–48; Woods, '"Our Awin Scottis Use"'.

[5] Brown, *Cult of Saints*, and *idem*, *Society and the Holy*; Bynum, *Fragmentation and Redemption*, and *eadem*, *The Resurrection of the Body*; Geary, *Living with the Dead* and *Furta Sacra*. See also, on saints' cults,

the wealth of artistic and documentary material on which such scholars have based their work, and material pertaining to this side of the saints is still, alas, often approached with some distaste or circumspection. Much more work has been put into establishing the historical parameters of historically dubious saints than has been spent on the probably more fruitful task of understanding how medieval churchmen and lay-people related to, publicised, and dealt with these saints.[6] But I think it is possible, and in this context appropriate, to go some way towards understanding the development of aspects of the cult of the saints in Scotland, and in the Gaelic world generally, by examining the material, much of it relating to Scotland, belonging to the cult of St Columba. Some of the attributes of this cult, and that of other saints, are familiar from elsewhere, but some seem to me to be distinctive to the Gaelic world, arising out of particular social and cultural circumstances.[7]

I should make it clear that this study focuses not on hagiographical texts in themselves. For Columba we are comparatively well-served both in terms of texts and critical studies of them, especially since the publication of Máire Herbert's superb work on Columban hagiography.[8] The centenary celebrations look likely to bring a new crop of research into the Columban granary. Rather, my interest is with the relationship between the living and the blessed dead, and hagiographical texts in the Gaelic world

---

Van Dam, *Saints and their Miracles in Late Antique Gaul* and Abou-El-Haj, *The Medieval Cult of Saints*, esp. chapter 1. Peter Brown's comments on the Gaelic world are stimulating, but somewhat disappointing: *The Rise of Western Christendom*, esp. 198–206.

[6] Ninian is a case in point: most work to date has focused on his historicity, e.g. MacQueen, *St Nynia*; Brooke, *Wild Men and Holy Places*; Hill, *Whithorn and St Ninian*. None of these dwells on the better documented cult aspects of the saint's dossier, though in his eighth-century Life and his Older Scots Life Ninian has probably the most interesting and informative collections of posthumous miracles, demonstrating his relationship with local communities, of any Scottish saint. See Clancy 'Scottish saints and national identities'.

[7] For a survey of Irish work on hagiography, and saints' cults generally, see Herbert, 'Hagiography'.

[8] Herbert, *Iona, Kells and Derry*; *The Life of St. Columba*, Reeves, *Saint Adamnan*; Anderson, *Adomnán*; Sharpe, *Adomnán*.

have comparatively little to tell us about this (Adomnán's *Life of Columba* being an exception to the rule). Although saints' cults had clearly caught hold in the British Isles long before the seventh century, certain aspects of the cult of saints remained de-emphasised, in the literature at least. Thus, in the earliest saints' Lives which we have (from the seventh century) there is a notable lack of posthumous miracles, little discussion of relics, and little sense of the meaning of the continuing patronage of the founder-saint, whether it be Brigit or Patrick, or more obscure saints.[9]

This is not to say that aspects of the cult of saints were not present, and it is certainly not to say that what the few incidents in these lives dealing with the relationship between the faithful and the saint after his death tell us is not important. The brief section of posthumous miracles in Cogitosus' *Life of Brigit* is instructive in its focus on the ornate shrine of Brigit and Bishop Conlaed as the source of miracles (a description of the early development of a saint's cult around a shrine which may have been less unusual in Ireland than literary sources suggest). It is also noteworthy for the extremely attenuated nature of the other main focus of her posthumous miracles, a huge millstone which she had, after death, helped the prior of Kildare to find, and which was later placed near the gate of the monastery where, we are told, 'it cures diseases of the faithful who touch it'.[10] That the focus of her power was a secondary relic is not surprising in a Gaelic context, and it is in keeping with the orientation of her miracles when living that this relic was connected with agriculture and the provision of food.[11]

Cogitosus shows us, then, that by the seventh century Brigit's shrine and relics had an active cult – that she was sought for help by her monks and by lay-people also. It is significant, though, that this early dossier of her posthumous achievements was not restated by later hagiographers who, despite using Cogitosus

[9] Concerning the scarcity of posthumous miracles, it should be noted that Máire Herbert has recently sounded a cautious note: 'Hagiography', 89.

[10] Cogitosus, *Vita Brigitae*, chs 31–2; translation in Connolly, 'Cogitosus's *Life of St Brigit*', 24–7.

[11] Though note the *Moelblatha*, a miraculous millstone on Iona said in the preface to *Altus Prosator* in *Leabhar Breac* to have been blessed by Columba. See Reeves, *Adamnan*, xcvi-xcvii.

closely, did not repeat these miracles. Local, native saints were developing strong cults, but hagiographers seemed less interested in recording their characteristics.

A number of seventh-century documents show us that the cult of saints and the use of relics had come to Ireland in the form of relics of the martyrs. It may be that some had come over with early missionaries, and it has been suggested that places holding such relics might be indicated by the use of the term *basilica* found in a number of place-names in Ireland.[12] The letter written in *ca* 632/3 by the southern Irish churchman Cummian to Ségéne, the abbot of Iona, and the hermit Beccán, trying to convince them to change their method of dating Easter, calls up by way of evidence a delegation of Irishmen who went to Rome around 630 and found people of many nations there celebrating Easter on the same day, though different from that of the Irish. The authority of the Roman method of dating is evoked by reference to the miracles wrought by the 'relics of the holy martyrs and books' which they brought back with them: 'We have seen with our eyes a girl completely blind have her eyes opened by these relics, and the paralysed walk, and many demons ejected.'[13]

Wherever we find relics of the early martyrs in seventh-century documents it is by way of authority and power: they seem to mark churches with a stamp of authenticity. That is what the *Liber Angeli* suggests of Armagh, certainly:

> Furthermore, it ought to be venerated in honour of the principal martyrs Peter and Paul, Stephen, Lawrence and the others. How much more should it be venerated and diligently honoured by all because of the holy admiration for a gift to us, beyond praise above other things, that in it, by a secret dispensation, is preserved the most holy blood of Jesus Christ the redeemer of the human race in a sacred linen cloth, together with relics of the saints in the southern church, where there rest the bodies of holy men from abroad who had come with Patrick from across the sea, and of other just men![14]

[12] Doherty, 'The use of relics in early Ireland'; 'The basilica in early Ireland'. On relics, see also the massively detailed, but unstratified survey in Lucas, 'The social role of relics and reliquaries'.

[13] Walsh and Ó Cróinín, *Cummian's Letter* De Controversia Paschali, 92–5.

[14] Bieler, *Patrician Texts*, 186–9; cf. Doherty, 'Use of relics', 93.

Tírechán, in his notes on Patrick written after 684, shows Patrick distributing authority to his disciples with the relics of martyrs. Two powerful, possibly rival churches are said to have been given such relics by Patrick: the old foundation of Baslick (*Basilica Sanctorum*) in Connacht, and Dun Severick. To one he gave 'a portion of the relics of Peter and Paul, Stephen and Lawrence which are in Armagh', to the other 'a portion of the relics of Peter and Paul and others and a veil to protect the relics'. It is unlikely that Armagh had such relics before the first half of the seventh century, and Tírechán may here be reflecting the power-relationships of his own time, but it is significant that he does so by means of these relics. As Charles Doherty points out, 'Armagh would appear to have used these relics in a manner similar to the papacy in an attempt to bring churches directly under her wing'.[15]

Tírechán's notes suggest that secondary relics connected with Patrick, such as chalices and patens, were thought of in much the same manner. Patrick's alleged distribution of such objects as these, as well as writing tablets and 'alphabets' (perhaps religious instructions)[16] demonstrate, for Tírechán, the authority of the founding saint. Fortified with such objects he goes into the west: 'Patrick took with him across the Shannon fifty bells, fifty patens, fifty chalices, altar stones, books of the law, books of the Gospels, and left them in the new places.' In one case he even gives his tooth to a bishop 'as a relic'.[17]

The pyrotechnic miracles associated with Patrick's body in Muirchú's Life of the saint illustrate well this association of authority with relics.[18] These miracles of power are devoted to preventing the saint's body from being used or disturbed, and to preventing fighting over it. Muirchú was firmly aware of, and perhaps somewhat embarrassed by, the lack of corporeal remains of its supposed founder in Armagh, but was equally aware of the potency such relics would have – power worth going to war for.

No doubt the secondary relics of Patrick, as well as those of the martyrs, were associated with healing, and the faithful prayed

[15] *Ibid.*; Bieler, *Patrician Texts*, 122, 160.

[16] See Márkus, 'What were Patrick's Alphabets?'; and for further discussion of the symbolic meaning of *elementa*, see O'Reilly, below.

[17] Bieler, *Patrician Texts*, 122–3, 158–9 (*in reliquias*).

[18] *Ibid.*, 120–3.

at their shrines. But neither Muirchú nor Tírechán tells us of such things. Their interest in shrines is the way in which they demonstrated vested authority, the *situation* of miraculous power. Tírechán gives us one other sight of the use of these relics: a nun, taking up residence on land near a church, swears a treaty of concord with that church on its founder-saint's relics.[19] The binding of earthly authority was one of the saint's powers.

In Armagh the locus of that binding authority was twofold: the shrine of the martyrs, and the insignia of Patrick, no doubt secondary relics of the sort which we later know as the Bachall Ísu and Patrick's bell. The fines levied for insult of these insignia, and the fact that later in the Middle Ages the Bachall Ísu was a binder of treaties *par excellence*, suggests that the honour and status of Armagh resided also in these relics.[20]

John Bannerman has shown quite clearly that the relics of Columba were to come, from the eighth century on, to represent the authority and honour of the *comarba*, the heir of Columba, and the Columban *familia* in general.[21] Iona in its earliest century and a half gives us a somewhat different picture of the development of the cult of saints. Before we turn there, however, it is as well to remember Iona's other close neighbours, Northumbria and the other English kingdoms. There, too, we witness in the seventh century two strands in the evolving cult of saints. It is most strongly present in the relics of martyrs and apostles, brought to the English church by missionaries, or sent by popes, or collected by English churchmen. Some such, like Acca, bishop of Hexham, and indeed Wilfrid his predecessor, were avid collectors of relics. The way in which both the sending of relics occurred, and the motives behind the collecting, suggests that, in common with Armagh and Ireland, continental relics were a mark of authority.[22]

At the same time, the English kingdoms were celebrating their own saints. Most prominent among them in the seventh century was the Northumbrian king, Oswald. His death as a martyr may

[19] *Ibid.*, 140–3.

[20] Doherty, 'Use of relics', 93; Lucas, 'Relics and reliquaries', 13–14.

[21] Bannerman, '*Comarba Coluim Chille*'; see also discussion in Ó Floinn, '*Insignia Columbae* I'.

[22] *HE* i.29–30, iii.29, v.20; *The Life of Bishop Wilfrid,* chs 5, 33, 55.

have given his cult the early impetus of association with the other martyrs. Certainly we know that his seventh-century cult involved many secondary relics: the cross he set up before his first battle, the stake on which his head was set, the ground into which his blood had soaked, as well as Oswald's hand and arm. This cult even reached Ireland, according to Bede, who tells of an Irishman cured during the great plague of 664 by a chip from the stake which held Oswald's head, dipped in water and given him by an English monk.[23] Adomnán, who visited the Northumbrian court of Oswald's nephew, Aldfrith, would no doubt have been aware of this cult, and it is interesting that one of the first posthumous miracles he records of Columba is one relating to Oswald.

Bede, in common with other Northumbrian authors, is more interested than Irish hagiographers in the posthumous miracles of the saints.[24] Indeed, he tells of the relics and shrines of certain Gaelic saints, such as the healing power of the post Áedán, first bishop of Lindisfarne was leaning against when he died, and of Fursa's shrine in Peronne. From Bede we know that Colmán divided up the relics of Áedán, taking some back to Iona with him when he left Lindisfarne after the Synod of Whitby.[25] The Lives of Cuthbert and Wilfrid both demonstrate the interest in the continued power of the holy man after death, and it is as well to remember this predilection when we consider the posthumous miracles of Columba recounted by Adomnán and their purpose.

My examination of the cult of St Columba begins, however, with another – and in some ways more important – event celebrated in 1997: the enactment in 697 at the Synod of Birr of *Lex Innocentium*, later called the Law of Adomnán, which protected non-combatants – women, clerics and children – from violence, with a later emphasis on the protection of women. The Law was signed by some fifty-one of the kings of Ireland and northern Britain, including the Pictish king, and forty of the leading

[23] *HE* iii.2, 6, 9–13, iv.14. On the cult of Oswald, see Stancliffe and Cambridge, ed., *Oswald*.

[24] For examples concerning Wilfrid, see *The Life of Bishop Wilfrid*, chs 66–7.

[25] *HE* iii.17, 19, 26.

churchmen of the Gaelic world.[26] It is a feat of international diplomacy, and should be celebrated alike in Geneva and Helsinki as in Birr. But I am interested not so much in the historical and political nature of the Law as in the way its framer, Adomnán, ninth abbot of Iona and best known as the author of the *Life of Saint Columba*, used the saints in the enforcement of the law.

The text of the Law is complicated, and as we have it it is a product of the Irish monastery of Raphoe, possibly in the late tenth or early eleventh century. Nonetheless it contains a number of earlier strata, including the signatory list (which has been shown to date from 697) and the details of the law itself and its enforcement.[27] One casualty of the text's composition in a monastery claiming Adomnán as its patron is St Columba: he is not mentioned once in the text, and has surely been written out in order to enhance the reputation of Raphoe and its patron saint. I have no doubt that initially Adomnán leaned on Columba as patron of his law, rather than on his own authority alone.

But not all saints have been written out. Immediately following the signatory list of kings and churchmen, we are told that Adomnán engaged the saints as guarantors of his law as well:

> The holy churches of Ireland, together with Adomnán, have also besought God with the orders of Heaven and the saints of the earth, that whosoever shall break the Law of Adomnán, both lay-men and clerics, whoever shall not claim it, and shall not fulfill it to the best of his power, and shall not levy it from every one, both chieftain and church: his life may be short with suffering and dishonour, without any of their offspring attaining Heaven or earth. Adomnán has also set down an order of malediction for them, to wit, a psalm for every day up to twenty days, and an apostle or a noble saint for every day to be invoked with it.[28]

The list of the saints which follows is intriguing, if one considers this to be an element created by Adomnán: alongside the apostles come Stephen, Ambrose, Gregory, Martin, Paul the Hermit, and,

[26] Text and translation in Meyer, *Cáin Adomnáin*; for recent translation, Márkus, *Adomnán's 'Law of the Innocents'*. Máirín Ní Dhonnchadha's edition is forthcoming. Commentary in Ryan, 'The *Cáin Adomnáin*'; Ní Dhonchadha, 'The guarantor list of *Cáin Adomnáin*, 697'; *eadem*, 'The *Lex Innocentium*'.

[27] Ní Dhonnchadha, 'Guarantor list'.

[28] *CA*, §§31–2.

strikingly, George. Gregory the Great's writings, the *Life of Martin*, the *Life of Anthony* with Paul the Hermit in it, were all sources for Adomnán's *Life of Columba* and, as we shall see, Adomnán elsewhere demonstrates considerable interest in St George as well.[29] These holy dead, the fathers of the church, are to be equal guarantors and potent enforcers of the Law. The later portion of the text also invokes saints as sureties, alongside the sun, moon and the elements. Legally, then, the Law charts interesting ground, revealing the saints as participants in the proper procedures of earthly society, able to take on the responsibilities of suretyship and enforcement.[30]

Such aspects are all the more emphasised in the later history of Adomnán's Law. In 727 the Law was renewed, accompanied by a circuit of Adomnán's own relics.[31] This is the first mention in the annals of the tradition of *commotatio*, the touring of a saint's relics in order to bind the saint's law and extract the due tribute. Indeed, Adomnán's is the first in a series of saints' laws enacted between church and secular leaders and relying heavily, it would seem, on the power of the saints and their relics for their effectiveness. Such laws include those of Patrick, of Dar-Í, and the 'Law of Columba', renewed frequently in the eighth century, the details of which are unknown. Máire Herbert has noted the active collaboration of Iona abbots and Uí Néill kings of Tara in the promulgation of this law, and the context of famine, disease and social unrest during which it was enforced, and has also pointed to the use of relic-circuits for the purpose of peace-making.[32]

The later text of the Law of Adomnán also presents its protagonist, Adomnán, as a frightening figure, capable of fasting and seemingly even dying in order to extract from God a law to protect women.[33] Moreover, he is presented as a vindictive and

[29] Clancy and Márkus, *Iona*, 213–19; *DLS*, 110–17.

[30] On the suretyship of supernatural elements, gods and God, see Stacey, *The Road to Judgment*, 199–221, though rather surprisingly she fails to discuss the role of saints in such transactions.

[31] AU 727.5.

[32] Hughes, *Church in Early Irish Society*, 167–9; Herbert, *Iona, Kells and Derry*, 60–6; for the Law of Dar-Í, see AU 813.8, 826.11 and see Ó Riain, 'A misunderstood annal'.

[33] *CA*, §§11–15; cf. Melia, 'Law and the shamanic saint'.

effective sheriff, his bell potent in cursing recalcitrant kings and their offspring, and this characterisation is continued in the tenth-century Life of Adomnán.[34]

Although Columba seems to have been written out of the text of the Law as it stands, Adomnán's reliance on Columba's power to guarantee the Law is made all the more likely by a series of miracles recounted by him in the *Life of Columba* which draw on the themes of the Law. Whether the Life anticipated the Law or reinforced it remains uncertain, since the date of the *Life* is still undetermined.[35] Yet certain episodes cannot be disassociated from the Law. Most notable is one in which a young girl, pursued by a man before the eyes of the young Columba and his teacher, and killed while sheltering beneath their robes, is avenged by the saint: 'In the same hour in which the soul of the girl whom he has slain ascends to heaven, let the soul of her slayer descend to hell.' Columba's teacher has spurred Columba on by lamenting that 'this crime, and our dishonour [goes] unavenged', and this miracle comes at the end of a series in which persecutors of exiles, churches and the innocent come to grief.[36]

What we see here is the standard literary means of indicating the efficacy of the saints in the Gaelic tradition. Unlike elsewhere, where tales told of miracles at the saints' shrines or done by their relics were the most important way to impress the public (and especially the nobility) that the saint was not to be trifled with, most Gaelic saints' Lives, whether in Gaelic or Latin, concentrate on the saint's effectiveness in life. As previously noted, posthumous miracles are scarce: it seems to me that this tendency in Gaelic hagiography reflects similar methods in praise-poetry, where the virtues of the patron could be evoked by describing and praising his ancestors as if they were still alive.

[34] *CA*, §§16–21; *Betha Adamnáin*, §§4–10, 13.

[35] For comments on the date, see e.g. Picard, 'Purpose', 169 ('the accumulation of evidence points towards a date around 700 rather than 690'); Anderson, *Adomnán*, xlii; Sharpe, *Adomnán*, 55. I lean towards Sharpe's suggestion that 'Adomnán may have begun it before 697; he worked on it for some time, revising the text in places, and he was obviously still writing after that date.' For further evidence and discussion, see Clancy, 'Personal, political, pastoral'.

[36] *VC* ii.25 and see ii.22–4: Anderson, *Adomnán*, 130–1 and 124–9.

Despite this apparent disparity between continental and Gaelic hagiography, Adomnán is an instructive exception in giving us a selection of miracle stories, some of them quite personal, which testify to Columba's power and patronage after his death. It is noteworthy that the sections of the *Life* which describe Columba's posthumous miracles, and Adomnán's own indebtedness to him, are set off as if to emphasise their importance. One group appears in the section on miracles of power which occurs (almost as a third preface) at the beginning of Book One on Prophecies, and the second group in a specially introduced part of Book Two, which closes that book. Moreover each of these posthumous miracles is given a clear pedigree with regard to their witnesses or sources; indeed Adomnán himself is witness to, and in some cases the instigator of many of them. The care Adomnán devotes to these miracles suggests that he was consciously attempting to do something at once significant and in need of particular highlighting, as if addressed to a particular audience. Given the greater interest of Northumbrian hagiographers in such miracles as confirmation of saintly power, it might be suggested that in these sections Adomnán is looking south. Be that as it may, both groups are of the utmost importance in understanding how the cult of saints had matured in Iona by the end of the seventh century.

First let us consider those in Book Two, then those at the beginning of Book One. The first posthumous miracle Adomnán recounts in Book Two is one which took place at the instigation of the elders of the monastery of Iona, including himself. We are given its date: seventeen years before Adomnán is writing. During a time of severe drought the elders decide to take Columba's relics on a circuit of the island:

> we formed a plan and decided upon this course: that some of our elders should go round the plain that had been lately ploughed and sown, taking with them the white tunic of Saint Columba, and books in his own handwriting; and should three times raise in the air that tunic, which he wore in the hour of his departure from the flesh; and should open his books and read from them, on the hill of the angels, where at one time the citizens of the heavenly country were seen descending to confer with the holy man.[37]

[37] *VC* ii.44: Anderson, *Adomnán*, 172–3.

This brings rain and fertility back to the land, and Adomnán's coda is instructive: 'Thus the commemoration of the name of one blessed man, made with his tunic and books, on that occasion brought saving and timely help to many districts and peoples.' The procedure adopted by the elders (or the story told by Adomnán) is drawn from Gregory the Great's *Dialogues*, which gives a similar account of the tunic of St Euthichius being carried through the fields of Lombardy during droughts.[38] This shows the way in which Adomnán's understanding of sanctity as culted on the continent informed the practice of the Iona monastery. Note, however, the innovation of reading from Columba's books, and the specific place on which the ritual is perfomed. Adomnán was concerned to introduce the particular into the generic. Note also his interest in the pattern of ritual, relic and place.

Adomnán invokes himself as witness to three miracles of wind-power in the next chapter. He is aware of the miracles of wind-power he described Columba as having performed in his lifetime, and here hastens to add his own personal witness. He notes at the start of the chapter: 'The credibility of miracles of this kind, that happened in past times and that we have not seen, is confirmed for us beyond doubt by those of the present day, that we ourselves have observed. For indeed we ourselves have thrice seen contrary winds turned into favourable ones.'[39] His own involvement in these particular miracles shows the way in which his understanding of the testimonies of others and of traditions concerning Columba has informed his relationship with his patron: his expectations are partly formed by his expert knowledge as a collector of miracle stories.

In the first, as a preventative measure before a difficult journey with timbers for a monastery building, Columba's name is invoked, with his relics. 'We adopted the plan of laying garments and books of the blessed man upon the altar, with psalms and fasting, and invocation of his name; in order that he might obtain from the Lord prosperous winds in our favour.' In the second account, it is abuse of the saint's name which persuades him. Their journey scuppered by an unfavourable wind,

[38] Anderson, *Adomnán*, lxviii; Herbert, *Iona, Kells and Derry*, 137–8.
[39] *VC* ii.45: Anderson, *Adomnán*, 174–5.

> we complained about the inconvenience of this contrary wind, and began in a manner as it were to upbraid our Columba, saying: 'Is this hindrance that opposes us pleasing to you, holy one? Till now, we have expected some consolation of help in our labours to be given by you, with God's favour, since we imagined that you were in somewhat high honour with God.'[40]

This technique works, and a favourable wind starts to blow. This is almost a foretaste of the later continental practice of the abuse of the saint and the humiliation of relics, in which a saint's relics were taken down from the altar and masses suspended until the saint righted some injustice.[41] The third miracle occurs in a like manner, with the monastic elders marooned before the saint's feast. A complaint is issued against the saint, and favourable winds return. This miracle touches the heart of the community of Columba: it allows the heads of Columba's family to return to the centre of his cult in time for his own important feast. At the end we are told, 'To the truth of the foregoing narrative there are still living not two witnesses only, or three, as law requires, but a hundred, and more.'[42]

The next chapter is the most personal. Adomnán attributes the freedom of Dál Riata and the Picts from the plague to the intercession of Columba, held in honour by many monasteries in those lands. But Adomnán also describes his own experience:

> We, however, give frequent thanks to God, who, through the prayers of our venerable patron on our behalf, has protected us from the invasion of plagues, both in these our islands, and in England, when we visited our friend king Aldfrith, while the pestilence still continued and devastated many villages on all sides. But both in our first visit, after the battle of Ecgfrith, and in our second visit, two years later, although we walked in the midst of this danger of plague, the Lord so delivered us that not even one of our companions died, nor was in any way smitten by the disease.[43]

[40] *Ibid.* Note the use of this sort of rebuke by Columba's teacher in ii.25 (Anderson, *Adomnán*, 130–1).

[41] See Geary, *Living with the Dead*, 95–124. For another Scottish example, see the abuse of St Kentigern's reputation in William of Glasgow's 'Song on the death of Somerled', in *ES* ii.256–8; trans. Márkus in Clancy, ed., *The Triumph Tree*, 212–14.

[42] Anderson, *Adomnán*, 178–9.

[43] *VC* ii.46: Anderson, *Adomnán*, 178–81.

Two different sorts of miracle story are recounted in the summary of miracles of power at the beginning of Book One. They are told more or less at the end of the summary, at greater length, and are not retold later, and it is likely that they are meant to be set apart from the other miracles. These too have detailed pedigrees. The first, we are told 'was confidently narrated to me, Adomnán, by my predecessor, our abbot Failbe. He asserted that he had heard the vision from the mouth of King Oswald himself, relating it to abbot Ségéne'. The second of these miracles has even more widespread and verifiable witnesses:

> Of this miracle it has been possible to produce not two witnesses or three, as law requires, but a hundred or more. For not in one place or time only is the same thing proved to have happened, but it has been established beyond doubt as having happened at various places and times, in Ireland and Britain, but in like manner and with the like cause of deliverance. We have learned these things, without room for doubt, from people who knew the facts in every district, wherever the same thing happened, with the same miracle.[44]

The contents of the two miracles are equally revealing. The first involves Columba as battle-giver: King Oswald receives a personal vision of Columba, huge, shining, above the battle-camp, prophesying victory. Adomnán prefaces the miracle with the words, 'This special favour was bestowed by God, who honours all saints, on him, not only while he continued in this present life, but also after his departure from the flesh, as on a triumphant and powerful champion.'[45]

Not only does the vision of the saint in Oswald's dream appear as one who would grant military success to kings, but also as one who thereby effects the conversion of nations. Through Oswald's rewarded devotion, his army is baptised, and the Christian king is 'ordained by God as emperor of the whole of Britain'.[46] Notice here Adomnán's distinctive argument: like the protection from the plague, like the relief of the drought, the personal connection between the 'one blessed man' and his disciples affects many nations and peoples.

[44] *VC* i.1: Anderson, *Adomnán*, 16–17.
[45] *Ibid.*, 14–15.
[46] *Ibid.*, 16–17: *totius Brittanniae imperator a deo ordinatus est.*

The second miracle takes the very opposite tack: it is not only holy kings to whom Columba grants his protection, but also baser people, violent criminals. Certain lay-people (and here we should note the probable use of *laicus* as 'warrior, bandit'),[47] and sinful ones at that, are saved from fire, sword and spear by the chanting of Columba's praises in Gaelic.[48] Those who scorn these verbal relics of the saint are the only ones killed. Columba, invoked, delivers his clients from the hands of their enemies.

Before moving on it is as well to note here the ways in which Adomnán is suggesting, recommending even, that Christians should use saints, should channel their prayer through them to God.

1. Direct imprecation: Adomnán's constant prayers save him from the plague, and the mild abuse of the saint's reputation grants favourable winds. The saint's *name* and his *honour* are at once the means and the target of the rituals here. And Adomnán is not afraid to employ the twin poles of the poet's art: satire as well as praise.

2. The use of relics: physical relics are used in rituals – lain on altars, taken on circuit, read from in special places, chanted over – to obtain the desired effect. It is noteworthy that books play a prominent role among these miracles. Note too that Columba's books elsewhere in the *Life* are shown to have marvellous properties. On the other hand, we may note that Columba's bodily remains play no role whatever in these miracles, though Adomnán mentions both Columba's pillow and the place where his bones lie as blessed locations.[49] It is also worth considering the way in which the procession with Columba's relics during the drought mirrors the later ritual of *commotationes*, relic-circuits, both in its procedure and in its context. Most of the instances of the proclamations of laws of saints mentioned above occurred during times of drought, famine, plague or unrest.

3. Poems or songs composed about Columba, mostly in the vernacular. This bears a striking resemblance to the use of secular

[47] Sharpe, 'Hiberno-Latin *laicus*, Irish *láech* and the devil's men'.

[48] *per quaedam scoticae lingae laudum ipsius carmina et nominis commemorationem* (Anderson, *Adomnán*, 16).

[49] *VC* iii.23: Anderson, *Adomnán*, 224–5, 232–3.

praise poetry. The patron saint here is swayed towards the supplicant by the use of panegyric. It is also striking that only really in Gaelic sources do we get this sense of poems composed about saints as, essentially, secondary verbal relics, whose use is tantamount to the veneration of physical relics.

These three methods of posthumous devotion Adomnán not only advocates but authenticates by his recipes for ritual and his clear delineation of the pedigrees and witnesses for each miracle. He related to the cult of saint Columba, not only as witness and storyteller, but also as instigant and creator. I find it hard, myself, to shake off the conviction that the ritual the elders of Iona enact during the drought was Adomnán's own experiment, a product of his reading of Gregory the Great and his devotion to his patron.

Some sense of Adomnán's lively interest in the cult of saints as practised elsewhere is provided by an examination of his earliest surviving work, *De Locis Sanctis*, the account of the Holy Places based on his own reading and the testimony of the Gaulish bishop Arculf. In it Adomnán gives us an opportunity to see his mind at work on the greater world of early medieval Christendom. It is thus most striking that some of his longest accounts in the text occur in the third book, when describing Arculf's visit to the city of Constantinople. Here we are treated to a detailed description of the veneration of the Holy Cross in the church built to house its relics. The description of the ritual associated with the veneration bears comparison with Adomnán's description of rituals employing Columba's relics in the *Life*.

> In the interior in the northern part a very large and very beautiful repository is on view. It encloses a wooden chest, and that in turn encloses a wooden reliquary, where the salutary wood of the cross is kept on which our Saviour was suspended and suffered for the salvation of the human race. Now according to the holy Arculf, for three consecutive days after the lapse of a complete year this famous chest, together with its precious treasure, is set up on a golden altar. It is only on three days a year . . . that the cross of the Lord is set up and placed on the altar, that is the day of the Lord's supper, on which the emperor and the soldiers of the army enter the church, approach the altar and kiss the salutary cross when the holy chest is opened.[50]

[50] *DLS* III.iii.

Here Adomnán shows an attention to the ritual of places and relics, an attention he had given earlier in the work to the use of Christ's shroud and to the Church of the Ascension in Jerusalem.[51]

More importantly, however, the third book of *De Locis Sanctis* gives two extended anecdotes about Saint George the Confessor, and one about an icon of the Virgin Mary. All three of these stories deal with images, with icons, and are well-written apologetic tales describing the miraculous power of the saints' images, and thus of the saints' power after death to continue to bless those who bless them and curse those who curse them. Particularly notable, in view of Adomnán's accounts of Columba's posthumous powers, is the bargain struck by an armed horseman with the image of George: 'I commend myself and my horse to you, George the confessor, that by virtue of your prayers we may both return safe from the expedition and reach this city, delivered from all dangers of wars and pestilences and waters.' The wonderful story of the horse-bargain that follows (with George the saint demanding more and more of the horseman until finally the saint receives the horse he has been promised, in return for the man's safety in many wars and dangers) underlines by parallelism the tale which precedes it, of the horseman who tried to damage the saint's image, and who was punished, and his horse slain in retribution.[52]

In St Adomnán, then, we find an eloquent and creative proponent of the efficacy of the blessed dead, patrons of good kings and desperate sinners, legal guarantors and enforcers of their rights, invokable through their names, their honour, their relics and through poetry. It is perhaps no accident, then, that later tradition connected Adomnán particularly with the cult of saints, ascribing to him poems such as 'The Martyrology of Adomnán', a prayer for aid to the saints of the four seasons, and 'The Reliquary of Adomnán', in which the contents of his obviously voluminous satchel are detailed as containing a whole anatomy of relics, including St Patrick's Tooth, St Brigit's Hair-Shirt and St Donnán of Eigg's Knee-Cap.[53] James Carney suggested that 'The Reliquary' could even be the work of Adomnán himself,

[51] *DLS* I.ix.23.

[52] *DLS* III.iv, and for the story of the Marian icon, III.v.

[53] Byrne, 'Féilire Adamnáin'; Carney, '*A maccucáin, sruth in tíag*'.

and while it seems to me that at the very least on the grounds of tone and content this is unlikely, another poem attributed to Adomnán is more probably of his authorship. This is the 'Prayer of Adomnán' found as a sort of coda to the longer and earlier *Amra Choluimb Chille*, the eulogy on Columba composed probably at the time of his death. 'The Prayer' imitates that poem's style and vocabulary, calling on Columba for protection after death:

Columb Cille	May Colum Cille
co Día domm eráil	commend me to God
i tías – ní mos-tías . . .	when I go – may I not go soon . . .
buidne co aingel airm	to the place of the angel host
(ainm huí násadaig Néil,	(the name of Níall's famous descendant,
ní súail snádud) . . .	not small its protection) . . .[54]

If Adomnán helps to establish the involvement of the saints in Gaelic law as sureties and enforcers, he also in this poem confirms their participation in a process of exchange which mirrors the conventions of contemporary praise-poetry. Like the criminals in his anecdote, protected from fire and sword by singing Gaelic poems in praise of Columba, Adomnán here invokes the might of Columba's protection. The word used is *snádud*, defined by D. A. Binchy as 'the power to accord to another person immunity from all legal process ... over a definite period of time which varies according to the rank of the protector'.[55] It was also the safe-conduct which could be offered by a free member of one tribe or kingdom to someone from outside that kingdom.[56] Both these meanings are in use in early poetry in praise of Columba, as well as other saints. The poets entreat the privileged member of the kingdom of heaven to grant them both safe conduct in the strange kingdom of the other-world, and also accord them immunity from due legal process, the trial and punishment which would be the due of the poet, a sinner, after his death. Columba and the other saints, the heavenly aristocracy, are appealed to as patrons, and in return for their patronage they are given poetry.

[54] Clancy and Márkus, *Iona*, 164–71.
[55] Binchy, *Críth Gablach*, 106.
[56] RIA, *Dictionary*, *s.v. snádud*.

This image is common to all the seventh-century poetry in praise of Columba. In the hostile territory of death, the saintly and powerful patron, Columba, a free citizen of God's kingdom, will provide his clients *snádud*, will convey them past the dangerous and fiery borderlands of hell, will protect them from the legal process which might be their due, and would help them in Sion, where, we are told, he has settled. It is this idea of Columba the protector in heaven which dominates the relationship between monk and patron saint in seventh-century Iona.[57]

This is certainly one of the images evoked in the poetry of Beccán mac Luigdech. This Beccán is the author of two poems in praise of Columba, and he may perhaps be the *Beccanus solitarius* to whom Cummian's Paschal letter of *ca* 632 was addressed (along with Ségéne, fifth abbot of Iona). He may also be identified with the Beccán of Rum who died in 677.[58] In his earlier poem on Columba, he opens with the language of clientship and protection:

> Bound to Colum, while I speak,
> may the bright one guard me (*snáidsium*) in the seven heavens;
> when I travel to fear's road
> I'm not lordless: I have strength.

He returns to this theme at the end of the poem:

> May he save me from fire – common fight –
> Colum Cille, noble candle,
> his tryst well-famed – he was bright
> may he bear me to the King who ends evil . . .
>
> No 'cry to wastelands' what's on my lips,
> I'll beg of my God my hero's prize;
> may he bear me past the king of fire,
> then my protection (*mo ráith*) is his.

Beyond this, however, Beccán gives a clear view of Columba as an ever-present guard, as a protector in life as well as after it:

> The shield of a few, a crowd's shield,
> a fort where all unsafe are safe;
> he is a tight fort – fair profit
> to be in Colum Cille's care . . .

[57] For a fuller discussion, see Clancy and Márkus, *Iona*, 152–4.
[58] *Ibid.*, 129–34.

greatly blessed in every plight
he who'd praise Colum úa Néill . . .

Colum Cille, while I live,
will be my chant, till the grave's tryst;
in every risk I'll call him,
when I'll praise him with my full strength.[59]

In his second poem, similar themes are expressed: Columba is *dín mo anmae / dún mo uäd* ('my soul's stronghold, fort of my poetic art'). Once again, the imagery of *snádud* returns:

Colum Cille, Colum who was, Colum who will be,
constant Colum, not he the protection to be lamented.

The last line (*ní hé sin in snádud ciäss*, literally 'that is not the protection which is lamented') plays on the idea of the time-limit of a patron's protection, one bounded both by the status of the patron and also by his life-span. Neither Columba's status nor his span of time in heaven's eternity knows any limit.[60]

This engagement of the saints in the ordinary exchange of praise poetry seems to me to be a product of the special circumstances of the professional poetry of the Gaelic world and the rapprochement between scholars of ecclesiastical learning and the native poetic guilds. Legend accorded Columba a prime part in the creation of this fruitful interaction, and in legend it was Columba's defence of professional poetry which moved Dallán Forgaill to compose the extraordinary elegy for him called *Amra Choluimb Chille*.[61] While there may be some truth in the legend, it is clear from that poem alone that the interweaving of native and ecclesiastical learning in religious praise poetry and other literary forms sprang as much from the poets themselves who must often have inhabited and been trained in both worlds.[62]

Such praise poems could also take on a salvific role of their own. Of the *Amra*, tradition had it that its recitation, not just its composition, would grant the reciter heaven.

[59] *Ibid.*, 136–43: §§1, 21, 23, 6, 9, 22.
[60] *Ibid.*, 148–9: §20.
[61] *Lebor na hUidre*, 11–15; discussion in Bannerman, *Studies in the History of Dalriada*, 160; Herbert, 'The preface to the *Amra Coluim Cille*', 67–75.
[62] See Clancy and Márkus, *Iona*, 99–100, 116–26.

> Whoever recites every day the Amra, whose meaning is difficult,
> will have from Columba the kingdom of heaven mightily.
> Whoever recites every day Columba's Amra with its sense
> will have prosperity on earth, will save his soul past pain.[63]

We should be reminded here of the bandits in the *Life of Columba* who recite Gaelic poems in praise of Columba and are saved from fire and death. The poems themselves had become a sort of secondary relic. Even the names of relics and poems seem to overlap. 'The Prayer of Adomnán', with which this discussion of praise poetry began, was called in some manuscripts *Cathbarr*, 'the battle-helmet'.[64]

It is to relics we must turn next, but first it should be mentioned that the role of Columba as protector in the poetry both of the Gaelic world and of Scotland in general did not end with the seventh century – far from it. As late as the fourteenth century, on the east coast of Scotland, in the island monastery of Inchcolm, we find monks invoking in poetry and prayer their patron saint, here cast, much as in Adomnán's Life, as patron of all Scotland. *The Inchcolm Antiphoner*, as it has come to be known, gives us liturgical settings for poetry and prayer in praise of Columba. It belongs to the first half of the fourteenth century, and to a period of warfare:

> Father Columba, splendour of our ways,
> receive your servants' offerings.
> Save the choir which sings your praise
> from the assaults of Englishmen
> and from the taunts of foes.

The prayers in the Antiphoner draw on stories which demonstrate a knowledge of Adomnán's *Life of Columba*, though others must be based on unknown traditions handed down to the monks in Inchcolm about their patron:

> You sweeten bitter apples; you restore the dead to life; you command the winds; you clear the air and put plague to flight. You draw water from a rock. You, mirror of the church and protector of this land,

[63] Stokes, 'The Bodleian *Amra Choluimb Chille*', 135.
[64] Carney, *The Poems of Blathmac*, xiii.

> look upon this choir . . . and may Christ's mercy by your prayer watch over this place dedicated to you.[65]

In a sense these prayers interweave both the images of the saint as effective in life and in death: as he was powerful and miraculous when alive, so he will protect his family and his land now. So in the perilous fourteenth century, Columba could still in eastern Scotland be called *spes Scotorum*, 'hope of the Scots'. In a century of plague, warfare, and the solidifying of the Scottish national image, Columba was still guarding and protecting it, as 'father of this land, excellent shepherd'.[66]

To the same century belongs one of an infrequent but significant series of appearances of Columba's relics in historical accounts. Bernard, abbot of Arbroath, returning from the battle of Bannockburn in 1314, gave over the *Breccbennach* of Columba to Monymusk, along with the lands of Forglen for its maintenance, and the military service which was the relic-keeper's obligation. The military service was without doubt the bringing of the reliquary into battle to ensure the saint's blessings on the army. This is the role in which we first find the reliquary in William I's reign, when it, its duties and its lands were granted to the monks of Arbroath.[67] This is not the only one of Columba's relics associated with victory in battle. One of the earliest of Gaelic manuscripts, the fragmentary psalter attributed by some to Columba's own hand, and traditionally his work, was called from

[65] *Pater Columba decus morum suscipe vota famulorum te laudantem serva chorum ab incursu anglicorum et insultu emulorum*; and *Mala amara dulcoras, mortuum vite redintegras, ventis imperas. Aerem serenas et pestem fugas. De rupe limphum extricas. Tu speculum ecclesie et patrie protector. Chorum hunc invisere ... locumque istum tibi deditum prece tua servet Christi clementia.* Translation of first extract, G. Márkus in Clancy, ed. *The Triumph Tree*, 318; translations of second extract, Preece, programme notes. For source, see note 4 above.

[66] *pater patrie, pastor egregie.* Note also the splendid series of miracles attributed to Columba and set during the fourteenth century which Walter Bower recounts in his *Scotichronicon*, in which Columba bests various enemies of Inchcolm and Scotland: *Scotichronicon* vii.108–11; 118–21; 398–403. I am grateful to Simon Taylor for calling these to my attention by reading them to me on Inchcolm on the feast of St Columba, 1997.

[67] *RRS* ii, no. 449; Anderson, 'Architecturally shaped shrines and other reliquaries'; Eeles, 'The Monymusk reliquary'. Discussion in Ó Floinn, '*Insignia Columbae* I', 144–9.

an unknown date the *Cathach*, or 'Battler'. In Mánus Ó Dónaill's compendious Irish Life of Columba, completed in 1532, the properties of the *Cathach* are described:

> And if it is borne three times sunwise around the army of Cenél Conaill when they go into battle, they will come back triumphant. And it is in the breast of a *comharba* or a cleric without mortal sin on him, as far as is possible, that it is proper for the *Cathach* to be when going around that army.[68]

Ó Dónaill tells this in the context of the tale of the Battle of Cúl Drebene, in which he has Columba participating as instigator and battle-winner, and the *Cathach* as the bone of contention. Whatever truth there may be in this, it is likely that Columba's persistent association with this battle, and Adomnán's claims for his involvement in granting battles to both Oswald of Northumbria and Áedán mac Gabráin, are the roots of Columba's reputation as an effective saint of war.

Nonetheless, it is significant that whereas the *Cathach* became identified with the battle fortunes of Columba's kin, the Cenél Conaill of Tír Conaill, in Scotland his relics became associated with the fortune of the nation. The *Breccbennach*, notice, was granted by the king to the monastery of Arbroath for keeping and bringing into military service. But the most explicit example of Columba's relics and their involvement with Scottish fortunes is in the Irish tale (embedded in a collection of annals) describing the battle of the men of Alba against Norse kings in the early tenth century. We do not know the original source of this tale. As it stands it is worked into a sequence of historical battle-tales concerning rulers in Britain and Ireland and their struggles against Viking rulers, and this sequence itself must be seen in the overall context of the annals in which it is found, which devotes a great deal of attention to tales about the behaviour of rulers, particularly Christian rulers, in war.

Be that as it may, the account describes the Scottish protagonists both as the men of Fortriu (*Foirtrennaig*) and as the men of Alba (*Fir Alban*). The account is worth quoting *in extenso*:

[68] *Betha Colaim Chille*, 182–5; on the *Cathach* itself, see Lapidge and Sharpe, *Bibliography*, §506. Discussion, in Ó Floinn, '*Insignia Columbae* I', 150–4.

> Almost at the same time the men of [Fortriu] and the Norwegians fought a battle. The men of Alba fought this battle steadfastly, moreover, because Colum Cille was assisting them, for they had prayed fervently to him, since he was their apostle, and it was through him that they received faith. For on another occasion, when [King Ívarr] was a young lad and he came to plunder Alba with three large troops, the men of Alba, lay and clergy alike, fasted and prayed to God and Colum Cille until morning, and beseeched the Lord, and gave profuse alms of food and clothing to the churches and to the poor, and received the Body of the Lord from the hands of their priests, and promised to do every good thing as their clergy would best urge them, and that their battle-standard in the van of every battle would be the Crozier of Colum Cille – and it is on that account that it is called the *Cathbuaid* (Battle-Triumph) from then onwards; and the name is fitting, for they have often won victory in battle with it, as they did at that time, relying on Colum Cille.[69]

As noted, the account needs to be read in the context of the author's particular interest in rightful action by kings and people in battle. Nonetheless, it provides a striking tableau, and a more sympathetic picture of how people, kings and armies were involved with the saint and his relics. We should picture, according to this tale, not simply a superstitious reliance on a crozier to win a battle, but a contract much like that involved in the relic circuits discussed earlier, where during plagues and famine, the relics of saints toured, not just enforcing law but also reinforcing a sense of order and security.[70]

John Bannerman has extensively explored the relationship between the relics of Columba and his successors, abbots successively of Iona, then Kells and Derry in Ireland, and at least Dunkeld in Scotland.[71] These abbots carried the insignia of the saints as their badges of office, and when the relics moved about (as they did frequently, for instance, in the early ninth century) we must suspect important events. The early ninth-century movements of the relics may well be connected with the foundations of monasteries at Kells and Dunkeld, and perhaps at

[69] FAI, pp. 168–71. For discussion of Columban croziers, including the *Cathbuaid*, see Bourke, '*Insignia Columbae* II', 173–83.

[70] See also Stuart Airlie's comments on kings, relics and patron saints, in 'The view from Maastricht'.

[71] Bannerman, '*Comarba Coluim Chille*'; for recent discussion, see Ó Floinn, '*Insignia Columbae* I'.

St Andrews.[72] Although we do not know in detail what these relics were, it is possible that they were corporeal remains. Bannerman has made a good case for the authority of the successor of the saint being closely connected with his control of the bodily remains of that saint. This is despite Gaelic sources showing a marked disinterest in corporeal relics: almost without exception the most important practical relics of any Irish or Scottish saint are secondary ones, usually books, bells or *bachla*. Those relics we know of which are associated with Columba and his authority are mostly of this type: the *Cathbuaid*, the *Cathach*, the *flabellum* which was at Kells, the Gospel of Martin at Derry, the *cochall* or covering which was destroyed on Iona by Ailén mac Ruairí in the early sixteenth century.[73]

Only rarely do we hear about Columba's body. Although the *Amra Choluimb Chille* remarked on the effectiveness of Columba's grave in troublesome weather,[74] Adomnán is pointedly guarded about Columba's body, making it clear that God prevented people by storms from attending Columba's funeral.[75] It is without doubt Columba's bodily shrine which Blathmac mac Flainn fatally defended in 825, when he and his companions were slaughtered on Iona.[76] The bodily remains were presumably split in some way in 849: his *scrín*, a shrine for his body, was forced to flee from Viking attacks around Dunkeld in 878, but we hear from an English list of the resting places of saints' relics in the tenth century that Columba's were at Dunkeld.[77] It is presumably at Columba's shrine in Dunkeld, as well, that St Cadroe's parents

[72] See Clancy, 'Iona, Scotland and the Céli Dé', 113–15. For Dunkeld, however, see Bannerman, below, p. 75 n. 1 and Broun, below, p. 105 n. 40.

[73] Reeves, *Life* (1874), lxxix-xcix; Watson, *Scottish Poetry from the Book of the Dean of Lismore*, 136–7: 'You made, and that is not all, / a raid on Iona and Reilig Odhrain; / and you madly ruined there / the *cochall* (shell/ cover shrine) of the orders and the masses' (translation mine). Discussion in Ó Floinn, '*Insignia Columbae* I', and Bourke, '*Insignia Columbae* II'. This reference to the *cochall*, which appears to have been different objects at different times and places, is not discussed by Ó Floinn.

[74] Clancy and Márkus, *Iona*, 110–11 (vii.18–19).

[75] *VC* iii.23; Anderson, *Adomnán*, 230–1; and see the comments of Márkus, below, pp. 124–6.

[76] AU 825; Metcalfe, *Pinkerton's Lives*, vol. 2, 293–7; *ES* i.263–5.

[77] Bannerman, '*Comarba Coluim Chille*', 29, 43; AU 878.9; Macquarrie, 'Early Christian religious houses', 121–2; Hudson, 'Kings and church in early Scotland', 153 and n. 39.

prayed for a child, and where Cadroe was given over to his kinsman Bean for clerical training.[78]

This last incident, recounted in the late tenth-century *Life of Cadroe* composed on the continent, is intriguing, since the Life in general gives us a very similar sense of the pervasive role of relics and saints in the lives of at least the nobility of Scotland in the tenth century. It may be that this is due to the Life's composition on the continent, and the audience to which it was addressed. Nonetheless it preserves many details of Gaelic life (such as fosterage) and political circumstances, and is an invaluable source for the period. In addition to the incidents at Columba's tomb, when Cadroe is about to set off for the continent, he is besieged in a church of St Brigit (perhaps Abernethy?) by people who do not wish him to leave:

> a crowd of nobles and peasants filled the church, having been summoned from different quarters. They all asked the man not to forsake his country . . . an outcry of the people arose; and they placed before him relics of the saints, and adjuring him by them besought him to yield to their wish.[79]

On the whole, however, in common with many other Gaelic saints, Columba's body did not have the same gory fascination for churchmen as we might observe with saints elsewhere. We do not find, as we do with St Oswald, the phenomenon of multiple heads, although other Gaelic saints, such as Patrick, developed

[78] *ES* i.432–4. For general discussion of bodily relics of Columba, see Ó Floinn, '*Insignia Columbae* I', 136–44, which concentrates on the Irish sources. There were still relics of the saint at Dunkeld around 1500. A superb account of the power of Columba to protect the people of Dunkeld diocese during a plague is preserved by Alexander Mylne. Priests in the diocese were giving water, in which had been dipped a bone of Columba's, to people to keep them healthy. One man was annoyed at being given water to drink, and had some beer instead, which was not blessed by the relic; he died of the plague. Mylne, *Vitae Episcopatum Dunkeldensium*, 43, cf. 40. I am grateful to Kenneth Veitch for drawing my attention to this account. Mylne also describes in detail a magnificent mural of the saint and his miracles painted at Dunkeld: *Fecit etiam ad magnis altare, ante murale depictum viginti quatuor miraculi Sancti Columbae, et duas de super ymagines eiusdem, duas columpnas, et desuper duos angelios*, p. 23.

[79] *Ibid.*, 440. For a discussion of the Life, see Macquarrie, *The Saints of Scotland*, 199–210.

multiple graves and bodies.[80] Rather, the saint's power focused not solely on his corporeal remains, but on a more proliferated power, in secondary and also oral relics.

Columba's relics may have been connected with the fortunes both of the church and of the kingdom of Alba after the Gaelic takeover of eastern Scotland in the ninth century. On a very earthly level, the relationship between Columba and the Scottish kingship can be seen in the involvement of the abbots of Dunkeld in the contests for the kingship during the tenth and eleventh centuries.[81] On a more abstract level, Columba's continuing identification with the dynasty descended from Cinaed mac Alpín is made clear in the names of successors to the kingship from the early tenth century: four kings between then and the twelfth century were called Mael Coluim, 'servant of Columba', certainly no accident of nomenclature. The cult of Saint Columba in Scotland continued to be a political as well as a personal and popular phenomenon.

In closing, I want to turn to one of the most exceptional and, on occasion, most personal of the attributes of saints' cults in the Gaelic world. I know of no real parallels in England or on the continent, outside popular liturgical plays, for the way in which Gaelic saints became characters – dramatic voices which could be wielded by poets to various ends. Probably no saint's voice was more used than that of Columba.[82] Sometimes poetry put in Columba's mouth is merely functional or antiquarian, sometimes it belongs to stories about the saint. Yet other times particular aspects of the saint's life as it came down in tradition – crisis points especially – could be appropriated by poets as vehicles for works of great literary beauty.

Such, for instance, are the series of poems in Columba's voice as he is leaving Ireland for the last time, longing for Derry or for the soil of Ireland, and playing on the nickname 'back turned towards Ireland'.[83] Or the well-known idealistic poem of the eremetic life, in which Columba wishes to live on an island:

[80] Though see Reeves, *Life* (1874), lxxix-lxxxv, and Ó Floinn, '*Insignia Columbae* I', 140–3 for traditions of Columba's body's resting place.

[81] Macquarrie, 'Early Christian religious houses', 121–2.

[82] See list and discussion by Kenney, *Sources*, 436–41.

[83] Murphy, *Early Irish Lyrics*, 65–9; Kinsella, *New Oxford Book of Irish Verse*, 64–9; O'Rahilly, *Measgra Dánta*, §45.

Delight I'd find in an island's breast,
on a rock's peak,
that there I might often gaze
at the sea's calm.

That I might see its heavy waves
over the brilliant sea
as it sings music to the Father
on its constant way . . .

That I might see its ebb and flow
in their sequence,
that this might be my name, a secret I tell:
'Back towards Ireland'.

That help of heart might come to me
gazing on it;
that I might lament all my wrongs,
hard to mention . . .

That I might ponder on some book,
good for my soul;
a while kneeling for dear heaven,
a while at psalms.

A while cropping dulse from the rock,
a while fishing;
a while giving food to the poor,
a while enclosed.

A while pondering the lord of heaven,
holy the purchase;
a while at work – not too taxing!
it would be delightful.[84]

Other frequent roles for Columba's voice in this later poetry is as a prophet, whether of specific historical events or of the day of doom; as a praiser of other saints, such as Mary; and as a writer. Some of the more prophetic poems have clear historical contexts. Such is the extraordinary long poem from Bodleian manuscript Laud Misc. 615, one of the main repositories of Columba poetry, which begins *Marbh anocht mo cholann-sa* ('Dead tonight is my

[84] O'Rahilly, *Measgra Dánta*, §42; translation in Clancy, ed. *The Triumph Tree*, 188–9. See also Jackson, *Celtic Miscellany*, 279–80.

body').[85] Here, probably in the context of the establishment of a Benedictine monastery by Raghnall mac Somhairlidh on Iona *ca* 1203 and the gradual fragmentation of the Columban *familia* under the new archepiscopal regime in Ireland, Columba laments the fate that has befallen his body, and curses Clann Somhairlidh and Irish kindreds for neglecting him:

> I am the son of Feidhlimidh,
> son of Ferghus, son of Conall.
> A grievance for Gaels the fate
> which will fall on my body.
>
> Myself, held captive by foreigners,
> and they themselves on raids;
> wretched I'll deem the foreign monks
> who'll be after me in my place.
>
> I will slay Clann Somhairlidh,
> both beasts and men,
> because they'll go from my counsel,
> I will lay them low and sap them.[86]

But whether the context be political or spiritual, these voices of Columba become in time the familiar ones: conversing with poets, ex-gods, pagan priests; confounding them or simply interrogating them; lamenting leaving Ireland; less frequently praising Iona. Although this may seem to have more to do with the literary history of the Gaelic world than with the cult of saints, in such poetry the creators drew near to their patron in a more intimate way than they did even in poems in praise of the saint. The propagandist of the Columban *familia* could don the mantle of the spurned saint, declaring, 'Myself, though I am long-suffering, a gush of rage will come upon me.'[87] The Columban cleric, leaving Derry for a journey to the Hebrides, could place himself alongside the weeping Columba, and be thankful his back would not be turned towards Ireland forever. The scribe could recall Columba's poetic voice lamenting, *Is scíth mo chrob ón*

[85] Ed. by Meyer, 'Mitteilungen aus irischen Handschriften', 392–5; translations in Clancy, ed. *The Triumph Tree*, 242–6. I hope also soon to provide a new edition and detailed discussion of the poem.

[86] Meyer, 'Mitteilungen', 393, §§5–7.

[87] *Ibid.*, §10.

scríbainn, 'My hand is weary from writing'.[88] With Columba, the cleric could reject divination and superstition, declaring 'It is Christ who is my druid'.[89]

These literary constructs – or rather, these multiple *personae* created by the poets – are in some ways the most lasting legacy of the medieval cult of St Columba. These poets were the earliest romanticists of the saint, and by bringing him closer to themselves and the audiences of these poems, the poets created a saint more personal, informal and attentive to nature than the earlier constructs of Adomnán or the poets of the seventh century. Their adaptations of Columba and the later synthesising of them in the compendious Life by Mánus Ó Dónaill continue to affect even our reading of Adomnán and other contemporary sources. Such is the nature of cult. It is not concerned with historicity. It is concerned only to establish a profitable, often salvific relationship between the holy dead and their living adherents. No matter how necessary the pursuit of the historical Columba may be, we must continue to be aware of how often we are peering through the incense around his shrines.[90]

[88] Murphy, *Early Irish Lyrics*, 70–1.

[89] *Martyrology of Tallaght*, 120; cf. Anne Ross, *Pagan Celtic Britain*, 329. This phrase has frequently been taken out of context to mean precisely the opposite. See M. Forthomme Nicholson's headlining of it in 'Celtic theology: Pelagius', 400.

[90] This chapter, which appeared previously in *Innes Review* 48 (Spring 1997) has benefited greatly from discussions with and criticism by Dauvit Broun, Stephen Driscoll, Roibeard Ó Maolalaigh, Simon Taylor, and particularly Gilbert Márkus. It is based in part on a lecture given to the Society of Antiquaries of Scotland in March, 1994, and more closely on a paper which was delivered at the Scottish Medievalists' Conference in Pitlochry in January, 1997, and I am grateful to both societies for inviting me to speak, and to all who took part in the subsequent discussions.

2

Seventh-century Iona abbots in Scottish place-names

Simon Taylor

NO single rule can be formulated regarding the significance of place-names which contain the names of saints or holy men and women. The subject has been extensively dealt with, and many views have been expressed.[1] A useful dimension to the debate was introduced by E. G. Bowen, who looked at the distribution of saints' cults, as evidenced mainly by place-names and dedications, in terms of route-ways or networks of communication and associated areas of cultural influence in early medieval Britain, Ireland and Brittany.[2] Most of the discussions stress that we cannot assume a church bearing the name of an early native saint (be he or she Irish, Cornish, English, Manx, Pictish, Scottish or Welsh) to have been established by that saint, or even by his or her immediate followers, and the more important the saint concerned, the more foolhardy such an assumption becomes. But the corollary of this is that the less important or kenspeckle a native saint, the more likely it is that dedications or place-names containing that saint's name point to genuine early associations.[3]

[1] The general issues are clearly set out in Watson, *Celtic Place-Names*, 148–50, while a necessary note of caution is sounded by Anderson, 'Columba and other Irish saints', especially regarding too much reliance on commemoration days (*ibid.*, 26–7). For comparative English material and methodology, see Binns, 'Pre-Reformation dedications to St Oswald in England and Scotland: a gazetteer', 241–2 and references.

[2] See especially Bowen, *Saints, Seaways and Settlements*, *passim*.

[3] Anderson, 'Columba and other Irish saints', 27.

Another generally agreed principle is that there is a marked tendency for dedications and other commemorations, such as place-names, to express control in some form or another of a cathedral or monastery, with the saint 'at the centre' being found in the form of dedications and place-names throughout that area of control, be it in a diocese or a monastic *paruchia*, as a stamp of ownership or authority, both material and spiritual.[4]

What is certainly true is that we cannot afford to disregard any evidence relating to the early saints, be it dedications, fair days, place-names, relics, saints' lives, or local legends.[5] Giles Dove is overcautious when he writes 'It is safest never to use the evidence of a place-name if it is not supported by some other source'.[6] Would that we had this luxury, especially in Scotland! But the paucity of sources other than place-names for early medieval Scotland makes it essential that we work place-names as hard as any other kind of evidence.

This chapter will attempt a complete survey of Scottish place-names which contain the names of the abbots of Iona from Báithéne (d. 600) to Adomnán (d. 704), in order to help define more precisely the networks and spheres of influence spreading eastwards from the mother house of Iona into Pictland and beyond in the seventh century. Ideally all names associated with Iona in the late sixth and seventh centuries should be included, but space permits only a representative sample.

It is instructive to look first of all at the distribution of place-name and dedication evidence for the founder of the monastery on Iona, and its first abbot, Columba or Colum Cille (*ca* 563–97).[7] As the most important of the 'indigenous' saints of the Scots,

[4] This has been especially well explored in a Welsh context in Chadwick, 'The evidence of dedications in the early history of the Welsh Church'.

[5] See Hughes' review of Bowen, *Settlement of the Celtic Saints in Wales.*

[6] Dove, 'Saints, Dedications and Cults in Mediaeval Fife', 70.

[7] I deal with Columban commemorations in more detail in Taylor, 'Columba east of Drumalban'. A full discussion of Columban commemorations and associations, including place-names, can be found in Redford, 'Commemorations of Saints', 36–45. I would like to express my thanks to Ms Redford for making available to me all her extensive material on early saints' commemorations in Scotland. A recently published list of commemorations in both Scotland and Ireland, with maps, can be found in Ó Muraíle, 'The Columban onomastic legacy', 193–218, 224, 226.

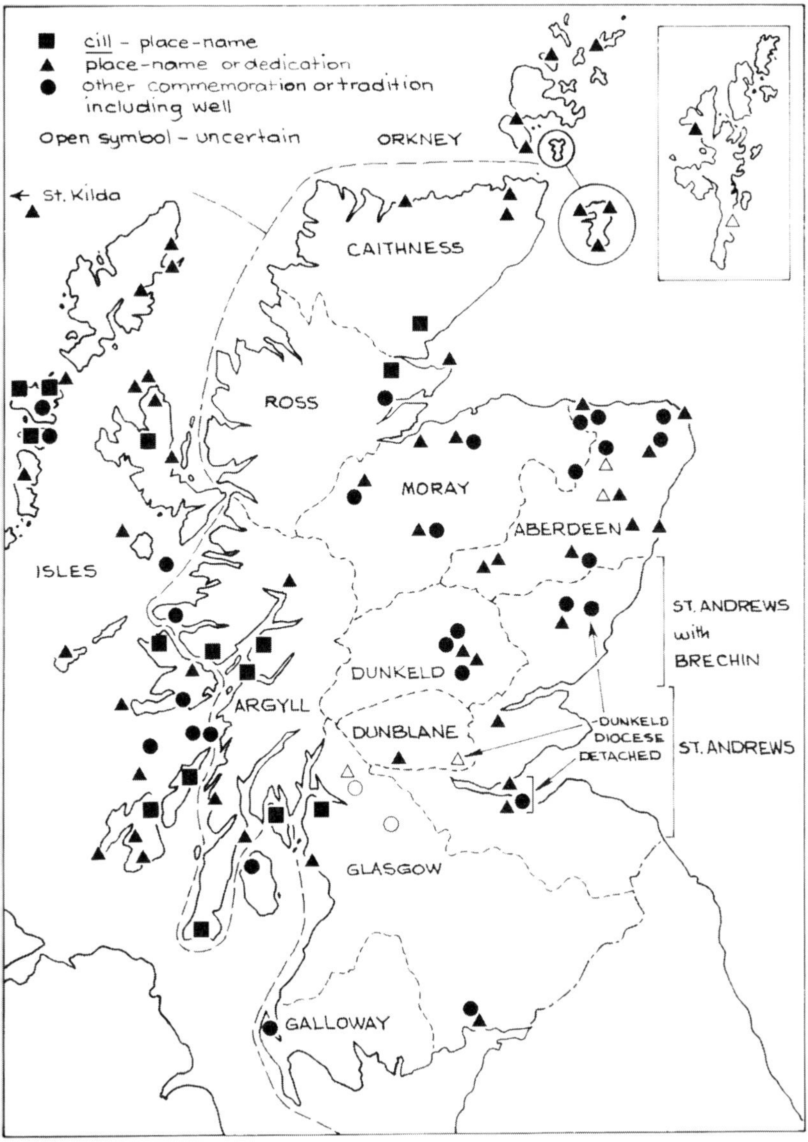

FIGURE 1. *Map of Scotland with the boundaries of the medieval dioceses* ca.*1300: commemorations of Columba* (Colum Cille), Colmán, Colmóc, Colm, *etc.*

it might be thought that he would exemplify much that we have been warned about in connection with major saints and secondary, later associations. Indeed, the distribution map (Fig. 1) of all forms of Columban commemorations, shows that, although predominant in Argyll and the Hebrides, they are reasonably well represented in eastern Scotland. This map, with additions and emendations, is a conflation of Redford's maps 1 and 11, as well as Ó Muraíle's maps 6 and 8.[8] In these they distinguish between *Colum Cille* commemorations, and those to Colum, Colmán and Colmóc, including in the latter those which contain Scots *Colm*. Given the frequent use of hypocoristic forms of saints' names in place-names and other forms of commemoration, as well as the fact that *Colm* was in Scots the full equivalent of *Colum Cille*, I do not think this is a very useful distinction to make. However, even those eastern commemorations which are often confidently ascribed to Columba of Iona must be treated with some circumspection. Those in and around Buchan are a case in point, stemming as they do from the association of Columba with Deer. This association, for all the protests to the contrary, does have the look of being a neat and tidy foundation legend, whereby a Pictish saint (Drostan), about whose life little was known by the early twelfth century, was associated with a saint (Columba) who was high in the estimation of the ruling class of the time.[9] The fact remains that the area where the more important Columba-commemorations are found (*cill*-names, parish patron saint, etc.) reflects more than anything else the lands and influence of the Benedictine abbey of Iona in the later Middle Ages, and should be compared with the map of the West Highlands showing estates and churches of Iona Abbey (as well as of the Iona Nunnery).[10] In fact, this close correlation between the distribution of Columba-place-names and dedications on the one hand and ownership by the Benedictine abbey of Iona

[8] Redford, 'Commemorations of Saints', 43 and 62; Ó Muraíle, 'The Columban onomastic legacy', 224 and 226.

[9] Clancy, 'Scottish saints and national identities', argues that the early grants to Deer are made to Drostan and God, while only the grants from the 1130s onwards include Columba as well. I am grateful to Dr Clancy for allowing me to see this material prior to publication. For another view, see Jackson, *The Gaelic Notes in the Book of Deer*, 4–7.

[10] RCAHMS, *Argyll* iv.146–7.

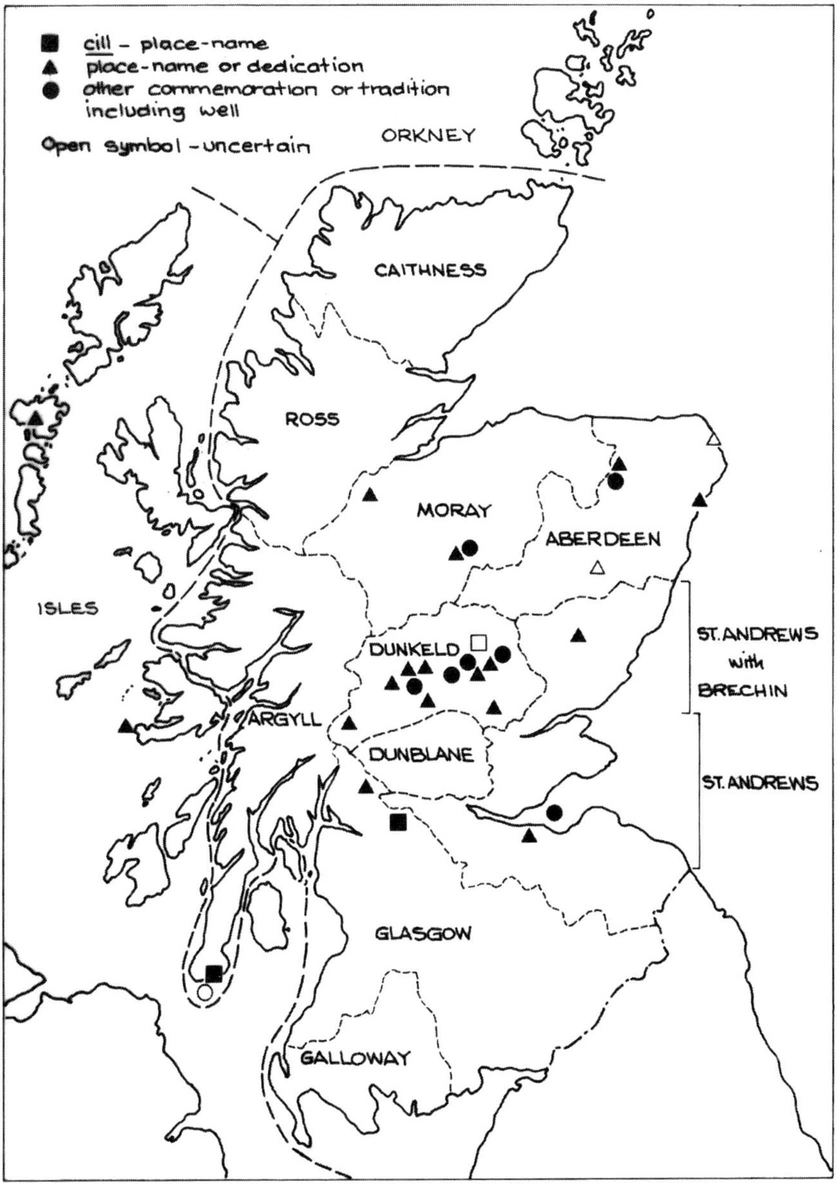

FIGURE 2. *Map of Scotland with the boundaries of the medieval dioceses* ca.1300: *commemorations of Adomnán*

on the other in Argyll and the Western Isles, may well reflect a historical and cultural reality which ante-dates the establishment of the Benedictine abbey on Iona *ca* 1203 by several centuries. Expressed another way, the possessions of the Benedictine abbey may have been based on a much older *paruchia* or sphere of Iona influence, which in turn is reflected by the place-name evidence.[11]

Turning to eastern Scotland, or Pictland, if we had no other evidence than the place-names and dedications, we would conclude that, compared with the later abbot of Iona, Adomnán (Fig. 2), or with Columba's contemporary, Mo Luóc,[12] Columba in fact made no greater impact there. And when we take into consideration his later popularity and status, which must inevitably have led to commemorations with no direct Columban or even Iona link, we could conclude that Columba's impact on Pictland was actually less than that of Adomnán or Mo Luóc. In effect, this accords well with what Adomnán implies, by his very silence, about Columba's mission to the Picts, and it would appear that place-names are more eloquent in this regard than is Adomnán himself in the *Vita Columbae*. It does not, however, accord well with the statements in the *Amra Choluim Chille*, an elegy on Columba written probably within a few years of Columba's death in 597, to the effect that Columba converted the 'tribes of the Tay'.[13] One of the most striking features of Columba commemorations (Fig. 1) compared with those of Adomnán (Fig. 2) is the almost complete absence of the former from Atholl (co-terminous with the core of the late medieval diocese of Dunkeld), in contrast to the seven or eight in that region linked to Adomnán. We would be hard pressed to find any explanation for this other than one which goes back to around the time of Adomnán himself. For if we were to assume that it reflected the later medieval prestige of Iona, for example through the moving of Columba's relics to

[11] We have very little direct evidence for the pre-Benedictine possessions of the abbey of Iona in Argyll and the Western Isles. However, the papal bull which first mentions the Benedictine abbey (1203) explicitly states that some of its lands in Islay belonged to the pre-Benedictine *abbacia* (see RCAHMS *Argyll* iv.143).

[12] For a distribution map of commemorations of Mo Luóc, see Bowen, *Saints, Seaways and Settlements*, 104.

[13] See Clancy and Márkus, *Iona*, 104, 112 and 118–19.

Dunkeld (in Atholl) in the ninth century, then surely it is Columba's name which would have come to dominate.[14] In fact, the only early commemoration evidence we have of him in all Atholl, Gowrie and Strathearn (i.e. all Perthshire except for Menteith), where most of the 'tribes of the Tay' must have dwelt, and which from the ninth century onwards became the heartland of the kingdom of Alba, whose patron saint Columba can be said to have been,[15] is the cathedral church of Dunkeld itself, which was dedicated to him.[16]

Atholl formed a recognisable sub-kingdom within the Pictish kingdom. As early as 739 it is recorded:[17]

> *Talorggan m. Drostain rex Athfoitle dimersus est, i. la Oengus*
>
> (Talorcan son of Drostan, king of Atholl, was drowned by Onuist [king of the Picts]).

[14] It should be noted, however, that Adomnán had his own status and prestige in the later Middle Ages in Scotland. Fordun, writing in the late fourteenth century, followed by Bower, writing in the mid-fifteenth century, mentions a prophecy of *Sanctus Adamnanus Iensis abbas* which foretold that Cinaed mac Alpín (*Kenedus filius Alpini*) would take possession of Scotland *de fluvio Tyne juxta Northumbriam ad Orchadum insulas.* The source of this prophecy cannot be found (*John of Fordun's Chronicle*, trans. Skene, 138; *Scotichronicon* ii, 278 and note at 446).

[15] Radner, *Fragmentary Annals of Ireland*, 17; see also Bannerman, '*Comarba Coluim Chille*', 29. See Clancy, at pp. 26–7 above, in which the passage from the *Fragmentary Annals* is quoted in full.

[16] See *Series Episcoporum* Series VI, vol. i *Ecclesia Scoticana*, ed. Watt *et al.*, 40, according to which the earliest reference to St Columba being the patron of Dunkeld Cathedral is from 1207. The only other possible traces of Columba commemorations in Atholl, Gowrie and Strathearn are: a St Colme's Well, Dunkeld and Dowally parish (NO0143) and a *Féill mo-Chalmaig* formerly held at the end of February in Moulin (by Pitlochry), first recorded in the *OSA*: see Watson, *Celtic Place-Names*, 279. Linked to this is a *Tobair Chalmaig* or St Colm's Well in Pitlochry, now covered over just south of the junction of Tober Argan Road and Lower Oakfield; see Liddell, *Pitlochry*, 64; see also below, p. 54. The parish church of Arngask was dedicated to St Columba, according to a charter of 1527 (*Camb. Reg.* no. 22). Although this parish now lies in Perthshire (Strathearn), it was in the sheriffdom of Fife (diocese of St Andrews) in the medieval period; for the complicated development of this parish, see Taylor, 'Settlement-Names in Fife', 94.

[17] AU 739.7. AT 739.6 similarly has *Talorcan mac Drostan, rex Athfotla, a bathadh la hAengus.*

The name 'Atholl', which means 'New Ireland', and is first mentioned in this annal, suggests significant early settlement from the Gaelic kingdom of Dál Riata in the west long before the establishment of Gaelic power in Pictland in the ninth century.[18] The concentration of Adomnán commemorations in Atholl, together with the strong and very localised commemorations to Coeti, the bishop of Iona associated with Adamnán (for whom see below pp. 58–9), and the cluster of *cill*-place-names around Logierait, the early secular centre of Atholl,[19] all suggest intensive Gaelic activity here, both secular and ecclesiastical, in the late seventh and early eighth century. In fact, we might go so far as to suggest that Atholl was the site of at least one of the *monasteria* of St Columba, so tantalisingly mentioned by Adomnán as existing in Pictland in the 680s.[20]

If we take the statements in the *Amra Coluim Chille* regarding Columba and the tribes on the Tay literally, and if we accept that Atholl was the *locus* of relatively intense Iona activity in immediate post-Columban times, one possible way of reconciling this with the remarkable dearth of Columba commemorations in the area would be as follows. It is possible that Adomnán and his contemporaries were indeed building on a Columban presence in Atholl which dated from Columba's own time, but that the drowning of Talorcan, king of Atholl in 739, which followed on Onuist's invasion of Dál Riata in 736,[21] seriously circumscribed this Iona-inspired activity. The place-names and commemorations there could then be seen to reflect this later stage of direct Iona involvement, frozen in time, as it were, by its sudden end. Of course, this hypothetical end might have come slightly earlier, with the much-discussed but little-understood expulsion of the community of Iona across Drumalban (the mountains dividing Atholl from Dál Riata) by Naiton king of the Picts, recorded in the Annals of Ulster under the year 717.[22] For a tenuous link to the period between Columba and Adomnán in Atholl, we might

18 Watson, *Celtic Place-Names*, 228–9.
19 See Taylor, 'Place-names and the early Church', 103.
20 Anderson, *Adomnán*, 178 (II. 46).
21 AU 736.1, 739.7; AT 736.1, 739.6.
22 *Expulsio familie Ie trans Dorsum Brittanie a Nectano rege*: AU 717.4; also AT 717.3.

point to the possible Fergna commemoration (abbot of Iona 605–23) in Pitlochry, Moulin parish, for which see below p. 54.

Baithéne

Columba was succeeded as abbot of Iona by his cousin Baithéne (597–600).[23] He appears as *Baitheneus* in Adomnán's *Vita Columbae*, and was also called Conin.[24] Although abbot for only three years, he had been amongst the monks who had accompanied Columba from Ireland to Iona,[25] and he 'seems to have been the saint's right-hand man'.[26] Two commemorations in Scotland can be ascribed to him with reasonable certainty. The first, and more certain, is the Berwickshire parish of Abbey St Bathans (St Andrews diocese, Merse deanery). It appears as *ecclesia Sancti Boithani* and *ecclesia Sancti Boythani ca* 1250.[27]

Approximately 20 kilometres north-west of Abbey St Bathans, on the other side of the Lammermuir Hills, lies the parish of Yester in East Lothian. The other name for this parish was *Bothan*[28] or *Bothanis*.[29] Watson confidently saw this name, too, as deriving from Baithéne, second abbot of Iona.[30] I would be more tentative in this ascription, in the light of the frequent use of the Gaelic *both* 'hut, sheiling' in a religious context.[31] However, it is a maxim of toponymics that a place-name should never be looked at in isolation, either geographically or historically. If this maxim is applied to Abbey St Bathans, a remarkable picture begins to emerge.

[23] For a full list of early abbots of Iona, and their relationships with each other, see Anderson, *Adomnán*, xxxviii ff.
[24] Anderson, *Adomnán*, 238 (Appendix).
[25] *Ibid.*
[26] Sharpe, *Adomnán*, 256, *q.v.* for a useful potted history of Baithéne's life.
[27] *Dunf. Reg.*, 205; and *St A Lib.*, 31. The 'Abbey' in the name appears to be a late (post-medieval) addition, and refers to a Cistercian nunnery founded there in the thirteenth century, for which see Cowan and Easson, *Medieval Religious Houses: Scotland*, 148.
[28] *ca* 1250: *St A Lib.*, 30.
[29] *ca* 1250: *Dunf. Reg.*, 204.
[30] Watson, *Celtic Place-Names*, 151.
[31] See Taylor, 'Place-names and the early Church', *passim*.

Abbey St Bathans lies on or near the southern end of several roads and tracks which traverse the long, inhospitable ridge of the Lammermuir Hills (see Fig. 3).[32] One of these begins its ascent into the hills on the northern or Lothian side at Yester or Bothan. The route now taken by the main road, the B6355, passes the Kell Burn in Whittingehame parish (NT6364) and, following the Whiteadder Water, it passes the Kilmade Burn (NT6663), which forms the march between East Lothian and Berwickshire (the parishes of Whittingehame ELO and Cranshaws BWK), and skirts the estate of Bothwell (*Bothkil*, between 1161 and 1164).[33] Still following the Whiteadder Water, the present main road leaves the river at Ellemford, while the Whiteadder continues about three kilometres to Abbey St Bathans, passing Shannobank (also known as Shannabank), which Watson derived from *Sean áth* 'old ford', remarking that it was already regarded as old at the time of the 'Gaelic occupation' (from the tenth century).[34] Two adjacent medieval parishes, Bunkle and Preston (now united), lie across this route as it emerges from the Lammermuirs south-east of Abbey St Bathans. Both were in the medieval period detached parishes of the diocese of Dunkeld, the only such south of the Lammermuirs, and amongst only five which lay besouth the Forth.[35] The name 'Bunkle' (*Bonekillesire*, between 1173 and 1178;[36] *Bonkel* in

[32] I have somewhat revised this section of the original article in *The Innes Review* 48 (1997) in the light of the very useful comments on roadways through the Lammermuirs made by Mr William Patterson of East Linton.

[33] From the royal confirmation of a grant made by Earl Gospatrick of Dunbar to Kelso Abbey of the *skalingas de Bothkil* ('the sheilings of Bothwell'). See *RRS* i, no. 217.

[34] Watson, *Celtic Place-Names*, 135.

[35] The other three are Abercorn WLO, Cramond MLO and Aberlady ELO. See *Atlas*, 353.

[36] *RRS* ii, no. 240. This original charter deals with the march between Bunkleshire and Coldinghamshire, and mentions a *Crhachoctrestrete* as forming part of that march. This indicates a paved or built road running from Oldhamstocks (to the north-west, north of the Lammermuirs) south-east via Causewaybank (NT8759) towards Berwick, probably along or near the present parish boundary between Coldingham and Bunkle-and-Preston. It is possible that any route coming from the direction of Abbey St Bathans might, in times of heavy rainfall at least, join this route in order to avoid crossing the Whiteadder, a difficult river which was very prone to flooding (see *OSA* iii.18).

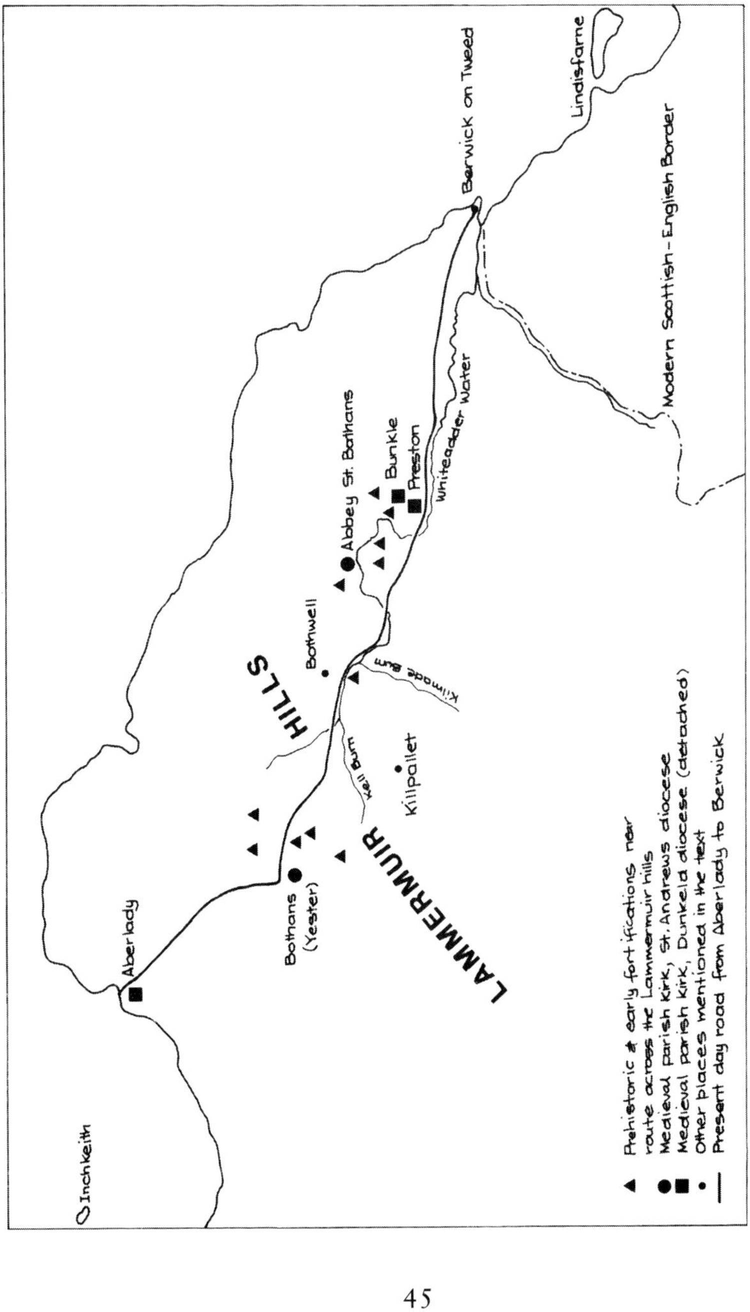

FIGURE 3. Map of East Lothian and Berwickshire showing the final section of the route from Iona to Lindisfarne, as it crosses the Lammermuir Hills

Bagimond's Roll, 1275),[37] seems to derive from Gaelic *bun chill* (earlier *bun chell*) probably meaning something like 'bottom church, church at the foot', which well describes its position: the medieval parish church of Bunkle lay at the very point where the flat plain of the Merse suddenly rises steeply up to the Lammermuirs (NT809596).[38]

The overwhelming impression given by the above litany of place-names is one of significant early Gaelic religious activity in and around the church which bears the name of Columba's immediate successor, Abbey St Bathans. Taken in isolation many of the minor names, such as those of the two burns, the Kell Burn and the Kilmade Burn, can be explained without resorting to Gaelic *cell, cill* 'church', as can the nearby Killpallet (*Gillpellet* and *Gibpallet* 1590; *Gilpallet* 1643; *Kilpallat* 1650).[39] Bothwell, given its early forms, and given the religious connotations of both its elements, is perhaps less easy to explain away, despite the specifically pastoral context in which it first appears.[40] The name 'Bothans' (Yester ELO) is strongly suggestive of early religious presence, whether it be interpreted as containing Baithéne's name, or Gaelic (or Gaelicised) *both*. Finally, both the name and the parochial status of Bunkle strongly signal the early religious nature of the site, and Columban connections are indicated by its close link with Dunkeld, not only as a detached parish but also as a mensal church of the bishop, 'at least since the early 12th century'.[41]

The extension of the kingdom of Alba south of the Lammermuirs is still not fully understood, but the best accounts suggest that Scottish power was firmly and irrevocably established there by the early eleventh century, after at least fifty years of Scottish

[37] Dunlop, 'Bagimond's Roll', 72.

[38] Or might it mean 'old or original church'? Compare *bun-nòs* 'old custom', *bun-fhàth* 'primary cause'.

[39] NT6260. All taken from *RMS*; see also Lang, *Whittingehame*, 186, who does not shy away from interpreting both the Kell Burn and Kilpallet as containing Gaelic *cill*. It should be noted here that none of the above place-names is mentioned in Williams, 'Non-Celtic Place-names of the Scottish Border Counties', which itself suggests that there are no obvious Germanic etymologies for them.

[40] See n. 33, above.

[41] Cowan, *Parishes of Medieval Scotland*, *s.n.*

penetration and settlement.[42] Evidence can even be adduced to suggest that the clergy of St Cuthbert, then at Chester-le-Street, had already lost their lands north of the Tweed by the 940s,[43] or even earlier.[44] The firm episcopal hold which the diocese of St Andrews exerted on all of Lothian (with the exception, of course, of the five Dunkeld detached parishes already mentioned) suggested to Barrow that 'the Scots held the upper hand in Lothian from the earlier part of the tenth century'.[45] This means that the Dunkeld episcopal connection with Bunkle and Preston cannot be earlier. Unfortunately, we do not know by what processes, or for what reasons, detached parishes, which are such a feature of medieval episcopal organisation in eastern Scotland, arose. Donald Watt writes:[46]

> Probably as a result of centuries-old loyalties dating back to missionary days, ... bishops retained authority over parishes which were geographically detached from the main area of the diocese.

Dunkeld may well have obtained Bunkle and Preston through some lingering Columban tradition, which finds toponymic expression in the adjacent parish of Abbey St Bathans.[47]

The place-name element *cill*, which is found at least in 'Bunkle', and possibly in one or more of those other names along the Abbey St Bathans–Bothans route mentioned above, has been the subject of several studies.[48] Nothing has fundamentally shaken

[42] See Barrow, *Kingdom of the Scots*, 148ff.; see also Anderson, 'Lothian and the early Scottish kings', and Duncan, *Scotland: The Making of the Kingdom*, 94.

[43] Barrow, *Kingdom of the Scots*, 152–3.

[44] Duncan, *Scotland: The Making of the Kingdom*, 94.

[45] Barrow, *Kingdom of the Scots*, 154.

[46] *Atlas*, 336.

[47] A similar Columban link, whether real or perceived, must lie behind the acquisition by the see of Dunkeld of the cluster of parishes on either side of the Forth surrounding Inchcolm, Aberdour parish FIF, where the Columban tradition was so strong that not only was the twelfth-century Augustinian house there dedicated to Columba, but three bishops of Dunkeld chose to be buried there in the thirteenth century. For more on this, see Taylor, 'Columba east of Drumalban'.

[48] For a full summary of these, see Taylor, 'Place-names and the early Church', 93–4 and endnotes 1 and 2. To this list can be added Redford, 'Commemorations of Saints', *passim*.

Nicolaisen's thesis that in eastern lowland Scotland *cill* ceased to be a productive place-name element before *ca* 800.[49] In fact, I have argued elsewhere that the *cill*-place-names in Fife and Atholl suggest that they were formed around 700.[50] If this is accepted, then the formation of the place-name 'Bunkle', would pre-date the acquisition of Lothian by the Gaels by two centuries or more.

The thread that holds together all the above toponymic and historical data is the aforementioned routeway. Not only is this one of the few routes which cross the Lammermuirs, it is also the most direct route from Edinburgh and Haddington to Berwick-on-Tweed, and, more significantly in the context of the present discussion, Lindisfarne.

In the seventh century we know that there was much coming and going between Iona and Lindisfarne. Oswald's victory over King Cadwallon in 634 made him king of all Northumbria, both Deira and Bernicia (the northern part of Northumbria), which by this time almost certainly included the Merse, though probably not the fertile lands north of the Lammermuirs.[51] Soon after this battle, as Bede tells us, Oswald asked 'the high-ranking men of the *Scotti*' (*maiores natu Scottorum*), amongst whom would have been Segéne, abbot of Iona 623–52, 'that a bishop (*antistes*) be sent to him by whose teaching and ministry the English people over whom he ruled might receive the blessings of the Christian faith, and the sacraments'. They sent him Bishop Aidan (*pontifex Aidanus, episcopus Aidan*), whom Bede describes as a monk (*monachus*) from the island called *Hii* (Iona). As a result, we are told that 'from then on many arrived in Britain (*Brittania*) day by day from the country (*regio*) of the *Scotti* and proclaimed the word of God . . . in all the provinces of the English under Oswald's rule'.[52] *Regio Scottorum* is here best translated 'Dál Riata', and may in fact simply mean Iona.[53] These 'many from Dál Riata' had several routes which they could have taken to Northumbria, and they no doubt varied according to local political

[49] Nicolaisen, *Scottish Place-Names*, 128–30 and 142–4.
[50] Taylor, 'Place-names and the early Church', 103.
[51] See Jackson, 'Edinburgh and the Anglian occupation', 35–6 *et passim.*
[52] Bede, *HE* iii.3.
[53] As Colgrave and Mynors point out in their notes, Bede, *HE* 220, n. 1.

conditions, which must often have been difficult, since whichever way was chosen would entail the traversing of border zones actively disputed amongst the various peoples of early medieval Scotland (see Fig. 4).

One of the most direct routes would have been to the Firth of Forth, either (1) overland by Strathfillan and Glen Falloch to Loch Lomond, where the choice could be made between a more mountainous route to Stirling via Inversnaid, Aberfoyle and the Lake of Menteith (Inchmahome); or to the Kelvin Valley via Balloch and Strathblane; or (2) via Crinan in Knapdale, then 'up the watter' to Glasgow, and up the Kelvin Valley. In the Firth of Forth there are the islands of Inchcolm (Aberdour FIF) with its strong Columban associations[54] and Inchkeith (Kinghorn FIF) with its tradition of Adomnán dating back to before the twelfth century (see p. 66 below). From here the choice was to continue by sea around the exposed Lothian and Berwickshire coast, or to head south-west by the shortest overland route through the Lammermuirs. If the overland route was taken, the most convenient landing-place would have been Aberlady, also a detached parish of Dunkeld diocese, whence over the Lammermuirs, perhaps via Gifford (Bothans) to Bunkle and Preston, passing through or near Abbey St Bathans.

If it is correct to assume that the second abbot of Iona is commemorated in two important place-names found at either end of this important hill-crossing, then we are justified in posing the question as to whether Iona influence was starting to penetrate into Bernicia along this route as early as the beginning of the seventh century, at the very time that Baithéne was abbot of Iona, about thirty years before Oswald invited Aidan to become bishop of Lindisfarne.[55] However, many of those making the long and difficult way from the abbey of Iona to Northumbria in the 630s and 640s would have been younger contemporaries of Baithéne, and these far flung commemorations to him might well have been

[54] See n. 47, above.

[55] Máire Herbert mentions political interaction between the Bernician royal dynasty and the secular patrons of Iona as having existed from the late sixth century. The fact that Oswald chose Iona as his place of exile in the early seventh century also points to close links pre-dating 634 (Herbert, *Iona, Kells, and Derry*, 41).

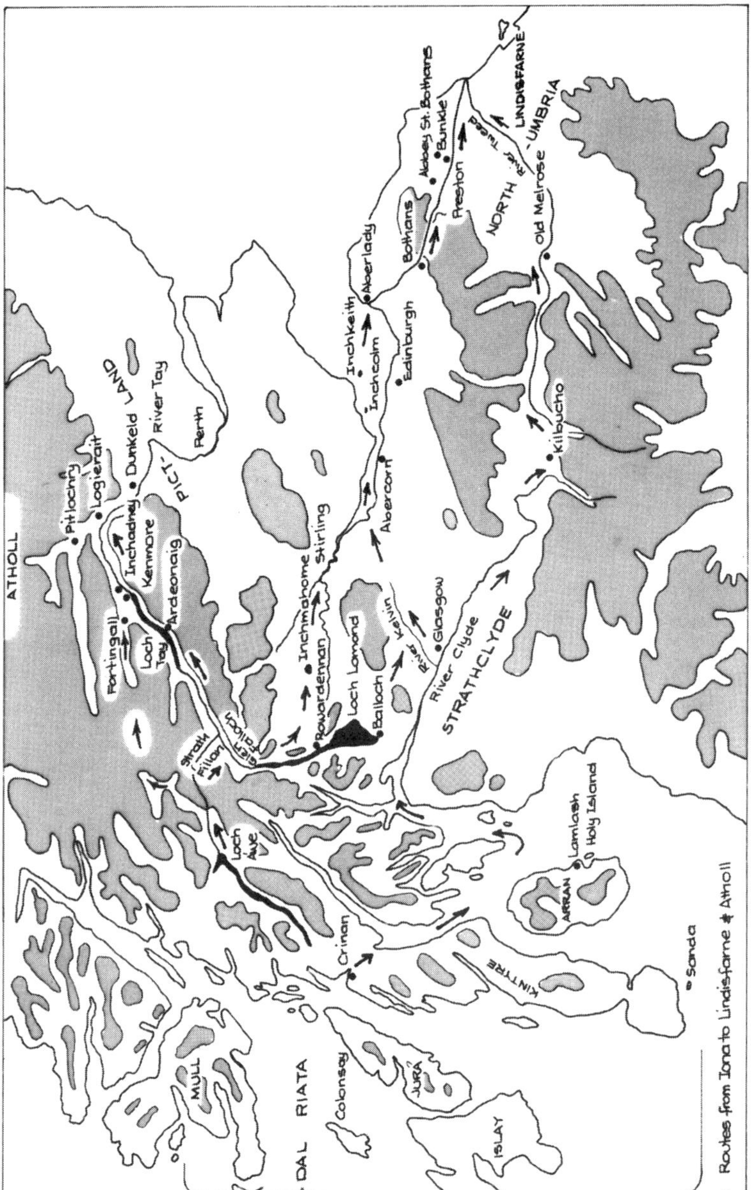

FIGURE 4. Routes from Iona to Atholl and Lindisfarne (Shading represents land over 250 metres)

due to some close relative of the second abbot, whether spiritual or familial or both.[56]

Another route which the 'many *Scotti*' had at their disposal was one which involved more overland travel, but was as direct as either of those described above. This involved passing through Glasgow, either by Strathfillan, Glen Falloch, Loch Lomond, Balloch and the Vale of Leven, or by the more maritime route described above, then following the Clyde up as far as Coulter LAN, whence an easy crossing through the hills could be made to the Tweed Valley near Drumelzier PEB.[57] It would then simply be a case of following the Tweed down as far as its mouth, only a few kilometres south of which lay Lindisfarne. It is perhaps significant that at one of the crossing-points between the Clyde and Tweed Valleys is the medieval parish of Kilbucho PEB, now part of the united parish of Broughton, Glenholm and Kilbucho, hitherto recognised as the farthest south-east example of a *cill*-name.[58] The most important early foundation in south-east Scotland which is related to this Clyde–Tweed route from Iona to Lindisfarne is the monastery of Old Melrose, established some time during Aidan's episcopate (635–51).[59]

Although intercourse between Northumbria and Iona must have waned somewhat after the Synod of Whitby in 664, it revived

[56] In the same manner that Baithéne himself was both cousin and *daltae* ('foster-son') of Columba (see Sharpe, *Adomnán*, 256–7).

[57] It is this last route, via the Crinan isthmus to Glasgow, then by Clyde and Tweed to Berwick that is shown as the only route between Iona and Lindisfarne on E. G. Bowen's map of the Western Seaways, after Crawford, 'Western seaways' (see Bowen, *Saints, Seaways and Settlements*, 10, fig. 2).

[58] I will not enter here upon the vexed question of the identity of the eponymous saint in Kilbucho: *Kilbevhoc ca* 1200 (*Melr. Lib.*), *Kilbeuhoc ca* 1200 and *Kelbechoc ca* 1230 (*Glas. Reg.*). It is generally accepted to be a female saint, Bega, with late seventh-century Northumbrian associations (see Watson, *Celtic Place-Names*, 151). However, as several writers have pointed out, there are many problems with a saint who might have started life as a holy bracelet. The arguments are best summed up in Todd, 'St Bega: cult, fact and legend'. I am grateful both to Dr Todd and Professor Robert Bartlett for discussion and enlightenment on this complex matter. The possibility also exists that we are dealing here with a late seventh-century saint called (Mo)Becóc, for whom see MacLean, 'Knapdale dedications to a Leinster saint', 58–9.

[59] See, for example, Duncan, *Scotland: The Making of the Kingdom*, 69.

again during the reign of Aldfrith (685–705), known also by his Irish name of Fland Fína, a friend of Adomnán, and with strong Irish and Iona connections: we know from various sources that Adomnán visited him in Northumbria twice in the late 680s.[60]

Cill Bheathain by Inverness has been associated with Baithéne.[61] However, according to Watson,[62] this commemorates St Beóán (Bean), and the early forms quoted by Mackay[63] *Kill Baine* 1649 and *Kilvain* 1666 would certainly support this, the *th* in the modern Gaelic spelling simply signalling the separate articulation of the vowels.

Laisrán

Baithéne's successor as abbot of Iona was Laisrán or Laisrén (mac Feredaig) (600–5) *Laisranus* in *Vita Columbae* another relative of Columba (son of a cousin), and closely associated with Columba in both Scotland and Ireland.[64] According to Watson he is not commemorated in any place-names in Scotland, although he considers a name-sake, who died in 639,[65] to be the saint whose name is found in Lamlash in Arran.[66] However, given the position of Lamlash and Holy Island near to one of the main routes from Iona to eastern (and south-western) Scotland, it is more likely that this place-name commemorates Laisrán the third abbot of Iona (see Fig. 4).

Fergna

Laisrán was succeeded by Fergnae or Virgno (*Virgnou(u)s* in *Vita Columbae*) (605–23). He was probably the first abbot of Iona

[60] Aldfrith's career and background are usefully summarised in Sharpe, *Adomnán*, 350–1.

[61] Redford, 'Commemorations of Saints', 55–6. 'The Estate of Bught of which Tor-a'-Bhean [now Torvaine NH6543] is a part, is called in Gaelic 'Kil a Bhean', or Bean's burying ground': Mackay, 'Saints associated with the valley of the Ness', 153.

[62] Watson, *Celtic Place-Names*, 312.

[63] Mackay, 'Saints associated with the valley of the Ness', 153.

[64] See Sharpe, *Adomnán*, 273–4.

[65] AU 639.5 (Do Laissi moccu Imdae, abbot of Leithglenn); AT 639.7 (Mo Laissi moccu Dima of Leithglenn).

[66] See Watson, *Celtic Place-Names*, 305–6.

not to belong to Columba's *cenél* or kin-group, and appears to have had British connections.[67] Watson considered that there were at least two place-names which contained his name, although both are recorded relatively late. Both are wells, both called *Tobair Fheargáin*, one in Kirkmichael parish BNF and one at Pitlochry PER. Both are described by Watson as 'famous wells', especially the Kirkmichael one,[68] and local traditions would seem to support this (see below). In addition there is Tir Fhearagain (*Tìr Fhearagáin*) in the parish of Kilvickeon (now Kilfinichen and Kilvickeon) in the Ross of Mull ARG. It lies only eight kilometres from Iona Abbey, to which it belonged (NM3318). However, its earliest recorded form *Teirgargane*, from 1588, suggests a different etymology.[69] It appears as *Tirergan* between 1769 and 1804 and 1802.[70] Besides Abbot Fergna there are two saints and one bishop of this name mentioned in the Irish genealogies.[71]

Tobair Fheargáin in Kirkmichael parish, near Tomintoul BNF, is on the south-east slope of Cnoc Fergan (*Cnoc Fheargáin*) (NJ1323). Both these features lie at the heart of Kirkmichael parish, with the parish kirk immediately north-east of Cnoc Fergan, on the other side of the River Avon. *Tobair Fheargáin* or Fergan's Well (as it is now known) is pictured in Peck, *Avonside Explored*, where it is stated that 'tradition tells of a busy sheep market held on this slope'.[72] It was certainly conveniently placed as a tryst for the inhabitants of Glen Lochy, Glen Broun and Stratha'an, which is no doubt why the parish church developed nearby.

These two place-names in the centre of Kirkmichael parish do suggest a local cult of a holy man called Fergan. Whoever this holy man was, it is noteworthy that his cult had been superseded by that of Michael already by the early thirteenth century, when

[67] See Herbert, *Iona, Kells, and Derry*, 39–40 and Sharpe, *Adomnán*, 370.

[68] Watson, *Celtic Place-Names*, 322.

[69] *RMS* v, no. 1492; see also *OPS* ii.306.

[70] The first in an unpublished lease belonging to the Argyll Estates; the second in a valuation roll. I am grateful to Dr Mairi MacArthur for these two references.

[71] See *CGSH*.

[72] Peck, *Avonside Explored: A Guide to Tomintoul and Glenlivet*, 34.

the land of *Lecheni*[73] *Michel* is mentioned as part of the lands of Stratha'an belonging to the bishop of Moray. Professor Barrow considers this to be the 'germ of the future parish of Kirkmichael', and the first part of the name is represented today by the place-name Achlichnie, which lies immediately south of the parish kirk (NJ1523).[74]

Tobair Fheargáin in Pitlochry, Moulin parish PER still exists. It is near the centre of the town, at the bottom of Well Brae, by Tobarargan Road, which preserves the name in Anglicised or Scotticised form.[75] It may be noted in passing that a well situated a few metres east of *Tobair Fheargáin*, and now covered over, is called locally *Tobair Chalmaig* or St Colm's Well.[76] According to the *OSA*, *Féill mo-Chalmáig* was held at Moulin beside Pitlochry at the end of February.[77]

Commán

We are on equally tenuous ground with dedications to Commán, not an Iona abbot, but the name of Fergna's nephew, and Adomnán's contemporary,[78] as well as the name of at least ten other saints.[79] Watson considered (for no particular reason, except probably that of proximity to, and early association with, Iona) that the Islay church and parish (both medieval and modern) of Kilchoman commemorates this Commán.[80] The only other commemoration of Commán in Scotland, and one not noted by Watson, is the dedication of the medieval parish kirk of Rossie (formerly **Rossieclerach*), now part of Inchture parish PER. In 1243 Bishop David de Bernham of St Andrews, as part of his

[73] As this name occurs in the early fourteenth century as *Lykeuyne*, and its modern reflex is 'Achlichnie', this is the more likely reading of this name than *Letheni* of *Moray Reg*.

[74] Barrow, 'Badenoch and Strathspey, 1130–1312: (2) the church', 2–4.

[75] Liddell, *Pitlochry: Heritage of a Highland District*, 64.

[76] *Ibid*.

[77] Note also the hill which dominates Strathtay to the north of Aberfeldy, which is called Farragon Hill (780 metres).

[78] See Anderson, *Adomnán*, 210 (III. 19).

[79] Watson, *Celtic Place-Names*, 302. According to Fergna's genealogy, the abbot's brother was also called Commán (*CGSH* 313.1).

[80] Watson, *Celtic Place-Names*, 302. *Kilchoman* 1426: *CSSR* ii.127.

efforts to (re)consecrate all the churches of his extensive diocese, consecrated the church of *Rossinclerach* to St Laurence and St Comanus confessor.[81] We have several indicators of the existence of an early religious centre here: our earliest reference to Rossie is from a charter of King Malcolm IV, referring back to one given by David I *ca* 1150, which mentions *abbacia de Rossim*, part of the land or revenues of which the king granted to Matthew, archdeacon of St Andrews.[82] The fine Class II Pictish cross-slab, which was found in the old burial ground of what was formerly the parish kirk of Rossie (NO292308), also indicates eighth-century Christian activity on the site.[83] Furthermore, in *ca* 1160 it is referred to as *Rosinclerach*, a Gaelic name meaning 'Rossie of the clerics', when it was given to St Andrews Priory by Archdeacon Matthew. It might be argued that the Gaelic *clerach* here refers to its possession by the clerics of St Andrews, but the *abbacia* and the carved stone suggest rather a much earlier group of clerics. The name of St Commán is also preserved in a now obsolete place-name referring to the upland immediately north-west of Rossie: it appears *ca* 1150 as *Hoctor Comon*,[84] where *Hoctor* represents Gaelic *uachdar* 'upland', the 'Auchter' of many Lowland Scots place-names.[85] This does not bring us any closer to identifying the Commán in question, but it does show that the cult of a Commán was firmly rooted in the vicinity of Rossie, an early Christian centre before the early twelfth century, and that Bishop David de Bernham was drawing on genuine local tradition in his (re)dedication of 1243.

Fergna died in 623, and was succeeded by Ségéne, a member of Columba's kin. His long abbacy of twenty-nine years saw the expansion of Iona's influence into Northumbria under Aidan (see above p. 51), as well as his staunch defence of Columban traditions

[81] *St A Lib.*, 348.
[82] *RRS* i, nos. 99 and 120.
[83] *ECMS* ii.306–8.
[84] *Dunf. Reg.* no. 24.
[85] For later forms such as *Ouchtircomon* and *Achtyrcoman*, and its identification with an area comprising Littleton and Lauriston in Longforgan parish PER, see *RRS* i.42 n. 7. A saint Com(m)án, who died *ca* 740, has given rise to the Irish Roscommon, for which see Joyce, *Irish Names of Places* i.495. See also Bannerman, '*Comarba Coluim Chille*', 25–6.

in the face of Roman custom.[86] Despite his long and influential period in office, there would seem to be no place-name or church-dedication in Scotland which commemorates him; which was also the case with his successor, Suibne moccu Urthri (652–7), during whose period of office Ionan influence was extended into Mercia.[87]

Cumméne

The next abbot of Iona whose name appears in a place-name is Cumméne (657–69) (*Cummeneus albus* in *Vita Columbae*). He was also of Columba's kin, and nephew of Ségéne. It was during his abbacy that the Synod of Whitby was held (664), after which the influence of Iona in Northumbria was, for a time at least, seriously diminished, and 'contributed to the adoption within the community [of Iona] of a defiant and somewhat embattled position in regard to the customs of its beloved founder'.[88] His name would seem to be contained in the alternative name Kilchumin, Gaelic *Cill Chuiméin*, for the medieval parish of Abertarff (Moray diocese, now Boleskine and Abertarff INV, at the south-west end of Loch Ness).[89] In 1431 we find mention of the vicarage of '*Ky[l]chommen* or *Abertarff*'.[90] Both Abertarff (*Abyrtorf*) and Kilchumin (*Kilwhuimen*) appear on Pont's map of 1590s.[91] Nearby the *OSA* has *Suidhe Chuiméin*, 'Cumméne's Seat'.

Suy Chummenn (for *Suidhe Chuiméin*) appears on a Pont manuscript map of Moray (NLS Pont Map no. 8) from the 1590s referring to the hill and hillfort one kilometre south of Dulsie Bridge, in Ardclach parish NAI (Moray diocese; NH933407). There are the remains of a chapel immediately to the north-east. The neighbouring farm, on whose lands the above features are situated, is Dunearn,[92] which must have been another, and presumably older, name for *Suy Chummenn*. Watson suggests that 'Dunearn' means 'fort of Ireland', referring to a district

[86] Herbert, *Iona, Kells, and Derry*, 41 and 42.
[87] Sharpe, *Adomnán*, 40–1; see also Herbert, *Iona, Kells, and Derry*, 43.
[88] Herbert, *Iona, Kells, and Derry*, 45.
[89] Watson, *Celtic Place-Names*, 303.
[90] *CSSR* iii.178.
[91] Stone, *Illustrated Maps of Scotland*, Plate 31.
[92] *Dunnern* 1507: *RMS* iii, no. 3068.

name which stretched as far as the Moray coast (Watson, *Celtic Place-Names*, 230).[93]

The other church north of the Forth–Clyde line, apart from that of Abertarff, which may have been dedicated to Cumméne was that of Glenelg INV (Argyll diocese; NG8219). It is *Heglis Kilchummerin* on Pont's map of 1590s as printed in Blaeu's *Atlas Novus* of 1654.[94] The form on Pont's manuscript map, however, seems to be *Kilchammerin*.[95] In 1671 it appears as *Kilchuman in Glenelg*,[96] and in the early eighteenth century as *Killchinnen*, *Kilchonen* and *Kilwhonan*.[97]

If these dedications are to Abbot Cumméne, then they perhaps reflect a renewed interest in Pictland on the part of Iona following the set-backs in England during his period of office.[98]

As with Ségéne and Suibne moccu Urthri, Abbot Cumméne's successor, Fáilbe (669–79), has left no recognisable commemorations in Scotland.

Adomnán

The next abbot of Iona was Adomnán (679–704); and with him the sparse and tenuous pattern of commemoration in Scotland, which we have observed in connection with his predecessors, changes dramatically. Twenty commemorations are listed by Redford,[99] twenty-one in Ó Muraíle,[100] and their distribution shows a distinctly eastern Scottish bias (see Fig. 2).

[93] But it may also be referring to the nearby River Findhorn (*Fyndaryn* 1226: *Moray Reg.* no. 29). See Watson, *Celtic Place-Names*, 230, as well as Nicolaisen, *Scottish Place-Names* (second impr.), 187. For more on this Dulsie Bridge–Cumméne reference, see Barrow, 'Macbeth and other mormaers of Moray', 114 and endnote at 122.

[94] Stone, *Illustrated Maps of Scotland*, Plate 31.

[95] According to *OPS* ii.207.

[96] Argyle Inventory, as quoted in *OPS* ii.207.

[97] *Geog. Coll.* ii.174 and 542–3.

[98] Note also Kirkcolm WIG, which was dedicated to St Cuimmíne or Cumméne. See Brooke, *Wild Men and Holy Places*, 75 and endnote at 192. I am grateful to Dr Thomas Clancy for this reference.

[99] Redford, 'Commemorations of Saints', 116–17; see also Watson, *Celtic Place-Names*, 270–1 and the Appendix below.

[100] Ó Muraíle, 'Columban onomastic legacy', 217 and map 10.

His career has been subjected to much competent discussion.[101] It involved recorded journeys to Northumbria (twice) and Ireland, although none to Pictland are explicitly mentioned in any of the sources. However, his relations with the Pictish king Bruide mac Derile (697–706) were such that the king appears as one of the guarantors of Adomnán's 'Law of the Innocents', the *Cáin Adomnáin*, proclaimed at the Synod of Birr in 697.[102] Whether or not King Bruide was present at the Synod of Birr in person, his inclusion in the list implies close diplomatic contact between Adomnán and the Pictish court. Furthermore, close and cordial relations with Pictland are implied by Adomnán's statement in *Vita Columbae* that there were several of 'St Columba's monasteries', i.e. monasteries belonging to the *paruchia* of Iona, within Pictland, which were held in great honour by the Picts.[103] As the well-travelled head of this *paruchia* for twenty-five years, and with good diplomatic links to at least one king of the Picts, it must be assumed that Adomnán visited Pictland more than once in his career.

This assumption is further supported by the place-name and dedicatory evidence, both directly and indirectly related to Adomnán. Of particular significance is the cluster of Adomnán-related place-names in Strathtay and central Atholl, already alluded to above (p. 40). The most important of these is the name for what was in the late twelfth century the principal church of Atholl. It became known as Logierait, but in the twelfth- and thirteenth-century record it is known as **Logie Mahedd*, that is 'Logie of St Coeti'.[104] Coeti was bishop of Iona. He died in 712, but was no doubt bishop there during Adomnán's abbacy, since he appears in 697 (as *Ceti epscop*) as one of the guarantors of the *Cáin Adomnáin*.[105]

[101] For some of the best accounts of his life, see Anderson, *Adomnán*, xxxix-xliii; Herbert, *Iona, Kells, and Derry*, 47–56 and Sharpe, *Adomnán*, 43–53. In Herbert, *Iona, Kells, and Derry*, 48, the chronology of the late 680s is thrown out by one year by the misdating of Egfrith's raid on Brega to 685 (for 684).

[102] See Ní Dhonnchadha, 'The guarantor list', 181 and 214.

[103] Anderson, *Adomnán*, 178 (II.46).

[104] *RRS* ii.341.

[105] See Ní Dhonnchadha, 'The guarantor list', 180 and 191.

To the long recognised place-names and commemorations to Coeti in the Strathtay area (in the parishes of Logierait and Fortingall)[106] can be added one more important probable Coeti place-name. Watson mentions that Coeti's name 'seems to appear also in Inchcad, conjoined with Clony (Clunie in Stormont), 1275'.[107] His reference is to Bagimond's Roll, where the form is *Inchecad*.[108] Although linked to Clunie to form a prebend for the dean of Dunkeld Cathedral, it is geographically quite separate. It appears also as *Inchcadin* in connection with Bishop Geoffrey of Dunkeld (1236–49), and as *Inchkadin* in 1506.[109] It forms the core of the later parish of Kenmore. The site of the medieval church is on the north bank of the Tay, immediately opposite Taymouth Castle (NN782467). Watson failed to make the link between this site, which is now known as Inchadney (Gaelic *Innis Chailtnidh* or *Innis Chaidnidh / Chaitnidh*), and the medieval parish of Inchcadin,[110] thus throwing subsequent researchers off the trail.

We therefore find Coeti linked to two important church sites within twenty kilometres of one another along a major route which leads from Argyll into the heart of Pictland via Strathfillan, Glendochart, Loch Tay and Strathtay (see Fig. 4). This must be significant of strong Iona influence, and since Coeti does not seem to have enjoyed great fame or prestige after his death, we can assume that his very localised cult found in Atholl was a result of contemporary presence in that area either of himself or of closely associated clergy.[111]

I have discussed elsewhere the wider implications of this, as well as of other place-name evidence in Atholl pointing to Iona

[106] See Watson, *Celtic Place-Names*, 314, and MacKinlay, *Dedications*, 417.

[107] Watson, *Celtic Place-Names*, 314.

[108] Dunlop, 'Bagimond's Roll', 73.

[109] *Dunk. Rent.*, 335 and 12.

[110] Watson, *Celtic Place-Names*, 314 and 517–18; *idem*, 'The place-names of Breadalbane', 258–9. The medieval church became disused *ca* 1762, and was subsequently demolished (see *ibid.*, 258).

[111] But see also n. 134 below. For references to a local cult of Coeti in a part of Co. Tyrone which lies near the important Columban centre of Derry, see *The Martyrology of Donegal*, at October 24 and 25, and note 2, 284–5. I am grateful to Dr T. O. Clancy for drawing my attention to this.

influence.[112] We would be justified in assuming that some of the other holy men commemorated in the place-names of this area, such as Coemi, whose name is found in Killiehangie in Logierait parish, were connected with Coeti and Iona at around this same period.[113] The Martyrology of Gorman at 2 November commemorates 'Cóemhi, i.e. a man of Alba (*Albannach*) from *Cell Cóeimhi*', which probably refers to Killiehangie and its saint.[114] Unfortunately we have no other information regarding him.

This survey of the place-names and commemorations relating to Iona abbots of the seventh century ends with the death of Adomnán. After him the succession of abbots is confusing, and, coming as it does at the height of the controversy at Iona regarding Roman usages, including the celebration of Easter and the form of tonsure, has led to much speculation about schism and rival abbots.[115] Both Anderson and Sharpe interpret the evidence more cautiously:[116] the latter writes, 'Rather than conjecture a schism, we should admit that it is impossible to interpret how the abbacy was occupied during this period'.[117]

One of these successors to Adomnán was Dúnchad or Duncan, who died in 717. His name seems to occur in two of the *cill*-place-names of east Fife, the significance of which I have discussed elsewhere.[118] In the eighth century there seems to be a general diminution of Iona influence in Pictland, and this may be reflected in the dearth of place-names which appear to commemorate eighth-century Iona abbots.

Concluding remarks

There is still much work to be done in Scotland before we can begin to talk with any confidence of the historical and onomastic

[112] See Taylor, 'Place-names and the early Church', 101–3 and 106.

[113] See *ibid.*, 106.

[114] See *The Martyrology of Gorman*, at 2 November. See also Watson, *Celtic Place-Names*, 314. The name as such does not appear in *CGSH*.

[115] See Herbert, *Iona, Kells, and Derry*, 57–67. The details of this succession are set out most clearly (in tabular form) in Anderson, *Adomnán*, xliii.

[116] *Ibid.*, xlii-xlv.

[117] Sharpe, *Adomnán*, 75.

[118] Taylor, 'Place-names and the early Church'.

reality which lies behind place-names and other commemorations referring to early medieval holy men and women, or at the very least to say 'we can go no further'. The basis must be the building up of a complete database of such references, with a full evaluation of the sources. The great place-name scholar, W. J. Watson, in his introductory remarks made to the paper given in April 1909 to the Gaelic Society of Inverness by W. Mackay entitled 'Saints associated with the valley of the Ness', said: 'I have often wished that some one would make an exhaustive list of Highland foundations by, and dedications to, ancient clerics and missionaries.'[119] If he had been speaking in the 1990s, he would have used the word 'database' rather than 'list'! J. M. MacKinlay went some way towards this list in his valuable *Ancient Church Dedications of Scotland: Non-Scriptural* in 1914, but the usefulness of his work is seriously limited by his uncritical use of sources, many of which he fails to cite. Watson himself made an important contribution to the task in Chapter 10 ('Saints of West and East') of his monumental *Celtic Place-Names of Scotland*. And more recently the work of Morag Redford (1988),[120] sadly unpublished, has pulled together many of the diverse strands, and will be of immense value for future scholars in this field.

Another important aspect in the interpretation of this material is one which has been more honoured in the breach than the observance in the above chapter. This is the comparison of commemorative material in Ireland and Scotland. Unfortunately Ireland lacks the equivalent of Watson's *Celtic Place-Names*, or even of MacKinlay's *Ancient Church Dedications of Scotland: Non-Scriptural*, which means that much of the basic material has still to be presented in an easily accessible form.[121] There is much scope for joint Irish–Scottish initiatives in this area.

[119] Watson's opening remarks are at 145–6.

[120] Redford, 'Commemorations of Saints'.

[121] However, expert local studies such as Mac Giolla Easpaig, 'Early ecclesiastical settlement names of County Galway', are beginning to remedy this situation. Also, since June 1997, there are in print the excellent comprehensive lists and maps of all Irish commemorations of Columba and Adomnán by Ó Muraíle 'The Columban onomastic legacy', 199ff.). I am grateful to Dr C. Etchingham and Dr C. Swift for information regarding Ireland.

In any wider analysis or interpretation of this data, the ideas advanced by E. G. Bowen regarding route-ways and networks of communication must play a prominent part, as I have tried to show in the above discussion of Baithéne dedications. It helps make sense of what is often a very confusing and disjointed picture, and opens up exciting new lines of approach for future research.

The inclusion of the name of a saint in a place-name often goes beyond the usual conventions of name-giving. As a kind of toponymic prayer, it can invoke the blessing and protection of the saint on the place so named, and as such bears witness to spiritual allegiances, hopes, and fears of the name-givers, as well as to the more material aspects of possession or route-ways.[122]

APPENDIX: ADOMNÁN

The following is based on Watson's list of Adomnán place-names and commemorations (*Celtic Place-Names*, 270–1), with additions and refinements, chiefly from Redford, 'Commemorations of Saints', 116–17.[123] Several of the following appear in such late forms, and rest on such slender evidence, that they must be treated with great caution. These have been represented by an open symbol on Fig. 2.

ABERDEENSHIRE

Aboyne and Glentanar parish (Aberdeen diocese)

St Eunan's Tree and Well, Aboyne: this appears as the Skeulan Tree and the Skeulan Well in the mid nineteenth century in the

[122] I would like to thank Mr James Renny for drawing the maps, and Dr Dauvit Broun, Dr Thomas Clancy and Ms Morag Redford for their help and encouragement in the writing of this chapter, as well as their comments on an earlier draft; also Mr William Patterson for so freely sharing his extensive knowledge of the eastern Borders. All mistakes remain my responsibility. I am also grateful to the Anderson Research Fellowship, which supported me during the writing of this chapter.

[123] See also MacKinlay, *Dedications*, 56–60; and Ó Muraíle, 'The Columban onomastic legacy', 217. Errors in the latter include the siting of Glen Falloch in Dunbartonshire, at the southern end of Loch Lomond: it is in fact at the northern end of that loch, and in Perthshire (217, no. 6); and the mistaking of Campsie, Cargill, Perthshire for the better-known Campsie in Stirlingshire (217, no. 14).

New Statistical Account, where the association with Adomnán seems to have first been made: 'They are still held in great veneration and the name seems to be a corruption of St Eunan, to whom the parish church of Aboyne was anciently dedicated. Within a short distance of the Skeulan tree there is another well called the Lady's Well.' (*New Statistical Account*, *Aberdeenshire*, 1060). Alexander, *Place-Names*, 374, adds that 'a mound now marks the spot' (NO530985, from Redford, 'Commemorations of Saints', 116).

Rathen parish (not in Watson, *Celtic Place-Names*) (Aberdeen diocese)

St Owen's Hill and Well, Rathen ABD are mentioned in 1723 in *Geog. Coll.* i.56. This appears in 1793 as 'St Oynes' (*OSA*; see also Alexander, *Place-Names*, 120, where they are described as being obsolete).

Slains parish (Aberdeen diocese)

'St Adamnan's Chapel': the ruins of this chapel are on the lands of Leask, Slains parish (NK030327). 'A fine old ruin' in the mid-nineteenth century, it is described in some detail in *New Statistical Account*, *Aberdeenshire*, 593, where it is referred to as 'St Adamannan's chapel'. It appears erroneously on OS 1" 7th series as 'St Fidamnan's Chapel'. It lay originally in Ellon parish, since the lands of Leask were disjoined from Ellon in 1606 and attached to Slains (*APS* iv.302). Forvie and Slains parishes were united *ca* 1573. It seems likely, however, that the dedication of this chapel had been transferred from the old parish kirk of Forvie, since the early sixteenth-century *Aberdeen Breviary* states that Adomnán (*Adampnanus*) was the patron saint there ('apud *Fur[u]i*').[124]

ANGUS

Tannadice parish (St Andrews diocese) or *Fern parish* (Dunkeld diocese detached)

Sanct Eunandis Seit, Fern or Tannadice ANG, is from 1527 (*ER* xv.655), where it is mentioned as one of the marches of part of

[124] *Aberdeen Breviary*, Pars Est., 114v.

the lands of Tullohill, Fern parish ANG. Watson includes this amongst his list of Adomnán place-names, and identifies it with St Arnold's Seat, a high hill (493 metres) in the parish of Tannadice (NO432640) (Watson, *Celtic Place-Names*, 271, followed by Redford, 'Commemorations of Saints', 116). However, from a cursory examination of these marches, it seems to me unlikely that *Sanct Eunandis Seit* is referring to this hill, which appears on Pont's map of Angus from the 1590s as *St Arne Seat*, and is *St Ernan's Seat* in 1744 (Watson, *Celtic Place-Names*, 271). Further work on the marches of the Tullohill should help locate *Sanct Eunandis Seit* more exactly.[125]

I can find nothing to support MacKinlay's assertion that Tannadice parish kirk was dedicated to Adomnán (MacKinlay, *Dedications,* 58).[126] Inshewan in Tannadice parish (*Inchchewin* 1474 *RMS* ii, no. 1174; *Inschewin* 1484 *RMS* ii, no. 1601) seems to contain the personal name *Eoghan* or *Éibhinn.*[127] However, if there are indeed early Adomnán associations in the area, it is possible that it contains a reduced form of that name.

ARGYLL

Campeltown parish (Kintyre) (Argyle diocese)

Killeonan NR690183. *Killewnane* 1481 *RMS* ii, no. 1485; chapel remains are noted here in 1873 (Redford, 'Commemorations of Saints', 116). It lay in the medieval parish of Kilkerran.

[125] A charter of 1528 issued under the Great Seal (SRO C.2.22. no. 77) may well furnish an earlier form of this place-name, as well as shed further light on the march, since it defines what is probably the same part of Tullohill as is found in *ER* xv, 655. It is printed as *RMS* iii, no. 539. Unfortunately, the printed version simply adds *inter limites specificatos*. This is frequently, and frustratingly, found in *RMS* to indicate that detailed marches have been omitted in the printed version.

[126] I have likewise been unable to corroborate the statement that there was a chapel which may have been dedicated to St Columba at the castle of Shielhill, which lies in Tannadice parish on the north side of the River South Esk beside Shielhill Bridge (Jervise, *Land of the Lindsays*, 342–3). See also Taylor, 'Columba east of Drumalban'.

[127] Note that there is also an Inchewan on the Tay immediately downstream from Birnam, Little Dunkeld PER (*Inchewin* [Easter, Middle & Wester] 1513: *Dunk. Rent.* 40); see my discussion in Hall, Henderson and Taylor, 'A sculptured fragment from Pittensorn Farm', 140. For *Éibhinn* see Watson, *Celtic Place-Names*, 271.

Iona (now Kilfinichen and Kilvickeon parish) (Isles diocese)

Crois Adhamnáin or Adomnán's Cross, Iona. 'A spot at the north end of the village, opposite *Port a Chrossain*, bears this name, although the object which gave occasion to it is gone.'[128]

Southend parish (Kintyre) (Argyle diocese)

The 'cell and sanctuary of St Adamnán in the isle of Sanda off the Mull of Kintyre'[129] must be treated with some caution. It is based on Bower's text, which refers to a *cella sancti Adamnani* there, as well as to a place of asylum for criminals.[130] However, Fordun's text, on which this passage is based, has *Sanniani*, *Anniani* or *Niniani* for Bower's *Adamnani* (see *Johannis de Fordun Chronica*, ed. Skene, 345). The manuscript stemma is uncertain, but an argument can be made for an original *Sannianus*, which militates against Adamnán as the saint involved.[131] It probably lay in the medieval parish of Kilblane.[132]

BANFFSHIRE

Forglen parish (Aberdeen diocese)

According to *OSA* the parish was also known as Teunan or St Eunan. There was also a St Adamnan's Well (Redford, 'Commemorations of Saints', 116). The old church stood above the River Deveron (NJ698499). The land of Forglen was linked to the custody of the reliquary of St Columba known as the Brecbennoch (see *RRS* ii, no. 499).

[128] Reeves, *Adamnan*, 421.

[129] Watson, *Celtic Place-Names*, 270.

[130] *Scotichronicon* i.186.

[131] I am grateful to Professor D. E. R. Watt and Dr D. Broun for help in the matter of manuscript relationships here. If 'Sannianus' is the correct reading, it represents Senán. There is a Kilmanshenachan (Southend parish) on the coast opposite Sanda (*Kilmosenchane* 1609: *RMS* vii, no. 126), which contains the name Senchán, a diminutive of Senach (see Watson, *Celtic Place-Names*, 309, where read *Belach Mugnae* [Ballaghmoon, Co. Kildare] for *Imlech Ibair*). But note also that Sanda and much of the neighbouring mainland belonged to St Ninian's priory, Whithorn.

[132] *OPS* ii.9.

FIFE

Kinghorn parish (St Andrews diocese)

According to Bower Adomnán (*Odamnanus*) was abbot on Inchkeith (*Incheketbe*), Kinghorn parish FIF, an island in the Firth of Forth, when he welcomed St Serf on the latter's arrival in Scotland.[133] It is likely that this is simply a misinterpretation of the passage from the *VS*. In a twelfth-century version of this 'Life' we are told that when Serf arrives in Scotland from Rome, *Sanctus Edheunanus*, who was *abbas in Scocia* at that time, goes to meet him on Inchkeith (*ad insulam Ked*) (*VS*, 140).[134] Since Adomnán was probably a contemporary of Serf, there is nothing inherently improbable about the fact that they were in contact, and there is no reason to assume, with Watson, that 'there may be confusion here with Adamnan of Coldingham' (Watson, *Celtic Place-Names*, 271).

INVERNESS-SHIRE

Insh parish (Moray diocese)

Watson's statement, that the church of Insh in Badenoch appears to have been dedicated to St Áibind, must be emended to read 'St Adomnán', especially in the light of Watson's own statement on the same page (and footnote 1) regarding Adomnán and Insh *viz.* that the dramatic knowe on which Insh kirk stands is called *Tom Eódhnain* (Watson, *Celtic Place-Names*, 271), while the early bronze bell still kept in the church there is traditionally associated with Adomnán.[135] In his detailed analysis of the early churches of Badenoch and Strathspey, Barrow writes: 'Perhaps the "Insh" [*Innis*], "the island" ... had been dedicated to the church at a

[133] *Scotichronicon* i, 14–17.

[134] This earliest reference to Inchkeith suggests that the specific may be Adomnán's contemporary, Bishop Coeti (for whom see above, pp. 58–9). The development of the dental fricative from the final /d/ (which would have been the phonetic realisation of the intervocalic *t* in 'Coeti') may have resulted from the assimilation to the more common place-name element 'keith', as found in Dalkeith, etc. which derives from Cumbric *coed*, 'wood(land)', and is singularly inappropriate for this exposed rocky island, which can never have supported many trees.

[135] Anderson, *Scotland in Early Christian Times*, 195–7.

very early period and, if it ever formed a thanage or shire, was in the possession of the clergy in such a way that secular lordship had no opportunity to develop' (Barrow, 'Badenoch and Strathspey, 1130–1312: (2) the church', 8).

Inverness and Bona parish; Urquhart and Glenmoriston parish (Moray diocese)

The church of the medieval parish of Abriachan (Moray diocese) stood at Killionan of Abriachan (Cowan, *Medieval Parishes*, 19). The late-nineteenth-century local antiquarian William Mackay was convinced that the saint in the name was Adomnán. In the adjacent parish of Urquhart (now Urquhart and Glenmoriston) a 'Crofta Sancti Adampnani' is mentioned in 1556. This appears in a document of 1647 as *Croft Indon*, and is Mackay's chief reason for his assertion that Killionan ('now pronounced "Eonan"') contains this saint's name.[136] Watson, on the other hand, was equally convinced that the saint involved was Fínán (Watson, *Celtic Place-Names*, 286), and Mackay and he politely but firmly disagreed on the subject at Mackay's talk to the Gaelic Society of Inverness in April 1909.[137] An entry in *Moray Reg.* no. 403 from 1544 proves Mackay wrong. It concerns the feuing to Hugh Fraser, Lord Lovat of the episcopal lands of Easter and Wester Kinmylies (*Kilmyles*), *Balnafare*, Easter and Wester Abriachan (*Abreoquhy*), *Kilquhynnane*, along with the mill of Bught (*Bucht*) and fishing on the River Ness. Given the fact that all these places which can be identified are within the modern parish of Inverness and Bona, on the west bank of the Ness, and juxtaposed as it is in this list with Abriachan, it is safe to assume that *Kilquhynnane* represents the later Killionan of Abriachan. Whether *quh* represents an original lenited *c*, or whether it is being used, as was often the case in Scots orthography, to represent *f*, which latter would prove Watson correct, it certainly rules out Adomnán as the saint contained in this name.

136 Mackay, *Urquhart and Glenmoriston*, 116, where the source is given as Fraser, *The Chiefs of Grant* iii, 121–4; see also Mackay, *Urquhart and Glenmoriston*, 335.

137 See Mackay, 'Saints associated with the valley of the Ness', 155, 160 and 162.

North Uist parish (Isles diocese)

According to Watson (*Celtic Place-Names*, 270) *Crois Adhamhnáin* was near Dun Rosail. It is the only Adomnán commemoration in the northern Hebrides.

PERTHSHIRE

Blair Atholl parish (Dunkeld diocese)

Possibly Kilmaveonaig, a medieval and early modern parish, now part of Blair Atholl parish (*Kilmeuenoc* 1275 in Dunlop, 'Bagimond's Roll', 73; *Kilmawewinok* 1595 in *RMS* vi, no. 348); despite Watson's assertions to the contrary (Watson, *Celtic Place-Names*, 310, n. 2), in the light of the other links with late seventh- and early eighth-century Iona expressed in Atholl names and dedications, the possibility that this is a hypocoristic form of Adomnán's name cannot be ruled out.

Cargill parish (Dunkeld diocese)

In Campsie, an estate on the east bank of the Tay, besides the *acra Sancti Adamnani* (*RMS* iv, no. 1809), mentioned by Watson (*Celtic Place-Names*, 271), there was also a chapel of that saint, to which the acre was attached. In the Coupar Angus Rental of 1542, in a list of the chapels belonging to that monastery, is 'Capella Sancti Adampnani in *Campsy*, cum una acra' (*CA Rent.* ii, 207). Campsie had been given to Coupar Angus Abbey by King William I *ca* 1175 (*RRS* ii, no. 154). In 1551 Abbot Donald set in feu the lands of Nether Campsie, including in the rent *sufficient wax to Sanct Adamnanis licht and chapell, conforme to the rentall* (*CA Rent.* ii, 70).

Dull parish (Dunkeld diocese)

Feil Eonan and *Tobar-Eonan* [*sic*] are mentioned here in Forbes, *Kalendars*, 266. Adomnán was also the patron saint of Dull parish kirk (Watson, *Celtic Place-Names*, 270).

Fortingall parish (Dunkeld diocese)

Muileann Eódhnain, 'Adomnán's mill', near Bridge of Balgie, Glen Lyon appears on the OS 1" 7th series map as 'Milton Eonan'. In

1632 this appears as *Mylntoun cum molendino Eonan nuncupato* ('with the mill called *Eonan*'). Watson also mentions a *Magh Eódhnain*, 'Adomnán's Plain' nearby (*Celtic Place-Names*, 270). For other traditions and minor place-names associated with Adomnán in Glen Lyon, see Forbes, *Kalendars*, 266, MacKinlay, *Dedications*, 58, and Watson, *Celtic Place-Names*, 271.

Kenmore parish (Dunkeld diocese)

The earliest recorded forms of Ardeonaig PER, formerly a parish in the diocese of Dunkeld, now in Kenmore, on the southern shore of Loch Tay, 'Adomnán's height', are from Bagimond's Roll (1274) (Dunlop, 'Bagimond's Roll', 47 *Erdonny*; 73 *Ardoueny*). The next occurrence in the record is the one mentioned by Watson (*Celtic Place-Names*, 270): *viz. Ardewnan* 1495 (*RMS* ii, no. 2235).

Killin parish (Dunkeld diocese)

Watson (*Celtic Place-Names*, 270) mentions a *Croit Eódhnain* ('Adomnán's Croft') in Glen Falloch, between Loch Lomond and Crianlarich.

Logierait parish (not in Watson, *Celtic Place-Names*) (Dunkeld diocese)

Lageonan (NN913530)[138] is a group of cottages east of Grandtully. Watson, however, mentions a *Fuaran Eódhnain* (Adomnán's Well) near Grandtully (*Celtic Place-Names*, 270).

STIRLING

Buchanan parish (formerly Inchcailloch) (Glasgow diocese)

Rowardennan is on the east shore of Loch Lomond, south of Inversnaid (for which see above p. 51) and at the south-west foot of Ben Lomond. It appears as *Row Ardenan* in 1748 (*Geog. Coll.* i.346), and seems to represent Gaelic *rudha àirde Eódhnain*, 'the point of Adomnán's height', or 'the point of [a feature called] *Airde Eódhnain*'.

[138] I am grateful to Dr Sheila Kidd for this information.

Fintry parish (Glasgow diocese)

Killunan NS607872. *Kille[u]nan* 1590s Pont/Blaeu. It lies on the Killewnan Burn, which forms the boundary between the parishes of Fintry and Killearn.[139]

WEST LOTHIAN

Dalmeny parish (St Andrews diocese)

In 1662 mention is made of the patronage of the chapel and altar of St Adamnan, in the parish of Dalmeny (*RMS* xi, no. 323).

[139] See also MacDonald, 'Gaelic *Cill* (*Kil(l)-*) in Scottish Place-Names', 11.

3

The Scottish takeover of Pictland and the relics of Columba

John Bannerman

UNTIL recently 'Union of the Picts and Scots' was the usual description of the process whereby the new Scottish kingdom of Alba or Scotia was formed. However, that has more to do with eighteenth- and nineteenth-century historiography than with history. Nor does the generally accepted date of this event, 842/3, inspire confidence, at any rate not for what is claimed for it. It should be said at the outset that contemporary or near contemporary evidence, such as it is, has no whiff of a negotiated settlement between two peoples as was often meant to be implicit in the use of the term 'union'. As far as the folk-memory of later Scots is concerned (and by these I mean the inhabitants of Alba, that is, of both Dál Riata and Pictland), the Picts were wiped out,[1] and if they survived at all, it was in some sort of limbo as daft wee folk making whisky out of heather.[2] It seems that 'union' in this context was first used in the eighteenth century, and probably has everything to do with the Union of Parliaments in 1707. The historian responsible was Thomas Innes who lived at that time, and who published his influential *Critical Essay on the Ancient Inhabitants of the Northern Parts of Britain or Scotland* in 1729.[3]

A study of what later Scottish historians (especially those writing with a Presbyterian and/or Anglo-centric slant) made of

[1] Hudson, *Kings of Celtic Scotland*, 42–3.
[2] Brown, *Scotland before 1700 from Contemporary Documents*, 87; Stevenson, 'The travels of Richard James', 115–16.
[3] i.141ff. See Ferguson, *The Identity of the Scottish Nation*, 190.

Innes' novel interpretation of the events surrounding the formation of Alba is an interesting one in its own right. Our aim here, however, is to have a fresh look at the evidence unencumbered by the trappings of Unionism. In so doing we are following in the footsteps of a number of historians who, within the last decade or so, have been moving away from the concept of 'union' between Pict and Scot in which it was often implied, if not always stated, that the Picts were the senior partners; away, in other words, from the notion of a Scoto-Pictish kingdom, towards a consensus which sees Alba as a military creation of the Scots supported by the Columban Church but at the expense of the Picts.[4] It is hoped that what follows will further amplify and confirm this view of events.

Let us begin with the hitherto generally accepted date *ca* 843 which I have already suggested is none too satisfactory or secure. It is a manufactured date. The Irish annals record Cinaed mac Alpín's obit in 858 and there is every reason to accept this. They were contemporary and, particularly in the case of the Annals of Ulster[5] (hereafter AU), remarkably well preserved. The Scottish Chronicle, a composite document compiled towards the end of the tenth century but apparently incorporating a set of contemporary annals beginning in the mid-ninth century,[6] states that Cinaed mac Alpín 'first of the Scots, ruled this Pictland prosperously for sixteen years'.[7] Subtract sixteen from 858 and you get 842–3 as the first year of Cinaed's reign over Pictland. But that is it; there is no specific evidence to support this date. We shall see that the Scots of the time apparently did not think that their takeover of Pictland had been successfully accomplished by 842 or 843.

However, it must have happened by 858, the year of Cinaed's death, for the statement just quoted from the Scottish Chronicle is supported by AU in so far as they refer to Cinaed in his obit as

[4] Broun, 'The origin of Scottish identity in its European context'; Wormald, 'The emergence of the *regnum Scottorum*'.

[5] All dates in the text are from AU unless otherwise specified.

[6] Anderson, 'The Scottish materials in the Paris manuscript, Bib. Nat., Latin 4126', 37–9; Cowan, 'The Scottish Chronicle in the Poppleton Manuscript'; Broun, 'The origin of Scottish identity', 40–2.

[7] *primus Scottorum rexit feliciter istam annis xvi. Pictauiam*: Anderson, *Kings and Kingship*, 249.

rex Pictorum, 'king of the Picts', the first king of Scots to be so entitled in the Irish annals.[8] The annalist did not necessarily intend to indicate that Cinaed had an hereditary right to the kingship of the Picts, as is sometimes assumed, although he may have had; rather it was laudatory in intent, recognition that he and his people had taken over Pictland. This is a feature of the period in Ireland and is sometimes extended to referring to the conquering people by the name of the conquered[9] which would adequately explain the continuing references to *Picti*, when *Scotti* were clearly meant for the next quarter of a century or so after the Scottish takeover of Pictland (865, 866, 871, 875).[10]

But we can be more precise than 858. I would submit that 849 is the year by which the Scots were satisfied that they had made a successful and permanent takeover-bid for Pictland. Like 842/3 this is something of a manufactured date, but it has more going for it. AU tell us that Indrechtach, abbot of Iona, came to Ireland with the relics of Columba in that year.[11] The Scottish Chronicle states that Cinaed 'transported the relics of Columba to a church (*ecclesia*) that he had built in the seventh year of his reign'.[12] The seventh year of his alleged sixteen-year reign over the Picts is 848–9, and long ago A. O. Anderson connected the two entries, pointing out that a division of the relics of Columba must have been made in this year, one part going to Kells in Co. Meath and the other to Dunkeld.[13] As before, AU give us the Irish side of the equation and the Scottish Chronicle the Scottish. That Kells and Dunkeld (unmentioned in either entry) were the respective destinations can be deduced from other evidence. In the Gaelic Church, the authority of the founding saint went with his most

[8] AU 858.2. The title *rex Pictorum* applied to Eochu Buide in his obit in AU 629.4 is a later interpolation from the lost Book of Cuanu. (No title is given to Eochu in his obit in AT 629.2.)

[9] Ó Corráin, 'Nationality and kingship in pre-Norman Ireland', 10.

[10] AU 865.2, 866.1, 871.2. AU 875.3 record a defeat suffered by *Picti* at the hands of the 'dark foreigners' which in the Scottish Chronicle is described as a defeat of the *Scotti* by the Danes (Anderson, *Kings and Kingship*, 250). But see Broun, 'The origin of Scottish identity', 40–5.

[11] AU 849.7. See also Broun, p. 105 n. 40, below.

[12] Anderson, *Kings and Kingship*, 250.

[13] *ES* i.279. A Columban Church precedent for this is visible in the similar division of the relics of Aedán of Lindisfarne after the Synod of Whitby in 664 (Bannerman, '*Comarba Coluim Chille*', 18–19, 25–6).

revered relics and the intention and the result in 848–9 was to split the Columban federation of monasteries in two. Kells became the administrative centre of the Columban monasteries in Ireland and Dunkeld the administrative centre of the church in Scotia.[14]

The plan was actually conceived long before 848–9 and, although this has been noted,[15] the significance thereof has not yet received the attention it deserves. Once again we have an Irish view of the proceedings to set beside a Scottish one. In 804, AU tell us that Kells was given 'without battle to the melodious Columba'. This is not normal annalistic reportage but a retrospective entry taken from an eleventh-century metrical source.[16] However, the year in which the event is said to have happened may be historically correct, for in 807, AU record 'the building of the new monastery (*civitas*) at Kells' and seven years later in 814 Cellach, abbot of Iona, relinquished the abbacy 'when the building of the church (*templum*) of Kells was completed'.[17] The Scottish evidence is less detailed; it is a note in the shorter Pictish king-list stating simply that Custantín son of Fergus 'built Dunkeld'.[18] Custantín's death is put by AU in the year 820 and the longer Pictish king-list gives him a reign of thirty-five years.[19]

[14] Bannerman, '*Comarba Coluim Chille*'.

[15] *Ibid.*, 32–3.

[16] AU 804.12. Herbert, *Iona, Kells and Derry*, 69.

[17] AU 807.4, 814.9.

[18] Anderson, *Kings and Kingship*, 266, 273, 287 (its omission at 281 in list I is clearly due to confusion with the note on the foundation of St Andrews in the following reign). The Pictish king-list survives in two versions. One is longer than the other by virtue of a lengthy pseudo-historical section added to the beginning (*ibid.*, 79–84). The longer version is referred to by Marjorie Anderson as 'P', the shorter as 'Q' (*ibid.*, *passim*); Miller, 'Matriliny by treaty', 159–61, classified them respectively under the titles *Series Longior* (SL) and *Series Brevior* (SB). It can not be demonstrated from the text-history of the shorter list that the note on Dunkeld's foundation by Custantín is older than between 1214 and 1249 (the date of the exemplar of Marjorie Anderson's 'X' group of Scottish king-lists: see Anderson, *Kings and Kingship*, 50, 52, 61). In the absence of a compelling case to the contrary, however, I see no reason to doubt its authenticity.

[19] AU 820.3. See Anderson, *Kings and Kingship*, 233. Witnesses of the shorter list read *xlv* (D), 42 (F), *xlii* (I), and *xl* (K): the exemplar of the 'X' group of lists (between 1214 and 1249) may therefore have read *xlii*. Marjorie Anderson (*ibid.*) suggested that *xxxu* in the longer list may originally have read *xxxii*.

Dunkeld, or more probably a new church dedicated to Columba within what was an existing monastery,[20] is likely to have been built at the same time as Kells, sometime between 807 and 814[21] which, of course, falls within Custantín's reign.

We have to decide now why such a plan could be conceived but not brought to fruition in the reign of Custantín. To help us there follows a list of the kings named in the Dalriadic and Pictish king-lists whose obits appear in AU between *ca* 740, when the annals, previously written up on Iona, were taken to Ireland (to be continued probably at Armagh),[22] and 858, the year in which they record Cinaed mac Alpín's death.

Dál Riata	**Fortriu/Pictavia**
	Aengus s. Fergus *rex Pictorum* d. 761
	Bruide (s. Fergus) *rex Fortrenn* d. 763
	Cinaed (s. Feradach) *rex Pictorum* d. 775
Aed Find s. Eochu *rex Dál Riati* d. 778	
	Alpín (s. Wroid *rex Pictorum*)[23] d. 780
Fergus s. Eochu *rex Dál Riati* d. 781	
	Dub Thalorg (Talorgan s. Aengus)[24] *rex Pictorum citra Monoth* d. 782

Dál Riata/Fortriu/Pictavia

Custantín s. Fergus *rex Fortrenn* d. 820
Aengus s. Fergus *rex Fortrenn* d. 834
Cinaed s. Alpín *rex Pictorum* d. 858

[20] Bannerman, '*Comarba Coluim Chille*', 23–4.

[21] This would rule out a link between the founding of this new church in Dunkeld and the transportation of Columba's relics to Scotland in 818 (see *Chronicum Scotorum*, ed. Hennessy, 130) suggested by Clancy, 'Iona, Scotland, and the *céli Dé*', 114. This and a similar annal entry in 829 need not be other than notices of the completion of two separate circuits of Irish Columban monasteries by the abbot of Iona, while a third entry recording the transportation of these same relics to Ireland in 831 may signify the beginning of another.

[22] Bannerman, *Studies in the History of Dalriada*, 25–6; Bannerman, '*Comarba Coluim Chille*', 39–40. See also Mac Niocaill, *The Medieval Irish Annals*, 22, 29.

[23] Alpín is erroneously entitled *rex Saxonum* in AU.

[24] Below, p. 84.

Custantín and Cinaed mac Alpín are given different titles in their respective obits, namely *rex Fortrenn*, 'king of Fortriu', and *rex Pictorum*, 'king of the Picts'.[25] In addition the Dalriadic king-list claims that they were both kings of Dál Riata which carried with it the title *rex Dál Riati*, 'king of Dál Riata'.[26] There are problems associated with all three titles.

It has been pointed out that the Dál Riata in Ireland and Scotland seemed to go their separate ways after Domnall Brecc's disastrous participation in the battle of Mag Rath (Moira) in 637.[27] The Irish Dál Riata can be traced in the annals thereafter pursuing an independent line in Northern Irish politics (691, 731, 741),[28] apparently under a new royal dynasty whose affiliations, when discernible, are Irish rather than Scottish. One of these seems to be Fiannamail whose obit in 700 informs us that he died as *rex Dál Riati*.[29] Another may be Donncorci, *rex Dál Riati*, who died in 792.[30] We have no knowledge of his antecedents, but like Fiannamail his name is not found elsewhere among the ruling families of the Dál Riata in Scotland about whom we have relatively full information. Furthermore, the obvious relationship between annals and king-lists, although yet to be elucidated satisfactorily, makes it worth noting that the king-list of the Scottish Dál Riata ignores Donncorci and apparently Fiannamail also.[31] It is true, of course, that AU in precisely this period were always careful to distinguish between the Cruithni or Dál nAraide

[25] AU 820.3, 858.2.

[26] Jackson, 'The *Duan Albanach*', 132. See also Anderson, 'Dalriada and the creation of the kingdom of the Scots', 107.

[27] Bannerman, *Studies in the History of Dalriada*, 7–8.

[28] AU 691.3, AU 731.5; AT 731.3; AU 741.10*a*. (All record battles between Dál Riata and Cruithni in Ireland.)

[29] AU 700.4; AT 700.3 (where he is erroneously entitled *rí Dál Araidhi*). Bannerman, *Studies in the History of Dalriada*, 7–8. It should be further pointed out that if Fiannamail was not king of the Irish Dál Riata, then they were the only major people of the historical province of Ulster unrepresented among the guarantors of *Cáin Adomnáin* (Ní Dhonnchadha, 'The guarantor list of *Cáin Adomnáin*').

[30] AU 792.4.

[31] But see Anderson, *Kings and Kingship*, 105, who remarked that 'Fiannamail bears a suspicious resemblance to an unexplained epithet attached to Eochu, Domnall Brecc's grandson [d. 697]': see further *ibid.*, 68 and n. 102.

of Northern Ireland and the Cruithni or Picts of North Britain by using Cruithni, both in the title *rex Cruithne* and elsewhere, for the Dál nAraide until switching to Dál nAraide itself in 776, and by using Latin *Picti* for the Picts. However, the Dál Riata were one people until the mid-seventh century, and when the split came there was no change of name on either side of the North Channel so that annalists would be unable to make a distinction between them that would not be unacceptably long winded in an annalistic context. All other kings so entitled in AU are demonstrably kings of Dál Riata in Scotland.[32]

Even if we had no other evidence, the title *rex Pictorum* surely implied sovereignty over all Picts both north and south of the Mounth, but nowhere are we ever specifically told that this was the case. However, the earliest historically authenticated Pictish king in AU, Bruide mac Maelchon (d. 584),[33] was described by Bede as a *rex potentissimus*.[34] More significantly Nechtan, son of Derile, described as *rex* in 713 and 717, was claimed by Bede to be 'king of the Picts who inhabit the northern parts of Britain' and to have exercised authority 'throughout all the provinces of the Picts'.[35] Yet another *rex Pictorum* was Aengus, son of Fergus, so entitled in 736 when, we are told, 'he laid waste the regions of Dál Riata and captured Dunadd', the main stronghold of the Dál Riata at this time.[36] It is true that after the defeat of his brother Talorgan by the Britons in 750 we read in the same annal of 'the ebbing of the sovereignty of Aengus' and significantly, since early Gaelic tradition appears to locate Aengus in the Pictish sub-kingdom of Circinn,[37] the battle of Asreth was fought two years

[32] In AU 616.1, Aedán, son of Mongán, is entitled *rex Dál Riati* in error for *rex Dál nAraide*.

[33] AU 584.3; AT (Stokes, *The Annals of Tigernach*, 2 vols (Felinfach 1993) i.114). His title *rex Pictorum* in AU (*rig Cruithneach* in AT) is, however, retrospective: see below, p. 81.

[34] *HE* iii.4.

[35] *per universas Pictorum provincias*: *HE* v.21. See AU 713.7, AT 713.8; AU 717.4; AT 717.3.

[36] AU 736.1, AT 736.1. Bannerman, *Studies in the History of Dalriada*, 113.

[37] To be precise Aengus is located in *Mag Gergind* associated elsewhere with Fordun and the Mearns: see Watson, *History of the Celtic Place-Names of Scotland*, 109. Although Watson admitted to being unable to reconcile linguistically *Gergind* and *Circinn*, he nevertheless equated Circinn

later in Circinn, 'between the Picts themselves'.[38] But Aengus seems to have retrieved the position, for he is designated *rex Pictorum* in his obit in 761.[39]

Three possible meanings have been suggested for the title *rex Fortrenn*: (*a*) king of the province or sub-kingdom of Fortriu, (*b*) king of a larger unit which included the sub-kingdom of Fortriu, and (*c*) king of all Pictland, synonymous with *rex Pictorum*. There can be no doubt about the first. As we have just noted, there were four traditional sub-kingdoms in Pictland south of the Mounth – Circinn, Atholl, Fife and Fortriu.[40] Almost certainly each had a king. Talorgan son of Drostan, heavily involved in the struggle for supremacy among the Picts in the first half of the

---

with Angus and the Mearns to accord with his interpretation of the geographical delineation of Alba south of the Mounth in the twelfth century *De situ Albanie*. His other equations are Atholl = Atholl and Gowrie, Fife = Fife and Fothrif, and Fortriu = Strathearn and Menteith (*ibid.*, 108). This seems to be largely acceptable, if only because it requires the least convoluted manipulation of the available evidence. I would add that if, as seems likely, the diocesan reorganisation of the early twelfth century was influenced by the traditional fourfold division of Southern Pictland, not necessarily because that division was remembered in the twelfth century but because the main Columban Church monastery in each of the four sub-kingdoms retained its preeminent position into the twelfth century and therefore naturally became the sees of the four new dioceses in the area, their positioning and their diocesan bounds seem to confirm Watson's scheme. These monasteries were Dunkeld and Kinrimont (or St Andrews) for Atholl and Fife respectively; Dunblane, whose diocesan bounds included most of Strathearn and Menteith, for Fortriu; leaving only Brechin in Angus for the remaining Pictish sub-kingdom of Circinn which should therefore have consisted largely of Angus and the Mearns as Watson suggested. (But see Broun, 'The seven kingdoms'.)

The entry recording the battle of Asreth in Circinn is from AT, but the words *inter Pictones invicem* indicate that it was once in the lost Chronicle of Ireland, the common source of AU and AT. Thus the unusual *Pictones* appears in AU in the annal for 750, and in 754 AU record a battle *inter nepotes Tuirtri invicem*, 'between the Uí Thuirtri themselves', phraseology which also appears elsewhere in AU. AT goes on to say that Bruide mac Maelchon was killed in the battle, but we can probably regard this as a later and erroneous interpolation. But see *ES* i, 241; also Grabowski and Dumville, *Chronicles and Annals of Medieval Ireland and Wales*, 124–6.

[38] AU 750.4, AT 750.3; AU 750.11, AT 752.3.

[39] AU 761.4, AT 761.4.

[40] See n. 37, above.

eighth century (713, 734) was *rex Athfoitle*, 'king of Atholl', in 739 when he was killed by Aengus, son of Fergus.[41] Aengus himself, as we saw, seems to have been a member of the ruling family of Circinn,[42] while it has recently been shown that lands of the family of Nechtan, son of Derile, another participant in the struggle, were located in west Fife.[43]

There was, however, an ecclesiastical unit called Fortriu which was larger than the province of that name. Thus, in 865 Tuathal, son of Artgus, died as *prím-epscop Fortrenn*, 'chief bishop of Fortriu' and abbot of Dunkeld.[44] Since Dunkeld was the administrative centre of the church by this time, the episcopal title, surely a reflection thereof, must mean that Fortriu in this context included Atholl whose centre was Dunkeld. Elsewhere Fortriu, at least in a geographical sense, seems to extend northwards to Dunottar near Stonehaven,[45] so Circinn must have been part thereof. Bede informs us that the Picts of the south were divided by mountains from those of the north,[46] while a political unit corresponding to Southern Pictland, from the point of view of an Irish annalist, appears in the obit of Dub Thalorg in 782 who was entitled *rex Pictorum citra Monoth*, 'king of Picts on this side of the Mounth'.[47] Finally, if it is accepted that the Moot Hill of Scone was originally a Pictish royal inaugural site,[48] then its central positioning *vis-à-vis* the four traditional provinces of Southern Pictland[49] is further evidence for a long-standing political unit comprising Pictland south of the Mounth whose overking would merit the title *rex Fortrenn* in its wider

[41] AU 713.7, AT 713.8; AU 734.6; AU 739.7, AT 739.6. In AU 713.7 and AT 713.8 he is described as Talorg, son of Drostan and brother of king Nechtan, almost certainly Nechtan son of Derile (Clancy, 'Philosopher-king: Nechtan, king of Picts (d. 732)'). I am indebted to Dr Clancy for giving me access to this material.

[42] Above, pp. 77–8.

[43] Clancy, 'Philosopher-king'.

[44] AU 865.6.

[45] Anderson, *Kings and Kingship*, 174. But see Broun, 'The seven kingdoms', forthcoming.

[46] *HE* iii.4.

[47] AU 782.1.

[48] Anderson, *Kings and Kingship*, 198–9; Duncan, *Scotland: the Making of the Kingdom*, 115–16.

[49] Above, n. 37.

sense. Presumably the ruling family of the sub-kingdom of Fortriu had provided the overking more often than those of the other three provinces.

The third suggestion that *rex Fortrenn* and *rex Pictorum* were synonymous should now fall without trace.[50] It was always unlikely in any case, if only because nowhere else do AU use different titles to describe the same kingship in the same period. It was in fact only the Pictish king-lists that encouraged such a view simply because they make no distinction between kings so entitled in the annals; all are included. The problem would be resolved immediately if they were perceived not as lists of the kings of Pictland but of the kings of Fortriu, inaugurated at Scone, who only sometimes, and incidentally as far as the lists are concerned, exercised control over Northern Pictland as well. The fact is that with one exception the main sphere of operations, when it can be discerned, of the Pictish kings common to the annals and the king-lists was in Southern Pictland. The exception is Bruide mac Maelchon (d. 584) who is never on record south of the Mounth. Adomnán has Columba travel up the Great Glen to visit him in his stronghold near Inverness and he further tells us that Bruide has a *regulus* or client-king ruling in Orkney from whom he took hostages for his good behaviour.[51] However, neither reference is incompatible with his being from Southern Pictland. As such he would surely require a stronghold north of the Mounth to maintain his authority over the Northern Picts, while his requirement for hostages from Orkney amounts to the same thing. Furthermore, it has been pointed out that the name *Bruide* was common among the royal families of Southern Pictland.[52] A southern orientation might also explain his father's name which is otherwise unrecorded in Scotland, whether in its Gaelic form *Maelchú* or its P-Celtic form *Maelgwn*. In other words his father may have hailed from Ireland or, as has been suggested, he could even have been Maelgwn, the famous king of Gwynedd in North Wales who died *ca* 548.[53] Finally, it should be pointed

[50] Anderson, 'Dalriada and the creation of the kingdom of the Scots', 107.

[51] *VC*, ii.33, 42; Anderson, *Adomnán*, 140–5, 166–7.

[52] Anderson, 'Ninian and the Southern Picts', 36.

[53] Chadwick, *Early Scotland*, 15.

out that a king from among the Northern Picts has yet to be identified in any context.

In AU, then, the title *rex Pictorum*, I suggest, was accorded to those kings on whose deaths the two halves of Pictland were conjoined, and *rex Fortrenn* to those who when they died were ruling over Southern Pictland only. The concept of a Pictland divided by the Grampians into Northern and Southern Pictland seems to be of long standing[54] and, indeed, as far as the annals are concerned, the latter title is the earlier of the two on record, given that the Iona Chronicle only became contemporary (or at any rate fuller and more detailed) at or shortly before the first precisely dated event was recorded therein in 686,[55] which means that the six obits of Pictish kings before 686 containing the title *rex Pictorum* (580, 584, 601,[56] 631, 653, 657) are retrospective entries.[57] *Rex Fortrenn* first appears in AU in 693, thirty-six years before the first contemporary record of *rex Pictorum* in 729.[58] Historians have tended to see the division of Pictland as more permanent at an earlier period than it later became, but it seems to me that the evidence of the above list of annal-obits from *ca* 740 to 858 indicates that the relationship between the two sections

[54] Wainwright, 'The Picts and the problem', 20–1, 50.

[55] Bannerman, *Studies in the History of Dalriada*, 25: for a discussion of the various views expressed on when the Iona Chronicle became contemporary, see Herbert, *Iona, Kells and Derry*, 22–3.

[56] This obit appears only in AT but it is similar to the others and was probably in the Iona Chronicle.

[57] AU 580.3, 584.3, 631, 653.1, 657.3; AT 580.2, 584, 599.2 (= 601), 631.2, 653.2, 657.4 (*ríg Cruithne*). However, the titles therein also indicate that the Iona annalists were themselves responsible. The Iona Chronicle, contemporary at least from 686 until its removal to Ireland in 740, makes sparing use of royal titles in records of events involving the Scots of Dál Riata or Picts. There are no examples of *rex Dál Riati*, only two of *rex Pictorum* (729, 736) and one each of *rex Fortrenn* (693), *rex Cinn Tíre* (721), and *rex Athfoitle* (739). If the early examples of *rex Pictorum* had been interpolated after 740 then similar interpolation would have been continued throughout the period 686 to 740. In fact it could be argued that contemporary reporting began at or sometime before the first annal in which a king of Picts did not receive the title *rex Pictorum*. This would be the obit of Domnall, son of Gartnait in 663 (the title *ríg Cruithneach* in AT is clearly a later interpolation). If this is correct, there is one example of *rex Dál Riati* (673) in the period of contemporary annal-writing on Iona.

[58] AU 693.1, 729.3.

continued to be unstable right up to Pictland's disappearance as a separate entity. Indeed, Scottish pressure on the Picts may have made a significant contribution to that instability in later stages.

It is worth noting in this context that despite the all-embracing struggle for supremacy in Southern Pictland visible in the annals for much of the first half of the eighth century which seemed to result in a final triumph for Aengus son of Fergus, the wording of the annals makes it clear that at all times the kingdom that they were struggling to control was not Fortriu but Pictland as a whole. The Scots at this time, far from being involved, were actually on the receiving end of Pictish aggression. So the annalist, in applying the title *rex Pictorum* to Cinaed mac Alpín in 858, besides glorifying the exploits of the Scots, is indicating that the two halves of Pictland were once again joined under the control of one king. It is for the same reasons that Cinaed's immediate successors continued to be entitled *rex Pictorum* in AU (862.1, 876.1, 878.2) until the achievement of taking over all Pictland had faded into the background, and the new and permanent persona of the greatly extended kingdom of the Scots demanded a new name *Alba* and a new royal title *rí Alban*, 'king of Alba',[59] first applied in AU to Domnall, son of Custantín and grandson of Cinaed, in his obit in AU 900.6.

Let us return now to the list of annal-obits as set out above[60] and consider them in conjunction with the other relevant entries in AU. The Scots could not do much about Aengus, son of Fergus, who died in 761 as king of all Pictland, judging by his title and by what we know of his career. He was the hammer of the Scots in his day and they showed no signs of stirring as long as he was alive. Bruide, his brother, died two years later as king of Fortriu only. It may be that the relationship between the two halves of Pictland had to be re-established as each new reign commenced and Bruide may simply not have had the time to do so. However, his successor Cinaed, son of Feradach, had to face an invasion of Fortriu by Aed Find, king of Dál Riata, in 768.[61] AU do not say who won the battle or what happened to the Scots, but if Aed Find is to be credited with initiating the Scottish policy of

[59] But see Broun, 'The origin of Scottish identity', 52–4.
[60] Above, p. 75.
[61] AU 768.7.

penetration into Pictland he himself seems not to have made any lasting gains therein. Cinaed died in 775 as king of Picts, while Aed Find's obit in 778 entitles him king of Dál Riata only.[62]

Aed Find was succeeded in Dál Riata by his brother Fergus who died three years later in 781. Alpín at his death in 780 was *rex Pictorum*, but two years later Dub Thalorg was only king of Fortriu when he died.[63] If we were to follow the evidence of the annals alone we would have to conclude that Custantín succeeded his father Fergus as king of Dál Riata in 781 and Dub Thalorg as king of Fortriu in 782. An annal-entry for 789 tells of a battle 'between the Picts' in which Custantín defeated Conall, son of Tadc. The latter bears a Gaelic name, and in 807 (the occasion of his only other recorded appearance in the annals) he was killed in Kintyre, the centre of Cenél nGabráin power.[64] Clearly by 789 Fortriu was in the control of Scots, and the annals do not allow us to conclude that the battle fought in this year was other than an unsuccessful challenge to Custantín's position by another Cenél nGabráin dynast. The longer Pictish king-list confirms this in so far as it gave Custantín a thirty-five-year reign[65] which, calculating from his death in 820, puts his accession in the year 785.

However, it is the king-lists, Pictish and Dalriadic, that disturb the picture drawn thus far from the contemporary annals. The longer Pictish king-list has four kings between Alpín and Custantín, and the shorter version three kings, at the same time as both apparently omit to name Dub Thalorg;[66] the king-list for Dál Riata (present at this point only in eleventh-century sources, the *Duan Albanach* and the Irish Synchronisms)[67] names four kings between Fergus and Custantín, besides giving the latter only an eleven-year reign which would mean that he did not

62 AU 775.1, 778.7.

63 AU 780.5, where *rex Saxonum* is an error for *rex Pictorum*: see AClon 773 (=780); 782.1 (*rex Pictorum citra Monoth*).

64 AU 789.11, 807.3; Bannerman, *Studies in the History of Dalriada*, 111.

65 On the longer list and this reign-length see nn. 18 and 19, above.

66 For the longer and shorter lists, see n. 18, above.

67 Jackson, 'The *Duan Albanach*', 132. The shorter version of the Synchronisms, Boyle, 'The Edinburgh synchronisms', 177; the longer version, Thurneysen, 'Synchronismen der Irischen Könige', 90. The verse naming Fergus and Eochu was omitted from the extant *Duan Albanach*.

succeed to the kingship of Dál Riata until 809, some twenty-four years after becoming king of Fortriu. All this, coupled with the fact that Custantín and his brother and successor Aengus appear in what was thought to be a list of the kings of Pictland, not to mention their respective titles in the annals, persuaded some historians that they were Pictish rather than Scottish kings who were succeeding to the kingship of the Picts in virtue of belonging to a royal matrilineage as was thought to be normal Pictish practice. Their possession of the kingship of Dál Riata was seen to be secondary and ultimately a result of the supposed continuing subordination of Dál Riata to the Picts ever since the *percutio Dál Riati*, 'smiting of Dál Riata' by Aengus, son of Fergus, *rex Pictorum*, in 741.[68]

How much credence should be given to the evidence of the Pictish king-lists? Here are the kings that appear between Alpín and Custantín:

Longer list	**Shorter list**
Drust s. Talorgan	Drust s. Talorgan
Talorgan s. Drostan[69]	Talorgan s. Drostan
Talorgan s. Aengus	Talorgan s. Aengus
Canaul s. *Tarl'a/Tang*[70]	

Talorgan son of Drostan has the same name as the king of Atholl who was killed in 734 and may not belong here. Talorgan son of Aengus may therefore be equated with Dub Thalorg of the annals. The fourth name, only to be found in the longer version of the list, is thought to be a corrupt form of Conall son of Tadc, Custantín's opponent in 789. If this is correct, it is not difficult to conclude that it was Conall's presence in this annal-entry which persuaded the original compiler of the longer version to include him at this point. Given then that Drust son of Talorgan is accorded only one year's reign in both versions of the king-list and could therefore have been easily overlooked by an annalist

[68] AU 741.10. Skene, *Celtic Scotland* i.306–16; Anderson, *Kings and Kingship*, 188–96; Duncan, *Scotland: the Making of the Kingdom*, 54–9.

[69] Absent from list A: Anderson, *Kings and Kingship*, 249.

[70] The name is rendered thus in lists A and B: Anderson, *Kings and Kingship*, 249, 263. In list C it is *Canul* s. *Tang*: *Lebor Bretnach*, ed. Van Hamel, 86.

writing in Ireland, the evidence of the annals and the Pictish king-list is not as contradictory as first appears.

In the Dalriadic king-list the third of the four kings interposed between Fergus and Custantín is none other than Conall son of Tadc, who is made to precede Conall son of Aedán,[71] his opponent in the annal-entry for 807 which recorded his death in battle in Kintyre. Once again the sole reason for the presence of these two in this king-list is likely to be the annal-entry of 807. The second of the four kings is named Domnall, son of Custantín. It has been suggested that Domnall ruled Dál Riata in a subordinate capacity to his father Custantín, son of Fergus.[72] It is more likely that there was confusion with Domnall, son of Custantín, who died as king of Alba in the year 900. Indeed it may be that Eochu, the first king listed, is the only genuine one.[73] He is present as Aed Find's son in straight-line royal pedigrees, the earliest of which was compiled in the reign of Custantín III who died in 997.[74] M. O. Anderson suggested that, since the sum of the years reigned by the kings noted in the *Duan Albanach* totals thirty-nine, precisely the number of years between the deaths of Fergus in 781 and Custantín in 820, then Eochu was probably king for only a few months at most.[75] This would also explain why he was ignored by the Irish annalist. Once again the evidence of the king-list and the annals can be reconciled more-or-less, leaving the way open for a view of Custantín's career and objectives other than the one most frequently predicated.[76]

Custantín was succeeded by his brother Aengus in both the Pictish and the Dalriadic king-lists and this agrees with the picture presented by the annals. But now the Scottish Chronicle comes into play, revealing that in respect of succession to the kingship of Fortriu there is a gap in the annals between Aengus who died

[71] Jackson, 'The *Duan Albanach*', 132; Boyle, 'The Edinburgh synchronisms', 177; Thurneysen, 'Synchronismen der irischen Könige', 91.

[72] Anderson, 'Dalriada and the creation of the kingdom of the Scots', 109.

[73] Boyle, 'The Edinburgh synchonisms', 177; Thurneysen, 'Synchronismen der Irischen Könige', 90.

[74] Bannerman, *Studies in the History of Dalriada*, 65.

[75] Anderson, 'Dalriada and the creation of the kingdom of the Scots', 108.

[76] Above, pp. 83–4.

in 834 and Cinaed mac Alpín who did not enter Fortriu until *ca* 843, and in respect of the kingship of Dál Riata there is a gap between the death of Aengus and Cinaed's accession there 'two years before he came to Pictavia', presumably therefore in 840 or 841.[77]

Between 834 and *ca* 843 both the longer and shorter Pictish king-lists name five kings.[78] Only the third of these received mention in the annals, namely Eóganán son of Aengus, who, together with his brother Bran and Aed son of Boanta, perished in a defeat inflicted on 'the men of Fortriu' in 839 by 'the heathens', probably Danes.[79] None is given a title therein but all three bear Gaelic names and clearly Fortriu had remained in the control of Scots. Eóganán's name is listed in the section devoted to kings in the *Liber Vitae* of the community of St Cuthbert alongside those of his uncle Custantín and of Aengus, son of Fergus (d. 761).[80] There can be no doubt that Eóganán was king of Fortriu as claimed by the Pictish king-list and its accuracy at this point is further vouched for by the fact that the combined reign-lengths of the five kings given therein amounts to ten years which is a reasonably close approximation to the gap in the annals between 834 and *ca* 843. According to the king-list Eóganán succeeded his first cousin Drust son of Custantín, who was in turn successor of Aengus.

The Dalriadic king-list, however, does not inspire confidence at this point.[81] Aengus' successor as king of Dál Riata is claimed to be Aed son of Boanta, who is made to precede Eóganán despite the fact that they were both killed in the same battle. Given recent precedent Eóganán's predecessor ought to have been Drust son of Custantín, and Aed's presence in the annal-entry for 839 could be the sole reason for his appearance in the king-list. Eóganán is succeeded by Alpín, Cinaed's father,[82] and the content and format

[77] Anderson, *Kings and Kingship*, 249–50.

[78] *Ibid.*, 249, 263, 266, 273, 281, 287.

[79] AU 839.9.

[80] Originally kept at Lindisfarne, now at Durham. See facsimile *Liber Vitae Ecclesiae Dunelmensis*, fos. 12vb, 12va, and 12ra respectively.

[81] Jackson, 'The *Duan Albanach*', 132; Boyle, 'The Edinburgh synchronisms', 177; Thurneysen, 'Synchronismen der Irischen Könige', 91.

[82] Not, however, in the *Duan Albanach* which seems to have lost another verse at this point.

of the statement in the Chronicle of Huntingdon[83] to the effect that Alpín was killed fighting the Picts may well be genuine.[84] But a second and unknown Eóganán interposed in the king-list between Alpín and Cinaed may simply be in error for Eóganán, son of Aengus.[85]

The rapid and, in Irish eyes, doubtless often obscure succession of kings in Fortriu and Dál Riata may well be a reason for the information-gap in the annals at this point. If the battle of 839 was the only event worthy of record, was that because it resulted in the Scots losing control of Fortriu for a time? The process may actually have begun in Drust's reign, for he is represented in the Pictish king-lists as reigning jointly with a Pict (judging by his name), while the uncompromisingly Pictish character of the names of Eóganán's successors in the Pictish king-lists and of a further three added in the shorter version[86] would suggest a resurgent Pictish resistance to Scottish control for which the result of the battle in 839 would surely have been a considerable stimulus.

This scenario would certainly explain the military dimension of the Scottish recovery. We have already noted that Alpín may have been killed fighting the Picts, while the Scottish Chronicle says of Cinaed that he 'destroyed' the Picts,[87] and the Prophecy of Berchán, recently shown to have been composed in large part by a Scottish poet in the reign of Mael Coluim III (d. 1093),[88] claims that Cinaed took 'the kingship of Alba by force of his strength'. It goes on to say that he 'conquered in battle' and that there was a 'slaughter of Picts'.[89]

It may be that the Pictish king-list was drawn up or concluded in a monastery which accepted that Cinaed became king of Fortriu in 842/3 and that an ancestor of the shorter version was then taken to an area of continuing Pictish resistance to Scottish control

[83] Ed. Skene, *Chronicles of the Picts, Chronicles of the Scots*, 98–104; Anderson, 'Dalriada and the creation of the kingdom of the Scots', 113–14.

[84] Anderson, *Kings and Kingship*, 273.

[85] Only in the shorter version of the synchronisms (Boyle, 'The Edinburgh synchronisms', 177).

[86] Anderson, *Kings and Kingship*, 266, 273, 281, 287.

[87] *Ibid*., 249.

[88] Ed. Hudson, *The Prophecy of Berchan*, 14–16, 116–21.

[89] *Ibid*., 42, 84.

which resulted in the names of a further three kings, leaders of that resistance, being added:[90] it is surely significant that the sum of their recorded reign-lengths amounts to six years, which added to 842/3 brings us to 848/9, the date at which Columba's relics were transferred from Iona to Dunkeld. I would suggest that 842/3 is the year of Cinaed's takeover of the kingship of Fortriu, not the kingship of all Pictland; not until 848/9 is that achievement marked by his transportation of Columba's relics to Dunkeld.

This might imply that Pictish resistance, as exemplified by the extra kings named in the shorter king-list, had retreated northwards across the Mounth,[91] which would bring Sueno's Stone, so-called, firmly into the picture. An upright cross-slab sculptured in relief on four sides and dated by art historians to the period 850–900, it is thought to celebrate Cinaed's takeover of Pictland. That view would tend to be confirmed by its location near Forres in what was once Moray (visible by the eleventh century at least as the most powerful province north of the Mounth), and by the depiction on the east face of what David Sellar has convincingly argued is a royal inaugural ceremony in prime position below the cross, emphasising in particular Cinaed's achievement in returning Northern Pictland to the fold.[92] The extraordinary display of military activity on the whole twenty-foot length of the west face depicting battle and slaughter, including decapitation, would then be convincing illustration of that aspect of the documentary record.

It may be that Custantín's career should be seen in much the same light; that already king of Dál Riata, he took over Fortriu by force of arms, in which case the presence of the title *rex Fortrenn* in the obit need have no other connotation than *rex Pictorum* in Cinaed's obit, namely, the glorification by the annalist of the Scottish takeover of Southern Pictland.[93] The Prophecy of

[90] Anderson, *Kings and Kingship*, 266, 273, 281, 287.

[91] Although the last of them Drust was killed at Forteviot or Scone according to List F (*ibid.*).

[92] Sellar, 'Sueno's Stone and its interpreters'.

[93] Associated with the title *rex Fortrenn* there is a similar tendency to refer to Scots as 'men of Fortriu' or as Picts (789, 839, 904): see above, p. 73.

Berchán supports this interpretation. There are five verses devoted to Custantín as a king of Scots in Pictland.[94] He is not portrayed as a Pict who succeeded to the kingship by right of inheritance. He is specifically associated with the Cenél nGabráin territory of Kintyre in Dál Riata. He comes 'eastwards' to do battle with the Picts and he was for the whole of his 'thirteen years' reign 'face to face, against a Pictish army'.

The same message comes through from the Dupplin Cross long thought to have commemorated Cinaed mac Alpín's exploits in Pictland. But the recent reading of Custantín's name in one of the two inscriptions thereon suggests that he, not Cinaed, was responsible for commissioning it and causing it to be set up on the banks of the River Earn overlooking the royal centre of Forteviot at the very heart of Southern Pictland.[95] It is to be seen as a record in stone of, and a thanksgiving to God and doubtless to Columba also for, the successful outcome of Custantín's Pictish adventures. That these were primarily military in character is surely witnessed in the east-facing panel depicting a phalanx of soldiers drawn up in battle order or perhaps in a victory parade.[96]

As part of a possible answer to the question of why Custantín was unable to implement his plan to remove Columba's relics from Iona to Dunkeld, let us look briefly at the career of the Pictish king Bruide mac Bili who died in 693. In 682, according to AU, 'the Orkneys were destroyed' by him and in 685 he won the famous battle of Dunnichen or Nechtansmere against the Angles of Northumbria.[97] He is given a comparatively long reign of twenty-one years by the king-list and looks very much like a king of all Pictland, a *rex Pictorum*, but by the end of his reign his authority had presumably diminished to such an extent that the contemporary annalist could only describe him as *rex Fortrenn* in his obit.

Custantín's career may have taken a similar course. He is given a reign of thirty-five years by the longer Pictish king-list,

[94] Hudson, *The Prophecy of Berchan*, 41, 83–4. A gloss confusing Custantín with Aedán mac Gabráin has misled commentators in the past (*ibid.*, 71, 83 n. 71, 197).

[95] Forsyth, 'The inscriptions on the Dupplin Cross', 237–44; see also Alcock and Alcock, 'Reconnaisance excavations', 219–41, 283.

[96] *Ibid.*, 240.

[97] AU 682.4, 686.1; AT 686.1.

thirty-one of them corroborated by AU, as we have seen,[98] that is, from 789 to his death in 820. A long reign is a mark of success in the Dark Ages. Was he so successful that sometime *ca* 800 he had managed to weld the two halves of Pictland together, becoming in other words *rex Pictorum*, apparently so securely that the plan of transferring Columba's relics to Dunkeld and Kells could be conceived and partially implemented, to the extent that the new buildings necessary to house these relics were actually completed by 814? And was it just at this point, 814, that Pictland fell apart again, ensuring that Custantín would only be described as *rex Fortrenn* in his obit six years later and forcing postponement of the final implementation of the plan until 849?

This scenario would best suit the presence of both Custantín and Cinaed in the Prophecy of Berchán.[99] The poem is concerned to celebrate the line of the kings of Alba from its beginnings up to and including the reign of Domnall Bán deposed in 1097. Cinaed is 'the first king from the men of Ireland in Alba to take kingship in the east' and 'he will be seventeen years, heights of valour, in the high kingship of Alba' when 'he dies on the banks of the Earn'. Yet the first king of Alba listed is not Cinaed but Custantín and the penultimate verse claims that there will be 'twenty-four kings . . . from the first king who will take Alba', clearly numbering from Custantín to Domnall Bán inclusively.[100] As already noted Custantín is constantly battling with the Picts but only 'for a short while will they be under his authority', and moreover 'at the hour he will die he will not be king'. This means that in the poet's opinion he was not king of Alba, or rather he was not *rex Pictorum* on his death, and presumably the period *ca* 800 to *ca* 814 (precisely 'thirteen years', if the Prophecy is to be believed) represents the 'short while' that he was *rex Pictorum*.[101] Although

[98] Above, pp. 83–4.

[99] Hudson, *Prophecy of Berchan*, 41–2, 83–4.

[100] *Ibid*., 56, 92.

[101] His appearance as Custantín, son of Fergus, *rí Alban* in a Middle Gaelic story about St Mochuda of Lismore is wholly unhistorical but in it Custantín, no longer himself a king, is made to say, 'Seven men were under my domination, every one a king'. This may be a memory of the traditional seven sub-kingdoms of Pictland over which he once reigned as *rex Pictorum* ('*Indarba Mochuda a rRaithen*', in *Bethada Náem nÉrenn*, ed. Plummer, i.300–11; ii.291–302).

Custantín was the first Scot to 'take Alba', that is, to become king of all Pictland, it was only temporarily, and Cinaed was the first to make all Pictland a permanent possession of the Scots. This is Cinaed's role in other sources but particularly in AU and in the Scottish Chronicle which, as we have already noted,[102] describes him as 'first of the Scots to rule this Pictland ... for sixteen years' ('until his death' understood). Custantín may have commissioned the Dupplin Cross at the point at which he became *rex Pictorum* rather than *rex Fortrenn*. This would mean a date for it round about 800 which accords with the dating of art historians.[103]

It has often been suggested that Viking raids or the threat thereof were responsible for the intended replacement of Iona as the centre of the Columban Church by Dunkeld and Kells, while the union of Picts and Scots so-called is sometimes represented as a drawing together of the two peoples in the face of a common enemy.[104] Now it may be that the decision to remove Columba's relics to Kells in Ireland was prompted in part by the special vulnerability of Iona to sea-borne attacks. It was devastated by the Vikings in 795, burnt again in 802, and no less than sixty-eight members of the community killed in 806.[105] But this cannot be the reason for the removal of Columba's relics to Dunkeld, if only because, despite the ever-increasing presence of the Norse in these waters and despite, for instance, the martyrdom suffered by Blathmac a monk of Iona in 825 for refusing to reveal where on the island these same relics (specifically *Scrín Choluim Chille*, Columba's portable shrine)[106] were hidden, it was almost a quarter of a century later that they finally went to Dunkeld. Moreover, as we have seen, Scottish pressure on Pictland began long before 795, the date of the first recorded plundering expedition by Scandinavians in these parts, while the sudden and apparently complete cessation of Norse attacks on Iona after 825 has been

[102] Above, p. 72.

[103] Forsyth, 'The inscriptions on the Dupplin Cross', 243; Wormald, 'The emergence of the *regnum Scottorum*', 146.

[104] Duncan, *Scotland: the Making of the Kingdom*, 86; Foster, *Picts, Gaels, and Scots*, 14, 111.

[105] AU 795; AU 802.9; AU 806.8.

[106] *Monumenta Germaniae Historiae: Poetae Latini Aevi Carolini*, ed. Dümmler, ii.297–301; translation in *ES* i.263–5.

attributed to the rapid Gaelicisation of Norse settlers in the area who, on becoming Christian, adopted Columba as their patron saint and may even have been allies of Cinaed mac Alpín in his takeover of Pictland.[107] Indeed, it has already been suggested that the perceived difficulty of overseeing the Irish Columban monasteries from east of Druim Alban had more to do with the foundation of Kells than any threat to Iona from the Norse.[108]

That the Irish venture was dependent on the move to Dunkeld rather than the other way about is also demonstrated by the fact that it did not happen until 849 despite Kells presumably being ready to receive its share of the relics any time after 814. Moreover, when the shareout did take place, among those relics that went to Dunkeld was Columba's portable shrine, *Scrín Choluim Chille*, his existing badge of authority on earth.[109] Finally, the plan to move to Dunkeld directly involved the kings of Scots in the persons of Custantín and Cinaed, thus reinforcing the continuing close association between the centre of the church and the monarchy first established by Columba and Aedán mac Gabráin in the sixth century.[110] Kells on the other hand seems to have been primarily an ecclesiastical project in that only abbots of Iona are mentioned in this connection, Cellach as builder of Kells, and Indrechtach who finally brought Ireland's share of Columba's relics from Iona to Kells in 849.[111]

It has been argued that Cinaed mac Alpín's origins were obscure and that therefore he is to be considered the founder of a new Scottish royal dynasty in opposition not only to the Picts but also to the house of Fergus which seems to have controlled Fortriu until 839.[112] But this ignores the straight-line pedigrees of later kings of Scots which have no doubts as to Cinaed's ancestry.

[107] Jennings, 'An Historical Study of the Gael and Norse in Western Scotland from c.795 to c.1000', *passim*; Bannerman, '*Comarba Coluim Chille*', 33–4; Wormald, 'The emergence of the *regnum Scottorum*', 139–40.

[108] Bannerman, '*Comarba Coluim Chille*', 42–3.

[109] *Ibid.*, 42–3.

[110] Bannerman, *Studies in the History of Dalriada*, 81–3; Bannerman, 'The Scots of Dalriada', 68.

[111] It is difficult to see any clear input from Ireland, whether ecclesiastical or secular (Herbert, *Iona, Kells, and Derry*, 68–70).

[112] Smyth, *Warlords and Holy Men*, 180–2.

The earliest of them, compiled only about a century and a half later in the reign of Custantín III who died in 997, shows Cinaed to have been a great-grandson of Aed Find and therefore a member of the mainstream Dalriadic royal dynasty, which of course included the house of Fergus, who was Aed Find's brother.[113] Their precise relationships are tabled as follows:

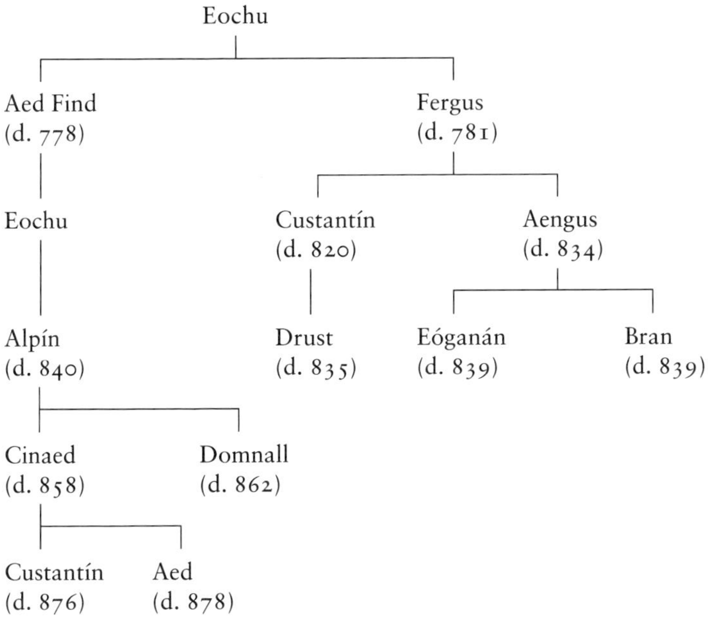

Opposition to Fergus' descendants hardly chimes with the fact that Cinaed named the older of his two recorded sons Custantín. Indeed, considering that his second son was called Aed, presumably after Aed Find, it is difficult to escape the conclusion that Cinaed intended honouring the memory of his two predecessors who had done most to prepare the way for his own achievement in attaining the permanent takeover of all Pictland.[114]

But perhaps the most compelling reason for claiming that Cinaed was following closely in Custantín's footsteps was the fact that he

[113] Bannerman, *Studies in the History of Dalriada*, 65.
[114] See Wormald, 'The emergence of the *regnum Scottorum*', 137; Wallace-Hadrill, *Early Germanic Kingship in England and on the Continent*, 106.

brought to fruition the project, first devised by Custantín and partially implemented by him, to transfer Columba's relics from Iona to Dunkeld, thereby establishing a new administrative centre for the church of what was to be known as Alba, the much-extended kingdom of the Scots. The formation of this entity by the year 849 was neither a negotiated union between two peoples nor, for that matter, the chance result of a plundering expedition by a wandering warlord aided by the fortuitous intervention of Scandinavians, whether Norse or Danes. Rather it was by dint of persistent and determined military pressure applied by the Scots over a period of more than sixty years, characterised, at least from *ca* 800, by concerted forward-looking and sophisticated planning on the part of both church and state.[115]

[115] I wish to thank Dr Dauvit Broun and Dr Thomas Clancy for valuable help and advice in the preparation of this chapter for publication.

4

Dunkeld and the origin of Scottish identity[1]

Dauvit Broun

IT is well known that from 900 the title *rí Alban* ('king of *Alba*') replaced *rex Pictorum* ('king of Picts'), which occurred for the last time in an extant contemporary record in the obit of Aed son of Cinaed mac Alpín in 878.[2] Also, from 918 *fir Alban* or *Albanaig* ('men of *Alba*', 'inhabitants of *Alba*') supplanted *Picti* ('Picts'), which is last found in a contemporary chronicle as the name of the people defeated by vikings at Dollar in 875.[3]

[1] This is a revised version of a paper given at the conference in May 1997 organised by the Department of Scottish History at Edinburgh University to mark the retirement of Dr John Bannerman after more than thirty years in the department. The core of this paper involves the analysis of extant texts in order to identify a chronicle which no longer survives, and I am very happy to acknowledge that I owe much of my understanding of how to go about this to John Bannerman's masterly demonstration of the existence of the Iona Chronicle in his 'Notes on the Scottish entries in the early Irish annals'. I would like to thank Dr Thomas Clancy and Prof. Máire Herbert for helpful comments and criticism, and members of the evening class on Pictish history held at Alloa in February and March 1997 for much interest and stimulation in these matters. I would also like to thank Dr Nerys Ann Jones for her constant support and encouragement. I am, of course, solely responsible for what is presented here.

[2] AU 878.2; AU 900.6. On the contemporary authority of these notices see below, pp. 100–2. They are noted, for instance, in Anderson, *Kings and Kingship*, 197–8.

[3] AU 875.3: *Congressio Pictorum fri Dubghallu 7 strages magna Pictorum facta est* ('The Picts encountered the dark foreigners and a great slaughter of the Picts resulted'). AU 918.4 (a lengthy account of a battle on the banks of a River Tyne between *fir Alban* and Ragnall, king of the 'dark foreigners'). It may also be noted that another title accorded to Pictish kings in

Alba is, of course, the modern Gaelic for 'Scotland'. This change in the name of the kingdom and its people may therefore be taken as marking the origin of Scottish identity.[4] *Alba* would not, however, have meant Scotland as we understand it territorially today; that stage was only reached in the thirteenth century, and was preceded by a rather bewildering range of meanings, including a region bounded by the Forth in the south, the central highlands in the west and Moray in the north, which may have been the original extent of the kingdom in 900.[5] In order to advance our understanding of this switch from Pictish to *Alba*-based terminology sometime between *ca* 875 to *ca* 900 it would be useful to identify the ultimate source of our evidence. Whose terminology does it represent? Unfortunately the severe limitations of the evidence will allow only a circumstantial answer to be offered. I will argue that our ultimate witness for the origin of Scottish identity is likely to be Dunkeld, which was itself established as the chief Columban church in the kingdom during the ninth century. There is no way of showing, however, whether Dunkeld actually initiated the coining of Scottish identity. Moreover, until we can say more about what *Alba* signified when it was adopted as the kingdom's name, we cannot be sure that this new Scottish identity was necessarily very different from Pictish identity.[6]

---

contemporary record was *rex Fortrenn*, 'king of Fortriu', which may have denoted southern Pictland or at least a large part of it. *Rex Fortrenn* appears for the last time in a contemporary chronicle in AU 834.1, but *fir Fortrenn*, 'men of Fortriu', is last found in a non-literary context in AU 904.4.

[4] See Broun, 'The origin of Scottish identity', 35–9, and most recently Dumville, 'Ireland and Britain'.

[5] See most recently Broun, 'Defining Scotland and the Scots'.

[6] The most convincing explanation will be the one which can account for how *Alba*, hitherto Gaelic for 'Britain', was deemed appropriate for a kingdom which occupied only a small part of Britain (especially so if it controlled only the area between the Forth, Moray and the central highlands). My remark that 'the coining of the term *Alba* . . . involved a dramatic, not to say outrageous, change of meaning' ('The origin of Scottish identity in its European context', 21) is certainly premature, and may prove to have been wrongheaded. For some suggestion that *Alba* as the kingdom's name may have denoted 'Pictland', see below, n. 57. It has been suggested in Dumville, 'Ireland and Britain', 183, that *Alba* was coined 'as a new territorial name for what had once been the kingdom of the southern Picts'. I intend to explore this issue in more detail on a future occasion.

Although the switch from Pictish to *Alba*-based terminology occurred in contemporary record between *ca* 875 and *ca* 900, it is generally held that the fate of the Picts and the creation of *Alba* was largely determined by events two generations earlier when Cinaed mac Alpín established himself as king of the Picts in the 840s.[7] The idea of Cinaed as founding father is so deeply ingrained that it has long been normal practice to number Scottish monarchs on the assumption that Cinaed was the first. The earliest example of this view of Cinaed is in the Scottish chronicle known variously as the 'Old Scottish Chronicle',[8] the 'Scottish Chronicle',[9] the 'Chronicle of the Kings of Scotland, version A',[10] or more recently the 'Chronicle of the Kings of Alba'[11] (the title I will use on this occasion). Here we are told that Cinaed destroyed the Picts, and that he had been king of Dál Riata for two years before he came to Pictland.[12] This cannot, however, be accepted as a contemporary account.[13] The Chronicle is a heavily annotated king-list

[7] See for instance Miller, 'The last century of Pictish succession', esp. 48, and Anderson, 'Dalriada and the creation of the kingdom of the Scots', 115–24. In general, see for example Duncan, *Scotland: the Making of the Kingdom*, 56–9; Smyth, *Warlords and Holy Men*, 210. For more recent views, see n. 19, below.

[8] Miller, 'The last century of Pictish succession'; Hudson, 'The conquest of the Picts'.

[9] Cowan, 'The Scottish chronicle in the Poppleton manuscript'; Anderson, 'Picts the name and the people'; Hudson, *Kings of Celtic Scotland*, *passim*. Anderson, *Kings and Kingship*, e.g. 197–8, opted for the longer 'Scottish Chronicle in the Poppleton manuscript'.

[10] *ES* i, 288–512, *passim*.

[11] The title used in Dumville, *The Churches of North Britain in the First Viking-Age*, 36, n. 107. The edition I have used for this article is Anderson, *Kings and Kingship*, 249–53. For the collection of Scottish historical pieces in which this appears (datable between 1202 and 1214) see Miller, 'Matriliny by treaty: the Pictish foundation-legend', 138–42; Crick, *The Historia Regum Britannie of Geoffrey of Monmouth*, iii: *Summary Catalogue of the Manuscripts*, 256–61.

[12] *Kinadius igitur filius Alpini primus Scottorum rexit feliciter istam annis xvi. Pictauiam. Pictauia autem a Pictis est nominata quos ut diximus <Cin>adius deleuit; Deus enim eos pro merito sue malicie alienos ac occiosos hereditate dignatus est facere, qui illi non solum Domini missam ac preceptum sp<re>ue<run>t set et in iure equitatis aliis equiparare* [?*u*/*n*]*oluerunt. Ist<e> uero biennio antequam ueniret Pictauiam Dalriete regnum suscepit.*

[13] *Pace* Hudson, 'The language of the Scottish Chronicle', 70–1.

which, as it stands, begins with Cinaed mac Alpín and concludes with Cinaed mac Maíle Choluim whose reign-length has been left blank: it is generally agreed that it assumed its current extent sometime during the latter's reign (971–95).[14] The Chronicle was probably written earlier – during the reign of Illulb (954–62), I would argue – and has been continued subsequently on more than one occasion.[15] This means that the Chronicle, a self-conscious essay in the history of the kingship of *Alba*, was written at a time when that kingship had been monopolised for half a century or more by a dynasty whose definitive ancestor was Cinaed mac Alpín. If descent from Cinaed mac Alpín had become a key ingredient in legitimating a claim to the kingship, then it would no doubt have been tempting to combine this with a consciousness that Picts had ceased to exist and so create an image of Cinaed as simultaneously founder of the kingship and destroyer of the Picts.[16] It can not be stated categorically, of course, that there was necessarily no substance to this notion of Cinaed; but it appears to conform suspiciously well with the propensity of historical texts to reflect the times in which they were written, especially when a highly-charged issue such as a kingdom's origins was involved.[17]

It is a notorious fact that identifiably contemporary evidence for Cinaed's career is alarmingly sparse. All that can be said with any conviction, indeed, is that he died at Forteviot as king of the Picts in February 858 and that he was instrumental in the removal

[14] However, in the light of the analysis of this text's composition in Howlett, *Caledonian Craftsmanship*, it may be necessary to give more heed to the contribution of the author of the compilation of Scottish historical pieces in which the chronicle appears.

[15] Hudson, 'The language of the Scottish Chronicle', 71–2, has commented that 'a copy of the chronicle seems to have been taken from Dunkeld to St Andrews sometime after the mid-tenth century ... probably during the reign of Cuilén [966–71]'; see also *ibid.*, 67.

[16] As David Dumville comments (*The Churches of North Britain in the First Viking-Age*, 36, n. 107), 'it is an interesting issue whether that chronicler was the first to propound his particular solution ...' to the question '... how is it that we are Gaels when formerly in this same territory Picts lived and ruled?'

[17] As Molly Miller has observed ('The last century of Pictish succession', 59), the Chronicle 'not only does not narrate the oral material on the fall of the Picts [discussed *ibid.*, 50], but also that instead the compiler gives the established alternative which written historiography provided'.

of St Columba's relics to Dunkeld (probably in 849).[18] Modern scholars have made a number of perfectly plausible attempts to overcome this dearth of information and assess the probability that Cinaed may or may not have conquered the Picts and deprived them of their heritage.[19] In this chapter I will not, however, discuss Cinaed mac Alpín in any detail. Indeed, the use of Pictish or *Alba*-based terminology in the late ninth century suggests that, as far as the end of Pictish identity is concerned, the spot-light should fall not on the 840s but on the period between the last references to 'Picts' and a 'king of the Picts' in a contemporary Gaelic source in the 870s and the first appearance in 900 of *Alba* as the term for the kingdom of Cinaed mac Alpín's successors.

The only readily accessible texts which preserve a contemporary record of the change from *rex Pictorum* to *rí Alban* and from *Picti* to *fir Alban* (or *Albanaig*) are Irish chronicles, in particular the Annals of Ulster, *Chronicum Scotorum* and the Annals of

[18] The evidence for the translation of Columba's relics to Dunkeld is discussed below, n. 40; its historical value has been questioned recently by David Dumville (*The Churches of North Britain in the First Viking-Age*, 20). Cinaed's death is recorded in AU 858.2; FAI §285; AI 858.3: see also *Annales Cambriae* (A text) 412 (= 856). The Chronicle of the Kings of Alba reads: *mortuus est tandem tumore ante idus Feb', feria .iij., in palacio Fothiurtabaicht* ... (see Anderson, *Kings and Kingship*, 250 n. 129 for reading of *ante*), '[Cinaed mac Alpín] finally died of a tumour on the Tuesday before the ides of February [i.e. 8 February] in the palace of Forteviot ...' Marjorie Anderson (*ibid.*) assumed that the Tuesday in question was Shrove Tuesday which was before the ides of February in 859 rather than 858. Hudson, *Kings of Celtic Scotland*, 46, has 8 February 858.

[19] See for instance Wormald, 'The emergence of the *regnum Scottorum*', arguing that Cinaed may straightforwardly be regarded as conqueror of the Picts; Bannerman, above, pp. 87–94, where Cinaed's military achievement is seen as the culmination of a plan initiated earlier in the century; Hudson, *Kings of Celtic Scotland*, 29–47, where it is emphasised that Cinaed's triumph should be placed in the context of a gradual increase of Gaelic political influence in Pictland, and that 'the beginnings of the permanent conquest should be dated to the eighth, rather than the ninth, century' (35) (see also Anderson, *Kings and Kingship*, 204); and Dumville, *The Churches of North Britain in the First Viking-Age*, 35–6, who has also pointed to eighth-century roots of the Gaelicisation of the Picts and has described how, at a time of Scandinavian pressure on three sides, 'the old ruling dynasty was displaced in the south at least by another, whose first prominent representative was one Ciniod son of Alpin'.

Clonmacnoise.[20] It has been shown that these chronicles are chiefly continuations and adaptations of an earlier chronicle which ran up to 911,[21] which Kathleen Hughes designated the 'Chronicle of Ireland'.[22] It is apparent that the Chronicle of Ireland was itself a compilation of more than one chronicle; as well as the Iona Chronicle (up to 740),[23] Kathleen Hughes suggested that it also included, for instance, material derived from Bangor in Ulster, Lismore in Munster, and Clonmacnoise (which supplied information on Connacht).[24] It has yet to be established when these various strands were brought together to create the 'Chronicle of Ireland', or how many stages of compilation this involved.[25]

Kathleen Hughes identified a major strain in the make-up of the Chronicle of Ireland as an 'Uí Néill chronicle', contemporary from the second half of the eighth century, which from at least the end of that century was written at Armagh.[26] It has also been

[20] AU, CS and AClon. Reference will also be made to FAI.

[21] Kathryn Grabowski, 'The Annals of Inisfallen, A.D. 431–1092: sources, structure and history', in Grabowski and Dumville, *Chronicles and Annals of Mediaeval Ireland and Wales*, 1–107, at 53–6.

[22] Hughes, *Early Christian Ireland*, 101. The idea of a core chronicle was earlier mooted in O'Rahilly, *Early Irish History and Mythology*, 258, and elaborated in Kelleher, 'Early Irish history and pseudo-history', esp. 126.

[23] Bannerman, 'Notes on the Scottish entries in the early Irish annals'. For general discussion see also Herbert, *Iona, Kells and Derry*, 22–3.

[24] Hughes, *Early Christian Ireland*, 138–42.

[25] For the most recent discussion of this question, see Etchingham, *Viking Raids*, esp. 5–6, and also 17–31, where there is an important analysis of the geographical distribution of certain classes of entry in the ninth century. Hughes observed a 'fall-off of Connacht and Munster entries about 850' which could suggest that 'they may have been incorporated about then' (Hughes, *Early Christian Ireland*, 142). Hughes' further comment remains true to this day: 'I can hardly stress too strongly that the evidence for the sources of the Chronicle of Ireland is difficult to interpret, and interpretation, I am afraid, will always depend to a considerable extent on individual judgment.' It is conceivable that the Chronicle of Ireland underlying all extant chronicles was only a brief stage in a continuing process of contemporary chronicling, compilation and adaptation. Note the comment by Etchingham (*Viking Raids*, 5) regarding the idea that all extant chronicles are variations of a core 'Chronicle of Ireland': 'whether or not this, rather than an admixture of local chronicling, best accounts for the partial divergence of the extant texts before the tenth century is a question which . . . may remain open'.

[26] Hughes, *Early Christian Ireland*, 129–35.

pointed out that the Annals of Ulster include an impressive series of obits of leading clergy in Armagh which continues beyond 911 up to 1189; indeed, as far as the office of *fer léginn* is concerned, a continuous succession has been identified from 780 to 1188.[27] A full and painstaking discussion of the history of the Chronicle of Ireland and the Annals of Ulster has yet to be published, but on current knowledge a reasonable hypothesis would be that an Armagh/Uí Néill chronicle kept from the late eighth century became in due course the 'Chronicle of Ireland'; a copy as far as 911 was made and formed a key element in other Irish chronicles (the 'Clonmacnoise group');[28] the Chronicle of Ireland continued to be maintained at Armagh until 1189 (incorporating at least one other chronicle in the mid-eleventh century); in 1189 it moved west (initially to Derry), and finally became the Annals of Ulster that we can read and touch today.[29]

It is likely, therefore, that the Scottish entries attributable to the Chronicle of Ireland (as well as entries or details unique to the Annals of Ulster) were a product of chronicling activity in Armagh. This is especially so in the decades either side of 900 when there was both a dynastic link between the Uí Néill and the family of Cinaed mac Alpín and also a close ecclesiastical

[27] Bannerman, '*Comarba Coluim Chille*', 39–40. The series would appear to include Joseph who died in 936 as abbot of Armagh, bishop, anchorite and *sapiens* (40 n. 1).

[28] On the Clonmacnoise group see Grabowski and Dumville, *Chronicles and Annals of Mediaeval Ireland and Wales*, 109–226.

[29] Bannerman, '*Comarba Coluim Chille*', 36–42; see also Mac Niocaill, *The Medieval Irish Annals*, 29–30. There were doubtless different phases of chronicling activity: Dumville, 'Latin and Irish in the *Annals of Ulster*, A.D. 431–1050', 330–1, has drawn attention to a significant change in the linguistic make-up of AU from 939, and has suggested that the section from 911 (or soon after) to 938 may represent the work of a single chronicler. Another complicating feature is the close relationship between AU and the Clonmacnoise group of chronicles apparent in a number of entries from the middle of the tenth century to the mid-eleventh century: see Grabowski and Dumville, *Chronicles and Annals of Mediaeval Ireland and Wales*, 56. Grabowski commented that this relationship ceased 'perhaps in 1054': both AU and AT (and CS), however, share the curious feature of recording the death of Lulach mac Gilla Comgáin in 1058 before that of his step-father and predecessor Mac Bethad mac Findlaích (who was killed in 1057), which suggests that this relationship between AU and the Clonmacnoise-group continued to 1058 at least.

connection between Armagh and the Columban federation. Both Aed Findliath mac Néill (d. 879) and his successor as king of Tara, Flann Sinna mac Maíle Shechnaill (d. 916), were married to Mael Muire daughter of Cinaed mac Alpín (d. 913).[30] On the ecclesiastical side the abbot of Armagh, Mael Brigte mac Tornáin, became abbot of Kells and *comarba Coluim Chille* ('heir of Columba') in 891 and ruled Armagh and Kells until his death in 927.[31] In both respects the likeliest channel for Armagh's interest in eastern Scottish affairs would have been Dunkeld. The removal of Columba's relics to Dunkeld under the auspices of Cinaed mac Alpín established Dunkeld as the chief Columban church in Cinaed's kingdom; it also illustrates that Dunkeld had a similar relationship with Clann Cinaeda meic Alpín as Armagh had with Uí Néill. The obits of two abbots of Dunkeld in 865 and 873 in the Annals of Ulster may be a further indication of this Armagh–Dunkeld link.[32] It would appear, therefore, that the change from Pictish to *Alba*-based terminology witnessed in Irish chronicles (and particularly the Annals of Ulster) is likely to reflect what was originally written in Armagh. How closely, however, can this also be said to reflect the change in terminology which occurred in southern Pictland, and maybe particularly in Dunkeld?

This question can only be answered with anything firmer than plausible conjecture if some material from a chronicle in southern Pictland itself could be identified. Ted Cowan has argued that the Chronicle of the Kings of Alba was originally created by splicing a king-list with material drawn from an annalistic source.[33] There are, indeed, seventeen items in the Chronicle between 849 and 952 which bear the hallmarks of originating in a contemporary year-by-year chronicle, either because they have been assigned to a regnal year or because they have been dated precisely to the day. These items alone in the Chronicle of the Kings of

[30] Hudson, *Kings of Celtic Scotland*, 45; Sellar, 'Warlords, holy men and matrilineal succession'.

[31] Bannerman, '*Comarba Coluim Chille*', 30, 32, 46. Herbert, *Iona, Kells and Derry*, 74–7.

[32] AU 865.6*b*; 873.8.

[33] Cowan, 'The Scottish chronicle in the Poppleton manuscript', 18; see also 5–6, 10. Contrast with Hudson, 'The language of the Scottish Chronicle', 70–1, where it is argued that the Chronicle was contemporary from 848/9.

Alba up to the mid-tenth century may be said without further investigation to have been derived ultimately from a contemporary source.[34] Unfortunately there is no obvious way of demonstrating how closely any of these items preserve the original wording of their annalistic source.

One feature of this run of seventeen items is that '*Alba*' replaced 'Pictland' at much the same time as would seem to have occurred at Armagh. *Pictauia* appears twice. In one item we are told that vikings devastated *Pictauia* in the mid-860s; in another we are told that Norsemen spent a year in *Pictauia* following their victory at Dollar in 875 and the ensuing slaughter perpetrated by them as far as Atholl. In 903, however, when there was another viking incursion in much the same region, the country they plundered is called *Albania* rather than *Pictauia*. This coincides so well with the switch from Pictish to *Alba*-based terminology in Irish chronicles that it suggests that there was a link between Armagh and the chroniclers who wrote this Scottish material.[35] It may be noted that the delay in abandoning *Pictauia* for *Albania* in the Chronicle of the Kings of Alba stands in contrast to its portrayal of Cinaed mac Alpín as founding-figure of the kingship of Alba. It would appear that the Chronicle's author has been happy to replicate the use of *Pictauia* and *Albania* in his annalistic source, although there is every reason to suspect that he has substituted *Scoti* for *Picti*, especially in view of the parallel between the survival of Pictish terminology in his source and in Irish chronicles.[36]

The suggestion of a link with Armagh immediately raises the possibility that these seventeen items in the Chronicle of the Kings of Alba may have been drawn from a Dunkeld chronicle, due to

[34] Eight can be directly corroborated by other contemporary sources. Two more items can be indirectly confirmed, while no serious objections can be raised against four others. Three are problematic, however, and are probably the unhappy result of centuries of copying.

[35] If the Chronicle of the Kings of Alba is considered in its entirety, it is notable that the only other use of *Pictauia* is found during the reign of Domnall mac Custantín, who died in 900. The possibility cannot be ruled out that this was taken from an annalistic source, but has not been associated with a regnal year because of the difficulty of reconciling reign-lengths with annals in what may have been a period of confusion (see below, p. 109).

[36] Especially AU. See further discussion in Broun, 'The origin of Scottish identity', 40–5.

the political and ecclesiastical connections which would have encouraged contact between Dunkeld and Armagh in this period.[37] The only way to suggest more convincingly that these items may indeed have originated in Dunkeld, however, would be if they revealed a marked concentration on Dunkeld and its environs.[38] Had the original chronicle used by the mid-tenth-century author of the Chronicle of the Kings of Alba survived it is likely that it would have betrayed a local bias. It does not survive, however, and all we have to go on is a selection made by the author of the Chronicle of the Kings of Alba who had an appetite only for events of regnal significance.[39] Despite this difficulty two of the seventeen items can be said to betray a local perspective, although in different ways; in the first instance the context suggests that it is significant that Dunkeld has *not* been mentioned, while in the second instance the context suggests that it is significant that Dunkeld *has* been mentioned. The first is the record of the translation of Columba's relics (probably in 849) to a church built by

[37] Three of these items concern the deaths of Irish kings: Mael Sechnaill mac Maíl Ruanaid king of Tara in 862, his successor Aed Findliath mac Néill in 879, and Cormac mac Cuilennáin king-bishop of Munster in 908, described as a 'most excellent king of the Irish and archbishop'. The interest in two Uí Néill 'high-kings' may, it is true, be expected of any important church in the Gaelic world, but it is particularly appropriate for Dunkeld given the ties of marriage between Dunkeld's royal patrons and the Uí Néill as well as the strong ecclesiastical links Dunkeld had with Ireland. The deaths of two more kings of Tara, Flann Sinna mac Maíl Shechnaill (916) and Niall Glúndub mac Aeda (919), are also noted in the Chronicle of the Kings of Alba, as well as the death of Domnall mac Aeda, king of Cenél nEogain (915) (identified in the Chronicle by Hudson, '*Elech* and the Scots in Strathclyde'); it can not be demonstrated, however, that this information comes from the Chronicle's annalistic source.

[38] Hudson, 'Kings and Church in early Scotland', 154–5, has argued that the Chronicle 'seems to have begun as a set of royal annals maintained at Dunkeld until the mid-tenth century; the monastery is mentioned by name four times more frequently than any other place, and the chronicle has a distinct Atholl orientation in its early sections'. See also Hudson, 'The language of the Scottish Chronicle', 69–72. Hudson does not, however, make a distinction between the seventeen items readily attributable to an annalistic source and the other material in the Chronicle.

[39] The text may also have been significantly reworked by the author of the compilation of Scottish historical pieces in which the Chronicle uniquely survives; for an analysis of the composition of the compilation, see Howlett, *Caledonian Craftsmanship.*

Cinaed mac Alpín.[40] We are not actually told where this church was. An explanation of this oversight could be that this was written at the same place as the church in question, in which case the chronicler may have instinctively taken the location for granted. This church was probably Dunkeld. Columba's relics were stated to be in Dunkeld in what appears to be the mid-ninth-century core of an early-eleventh-century document.[41] The

[40] *Septimo anno regni sui reliquias sancti Columbe transportauit ad ecclesiam quam construxit* ... 'In the seventh year of his reign [Cinaed mac Alpín] transported the relics of St Columba to a church which he built ...'. The Chronicle gives Cinaed a sixteen-year reign; he died in February 858 so his seventh year would appear to have been 848–9; reign-lengths in the Chronicle are sometimes problematic, however (e.g. sixteen years for Cinaed's son Custantín, although he evidently reigned 862–76; see also n. 59, below). A link has been suggested with the transportation of Columba's relics recorded in AU 849.7: *Indrechtach, abbas Iae, do thiachtain dochum nErenn co mindaibh Coluim Cille*, 'Indrechtach, abbot of Iona, came to Ireland with the relics of Columba.' This has been seen as the Irish half of a division of the relics between Kells and Dunkeld; *ES* i, 279 n. 4 and most recently Bannerman, above, pp. 91–2. Although the coincidence in date is suggestive, the movement of relics was itself not uncommon. The movement of Columba's relics noted in AU 849.7 may thus be compared with the almost identically phrased entry in AU 831.1: *Diarmait do tiachtain i nHerinn co mindaibh Coluim Cille*, 'Diarmait [abbot of Iona] came to Ireland with the relics of Columba'. In this instance no division of relics was apparently involved. Note, therefore, David Dumville's reservation when he wondered 'if the legends of the transfer of relics of Columba from Iona to Dunkeld (Perthshire) in the decade 849–858 have any historical value' (Dumville, *The Churches of North Britain in the First Viking-Age*, 20). Clancy, 'Iona, Scotland and the *céli Dé*', 114–15, has argued that these (and the movement of Columba's relics noted in CS 818.4) were associated with the founding of churches, respectively Dunkeld by Custantín son of Uurguist (789–820), St Andrews by Custantín's brother Onuist (820–34), and Cinaed's foundation in Dunkeld; this is not, however, accepted in Bannerman, above, p. 75 n. 21. My own view is that the attribution of the movement of Columba's relics to a regnal year in the Chronicle of the Kings of Alba suggests that this information has been derived from the Chronicle's annalistic source, and that this on its own is sufficient reason to accept that the statement is likely to be accurate, even if what was intended by Cinaed's seventh year can not be established with as much confidence.

[41] Rollason, 'Lists of saints' resting places', 61–8 and 87. This would suggest that the relics were returned to Dunkeld as their original place of keeping after being taken for safety to Ireland in 878 (see below, p. 108). Dunkeld itself may have been founded earlier in the ninth century as part of a scheme to remove some or all of Columba's relics from Iona; see Bannerman, above, esp. pp. 74–5.

other item which may betray a local perspective is the record of the viking incursion in 903. This is put in a curious way: 'the Norsemen plundered Dunkeld and all Alba.'[42] Presumably many places were attacked apart from Dunkeld; only Dunkeld, however, is mentioned. This would be natural enough if these words were written in Dunkeld; if they were written elsewhere, however, then it is odd that the author has not recorded the vikings' assault on his own church or locality. It is a welcome coincidence that one of these items which seem to betray a Dunkeld perspective is also the vital item in which *Albania* appears rather than *Pictauia*.

Two possible explanations come to mind. The first is that the mid-tenth-century author of the Chronicle of the Kings of Alba belonged to Dunkeld, and that this has influenced the way he selected or adapted material from the year-by-year chronicle at his disposal.[43] Alternatively, the year-by-year chronicle-source itself may have been written at Dunkeld, and the Dunkeld perspective may have survived in two items which were incorporated into the Chronicle of the Kings of Alba. If the latter explanation is true, then we can posit that a 'Dunkeld chronicle' contemporary from at least 849 to 903 (and doubtless beyond) was the probable source for most or all of those items in the Chronicle of the Kings of Alba which are likely to have been derived from a year-by-year chronicle. The existence of such a 'Dunkeld chronicle' could still be postulated, however, if the Dunkeld-perspective was deemed only to reveal directly the provenance of the mid-tenth-century Chronicle: if the Chronicle was written in Dunkeld, then a year-by-year chronicle kept at Dunkeld would be a likely source for the contemporary information used by the Chronicle's author.

[42] *Cuius tercio anno Normanni predauerunt Duncalden omnemque Albaniam.* 'In his [Custantín mac Aeda's] third year the Norse plundered Dunkeld and all Alba.' The date of 903 is established in relation to the next item: *In sequenti utique anno occisi sunt in Sraith hErenn Normanni.* 'In the following year, in any event, the Norse were killed in Strathearn'; this is reported in AU 904.4.

[43] The continuation of the Chronicle as far as the reign of Dub mac Maíl Choluim (962–6) includes a battle in which the casualties named are the abbot of Dunkeld and the mormaer of Atholl: this battle is also recorded in AU 965.4, noting the death only of the abbot of Dunkeld. This may be evidence that the Dunkeld–Armagh link existed at a later stage in the Chronicle's evolution, so that perhaps the Chronicle and its initial continuation were written at Dunkeld.

Dunkeld, of course, is also the church suggested by other considerations, most notably the link between the source of these items and Armagh chroniclers. The change from *rex Pictorum* to *rí Alban* made by Armagh chroniclers betwen 878 and 900 thus seems to coincide with a similar change in terminology from what may have been a Dunkeld chronicle. On current knowledge the likeliest scenario is that the switch from Pictish to *Alba*-based terminology reflected Dunkeld's usage and was picked up in Armagh through the close ties between the two churches.[44]

The use of *rex Pictorum* up to at least 878, its replacement by *rí Alban* no later than 900, and no doubt the concomitant use of *Picti* and *fir Alban* would seem, therefore, to have been generally approved in Dunkeld and, by implication at least, by Cinaed mac Alpín and his sons. This could have a number of important consequences for how we might think about the fate of the Picts and the origin of Scottish identity. First of all, it has been argued that this period witnessed not only Gaelicisation but also ecclesiastical reform;[45] evidence for this is found in one of the items attributable to the putative Dunkeld chronicle, a convention between King Custantín and Bishop Cellach at Scone in 906.[46] It has also been suggested, moreover, that ecclesiastical reform was associated with a resurgent cult of Columba in Pictland (attested

[44] It would be helpful if it could be shown that Armagh chroniclers at some stage actually incorporated a Dunkeld chronicle into their work; the Armagh chronicle could therefore be direct testimony of this putative Dunkeld chronicle. No study, however, has been carried out to support this.

[45] Wormald, 'The emergence of the *regnum Scottorum*'; see also Clancy, 'Iona, Scotland and the *céli Dé*'.

[46] *Ac in .ui. anno Constantinus rex et Cellachus episcopus leges disciplinasque fidei atque iura ecclesiarum ewangeliorumque pariter cum Scottis in colle credulitatis prope regali ciuitati Scoan deuouerunt custodire. . . .* 'And in the sixth year King Custantín and Bishop Cellach on the hill of belief near the royal monastery of Scone vowed together with *Albanaig*(?) to preserve christian laws and disciplines and protect the rights of churches and gospels . . .' There are significant differences in how this passage has been translated in the past; in particular, the phrase *pariter cum* has been taken to mean 'in conformity with' (*ES* i.445 and n. 1); the translation of this phrase adopted here was first suggested in Anderson, 'Dalriada and the creation of the kingdom of the Scots', 127. Anderson, *Kings and Kingship*, 251 has read *custodire* rather than *custodiri* (as in *ES* i.445 n. 1).

by the movement of his relics to Dunkeld) to produce a vigorously pro-Gaelic anti-Pictish ideology, and that this, combined with a Gaelic military conquest led by Cinaed mac Alpín, served to undermine the Picts politically and culturally.[47] It would appear, however, that the chief Columban church in the kingdom did not go so far as to reject Pictish identity until two generations after Cinaed mac Alpín (if rejection was indeed what happened). If ecclesiastical reform was a key agent in the abondonment of Pictish identity then it would seem only to have become vigorously anti-Pictish some considerable time after a conjectured conquest of the Picts by Cinaed.

Dunkeld's acceptance of Pictish identity up to at least 878[48] raises another issue. It is tempting to regard the delay between Cinaed's takeover and the adoption of *Alba* as the kingdom's name as evidence of a gradual, almost inevitable transition as a consequence of Gaelic dominance politically and culturally.[49] This would not, however, appear to have been Dunkeld's experience. In 878 the Chronicle of Ireland recorded that 'the shrine of Columba and his other insignia arrived in Ireland, having been taken in flight to escape the foreigners'.[50] Since Columba's relics had apparently been shared between Kells and Dunkeld in 849, it seems likely that the shrine and relics which came to Ireland in 878 were from Dunkeld.[51] This was not the only occasion Dunkeld suffered from viking aggression;[52] the extreme measure taken on this occasion, however, suggests that the situation in 878 had become particularly desperate. In the same year Aed son of Cinaed

[47] Wormald, 'The emergence of the *regnum Scottorum*'.

[48] Possibly into the reign of Domnall mac Custantín (d. 900): see n. 35, above.

[49] This is either stated or implied in the works referred to in n. 7, above.

[50] AU 878.9: *Scrín Coluim Cille 7 a minna olchena du tiachtain dochum nErenn for teicheadh ria Gallaibh*; CS 878.4 has the same words, except *archena* for *olchena* and omission of *du tiachtain.*

[51] Bannerman, '*Comarba Coluim Chille*', 28–31. It has been assumed that the relics came from Iona (Dumville, *The Churches of North Britain in the First Viking-Age*, 21; more cautiously in Herbert, *Iona, Kells and Derry*, 73).

[52] As well as the plundering suffered in 903, the Chronicle of the Kings of Alba also noted an attack during the reign of Cinaed mac Alpín (d. 858) (although the source for this can not be established).

mac Alpín was killed by his own followers:[53] as a result the dynasty which had established Dunkeld's pre-eminence not only lost the kingship but would appear to have broken its cohesion, and would hardly have been in a position to protect Dunkeld from indigenous rivals, never mind the next wave of viking attack. It may be no coincidence that the evacuation of Columba's relics is the last event relating to succession to the kingship or Dunkeld found in Irish chronicles before 900: perhaps the link between Dunkeld and Armagh had temporarily ceased to operate.

It is hard to avoid the conclusion that in 878 the most tangible achievements of Cinaed mac Alpín – his family's dominance of the kingship and the housing of Columba's relics in Dunkeld – suffered a devastating reverse. It is with hindsight that we know this was to be only a temporary setback. The ultimate success of Cinaed's dynasty, therefore, was due to the efforts of his grandsons, Domnall mac Custantín (d. 900) and (in particular) Custantín mac Aeda (d. 952). It would be a mistake, I would argue, to regard their achievement as simply piecing together the fragments of what Cinaed had established. A likely example of Custantín's markedly different approach was the setting up of Cennrígmonaid (St Andrews) as the chief church of the kingdom.[54] Moreover, there is no evidence to link Columba's relics with Cennrígmonaid:[55] the basis of its authority would again appear to have been different from what Dunkeld's had been.

The demise of Pictish identity may therefore have been one of the consequences of the destruction of Cinaed's immediate legacy.[56] There is no need to suppose that Cinaed or Dunkeld (at least up to 878) actively wished to abandon Pictish terminology. It is conceivable that, if what Cinaed established had endured, the kingdom would have remained Pictish at least in name, and

[53] AU 878.2: *Aedh m. Cinadan, rex Pictorum, a sociis suis occisus est*, 'Aed son of Cinaed, king of Picts, was killed by his own associates'.

[54] The Bishop Cellach who appeared with Custantín at Scone in 906 is found as the first bishop of St Andrews in fifteenth-century lists; see Miller, 'The last century of Pictish succession', 48. It is an assumption that these lists were actually of bishops of *Alba* based at Cennrígmonaid (St Andrews).

[55] *Pace* Bannerman, '*Comarba Coluim Chille*', 31.

[56] Not necessarily an immediate consequence, however; Pictish identity may have continued into the reign of Domnall mac Custantín (d. 900); see n. 35, above.

its people would have continued to identify themselves as Picts (regardless of how strong Gaelic culture may have become). The evidence, such as it is, suggests that Pictish identity (and, it seems, their language) was a casualty of the new kingdom built by Cinaed's grandsons rather than a necessary consequence of Cinaed's own achievements.

How, then, might we explain the final demise of the Picts and the emergence of *Alba*? Cinaed's grandsons no doubt exercised military might and may have sought to harness a prevailing climate of ecclesiastical reform; they may, for all we know, have forcibly ousted the Pictish nobility and developed a vigorously anti-Pictish ideology. To understand more, however, we need to know what *Alba* signified at this time; whether, indeed, it necessarily represented a wholesale and deliberate break with Pictish identity.[57] From what we know so far, however, I would argue that the immediate context of the coining of Scottish identity is most likely to have been the instability and social dislocation which followed in the wake of the worst phase of Norse devastation inflicted on southern Pictland in 875–6 and 878.[58] The confusion in extant

[57] The switch from *rex Pictorum* and *Picti* to *rí Alban* and *fir Alban* could, conceivably, signify no more than an instance of a change by chronicle-scribes from Latin terminology to Gaelic (although it also involved replacing a people term with a territorial one; see Broun, 'The origin of Scottish identity', 47–54, and also Dumville, 'Ireland and Britain', 183). If so it may therefore be compared with other changes in linguistic usage in AU; see Dumville, 'Latin and Irish in the *Annals of Ulster*, A.D. 431–1050', 320–41, esp. 330–1, where he noted, for instance, the last appearance of *abbas* in 922 and *princeps* in 938 (with a final occurrence in 948), and the frequent use of *airchinnech* only from 941, and that *Goídil* 'is very noticeable in the 940s, but not before'. Perhaps, then, *Alba* was intended simply as a translation of *Pictauia*. For other evidence pointing to *Alba* as equivalent to Pictland see Broun, 'The origins of Scottish identity in its European context', 24–5 (although the argument there is in need of revision). It should not be forgotten, of course, that the Pictish language died out. The change in terminology may therefore reflect the final decline in the Pictish language; it does not on its own, however, necessarily represent a determined rejection of Pictish identity.

[58] See further Broun, 'The origins of Scottish identity in its European context', 27–30, although note that I would now place more emphasis on the late 870s and its aftermath than I did in that article. Social change as a key to understanding the creation of Alba and 'disappearance' of the Picts (although without highlighting destabilisation caused by Scandinavian

records relating to the kingship after 878 may reflect genuine political uncertainty. By the time *Alba* had replaced Pictland in Dunkeld's vocabulary the process of reconstructing the kingdom had been sufficiently established to defeat a serious viking incursion in 904 – the first recorded victory over the Norse in the kingdom's heartland. The successful defence of the realm and the long reign of Custantín mac Aeda provided the necessary stability for the new kingdom of *Alba* to endure.[59]

---

devastation) has also been discussed in Duncan, *Scotland: the Making of the Kingdom*, 100–3, and especially (from an archaeological perspective) by Stephen T. Driscoll, 'Power and authority in early historic Scotland', and *idem*, 'The archaeology of state formation in Scotland'.

[59] See also Broun, 'The origin of Scottish identity in its European context', 29. Another key element of this new political structure could have been the office of *mormaer*, which is first attested in contemporary record along with the first appearance of the term *fir Alban* (AU 918.4). Custantín abdicated to become abbot of *céli Dé* at Cennrígmonaid for five years (according to thirteenth-century king-lists; Anderson, *Kings and Kingship*, 267, 274, 283, 288). Custantín's reign is given as forty years in the Chronicle of the Kings of Alba and in Marjorie Anderson's X-group of king-lists, and forty-five years in Anderson's Y group and her list B (*ibid.*, 251, 263, 267, 274, 283, 288), as well as her list C (*Lebor Bretnach*, ed. Van Hamel, 86). The Chronicle of the Kings of Alba stated that Custantín died in the tenth year of the eleven-year reign of his successor: his death is noted in AU 952.1*b*. None of this adds up. A possible series of amendments would be to suppose that his reign-length was forty-two years (*xlii* becoming *xlu* and *xl*) and that the five years he spent as abbot of *céli Dé* at Cennrígmonaid either related to only part of his retirement or was actually ten years (*x* misread as *u*). The exact chronology is destined always to remain uncertain.

PART II

Adomnán the writer

5

Iona: monks, pastors and missionaries

Gilbert Márkus OP

WHILE helping to demolish certain myths about Columba and 'Celtic Christianity', Professor Donald Meek recently referred to the well-known and much-loved story which Adomnán tells in his *Life of Columba* about the storm-tossed crane which flaps its way over from Ireland, and arrives exhausted on Iona.[1] The saint gives orders that it should be fed and treated as a guest until it is strong enough to fly back home again.

Professor Meek suggests that this story has little to do with Columba's eco-friendly animal-loving credentials, and a lot to do with his political consciousness, his continuing connection to his own family and their interests in the northern part of Ireland. Columba himself gives the reason for his hospitality towards the animal: 'I commend it to you so carefully for this reason: that it comes from our own fatherland' – *de nostrae paternitatis regione*. This crane does not represent 'nature' which is to be loved and cherished. Nor is there any reason to think that it represents the last gasp of 'ornithomancy', or a pagan belief in cranes as sacred birds.[2] The bird is significant, as Columba says himself, because

[1] *VC* i.48; Meek, 'Surveying the Saints'; and see Meek, below, pp. 263–4.

[2] Finlay, *Columba*, 23–5. Even if there were some echo here of the idea that bird-flights could be interpreted, and we have no evidence that Adomnán was aware of such beliefs, we should notice that in this story Columba is not magically discerning the truth by watching the bird; he already knows the truth prophetically, and the incident of the bird merely establishes the truth of his prophetic knowledge. Is this a story where the saint is painted trumping the card of a pagan belief? Something similar may be involved

it represents the interests of his own family, the Cenél Conaill, and of course the family of Adomnán who wrote the story.

This reading of the crane as a political animal is confirmed if we set it in the wider pattern of the saint's encounters with other animals in the *Vita Columbae*. In all the other stories, we find that they reveal a kind of mental map whose chief outlines are determined by the political geography of Scotland as seen by a monk on Iona.

There are two tales of animals encountered by Columba in areas of Pictish control. One takes place on Skye, where Columba meets a boar of amazing size and commands it, 'Go no further, but die where you are now.' Needless to say the animal fell dead, slain by the power of his terrible word.[3] The other Pictish animal encountered in the *Vita Columbae* is of course the dreadful water-beast, the monster in the River Ness.[4] It has already killed one man by the time Columba arrives on the scene, and he is determined to oppose it. In order to do so, he first orders one of his monks to take off his clothes and swim across the river. Using him as bait, Columba lures Nessie out of her hiding place. As the monster is bearing down on the swimming monk with a great roar, Columba invokes the name of God and sends her fleeing in terror. 'The beast fled terrified in swift retreat, as if it was being pulled back by ropes.' These are the only two stories of animals which take place in Pictish territory, and they both involve open hostility, an act of power by the saint in which the animal is destroyed or put to flight.[5]

The animals we meet in Dál Riata are treated quite differently. In Dál Riata we are among Columba's local Christian people, his

---

with the horse at his death, or in the strange threefold death of Guaire: the saint out-shamans the shamans. On pre-Christian sacred and magic birds, see Ross, *Pagan Celtic Britain*, chapter 6.

[3] *VC* ii.26. Sharpe, *Adomnán*, 175.

[4] *VC* ii.27.

[5] The motif of saints as well as secular heroes destroying monsters is not uncommon. Colmán Elo does it for the king of Kintyre, for example, and Mac Creiche destroys one in the Shannon. See Plummer, *Lives of Irish Saints*, vol. 1, 175 and vol. 2, 169; Plummer, *Miscellanea Hagiographica Hibernica*, 41f. and 80f. On monsters in Irish sources see Borsje, *From Chaos to Enemy:* and 'The Monster in the River Ness'.

protégés, the kingdom whose rulers have given him land and to whom he is the emerging patron saint. So Columba is still an agent of divine power in Dál Riata, but the animals here play a different role. Instead of hostility, they fit rather into a pattern of social usefulness, hospitality, food, property rights and decent Christian behaviour. So the Dál Riata miracles include a prophecy which prevents a man from killing and stealing seals from Iona's own breeding ground,[6] reflecting a concern with Iona's legal rights over certain resources. The thief is later given sheep by Iona monks to satisfy his hunger instead. Other miracles reveal a similar monastic vision of feeding the hungry: the miraculous catch of salmon for fishermen in the River Shiel[7] and the multiplication of poor farmers' cattle herds after they have shown hospitality to Columba on his journeys.[8] Importantly, the miraculous feeding of the poor and increase of their wealth depends on their first having shown hospitality and generosity to Columba when he comes to their homes. In another instance, a bull has been bewitched by someone, and appears to be giving milk until it is blessed by the saint. In another case, Columba gives a sharp stake to a poor man who had no means to feed his wife and children. When he planted this stake in the ground, some large wild animal impaled itself on it every day, enabling the poor man to feed his family and sell his surplus. Not much sign here of Columba the nature-lover, as stags, hinds, goats and salmon, and eventually dogs and ravens all impale themselves on his big sharp stick.

All the miracles of this group whose location can be identified are performed in the territory of Dál Riata. In fact, they are even more local than that, as most of them take place in the territory of Cenél Loairn or at its very limits – that is the particular kingdom within Dál Riata where Iona happens to be situated.[9] They are all domestic miracles in one way or another, supporting the

[6] *VC* i.41.

[7] *VC* ii.19.

[8] *VC* ii.20 and 21.

[9] *VC* i.41 is on or near Mull; ii.19 in the River Shiel at the northern edge of Cenél Loairn territory; ii.21 (Colmán of Ardnamurchan) and ii.37 (the hungry man) in Lochaber around the River Lochy; ii.22 in Ardnamurchan. Cainle, the location of the episode in ii.17 cannot be identified, but the names of the people concerned are Gaelic, so it should be sought either in Dál Riata or in Ireland.

material needs of the farming and hunting-fishing people who lived around Iona. They also reinforce the kinds of claims that Iona would make on these people, and the claims of Iona's abbots: the right to hospitality, for example[10] or the authority of the abbot as a judicial figure in a legal dispute.[11]

It is worth pointing out here that Adomnán wrote the *Vita Columbae* during a long period of Cenél Loairn control of Dál Riata, and that Iona is situated in Cenél Loairn territory. We might suspect that Adomnán is wooing their leadership with these stories, especially since Iona's earlier links had been with Cenél nGabráin, notably through Columba's alleged role in the inauguration of Cenél nGabráin kings. Note also that in these miracles which benefit Cenél Loairn people, there is sometimes a Cenél nGabráin or Cenél nOengusso opponent.[12]

The third group of stories involving animals are those that relate to animals from Iona itself. There are three such stories, and all of them portray a close and even un-naturally harmonious relationship between man and beast, and even between the beasts themselves. The best known of these is the story in which a horse comes to Columba shortly before his death and weeps over him.[13] Less well-known are two stories that occur in succession in Book II of the *Vita*, in which Iona's animals become signs of almost biblical harmony and well-being. In one, Columba blessed the island shortly before his death, and thereby guaranteed that 'all poisons of snakes shall have no power to harm men or cattle in the lands of this island for as long as the people who dwell here keep Christ's commandments'.[14] He does not actually expel the snakes or do them any harm, but only prevents them from harming

[10] *VC* ii.21 and 22.

[11] *VC* ii.17.

[12] *VC* ii.22 (Ioan of Cenél nGabráin is cursed and drowned); ii.23 (Feredach of Islay, in the territory of Cenél nOengusso, is cursed and damned for violating sanctuary); ii.24 (Lam Dess of Cenél nGabráin dies cursed for trying to kill Columba). Of course, there may also be a more religiously motivated form of distancing going on here: Adomnán reminding his monks that though they are supporters of the strong king-theory of their pro-Cenél nGabráin history, they should remember that these powerful people are often violent and unjust, and that good monks should keep their distance from such worldly powers.

[13] *VC* iii, 23.

[14] *VC* ii.28; Sharpe, *Adomnán*, 177.

other creatures. At another time one of the monks got Columba to bless a knife he was carrying. Columba absent-mindedly waved his hand about over it, then prayed – perhaps remembering the damage his sharpened wooden spike had done – that the tool he blessed would never harm man or beast. So when the monk Molua tried to kill a bullock with the knife an hour later, though he tried very hard three times, the knife would not penetrate the skin or harm the beast. Finally it was melted down and its metal used to coat all the other iron tools in the monastery, and afterwards all of these implements were rendered completely harmless to all flesh. Thus two blessings by the saint produce an island where neither snake nor weapon can harm living creatures. It is a little paradise, a centre of harmony in a world of conflict. Perhaps there is a reference here to the prophecy of Isaiah about Jerusalem:

> The wolf and the lamb shall feed together, the lion shall eat straw like the ox; and dust shall be the serpent's food. They shall not hurt or destroy in all my holy mountain. (65:25)

Adomnán paints a picture of his monastery almost as if it were a foretaste of heaven where the peacefulness of God's reign is already apparent.[15]

Scottish space is therefore divided into three parts in Adomnán's 'mental map',[16] and this tri-partite division informs not just the behaviour of the political animals, but also the way that Columba relates to the people he meets. The appearance of the saint on Iona is almost constantly one of benign paternal care, blessing and protecting his monks, ministering salvation and showing forth

[15] Mark 16:18 offers a similar suggestion of the reign of God made visible in a similar way among believers.

[16] I am grateful to Thomas O'Loughlin for his comments in regard to mental maps here. See his work, on more large-scale mental maps in Adomnán's writings, 'Living in the Ocean', and 'The View from Iona: Adomnán's Mental Maps'. See also Michael Richter, 'The European Dimension of Irish History'; Downs and Stea, *Maps in Mind*; Gould and White, *Mental Maps*. I leave aside here the two animal stories that take place at sea, *VC* i.19 (featuring a whale) and ii.42 (with its 'foul and very dangerous little animals'), because the open sea is space outside the sphere of any nation or culture, and the animals should perhaps be seen as representatives of the watery chaos of the sea, if they represent anything at all.

the grace of God in prayer and prophecy. His apparitions in Dál Riata and particularly Cenél Loairn, as we have seen, involve his receiving the loyal support and hospitality of the people there, occasionally punishing them if they go astray, judging in their disputes and supporting them in their hardships. Finally in Pictland he is mostly involved in some kind of confrontation with the local people – with the king or his wizards usually – cursing them, punishing them, or merely defeating their wicked anti-Christian tricks. There are occasional healing and saving miracles, but on the whole Pictland is represented as hostile.

Confirmation of the hostility of Pictland, both human and animal, is also found among angels. Professor Máire Herbert has observed that different kinds of stories in the *Vita Columbae* appear in different parts of the country. She is more concerned with the sources of the stories which Adomnán has recorded, the idea that different kinds of story were told in different places. But an additional feature of her useful breakdown of the stories and their locations is that it shows that there are almost no angels in Pictland.[17] There are twenty-three angelic visions in the Third Book of the *Vita*, of which four take place in Ireland and they are angelic visions by other people concerning Columba, rather than visions enjoyed by Columba himself. All nineteen of Columba's visions of angels take place in the monastery of Iona or in his nearby monastery of Hinba[18] except for one, the only angelic vision outside the monastic environment, and it takes place in Pictland, when the saint is travelling on the other side of Druim Alban: a vision of angels revealed to the saint that a man was dying at Urquhart, a Pict by the name of Emchath who had lived a good life and now wanted to be baptised before he died. When the saint got to Urquhart, on the northern shore of Loch Ness, Emchath and his son and all his household believed and were baptised.[19] In this story we can perhaps see the first evidence of a Columban church in Pictland. Angels are often seen in Irish stories at the moment of death of a holy person as they come to take his or her soul to heaven, and they are seen subsequently flying over their graves, as a kind of power cable joining heaven and earth,

17 Herbert, *Iona, Kells and Derry*, 15.
18 *VC* iii.5, 17, 18.
19 *VC* iii.14.

signifying that the divinely given powers which that saint manifested in his lifetime are still present in the place where his body is buried.[20] The angels around Emchath and his family look suspiciously like a sign that there was a church at Urquhart, known to Adomnán and his community, which they believed that Columba had founded. Even today it is clear that there was an important church in the vicinity at an early date, as only a couple of miles to the east of Urquhart is an *Achnahannet*, which we might translate 'the field of the mother-church', signifying a pastoral centre and ancient church site in the vicinity to which the field belonged.[21]

Iona

The foregoing suggests that Adomnán has a mental map of Scotland which is divided into three distinct spaces. It is worth looking a little more closely at just how these three spaces differ from each other in the picture he paints. But at this point it is worth sounding a little caveat about this picture. Any incident described by Adomnán may reveal one of several things:

a] how things really were in Iona in the sixth century, when Columba was alive;

[20] For a handful of examples, see *VC* iii.6, 7, 9–14, 23; Stokes, *Martyrology of Oengus*, 7 and 9; Herbert, *Iona, Kells and Derry*, 64 for the death of Colum Cille; Stokes, *Lives of the Saints from the Book of Lismore*, 221 for the death of Senán, and 278 for the death of Ciarán; Bieler, *Patrician Texts*, 119, for the death of Patrick.

[21] NH512.262 Alcock's discussion of excavation at Urquhart is in Alcock and Alcock, 'Reconnaissance Excavations on Early Historic fortifications'. For the meaning of *annat* as a formal and legal description of a church of a certain status, see Clancy, 'Annat in Scotland'. Given the presence of a holy grave at Urquhart, the presence of the relics of the 'founder' who might be Emchath or his pious son, Virolec, might be sufficient to constitute the church there as an *andóit* (whence the name *annat* comes) as either of these men could be seen as the founder or *érlam* of the church. Part of an *andoit*-church's claim to precedence over others is its possession of the relics of the *érlam*. MacKinlay, *Folklore of Scottish Lochs and Springs*, 41, finds an association of Urquhart with Drostan in its appellation *Urchudain Maith Dhrosta[i]n*. Watson, *Celtic Place-Names* 318, is preferable here, telling us that in Gaelic Urquhart is *Urchardan Mo-Chrostáin* (leg. *Mo-Dhrostáin*). Furthermore, there were his relics here, too, under the charge of a *deoir*, who had a croft called *Croit an Deoir*.

b] how Adomnán *thinks* things were in Iona in the sixth century;
c] how things are in the late seventh century, when he himself is writing;
d] how he would *like* things to be in the seventh century, so that they are prescriptive rather than descriptive.

In any given case it may not be easy to say which of these four possibilities is the most likely. Sometimes it will be impossible, while at other times we must guess as best we can on the evidence available to us.

But turning to Adomnán's description of Iona and the events that take place there, we can see a clear emphasis on the strictly monastic routines of this harmonious community: prayer, asceticism, fraternal charity, study, labour. One important thing that should be noted is that only monks live on the island in Adomnán's picture. This is made quite clear when Columba dies and the only people who can come to his funeral are his family of monks, as lay-people are kept from crossing the water to the island.[22] There are no stories in the entire *Vita* which suggest that non-monastic persons regularly lived on the island. When penitents arrive they come to confess, but they do not do their penance on Iona itself. They are sent rather to other places: to Tiree for example,[23] or to the unidentified island of Hinba.[24] In one extreme case a man's sin is thought to be so dreadful that he is sent to live among the Britons to do penance.[25] Clearly Adomnán does not see Iona as a place of penance for lay-folk, and when two visitors are admitted to the monastery as pilgrims, they are told they can stay on the island only if they first receive the habit and become monks.[26]

Other reasons for visiting the island include a search for medical help,[27] the royal ordination of a king,[28] help with getting food[29]

[22] *VC* iii.23.
[23] *VC* i.30; ii.39.
[24] *VC* i.21.
[25] *VC* i.22. 'This man has acted like Cain and killed his own brother and debauched his mother.' He is given twelve years penance, but fails to fulfil them and returns to Ireland and is murdered.
[26] *VC* i.32.
[27] *VC* i.27.
[28] *VC* iii.5.
[29] *VC* i.41.

and burial of the dead.[30] None of these would require residence on the island, or at least not for more than a day or so.[31] None of these are, for that matter, strictly pastoral functions, but mostly part of the normal routine of monastic hospitality.[32] Interestingly, when Columba baptises people, performing a priestly rather than an essentially monkish task, he is never seen doing so on Iona. If the bishop Uinniau who taught Columba is the author of the *Penitentialis Vinniani*, an important sixth-century penitential, then we can see how Columba might have inherited a sense of the clear distinction between the roles of monk and priest, for Uinniau says: 'He ought not to be called a cleric or a deacon who can not baptise, nor should he receive the dignity of a cleric or a deacon in the church. Monks, however, ought not to baptise or to receive alms. But if they should receive alms, why will they not baptise?'[33]

There are other signs that Iona was not much interested in ordinary pastoral activity, apart from the fact that no lay-people lived on the island. We do not know of a single bishop of Iona before Cóeti (d. 712), though for pastoral work a bishop was deemed necessary. For much of the time there was no bishop on the island.[34] Yet when Iona was involved in establishing a missionary church, and then running it as a pastoral concern, she sent bishops. We know of four Iona monks who became bishops

[30] *VC* i.16.

[31] There seems to have been a guest house on the western side of the island for temporary visitors, keeping them out of the monastery's way. This is where the Cenél Conaill crane stays (*VC* i.48). Columba himself was, according to Adomnán, frustrated by crowds of people coming to the island asking questions. For this reason he kept many of his miracles secret (iii.7). A guest house or *hospitium* was also used for visiting monks of the Iona *familia*, such as Cailtán, who stayed there until he died (*VC* i.31). See MacDonald, 'Adomnán's Monastery of Iona', 39.

[32] These are the kinds of functions envisaged by the *Amra Choluimb Chille*: 'He was a shelter to the naked, he was a teat to the poor.' Clancy and Márkus, *Iona: the Earliest Poetry*, 109.

[33] Bieler, *Irish Penitientials*, 92; for Uinniau see*VC* ii.1. The distinct character of these roles is confirmed by Columbanus in his second epistle: 'For the patterns (*documenta*) of monks and of the clergy are different, widely separated from each other,' in Walker, *Sancti Columbani Opera*, 20.

[34] *VC* i.44 suggests this in its description of a eucharistic celebration, when Columba suddenly realises that one of his concelebrating guests is a bishop in disguise. He asks him then to preside alone as bishop.

of Lindisfarne in the seventh century, and one or possibly two who were bishops of Mercia and the Middle Angles.[35] Iona clearly understood the centrality of the bishop to the pastoral life of the church, and the absence of a bishop of Iona is all the more suggestive of a community with very little immediate pastoral involvement.[36]

Another feature of the monastic isolation of Iona is that Adomnán seems to have no interest in encouraging a view of Iona as a place of pilgrimage. Where other churches might find revenue and influence in developing a cult of the enshrined saint's body, Adomnán never mentions the grave of Columba as the site of miracles.[37] This is strange, because the *Amra Choluimb Chille,* probably written only a year or two after Columba's death, had already made that claim: *Fó lib lige a aí, ar cach saeth sretha sína,* 'You find his grave good in its virtue, appointed for every trouble of weather.'[38] These lines suggest that there was a very early cult at the grave of Columba, and though Adomnán must surely have known of such a reputation he never exploits it or even mentions it. The cult of relics in a grave would be an advertisement for a church of pilgrimage, but Adomnán's Iona is not to become such a shrine. That churches did place corporeal relics in prominent positions and use them as cult objects is well-known and apparent, for example, from Bede's description of the bones of Áedán, placed by his successor Fínán beside the

[35] See the discussion of Irish bishops in England below: *Austerior*, Áedán, Fínán and Colmán were bishops of Lindisfarne in succession. The first bishop of Mercia is an Irishman called Diuma, succeeded by the Iona monk Cellach, who retires to Iona.

[36] There is a story in which Columba abandons a dying monk, so as not to be rendered impure by being in the same house as a corpse (*VC* iii.6), as some monasteries seem to have had a pollution fear for their priests based on that of Leviticus 21:1, 10–11. The difficulty of a priest offering pastoral care of the dead and dying while following this taboo is evident. If there were a bishop present, or near at hand, it would be possible to be 're-consecrated' as the taboo requires, and so the difficulty would be somewhat eased in pastoral situations when a bishop's proximity could be more or less relied on.

[37] I exclude the 'light of heaven' that shines there while angels visit in *VC* iii.23, which is simply a sign of his sanctity rather than a miracle from which a pilgrim might benefit.

[38] Clancy and Márkus, *Iona*, 110–11; for further thoughts on this subject, see Clancy, above, p. 28.

altar of a church in Lindisfarne, where they work all sorts of miracles, while Cogitosus' *Vita Brigitae* makes her grave and church a place of miracle-working pilgrimage: 'Who can count the diverse crowds and innumerable people coming in from all the provinces? – some for healing of their infirmities, others for the spectacle of the crowds, others coming with great gifts?'[39] Of course, Adomnán does mention miracles generated by other non-corporeal relics of Columba – his tunic, for example, and books written by his own hand – but not in ways which might suggest that he was promoting a cult of pilgrimage to the island.

Columba's remains were buried in Iona, Adomnán tells us. In fact, this is an absolutely necessary feature of the monastery from Adomnán's point of view: his own status as abbot of Iona is dependent on the fact that he possesses the relics of the founder saint.[40] But lay-folk would be expected to make contact with Iona's relics not by making a pilgrimage to the monastery, but rather when the relics were taken out by the abbot on a tour or 'circuit' as is recorded in AU 727: 'The relics of Adomnán are brought over to Ireland, and the law is promulgated anew.' It was the use of these touring relics which expressed and reinforced the power of the abbot among the people, among other churches and rulers, not the monastery's status as a pilgrimage destination. Interestingly, there are suggestions of this process already apparent in the *Vita Columbae*. In *VC* i.3 for example, the saint is processed into the monastery of Clonmacnoise by the monks there, who 'bowed their heads and kissed him reverently, and to the accompaniment of hymns and praises they brought him with honour to the church.' A young boy contrives to touch the hem of his garment and receives gifts of wisdom and judgement from the saint. Most interestingly, the monks have fashioned for the saint a square wooden structure, *de lignis piramidem*, with which

[39] *HE* iii.17 and *PL* 72.790. Adomnán also seems to be impressed by vast crowds of pilgrims who go to venerate the tombs of patriarchs, as he makes constant mention of them throughout his other major work: see *DLS*, *passim*.

[40] For the role of relics in the authority of an abbot or *comarba* of a church, see Bannerman, '*Comarba Coluim Chille*'. Bede also seems to link Iona's authority to the presence of Columba's relics: 'The island in which his body lies' holds pre-eminence over the monasteries established by his disciples' (*HE* iii.4).

they surround him, and this surely echoes the stone surround, *lapidea piramis*, which Adomnán describes on the graves of King David in Jerusalem and of Rachel in Effrata. Columba is practically becoming a relic in his own life-time.[41]

Other relics of the saint are also portable and located away from the island: the stone he leaves at the fortress of Bruide, for example, which gave healing to the sick,[42] and more portable yet, a song in praise of Columba which was sung by certain blood-stained brigands who were then saved from being slaughtered themselves.[43]

Iona is therefore, properly speaking, a cloister, a *clausura* or space closed off to the rest of the world, to its turmoil and disturbance. The only people who come to spend time on the monastic island and who are not sent somewhere else are clergy and monks.[44] It is not portrayed by Adomnán as a pastoral centre.

Dál Riata

To turn to the next of Adomnán's three spaces, we move from Christian monastic space to Christian secular space, to Dál Riata. It is worth saying to begin with that in Adomnán's historical imagination, Dál Riata was already a pretty thoroughly Christianised territory by the time Columba arrived there in 563. Columba never preaches the gospel to these people in order to

[41] See *DLS*, 76 and 78. Perhaps a similar process is under way in the constant references to the saint's upraised right hand as the instrument of his power. On the saint's death-bed, his weakened right arm is finally raised by his own faithful attendant, Diarmait, who manipulates it over the assembled monks to effect the saint's final blessing. Could there have been an arm-relic of the saint by Adomnán's time, as appeared in some reliquaries for various saints, including Columba himself, in later centuries? See Ó Floinn, '*Insignia Columbae* I', 144. Although the division of relics was not an established practice in the seventh century, recall that the hand and arm of the holy king Oswald had been cut off in battle and become a relic preserved in a silver shrine in Bamburgh [*HE* iii.6], which Adomnán must surely have known, and that Aidán's bones at Lindisfarne had been divided in 664 [*HE* iii.26] and a portion taken first to Iona and then probably to Ireland.

[42] *VC* ii.33. Bruide kept the stone for a while, and only died when it was lost.

[43] *VC* i.1. See also Clancy, above, pp. 18, 23–4.

[44] *VC* i.4, 5, 6, 17, 26, 44; ii.14, 15; iii.7, 17.

convert them to Christianity; the only baptism he performs is of a child on Ardnamurchan who has been brought to him by his presumably already Christian parents,[45] and wherever he goes he is, by and large, treated with the kind of respect and reverence that an abbot would look for among a Christian population. When Adomnán thinks about sixth-century Dál Riata, then, he is thinking of a population much like that of his own day.

And Adomnán is probably right. When Columba arrived in Dál Riata he was moving from one part of a Christian Gaelic milieu to another. He was not going to live among absolute strangers, but among people who shared his language and his culture. Scottish Dál Riata was simply the eastern half of an Irish kindred, the other half of which lived in northern Ireland, Columba's former neighbours. There is no reason to think that they had all this language and culture in common but that they had different religions.

When Columba arrived in Dál Riata, he was given land, a whole island, by the king, Conall mac Comgaill, which would have been unlikely if the king were a pagan. On Conall's death we hear that Áedán mac Gabráin becomes king and that he seeks ordination as king, a Christian inauguration, at the hands of Columba on the island of Iona. Again, one can only imagine a king behaving like this and thinking that ordination might do him any good or make his reign more secure, in a fairly Christianised establishment, especially since this whole ritual seems to be something of an innovation, either grafted onto or replacing the former inauguration rites.[46]

Columba is not the only monastic founder to appear in this part of the world. There are monks and monasteries which have nothing to do with Columba on Tiree, Lismore and probably Eigg during Columba's life-time, not to mention Iona's own daughter-houses, and other foundations such as Applecross by the time Adomnán is writing.[47] It is hard to imagine a non-Christian society allowing an alien church to arrive and grab all this land.

[45] *VC* ii.10.
[46] Enright, *Iona, Tara, Soissons.*
[47] Applecross was founded in 673 (AU 673.5), apparently a daughter-house of Bangor.

If there was a reasonably well established church in Dál Riata by the time of Columba's arrival, there is no reason to doubt that it had bishops and clergy. A king or prince who had accepted the Christian faith would also import as much as possible of the Christian organisation, because Christianity never arrives simply as an abstract set of religious propositions. It always appears in a particular form, and here the only form known to Christianity is this: bishops, sacraments, scripture, monasteries, canon law, altar equipment and so on. As David Dumville remarks, 'we must suppose that by the mid-sixth century an ecclesiastical infrastructure had already been created (in Dál Riata), to which Iona was in the first instance but a monastic appendage'.[48]

So there must have been bishops in Dál Riata, but we know almost nothing about them in this part of the world until the very end of the seventh century when Iona had a bishop Cóeti. According to the Annals of Ulster he died in 712. Cóeti appears in the guarantor list of the *Cáin Adomnáin* in the year 697 alongside two other men described as bishops: Curetán and Conamail.[49] Curetán's sphere of influence seems to be in the north-east of Scotland around Rosemarkie, while Conamail, if he really was a bishop, is probably the same man as became abbot of Iona and died in 710.[50]

[48] Dumville, *Saint Patrick: AD 493–1993*, 188. Note that Iona was not only an appendage to the Dál Riatan church, it was a foreign appendage, its abbots and its political ties being to another, albeit allied, political entity – the Cenél Conaill of the northern Uí Néill. What are we supposed to think that the senior Dál Riatan clergy did when Columba arrived? Did they just roll over? It is not the kind of behaviour one expects of bishops. There was resistance to the Columban project both in Pictland and Dál Riata, as is very clear from Adomnán's lament in *VC* ii.46, on which see below, pp. 136–7.

[49] Thomas Clancy has wondered whether 'Mael-Dub epscop', number 37 in the *Cáin Adomnáin* guarantor list, might not also be a bishop in what is now Scotland. As well as appearing in the guarantor list, his name appears in the prologue immediately after that of Curetán. See Ní Dhonnchadha, 'The guarantor list', 196; Márkus, *Adomnán's 'Law of the Innocents'* 13. The name is also found in Scottish dedications: *Kylmalduff* at Inveraray, (Watson *Celtic Place-Names*, 305) and Crossmyloof, south of Glasgow. However, the name is not uncommon, so this must remain speculative.

[50] We may doubt whether he was a bishop. Ní Dhonnchadha, 'The guarantor list', has shown that while the names in the guarantor list seem to be largely authentic and fit the year 697, the titles given to the names,

There are traces of other bishops in Dál Riata. The *Aberdeen Breviary* says that Mo Luóc, the founder of the church on the island of Lismore, was a bishop, and though that is not supported by other sources, neither is it contradicted.[51] Another bishop appears in the Book of Armagh in a reference to *eps(cop) Ném i Telich Ceniuil Oingus(so)* which may well refer to a bishop in Dál Riata. It is not certain, but the presence in Cenél Oengusso territory, on Islay, of *Aird-Néimh, Cill Néimh* and *Eilean Néimh* might support the claim.[52] More concretely, Adomnán tells us that a cleric was ordained in a monastery on Tiree, not the Columban monastery but one of its competitor churches.[53] It was an illicit ordination of a murderer, but the priest who organised the ordination is described fetching a bishop to do it. Sadly, we do not know where the bishop came from – Ireland or Dál Riata?

There are several other bishops who were definitely in Dál Riata during the seventh century. There is to begin with the first bishop sent to Northumbria, sent at the request of Oswald when he became king and his exile in Dál Riata was over. Bede describes him as *austerior*, of a harsher disposition, but does not name him. *Austerior* is unable to make any impression on the Northumbrians, being so harsh, and he returns to Iona to be replaced by the gentler Áedán.[54] So from some period after 634

---

bishop, abbot, king or whatever, are not always appropriate. However, there is a *Convall* in the Dunkeld Litany immediately after Kentigern in the section of bishops, and this may be a reference to our man from Iona, or perhaps to the Conval whose memory is preserved in the dedication of Inchinnan – or both. See Forbes, *Kalendars*, lviii.

[51] S. *Moloch* appears in the Dunkeld Litany in the section addressed to bishops, but I am not sure how good this evidence is. Though it probably refers to Mo Luóc, it may depend on the Aberdeen Breviary. See Forbes, *Kalendars*, lviii; *Aberdeen Breviary*, vol. II, pars estiva, pt. 3, fo. 5v–8v.

[52] In the *Notulae*, folio 18b. See Bieler, *Patrician Texts* 180. We cannot date this reference at all: if the *Notulae* were prepared around or shortly after 750, that would offer a *terminus ante quem*. We cannot be sure that the Ném in question was a Dál Riata bishop (there are Cenéla Oengusso elsewhere), but Watson's list of *Ném* dedications on Islay is suggestive if not persuasive. Watson, *Celtic Place-Names,* 307.

[53] *VC* i.36.

[54] *HE* iii.5.

until his death, there was a bishop who was also a monk of Iona, back home 'in his own land'. But he disappears completely. There is no obvious record of his death, or of what he did in the meantime. Did he return to simple monastic life, or did his episcopal state mean that he would continue to be used pastorally, in mainland Dál Riata perhaps?

Then of course there is Colmán, the bishop of Lindisfarne who was defeated at the Synod of Whitby and left Lindisfarne in 664, along with those of his brothers who still rejected the decision of the synod, and some of the bones of Áedán.[55] He went to Iona to consult his brothers, and so there was another bishop in Dál Riata from 664, until we are told in the Annals that Colmán left for Ireland, for Inis Bó Fínne, in 668.[56]

The first bishop of the Mercians and Middle Angles after the baptism of their *princeps* Peada, the son of king Penda, appears to have been another Iona monk (certainly an Irishman) called Diuma. On his death, Fínán of Lindisfarne consecrated an Iona monk called Cellach as the second bishop, but Cellach took early retirement shortly afterwards and, Bede tells us, returned to Iona.[57] Again, on leaving his diocese, Cellach seems to disappear from the record. We are left to speculate as to what this bishop did on his return to Dál Riata and to his monastery.

But all this string of bishops coming and going is suggestive of a strong sense of the episcopal character of pastoral work. Oswald was an exile in Dál Riata among Columban clergy, together with his thegns, until 634, and he learned his faith there and was baptised there. When he returned to Northumbria, he asked Iona for bishops and got them. This suggests that he himself knew, and had learned on Iona, that bishops were necessary for pastoral organisation. We might add that it is likely that all these bishops which Iona had sent to Lindisfarne and elsewhere were consecrated by three other bishops. Certainly that was what the law

[55] *HE* iii.26 and iv.4. This made him *comarba Áedáin* wherever he went, perhaps, taking this dignity to Mayo with him eventually.

[56] AU 668.3.

[57] *HE* iii.21. This seems to be in the mid-650s, but we can not date it precisely. The fact that he is succeeded by an Englishman (though one taught by the Irish) may suggest a fairly loose grasp on the election process by the Lindisfarne *Scotti* in what might otherwise be regarded as their 'patch'.

required,[58] and Bede actually mentions in one of his consecration stories that when Fínán ordained Cedd as bishop of the East Saxons, he summoned two other bishops to help him, fulfilling the legal requirements. And one can be quite certain that, given the controversies surrounding Iona's dating of Easter and their unorthodox hair-style, if there were any irregularities in their rites of ordination people would have made an issue of that as well, if only to discredit their position on the Easter date. But this allegation is not made at Whitby, and it is hard to believe that the English would have overlooked such a glaringly obvious heteropraxis. Iona must be having her bishops ordained legally, with three other bishops laying on their hands. Unfortunately, we can not tell whether Iona sent her candidates to Ireland to be ordained, or whether there were enough bishops on mainland Scotland to do the job. But wherever it was done, we can be fairly certain that Iona's understanding of pastoral organisation involved a strong sense of episcopal authority.

To return now from Northumbria to Dál Riata itself: Iona, for all its monastic character, contributed clergy to the pastoral work of the local church, as monasteries did all over Europe. Why would we assume that the Iona clergy and their churches in Dál Riata would be any different from those who had gone from Iona to Northumbria? We do not see many of them in Adomnán's writing: in fact we only see one with any clarity, and that is a cleric by the name of Cailtán who occupied a church on Loch Awe which was known to Adomnán himself as *Cella Diuni*, the church of Diún – who was actually Cailtán's brother. The cleric is referred to as a *praepositus*, a title which suggests that his

[58] A law which is affirmed by the first book of *Collectio Canonum Hibernensis*, a work with close connections to Iona in the early eighth century: *Porro episcopus non ab uno, sed a cunctis comprovincialibus ordinetur . . . ab omnibus convenientibus constituitur ac non minus ac tribus praesentibus, caeteris tamen consentientibus, testimonio litterarum.* Sinodus Cartaginensis ait: *Tunc consensu clericorum et laicorum et totius provinciae episcoporum maximeque metropolitani vel epistola vel auctoritate vel praesentia ordinetur episcopus* (*CCH* i.5). Note, however, that one manuscript does mention *conepiscopi, i.e. vicarii episcopi* (*CCH*, p. 5, note i). There is no doubt that to have three ordaining bishops was the norm, though *corepiscopi* (Wasserschleben's *conepiscopi* appears to be a misreading) remained a problem in Europe as council *acta* make clear by their prohibitions: Meaux in 845, Chalons in 873 and Metz in 888.

church had a small community, that he is the prior of a monastic daughter-house of Iona. But its location at Loch Awe, in the heart of what we might think of as a residential area, and in a place where we have an *Annat* place-name close at hand, suggests that this is a pastoral centre and not an ascetic foundation.[59] Shortly before he dies, Cailtán is recalled to his monastic home 'in true spiritual obedience', to die and rest his bones in the graveyard of Iona.[60] One story about one clergyman from Iona – the only one we know of working in Dál Riata. Who was he working for? Who was his bishop? This little anecdote tells us nothing about what kind of jurisdiction Iona had, if any, among the clergy of Dál Riata, not all of whom, presumably, were Iona monks.

Pictland

What about the third of Adomnán's territories: Pictland? Bede says that Columba came to Scotland as a missionary, sailing east to convert the northern Picts, and that he preached and baptised Bruide mac Maelchon who was then king.[61] For Bede, Columba is a missionary, but that is very much part of Bede's ideal anyway, inspired as he is by Gregory the Great and his mission to the English.

Adomnán, on the other hand, was better placed than Bede to know what Columba thought he was doing, and he says quite clearly that Columba came to Britain as an ascetic: 'In the second year following the battle of Cúl Drebene, when he was forty-one, Columba sailed away from Ireland to Britain, choosing to be a pilgrim for Christ.'[62] Pilgrimage for Christ, the white martyrdom, took a man away from his kin, his own country, and many of his rights and privileges. It was a form of asceticism, not a technique of conversion or evangelical persuasion. The fact that some pilgrims ended up converting pagans does not mean that that was their motive, nor that Columba expected to convert anyone. And if Columba had come to convert the Picts, you would not

[59] On the significance of *annat* in church organisation, and on Kilchrenan in particular, see Clancy, 'Annat in Scotland'.
[60] *VC* i.31.
[61] *HE* iii.4.
[62] *VC* Second Preface.

expect him to have established his centre on one of the most western parts of Scotland.

Columba came as a monk, as an ascetic, to establish a monastery which would be a centre of prayer, of study and work. He settled in a place which was reasonably remote even from Gaelic power centres such as Dunadd and Dunollie, let alone from Pictish centres. But for Adomnán Pictland is still important: it represents that third region of the mind, the un-Christian territory, wild and oppositional, barbarian he would say.[63] He has two very confrontational animal-stories, as we have seen, and a good number of confrontations – sometimes quite violent – with Pictish people. Picts try to set fire to his boat,[64] Pictish magicians interrupt him and his monks during their prayers,[65] he overwhelms a poisonous well which was venerated by the Picts as a god, and beats the wizards by turning it into a healing well,[66] he forces the wizard Broichan to release his Irish slave by very nearly killing him with a curse and then defeats him in a wind-directing competition.[67] Finally, finding himself refused entrance to king Bruide's fort, Columba makes the sign of the cross over the gates, knocks and lays his hand on them, and the doors spring open,[68] like one of our modern door-step evangelists, only without the suit and tie and stick-on smile.

The most confrontational material involves the saint having power-contests with magicians, *magi*. It is very much like Sulpicius Severus' *Vita Sancti Martini* in that respect: the saint in conflict with the representatives of the old gods and their cult. But it differs from that genre in one very important respect: Adomnán nowhere describes Columba founding a church. Nor, importantly, does he mention Columba's baptism of king Bruide mac Maelchon

[63] He does call some people *barbari*: the *Meati* when they are beaten in battle (*VC* i.8); the raiders of a little man's farm in *Crog Reth* (i.46) identified by Watson, *Celtic Place-Names,* 78, as *A'Chruach*, to the west of Loch Rannoch; the Picts at his showdown with Nessie (ii.27, *gentiles barbari*); and the nations who will one day bestow special honour on Iona (*barbararum et exterarum gentium*, iii.23).

[64] *VC* i.34.

[65] *VC* i.37.

[66] *VC* ii.11.

[67] *VC* ii.33, 34.

[68] *VC* ii.35.

– though we can be sure that if there was any basis for making such a claim Adomnán would have made it. There is something quite different going on between Columba and the Picts in Adomnán's picture. While the magicians are opposed and routed by the saint, he has a much more delicate approach to other Picts. There is one instance where he preaches the gospel and converts someone,[69] and the two baptism stories we have already mentioned on Skye and at Urquhart. But that is all. Adomnán has no stories to tell about great preaching crusades, mass conversions and church-foundations. And after all it is likely that Columba and his monks were only part of the story of conversion in Pictland, with other monks from other monastic families having a role, as well as Dál Riatan clergy perhaps, British Christians in the south, inter-marriage between Pict and Scot and so on.[70]

But Adomnán has other more subtly told stories: like the leader of a Pictish war-band who comes to Columba on Skye seeking baptism,[71] and a Pict called Tarain who comes to him as a refugee seeking asylum.[72] Then there are Columba's visits to king Bruide in which we see a certain cordiality between the king and the saint. He leaves a miraculous healing stone for Bruide in his house,[73] he asks protection for a monk in Orkney, which is evidently within Bruide's military sphere of influence. Perhaps

[69] *VC* ii.32.

[70] There is evidence of early Christianity in Pictland which is not a result of Columba's preaching. St Patrick refers to 'apostate Picts' (*Epistola*, §2; Hood, *St Patrick*, 35; but cf. Dumville, *St. Patrick*, 129–32); *Y Gododdin* has Pictish allies of the Christian British warriors attacking the 'heathen' (Jackson, *Gododdin*, 100); Áedán mac Gabráin (d. 606.2, AU), ordained by Columba, may have had Pictish connections as suggested in the prophecy of Berchan and in the name and destiny of one of his sons – Gartnait is a Pictish name – recorded by Annals of Tigernach (*ca* 601) as 'King of the Picts' and therefore likely to have had a Pictish mother. Archaeological evidence of early Christianity in Pictland is not so easy to identify, but the long-cist cemeteries at Hallow Hill by St Andrews and on both sides of the Forth, and perhaps the Catstane at Kirkliston (near Edinburgh Airport) offer glimpses (Foster, *Picts, Gaels and Scots*, 79). However, I do not think Ninian is likely to be of much help to us here, as stories of his preaching to the Southern Picts are likely to be eighth-century English propaganda for Whithorn.

[71] *VC* i.33.

[72] *VC* ii.23.

[73] *VC* ii.33.

most important are those stories which end up with Columba and his God being honoured and praised by Pictish people, because this is what Adomnán is really looking for, part of the agenda of the *Vita* itself: the establishment of Iona's monks as the favoured church body in Pictland,[74] and as the favourite of the Pictish king. Perhaps a key moment in the creation of this bond between king and saint is in the story of Columba singing outside Bruide's fortress, while the wizards are trying to stop him. Adomnán says that Columba lifts up his voice 'like some terrible thunder'. But perhaps it is not just the number of decibels that is important here, but the psalm-number. Adomnán says that Columba sang Psalm 44:

> My heart overflows with noble words,
> so I speak my song to the king . . .
> O mighty one, gird your sword upon your thigh,
> in splendour and beauty go forth . . .

Of course, the monk singing the psalm is usually addressing the king of heaven, the God of Israel, but the resonances of the song in terms of blessing an earthly king are unmistakable, and it even concludes with that promise so often made by Gaelic saints to kings: 'sons shall be born to you in place of your fathers'.

Is Columba not portrayed here as wooing the Pictish king, seeking that contract of mutual honour between saint and ruler, between monastery and kingdom, between church and *túath*, which underlies so much hagiography, especially in the Columba dossier? And is this not what Adomnán is really concerned about? At the end of the seventh century Iona is probably, in spite of the many other churches, monasteries, missions to the Picts, still the most influential of them all. But not everyone accepts Iona's position. We have seen Iona was initially a monastic appendage to an existing church in Dál Riata. Would we expect the non-Columban clergy simply to roll over and accept Iona's claim to jurisdiction over the whole of their territory? There was some form of ecclesiastical organisation in Pictland, too. Would all their clergy accept Iona's claim of authority? We have got used

[74] *VC* ii.27 (the Picts glorify the God of the Christians); ii.32 (raising the dead child, the God of the Christians is glorified); ii.35 (after forcing open Bruide's doors, the king holds the man in great honour).

to hearing Bede's description of Iona as the church whose abbot had jurisdiction over the whole Church in Scotland,[75] but we do not hear the other voices so easily, the voices of the churches whose independence may have been threatened by such a claim. But we can hear them distantly in the background in Adomnán, a faint noise of protest. Adomnán tells us that Columba's monasteries are held in great honour among the Picts and the Irish in Britain, and this is due partly to the fact that Columba saved them from the plagues which afflicted everyone else. But he goes on in a tone of lament: 'What we are now going to say is, we reckon, not to be heard without sorrow, for there are many extremely stupid folk in both peoples (Picts and Scots) who do not know that they have been protected from disease by the prayers of the saints, and these ungrateful people abuse God's patience.'[76] This is an important passage, a cardinal point in the work, concluding the whole of Book II and its recitation of Columba's miracles of power with an appeal for recognition of his, and therefore Adomnán's, authority.

It was an appeal which failed. Iona's century and a half of service, her monastic expansion, her faithful propagation of the gospel in Pictland, do not qualify her in the minds of many clergy to have some kind of jurisdiction over the whole territory. It may be that Iona got herself a bishop some time before 697, bishop Cóeti, as part of a campaign to consolidate her ecclesiastical claim, to make herself more credible as a leader of churches by having episcopal as well as abbatial authority.[77] But this is guess-work.

[75] *HE* iii.3, though notice that by the time Bede is writing the jurisdiction of Iona is described in the past tense, *arcem tenebat*, though in the following chapter the suggestion is that there is some continuing subjection to Iona, even of the bishops, *ordine inusitato*.

[76] *VC* ii.46.

[77] His episcopal jurisdiction seems to have included a swathe of land in Strathtay and central Atholl where dedications to him are found in several places: Simon Taylor, above, pp. 57–60. Taylor notes that the area of dedications to Cóeti is remarkably close to a significant cluster of dedications to Adomnán, probably Cóeti's abbot, in Glen Lyon and Strathtay. See Taylor and Ó Muraile, 'The Columban Onomastic Legacy', 217, 228, for *Craig Euny, Magh Eódhnain, Muileann Eódhnain, Tobar Eonan* in Glen Lyon; Dull (where Adomnán is the patron saint) two miles north-east of Kenmore; *Fuaran Eódhrain*, a few miles east again near Grandtully; *Ard Eódhnaig* (Ardeonaig) on the south side of Loch Tay.

We do not even know what kind of jurisdiction it was that was in dispute – was it the right to receive tribute from other churches; was it Iona's special relationship with kings that was at stake; was she claiming a provincial appellate jurisdiction in legal disputes between Scottish churches;[78] was she claiming the right to appoint bishops, or was it merely a primacy of honour? We do not know.

It might be, then, that we can see Adomnán fighting off the rival claims of other churches in Scotland, other monasteries and bishops, in the negative way he treats them in the *Vita*. He tells us of many senior ecclesiastics from Ireland, bishops and abbots, who visit Columba on Iona, or who receive him in their own monasteries, with great reverence and honour. But what about Adomnán's treatment of Scottish churches, Iona's competitors? We hear that God punished the rival monasteries on Tiree, ravaging and killing off their monks with plague, but that Columba's monastery was protected by the fasts and prayers of its monks – implying that the other monks deserved their fate perhaps.[79] As to the other churches, Adomnán ignores them: Mo Luóc of Lismore, Columba's contemporary, never appears. Neither does Donnán of Eigg. Bláán's church at Cenn Garad (Kingarth) and its bishops, Applecross founded a little later, the other churches in Pictland, are all ignored. Iona and its mission is the focus of our attention throughout, and its holiness and spiritual power are manifested consistently in the three regions of Adomnán's spiritual map: the ascetic, the pastoral and the missionary, three functions in three regions – three functions which embrace all those of the church, and three spaces which embrace the whole of northern Scotland.

Ultimately, in spite of spectacular success in 697, when everyone who is anyone seems to be signing Adomnán's Law, a few years later we can see the apparent failure of Iona's claim.[80] Around

[78] This appellate jurisdiction is a feature both of Patrician texts making claims for Armagh (*Liber Angeli*, § 28 in Bieler, *Patrician Texts*, 188, and of the Iona–Dairinis text of *CCH* xx) where a more provincial arrangement is envisaged which would better serve Iona's claims.

[79] *VC* iii.8.

[80] Ironically, as Thomas Clancy has speculated, we might in fact regard this as a kind of success story for Iona abbots at one level, given that Adomnán himself was convinced of the correctness of the new Easter dating

710 or shortly afterwards, Nechtan is wooing the Northumbrian church, writing to Ceolfrid for help in reforming the Church in Pictland. In 717 the Annals of Ulster record 'the expulsion of the family of Iona by King Nechtan beyond the Spine of Britain' – that is, back to the west side, back to Dál Riata. I am not sure what we should imagine as happening here. Do we have to picture hundreds of Columban monks packing their haversacks and trekking back to Argyll? Or might it not simply be a decision by other churches that Iona's claims to authority are not convincing or binding? The Iona monks might have stayed put, then, only now subject to the authority of the newly reformed and royally backed church of Nechtan's domain. Eight years later, in 725, a man called Brecc of Fortriu dies. He looks like a cleric in his entry in the Annals of Ulster.[81] With a title like that, is he not likely to be a bishop, representing the first appearance[82] of a newly beefed up, episcopally organised centre in the heart of Pictland, and the ultimate and inevitable redundancy of Adomnán's old tripartite mental map?[83]

---

system, and that Iona's abbot Dúnchad (d. 717.1, AU, possibly in some kind of exile in Pictland as his successor had taken over the *cathedra Columbae* the previous year) may well have been one of the promotors of Nechtan's reform in Pictland, especially as there are dedications to him in Pictish East Fife. See Taylor, 'Place-names and the early Church in Eastern Scotland', 100. For similar arguments, see now Veitch, 'The Columban Church'.

[81] *Conghal m. Maele Anfaith, Brecc Fortrend, Oan princeps Ego moriuntur*, AU 725.7. Thomas Clancy has suggested that we might consider that Falkirk, formerly *Ecclesbrec* [also Egglesbreth, Egelilbrich, Eaglesuret, Eglesbryth, Eiglesbrich, Eiglesbrec, Egelbrech, Eglesbrigh, listed by Nicolaisen, *Scottish Place Names* (1976), 7–15] may have originally been 'the church of Brecc', dedicated to this cleric.

[82] Or perhaps the second appearance, if we accept the suggestion by Simon Taylor that stories of St Serf represent an early episcopal re-organisation of the Pictish church after the Anglian withdrawal from Abercorn in 685 (S. Taylor, 'Place names and the early Church in Eastern Scotland', 101). See also Alan Macquarrie, '*Vita Sancti Servani*', 133, who saw Serf rather as a proponent of Gaelic organisation.

[83] An earlier version of this paper was delivered at the Scottish Catholic Historical Association's conference in Edinburgh, in June 1997. It reached its present form after Thomas Clancy and Thomas O'Loughlin offered their own comments and suggestions, and I would like to thank them for the generosity with which they did so.

6

Res, tempus, locus, persona:[1] Adomnán's exegetical method

Thomas O'Loughlin

Adomnán as exegete?

Despite Bede's description of him as *uir ... scientia scripturarum nobilissime instructus*,[2] Adomnán as exegete is still a far less known figure than Adomnán as the hagiographer of Columba.[3] Locating the exact causes of this neglect of a major part of the legacy of seventh-century Iona is a complex business, but part of the explanation lies in the fact that much of Adomnán's work has been seen as simply the description, at second-hand, of places in Palestine, rather than as an attempt to come to grips with the problems of consistency and coherence which the Christian Scriptures could throw up for the careful reader.[4] To date, although J. F. Kelly has included the *De Locis Sanctis* [*DLS*][5] in his catalogue of Irish scriptural works,[6] it is not considered by most who study the history of exegesis. Indeed, apart from an article by D. A. Bullough, there is, to my knowledge, no work

[1] Isidore, *Etymologiae* II.16.1 (see below).

[2] Bede, *HE* v.15.

[3] This is the reverse of the medieval situation, cf. O'Loughlin, 'Adomnán the illustrious'.

[4] Cf. O'Loughlin, 'The exegetical purpose of Adomnán's *De Locis Sanctis*'.

[5] The edition of D. Meehan and L. Bieler (*Scriptores Latini Hiberniae* 3, Dublin 1958) will be used here.

[6] Kelly, 'A catalogue of early medieval Hiberno-Latin biblical commentaries: II', 393.

explicitly devoted to analysing Adomnán's skills as an exegete.[7] Bullough wrote:[8]

> The *De locis* is best regarded against the background of the methods of biblical exegesis current in seventh-century Ireland. . . . The final chapter of the first book of the *De locis* is indeed a mature, if not entirely characteristic, example of 'modern' literal exegesis. Arculf had apparently been unable to give any usable information about 'a church at the right-hand side of Bethany' which is its nominal subject. So Adomnán examines the evidence of the Synoptic Gospels for the discourse Christ was said to have given in that place in the light of the question 'Where?' 'Of what sort?' 'At what time?' 'To what persons?'one of the earliest examples (perhaps even the oldest still extant) of the tetrad of questions in Irish biblical criticism.

But this raises even more questions: if *DLS* was intended as a travel guide, why bother to find material on places that were of little interest? If Arculf is the occasion for its composition, why is he not mentioned in the body of one of its longest chapters? And if this is a 'mature' piece of exegesis, in what does that maturity consist? Essentially these are one question, but they relate to different aspects of Adomnán's aim in writing. The Scriptures did pose a set of problems of a specific sort to exegetes: *aenigmates* where the information in one place in the Scriptures did not accord with information found elsewhere. In such cases it was the primary duty of the exegete to bring the conflicting evidence in harmony.[9] For instance, a tomb is said to be in one place in one biblical book, but somewhere else in another (Jacob was buried near Hebron according to Gen 50:13, the position taken by *DLS* II.10.2, but at Shechem according to Acts 7:16). Thus the exegete must not only decide which is the true account, but must do so in

[7] Bullough, 'Columba, Adomnán and the achievement of Iona'. When Meehan in his introduction (*DLS*, 6) realised that *De Locis Sanctis* was a work requiring a high level of scriptural sophistication he thought of Arculf as the genius, not Adomnán, see O'Loughlin, 'Why Adomnán needs Arculf'. I have tried to draw attention to Adomnán's skill *en passant* in articles relating to other aspects of medieval exegesis, e.g. in O'Loughlin, 'Julian of Toledo's Antikeimenon and the development of Latin exegesis'.

[8] Bullough, 'Columba, Adomnán and the achievement of Iona', at 122.

[9] The background to this is surveyed in O'Loughlin, 'Biblical contradictions in the *Periphyseon* and the development of Eriugena's method'.

such a way that does not assert that Scripture is in error. One route to the solution of some of these problems was proposed by Augustine: study the actual geography of the places mentioned and then, with first-hand evidence of where the places were actually located, one might be able to see that many disagreements were only matters of differing wording or were only apparently contradictory.[10] But such solutions would require books, based on empirical evidence, about places mentioned in Scripture, and these works were still to be written. Adomnán took up this challenge and used the device of Arculf, a suitable expert in these matters,[11] to guarantee the validity of his solutions to these *aenigmates*. It is as the author of such a technical work of exegesis that we must study Adomnán the exegete. However, since such scriptural difficulties underlie much of *DLS*,[12] if we are to gain a proper appreciation of Adomnán's method we must examine a substantial case, where he would have considered the problem to be particularly thorny and significant, and view his reconciliation of 'apparent' contradictions in detail. Such a case would not only show us his method at work, but would enable us to compare his method, and skill, with that of predecessors or contemporaries who were concerned about the same problem. For such an examination I know of no better case than the chapter, entitled *De alia*

[10] This solution was older than Augustine. Eusebius of Caesarea had this in mind when he compiled his work on biblical geography. From the introduction to the one part of it that survives (the *Onomasticon*) we know that the entire work contained a guide to ethnological terms, a topography of Jerusalem, a plan of Jerusalem and the Temple, and the onomasticon of the places mentioned in the Scriptures, and that it was his aim that this work would supply the key to many exegetical difficulties (cf. Curti, 'Eusebius of Caesarea', 300). But by the end of the fourth century, when Jerome translated the *Onomasticon* into Latin, the first three parts of this work must have been, to all intents, already lost. This Latin work was praised by Augustine, but he presumed that other useful works using geography still needed to be produced so he too had no idea that Eusebius had already produced such works (Augustine's thoughts on these questions can be found in the *De Doctrina Christiana* II.39).

[11] *Arculfus ... peritus locorum uerax index et satis idoneus ...* (*DLS*, *procemium*).

[12] I have examined some simple cases in 'The exegetical purpose of Adomnán's *De Locis Sanctis*', 'Why Adomnán needs Arculf: the case of an expert witness'; and in 'Adam's burial at Hebron: some aspects of its significance in the Latin tradition'.

ecclesia ad dexteram Bethaniae partem constructa, already identified by Bullough as a piece of 'mature exegesis,' which concerns the movements of Christ in the days before the crucifixion.[13]

The problem in the Scriptures

Let us first lay out the problem as it is found by reading the scriptural accounts without a modern heuristic of the nature of the inter-relationships of the synoptic gospels (Matthew, Mark, Luke), and the relationship of the synoptics to John.[14] In the four gospels we are presented with very different accounts about where Jesus was, what he said, and when he said it, in the week before his death. For instance Matthew's account of the warnings of Jesus about what will happen 'at the end' (known today as the 'synoptic apocalypse' [Matt 24:1–25:46 // Mark 13 // Luke 21:5–38]), while agreeing with Mark as to places and dates, is nearly twice as long. Luke's account is about the same length as Mark's, but differs as to places, is less exact about times, and some of the material is used elsewhere in his gospel.[15] But even if these differences can be ironed out, there is still the problem of John. John not only does not mention the warnings about the future, but gives Jesus a different set of movements, mentions different places and houses, and all of this takes place on a different time-scale. The problems of these passages, since they touched on the central Christian event, the Crucifixion, and on equally important events connected with it, such as the Last Supper, gave this problem a unique status among the difficulties to be resolved relating to the harmonisation of the gospels.[16]

[13] This chapter is numbered 'xxv' in the Latin text (p. 70) and '27' in the translation (p. 71); in the basic modern edition (P. Geyer, *CSEL* xxxix) it is 'xxvii' (pp. 251–3). In Bieler's 1965 edition (*CCSL* clxxv) it is ch. 'xxv' (pp. 202–3). Here Bieler's numbering will be followed for convenience.

[14] The various modern (i.e. post-eighteenth century) approaches to this problem are sketched out by Neirynck, 'Synoptic problem'.

[15] The problems can be followed most conveniently in Huck and Greeven, *Synopse der drei ersten Evangelien*, 217–31; the general complexity of the question can be seen in Barr, *A Diagram of Synoptic Relationships*.

[16] We can gauge this importance by the attention devoted to it among theologians and exegetes. For instance Thomas Aquinas discusses the discrepancy between John and the Synoptics on whether the day of the crucifixion was the same as the day of the Passover in his *Super Euangelium*

The four gospels come into complete agreement on only two points: first, that Jesus was crucified on a Friday[17] just outside Jerusalem; and second, that on the previous evening the meal known traditionally as the Last Supper took place. It is on the basis of working backwards from this one fixed date that attempts to reconcile the preceding narratives in all four gospels were made. The points of conflict can be more clearly seen thus:[18]

MATTHEW	MARK	LUKE	JOHN
			11:17 At Bethany.
			11:54 Goes to Ephrem when Passover is near (11:55).
24:1 At Jerusalem.	13:1 At Jerusalem.	21:1 At Jerusalem.	

S. Ioannis, XIII.1 (ed. R. Cai, Turin 1952), 324, and makes the solution a matter touching the whole credibility of Christianity when he says of it: *haereticum est dicere, quod aliquid falsum, non solum in Euangeliis, sed etiam in quacumque canonica Scriptura inueniatur.* As late as the 1950s it was still an issue that called for apologetic accommodation in Roman Catholic scholarship: in the 1957 edition of his translation of the New Testament (first published in 1945) R. A. Knox added two footnotes, attempting to reconcile – in a way similar to Adomnán – Matt with John to show that one could 'avoid any appearance of discrepancy' (New Testament: London 1957, 28). The problem can be seen in a more modern guise in other works: cf. Corbishly, 'The chronology of New Testament times', at n. 676 be (and cf. W. Leonard, 'St John', 1004, n. 802b); and Jeremias, *The Eucharistic Words of Jesus*, trans. Perrin, 15–89 and especially 36–41. The 'classic' modern attempt to settle this question 'historically' (used by both Corbishly and Jeremias) is Fotheringham, 'Astronomical evidence for the date of the Crucifixion'. Fotheringham returned to this topic later ('The evidence of astronomy and technical chronology'), but did not add anything of relevance to this question.

[17] This is based on the coherence of Matt 27:62, Mark 15:42, Luke 23:54 and John 19:31 (cf. Jones, 'St Matthew', 898; O'Flynn, 'St Mark', 928, n. 739e, and 932, n. 742h).

[18] I offer this simple parallel as the standard fourfold parallel of these passages (Aland, *Synopsis Quattuor Evangeliorum*, 425–30) is primarily concerned with textual parallels rather than with details about times and places, and therefore does not bring out the pre-modern problematic sufficiently clearly.

Matthew	Mark	Luke	John
24:3 Goes to Mt of Olives.	13:3 Goes to Mt of Olives.		
Some disciples come to Jesus.	Named disciples: Peter, James, John, & Andrew.	Some disciples come to Jesus.	
Apocalyptic Discourse (on Mt of Olives).	Apocalyptic Discourse (on Mt of Olives).	Apocalyptic Discourse (in Jerusalem).	
		21:37 Goes to Mt of Olives at night, but daily in Jerusalem teaching.	
26:2 'Date' given two days to Passover.	14:1 'Date' given two days to Passover *et azyma*	26:2 'Date' given Passover to Passover. *et azyma* drawing near.	12:1 'Date' given six days
26:7 **At Bethany** in house of Simon the leper.	14:3 **At Bethany** in house of Simon the leper.		12:1 **At Bethany** house not named, but since the family of Lazarus present, it might be his.[19]
26:7 Anointing by a woman.	14:3 Anointing by a woman.		12:3 Anointing by Mary.
			12:13 On the 'next day' he enters Jerusalem in triumph.
26:17 First Day of Unleavened Bread; to city from Bethany.	14:12 First Day of Unleavened Bread; to city from Bethany.	22:7 Day of Unleavened Bread.	

[19] This aspect of the problem has a long history in that the Old Syriac version seeks to make it explicitly Lazarus' house (cf. Brown, *The Gospel According to John* i.448). Another curious attempt to reconcile everything to harmony is the suggestion that Simon was the father of Lazarus (Sanders, '"Those whom Jesus loved" (John xi.5)'), unfortunately there is not a shred of evidence for such a link!

Matthew	Mark	Luke	John
26:20 **Last Supper**	14:17 **Last Supper**	22:14 **Last Supper**	13:1 **Last Supper**
26:36 To Gethsemani on Mt of Olives.	14:32 To Gethsemani on Mt of Olives.	22:39 To Mt of Olives.	18:1 To garden across Kedron valley.
27:1 Day of Crucifixion.	15:1 Day of Crucifixion.	22:62 Day of Crucifixion.	18:28 Day of Crucifixion.

We can now describe the problem in a series of steps.

First, Matt and Mark present a major problem with regard to the text of the Apocalyptic Discourse as they vary so greatly in length and details; but they present no difficulties as to times and movements – wherever they differ in historical detail they can be seen as complementary to one another.

Second, taking Matt and Mark together against Luke we find that the textual difficulties over the content of the Apocalyptic Discourse are now minor.[20] Likewise with regard to time there is no difficulty, the Lucan narrative is less precise in that numbered days are not given, but since these time-notes in no way disagree with Matt and Mark, they can be seen as fitting in with Matt and Mark. However, the sequence of Jesus' movements presents a major problem: in Luke the place of the discourse appears to be Jerusalem itself and not the Mount of Olives. The Mount of Olives is only mentioned as the place to which Jesus goes at night, with the implication that he is commuting each day between there and the city. There is no support for this going to and fro between Jerusalem and the Mount of Olives in Matt and Mark. Likewise there is no mention of a trip to Bethany, but this difficulty is lessened in that there is no mention of an anointing of Jesus in Luke, so its absence could be presented as an entire episode that fails to be recorded – and hence does not contradict – Matt and Mark.

Third, the problems become critical when the accounts of the three synoptic gospels – however they be internally reconciled – are placed alongside John. The textual difficulties about what

[20] What difficulties there are can be resolved by the same method, and with less bother, as that used in harmonising Matt and Mark.

Jesus said (different teachings and topics) can be easily solved using the standard explanations for the differences between the synoptics and John, but the difficulties about times and places are far more serious. However, there are two 'anchor points' between Matt/Mark and John: first, Jesus is anointed in Bethany; and second, some time after that he is present in Jerusalem with the disciples at the Last Supper. Because of these common elements in space and time, a reconciliation – if the texts be historically true (which is the basic presupposition underlying the whole problem) – must be presumed to be possible. If one abandons this notion then one must ask what is meant by truth in the gospels; while if one fails to reconcile the account, then one must abandon any notion of certain truth for all four gospels. With regards to movements, John presents a completely different sequence. In Matt and Mark the sequence is Jerusalem, the Mount of Olives, [?], Bethany, Jerusalem; in Luke it is, or could be construed to be, Jerusalem, the Mount of Olives, [[?], [?] ?], Jerusalem (essentially: Jerusalem, . . . , Jerusalem). In John, by contrast, it is Somewhere-not-Jerusalem, Bethany, Ephrem, Bethany, Jerusalem (essentially from somewhere outside the city to the city). These accounts are in open contradiction, but since one can be in the same place on different occasions this problem is less troublesome for reconciliation than the problems in the time sequence – for each designated moment in time is unique. The essence of the difference concerns a discrepancy of four days: Matt and Mark (Luke is irrelevant here) say there are two days between the arrival in Bethany and the Passover, while John says there are six days.

Fourth, for later-patristic and medieval exegesis there was a further problem: the liturgical calendar follows John – the great entry into Jerusalem (John 12:13ff.) takes place on the fifth day (Palm Sunday) before the Day of Crucifixion (Good Friday).[21] However, most of the remembered details about the events before the crucifixion, e.g. the plots against Jesus, come solely from the Synoptic accounts.

Today, these problems would not even be raised in a study of the gospels except as items illustrating the varying mind-sets of

[21] In John this day of entering Jerusalem is the 'next day' after the arrival in Bethany.

the writers, but this disregard is not part of the tradition. And to this we must now turn.

Augustine's *De Consensu Euangelistarum*[22]

While several early Christian writers were concerned with this question in their attempts to harmonise the gospels, I shall concentrate here on just this one work of Augustine[23] since it was Adomnán's source in *DLS*.[24] While Augustine expressed his interest on several occasions in having works of scriptural scholarship that cleared up biblical problems and contradictions – and we can see *De Consensu Euangelistarum* in this light – we must remember that it is also a work of apologetic. It was written to rebut those who pointed to the contradictions in the gospel accounts as evidence that Christianity lacked historical credibility, and since it laid an emphasis on history, it was consequently a fraud.[25] Since such a defence of the historicity of the gospels must be all or nothing (allowing even one error put the whole in doubt), Augustine had to take the high ground and defend every detail. The theory laid out in Book I of *De Consensu*, and again in the opening lines dealing with our problem,[26] takes this form: every direct statement in the Scriptures *must* be true, for whatever the evangelist wrote – even if it is not part of what God wanted to communicate – can be read as revelation, and hence is guaranteed by God's word who inspired the writer to set out upon the work.[27] There can never be a mistake in scripture, so if one thinks one has found an error then either the text is faulty, or the translation is faulty, or one's understanding is faulty.[28] This dogmatic *a priori*

[22] Ed. J. Weihrich, *CSEL* xliii (Vienna 1904).

[23] Cf. Penna, 'Il *De consensu euangelistarum*', for the general problem; and Ray, 'Augustine's *De Consensu Evangelistarum*', for its later use in Latin theology.

[24] The evidence that the *De Consensu Euanglistarum* lies behind the text of Adomnán, cf. O'Loughlin, 'Adomnán's *De locis sanctis*: a textual emendation'.

[25] Cf. Portalié, *A Guide to the Thought of St. Augustine*, 62.

[26] See below.

[27] Portalié, *A Guide to the Thought of St. Augustine*, 122.

[28] Cf. *Contra Faustum* XI.5 (*PL* xlii.249) for this pithy summary of his position; and cf. my 'The controversy over Methuselah's death: protochronology and the origins of the Western concept of inerrancy', *Recherches de Théologie ancienne et médiévale* 62 (1995) 182–225.

had two effects on the tradition. First, it not only did not help towards a solution, but it exacerbated the debate by making such questions a matter of basic Christian faith. And second, it meant that Christian scholars believed that there was a solution which would reconcile all the problems. So no matter how many scholars failed to harmonise the texts, it was always worth new endeavours and more labour for the solution *must* exist (or Christianity was false) if only someone bright enough or holy enough could find it. Furthermore, if earlier strategies had failed to find a way to unravel 'the knot',[29] then *a fortiori* every new strategy was worth exploring, no matter how strange. It was this understanding of these gospel problems that would inspire Adomnán in *DLS* I.xxv, but first we must look in detail at Augustine's solution.

Augustine tackled the problem in two parts: first, the textual discrepancies between Matt, Mark and Luke in the Apocalyptic Discourse;[30] and second, the chronological difficulty between Matt-Mark and John, as to when the anointing at Bethany took place.[31] In dealing with the first he ignored the problem of location and assumed that the three evangelists locate the discourse on the Mount of Olives. He began by setting out his basic principles: in accepting what each gives in his gospel we must not suspect contradictions. But this only applies where there are exactly parallel passages – what is found in one may be omitted altogether by the others, and so it is only in these specific cases that the exegete must demonstrate that there is no conflict. Augustine, however, did accept that in this case, since the accounts relate a single historical discourse by Jesus, that the common solution that different statements might be explained as referring to different moments in Christ's ministry cannot be used. That said, Augustine's explanation of the differences is a very simple and standard one. Each evangelist recalled the exact same message but used different words and phraseology.[32] When these

[29] For the background of 'the knot' metaphor which belongs to the world of Adomnán and early medieval exegesis, cf. my 'Biblical contradictions in the *Periphyseon* and the development of Eriugena's method'.

[30] II.77.147–51, pp. 251–6.

[31] II.78.152–3, pp. 256–60.

[32] At the beginning of Bk I of the work he had pointed out that the information came to the evangelists by different routes: Matthew and John were eye-witnesses, Mark and Luke by way of the apostles. Cf. Ray, 'Augustine's *De Consensu Evangelistarum*', 559.

differences of expression are compared – and he examined more than half-a-dozen cases – it becomes clear that the meaning is exactly the same in each gospel. Thus the first problem can be easily overcome. It is clear that Matt is the fullest and most accurate text – indeed he takes it as the basic text[33] – and the others omit passages, or add only incidental details.

Things are not nearly so straightforward in the second problem. Augustine began by noting that at the end of the discourse there is agreement between Matt, Mark and Luke (he accepted 'drawing near' as equivalent to 'two days'). He then asserted that on three occasions John declares the feast to be near (presumably he was thinking of John 11:55, 12:1, and 13:1). Augustine inferred that this means that the feast was imminent – and so there is no dispute! So why the controversy? This is due to those who do not read the gospels with sufficient care, and so are betrayed by their carelessness into the error of thinking that there is a contradiction between the date of the anointing in Bethany between Matt-Mark (he notes that Luke omits the whole incident) and John. By repeating his assertions, he hoped to persuade the reader that all that really has to be explained is how these less careful readers are so easily trapped. The answer lies with one of the standard 'rules' of interpretation for the Scriptures: 'recapitulation'. This is a notion which Augustine took over from Tyconius, and which he expounded as one of the special tools one had to keep in mind when reading Scripture.[34] Essentially, it is something like a 'flashback' in modern film; a 'recapitulation' occurs when the narrative order in a biblical text is not in the same sequence as the historical events, when an event is narrated after other items of narrative, yet the event took place before the items already narrated.[35] Thus John's chronology stands as the basic time-sequence, and Matt-Mark do not depart from it. The anointing

[33] On taking Matt as the basic text, cf. my 'Tyconius' use of the canonical gospels'.

[34] The is Rule VI in Tyconius (*The Book of Rules of Tyconius*, 66–70) and is taken over from him and explained in *De Doctrina Christiana* II.36.52–4.

[35] The historical events occur in lineal sequence (1,2,3,4,5) and normally in the historical books we find the same sequence in narration. But when the narrative has this sequence: 1,3,4,2,5 then item 2 can be considered a 'recapitulation'.

took place six days before the Passover, but it features out of chronological sequence in Matt-Mark after they have told of what Jesus said two days before the Passover. Augustine did not suggest a reason for the 'recapitulation', and his proof that it is such is based on a most legalistic reading of Matt and Mark. He said that they do not imply that Bethany occurred after the Discourse – for then they would have said *post haec cum esset Bethaniae* – but only that there was an anointing at Bethany: *sed Mattheus quidem 'cum autem esset' inquit 'Iesus in Bethaniae', Marcus autem 'cum esset Bethaniae'*. The careless readers! They thought that because this was the next thing written down, this was the next thing that happened – they should have remembered that on any occasion when one event succeeds another, then the writer should state this explicitly by using *post*!

Augustine's whole solution has a hollow ring to it. By dividing the problem into two he was able to suggest that it could be tackled in little pieces. But it is a single unified problem – and by dividing to conquer he ignored the totality of the problem; while by addressing it severally he was able to divert his reader's attention from the fact that the whole is more than the sum of the parts.[36] Moreover, by suggesting that Luke simply omits certain events, and in other cases agrees with Matt and Mark, he ignored the whole problem of place. As for 'recapitulation' as an explanation, this can be seen as the mechanical use of a tool; and he failed to explain why two evangelists used it at the same point in their narratives. Furthermore, his close literal reading of their accounts was a rather tenuous one. All in all, what we have is a feat of rhetoric: he makes his assertions and judgements with authority rather than justification, and while he repeats his first principle several times (there can be no contradictions or errors in the gospels) these are little more than instances of begging the question.

[36] Modern exegetes often find themselves, by accident, in agreement with Augustine's approach for today the problem would be tackled in two parts: first, the synoptic problem of relating Matt, Mark and Luke; and second, the problem of relating the synoptics to John. But this agreement is only coincidental for Augustine did not have the modern distinction between Matt, Mark and Luke *as the synoptics*, and John. For him, the gospels were four parallel accounts each equally, though individually, and independently relating the same events.

Adomnán's approach

Whether or not this was Adomnán's judgement of Augustine's solution we shall never know, but clearly he believed that the true solution had not yet been found for he approached the whole problem from a new angle using a different, if equally mechanical, exegetical strategy.[37] The most striking differences in their methods is that Adomnán approached the question as a single whole. Since he had Augustine before him while he wrote, this approach to the problem must reflect a conscious decision on his part, and a recognition that the problems of locations and timings in the four gospels must all be consistent or the solution unsatisfactory. Therefore his solution deals with all the places mentioned in the time between Christ's arrival in the environs of Jerusalem (when all four gospels are in agreement) and the next occasion when all agree: the Last Supper. Adomnán also prepared the ground for his solution in another way by stating at the outset the basic geographical fact that the Mount of Olives and Bethany are close together – indeed the Mount is in the southern part of Bethany (*DLS* I.xxv.1) – and this proximity removed any difficulty that might be posed by saying how could Jesus be in Bethany and/or on the Mount of Olives and/or Jerusalem.[38] This crucial piece of geographical information Adomnán took from his principal source of such detail, Jerome's *Liber de Situ et Locorum* who wrote thus:

> Bethania uilla in secundo ab Aelia miliario in latere montis Oliueti, ubi saluator Lazarum suscitauit, cuius et monumentum ecclesia nunc ibidem extructa demonstrat.[39]

[37] The method is used twice in the *DLS*, here, and at I.xii.3.

[38] In *DLS* I.xxii it is pointed out that the Mount of Olives and Mount Zion (=Jerusalem) are close together separated by the Valley of Josaphat.

[39] I have used P. de Lagarde's edition of Jerome's *Liber de Situ et Locorum* (i.e. the Latin version of Eusebius' Περὶ τῶν τοπικῶν ὀνομάτων) published in *Onomastica Sacra* (Göttingen 1887, *ed. altera*) as printed facing the Greek in E. Klostermann's edition of Eusebius (*GCS* xi.i, Leipzig 1904), 59 (I refer to Jerome as Adomnán's source as Jerome added the detail about the church built there to what he found in Eusebius). On the use of this work in *DLS*, cf. my 'The library of Iona in the late-seventh century: the evidence from Adomnán's *De locis sanctis*'. This sentence of Jerome's contains several difficulties of its own; but we could roughly render it thus:

Location is not *really* a problem as all the places are close to one another, so travel between them is not a problem. The actual site of the Lord's sermon can be identified by the church built there. While Adomnán obviously agreed with this identification, he did not make that assertion the beginning of his argument: 'there is the spot we adjudge (*arbitramur*) the Lord's sermon to his disciples to have taken place' (*DLS* I.xxv.1). To have simply stated this as a fact would have begged the ensuing question as to where events took place. This hesitation, in contrast to Augustine who equiparated Luke with Matt and Mark, is in deference to Luke where the Apocalyptic Discourse seems to take place in Jerusalem. However, and again in contrast to Augustine, the actual problem that Adomnán is addressing is not explicitly stated. We must infer what he is about from the fact that 'diligent investigation' (*non neglegenter inquirendum*) of the gospels is required about Bethany and the Mount of Olives.

The technique that will resolve the problem involves noting the nature of the sermon,[40] time of occurrence, and who is involved (*DLS* I.xxv.2). While he does not mention place in this list, we can take this as implied as 'place' is the basic category in the book, and as such it is involved in the solution. This technique of *tempus*, *locus*, and *persona* has been mentioned in connection with Irish exegesis by many scholars,[41] and here we have, if not,

'Bethany is a town two miles from Jerusalem [*Aelia*] on the side of the Mount of Olives. This is where Jesus raised Lazarus [N.B. that Jerome here echoes John 12:1, which is also echoed by Adomnán in *DLS* I.xxix]; and there now a church has been built which points out his tomb.'

[40] Nature in the sense of its essence: what it actually contained.

[41] The scholar who most drew attention to this was Bischoff, 'Wendepunkte in der Geschichte der lateinischen Exegese im Frühmittelalter', 205 (= *Mittelalterliche Studien* i.217–18) who considered it one of the characteristics of Irish exegesis (but cf. Stancliffe, 'Early "Irish" biblical exegesis'). This is not the place to trace its history as methodological tool in the exegesis of texts, it suffices to say that it was a formal method used both in Irish circles (cf. Bieler's list of uses in his edition of *The Patrician Texts in the Book of Armagh*, 194) and elsewhere (Bischoff himself pointed to its use by Bede in his commentary on the Book of the Apocalypse (*PL* xciii.135); Bischoff, 'Wendepunkte in der Geschichte der lateinischen Exegese im Frühmittelalter', n. 57). It was used by writers both earlier (e.g. Sulpicius Severus and Isidore) and later than Adomnán in the studies of textual

perhaps, the earliest occurrence of the use of the method, certainly one of the most elaborate.[42] The method, which has its origins in grammatical theory,[43] can establish the uniqueness of each event (particular persons in a specific place at a given time). Since each human event has this unique threefold signature, then once several such signatures are known the events can be inter-related; and given that all three elements are needed to isolate one event from another, where one source only supplies one or two elements we can legitimately combine sources to provide a full description. For example, if one source mentions time and place, but not persons, then the omission can be made good from the other source dealing with the same event. The method is clearly ideally suited – if the evidence is supplied in the texts – to the harmonisation of the gospels; and it coheres perfectly with Adomnán's own axioms. First, since each event is uniquely identified there can never be clash or contradiction between events: the logic of the method (the Law of Contradiction) insures that two distinct human events cannot be in the same place at the same time, nor the same event in two places or at two times; and second, the Scriptures cannot contain errors of historical fact: without this assumption (the Principle of Inspiration) they could not be treated as the word of God. Neither principle was doubted by Christians in the period. Adomnán's confidence in his method can be seen in his statement that 'if we choose to open the three evangelists, Matthew, Mark, and Luke, that it will become manifestly clear to us that they speak together in harmony' (*DLS* I.xxv.3–4).

---

evidence (e.g. Gratian, *Decretum*, D. XXIX c.1: *Ex tempore et loco et persona et causa regulae canonum intelligantur*; and cf. also D. XX *dictum ante* c.1: cf. McIntyre, 'Optional priestly celibacy', 116, for pointers as to its use in early canonical jurisprudence).

[42] Cf. Bullough, 'Columba, Adomnán and the achievement of Iona'; and note that Bischoff drew attention to the use of the schema of *tempus*, *locus*, and *persona* by Adomnán both here, and in *DLS* I.xii.3 ('Wendepunkte in der Geschichte der lateinischen Exegese', n. 56).

[43] It is noted in relation to the nature of speech (*De elocutione*) by Isidore in the *Etymologiae* (II.xvi.1)which was present on Iona that *res*, *locus*, *tempus*, and *persona* affect how a message is to be delivered; while Sulpicius has a speaker say that the advice of the grammarians to note the place, time, and person may assist in unravelling problems (*Dialogi* II.vii).

Adomnán's first concern was to establish the nature of the event (the speech we call the Apocalyptic Discourse). Here, as with Augustine, the basic text is Matt in that he gives both the beginning (quoted at I.xxv.4) and end of the discourse (quoted at I.xxv.6). Matthew's text is the fullest (here Adomnán quoted Augustine: *Matheus prolixo sermone*), and it is to be taken as the account of what was actually said. The beginning of the sermon is the introduction by Matt, *Sedente autem eo super montem Olitueti* ..., and the apostles' question, *Dic nobis quando* ... (Matt 24:3). The actual speech ended with the words of Christ: *Scitis quia post biduum pascha fiet et filius hominem tradetur ut crucifigatur* (Matt 26:2).[44] The question of place is also given by Matt: the Mount of Olives – this is beyond doubt as it is explicitly given there (I.xxv.4). Luke, presumably, has to be fitted to this. Since Matt positively states 'the Mount of Olives', we can conclude, on Adomnán's principles, that Luke simply failed to note the change in location, and this omission is what gives rise to the impression that the speech took place in Jerusalem. This is a case of one evangelist (Matt) supplying an omitted element in another (Luke), and a similar combination of sources supplies the details about the persons involved. In this case Matt simply says 'disciples' and is silent about specific names, 'but Mark is not silent, and writes the names down' (I.xxv.5). Here Mark supplies details omitted by Matt and informs us that apart from Jesus there were Peter, James, John, and Andrew (Adomnán quoted the verse (Mark 13:3) in full). Already there is a sense that the limitations of each are being balanced out to provide a complete picture.

[44] I have suggested textual emendations within this chapter: (1) see 'The exegetical purpose of Adomnán's *De Locis Sanctis*', 47, where I give reasons for reading the text of I.xxv.3–4 thus: [3] ... *nobis manifeste clarebunt qui de sermonis qualitate concinnentes loquntur.* [4] *De loco ipsius* ... (which is the reading adopted here); (2) in 'Adomnán's *De locis sanctis*: a textual emendation and an additional source identification', I show that in I.xxv.5 the *Vetus Latina* reading of Mark 13:6 should be retained (with MSS PZ) as this is the form in Adomnán's source, Augustine, and read *quia ego sum Christus*; (3) at the end of I.xxv.6 the phrase *et cetera* after the quotation of Matt 26:2 should be omitted (with MS B); since, as should be clear from the above, Adomnán thought of this verse as the end of a section, and the '*et cetera*' implies reading on into the account of the plots against Jesus (Matt 26:3 and following).

The situation is more complicated when it comes to establishing the time of the event. By defining the length of the speech as running from Matt 24:3 to 26:2 (the obvious textual unit in Matt), Matthew also supplies the time: it took place – according to the words of Christ himself at the end of his discourse (26:2: '*Scitis* ...) – two days before the Passover (I.xxv.6). Since these are the Lord's words (Matt 26:2),[45] and there he gives the time, that is when it took place.[46]

Thus Adomnán established a complete description of an event in space and time: his sense of the completeness of what he had done can be seen in I.xxv.7: 'so it is now clearly shown that ...' (*Aperte ergo ostenditur* ...), and he summarised his position. So the complete signature of the event is this:

PLACE: Mount of Olives – the direct evidence is Matt which fills out the omission in Luke.

PERSONS: Christ, Peter, James, John, Andrew – the direct evidence is Mark which fills out the omissions in Matt and Luke.

NATURE OF EVENT: The speech as found in Matt 24:3–26:2 – the direct evidence is Matt which fills out the omissions in Mark and Luke.

TIME: Two days before the Passover – the direct evidence is Matt which fills out the omission in Luke, and against which, presumably, we read other evidence: John.

There can now be no confusion about what took place on that day – a unique event had been adequately defined – and in relation to such a fact we can legitimately fit all other evidence. Adomnán may not have solved all the problems, as Augustine thought he had, but he had established a basic fact about the last days before the crucifixion.

[45] Augustine's argument hints at the speech ending before the statement at 26:2; and he further strengthened his case by noting that in Mark and Luke the statement about time ('two days' in Mark, 'near' in Luke) are not put into the Lord's mouth, but only the words of these writers (II.lxxviii.152, p. 256).

[46] Using the same argument of Augustine, that in two gospels the time is given not by Jesus but by the evangelist 'in his own person', the time given by John in John can be dismissed in favour of the better authority of the words of Christ himself in Matt.

There are two possible weaknesses in Adomnán's argument. He pressed for further precision of what 'two days before the Passover' means and defined this as 'two days before the first day of unleavened bread, that is the Passover' (this is based on Mark 14:1: *erat autem pascha et azima*, while Matt 26:2 – which he quoted – simply has *pascha*) putting the event on the 'fourth feria' (i.e. Wednesday). But this dating ignores Matt 26:17 (*prima autem azymorum accesserunt* – but which is echoed in I.xxv.7) and Mark 14:12 (*et primo die azymorum quando pascha immolabunt*) which state that this is the day of the Last Supper (which if the crucifixion took place the day before the Sabbath – Friday[47] – then the day of the Supper is one day before that – Thursday. But if the discourse took place two days earlier (i.e. 'the day before yesterday'), then it took place on Tuesday (*feria tertia*). How can such a weakness be explained from someone as sensitive to dating matters as Adomnán? I do not believe that it is a slip, but based on a particular reading of Matt 26:2 and Mark 14:12 – against which all the other evidence is fitted. The day of the Passover is the day that the paschal lamb is sacrificially slain (Matt 14:12). Christ is the paschal lamb of the Christians (1 Cor 5:7: *pascha nostra immolatus est Christus*) and the immolation takes place at the crucifixion. Therefore, the moment of the paschal immolation and that of the crucifixion must coincide. In this reasoning Adomnán is at one with John which places the death of Jesus on the 'Day of Preparation': at the very moment 'the true lamb' was being killed on the Cross, so the ante-types of him, actual lambs, were being slaughtered in the temple precincts in Jerusalem.[48] In this case he read Matt 26:2 in the sense that the focus of the sentence is the crucifixion: after two days will be the Passover and, the significance of this is, Christ's crucifixion – the mention of the betrayal points simply to an event which must precede it. Thus the emphasis on 'the fourth feria' may point towards an aspect of Adomnán's christology.[49]

[47] The evidence for this, available to Adomnán, is set out above.

[48] Cf. R. E. Brown, *The Gospel According to John* (London 1971) ii.883.

[49] See his use of Cassiodorus in III.v.9 on Jesus as 'the anointed one,' cf. my 'The Latin version of the scriptures in use on Iona', 23–5.

The other possible weakness of Adomnán's position is that, while he had to be conscious of the whole problem or he would not have written this chapter, he completely avoids the difficulties posed by John. In his defence he might argue that he had contributed to the solution by getting one date absolutely fixed, and that it is against this that John be read. This is, moreover, all that he explicitly claimed to attempt for he mentioned only Matt, Mark, and Luke by name. In this case, there is no reason why the Augustinian solution of a 'recapitulation' cannot be used to explain the date of the anointing at Bethany: it took place six days before the crucifixion, but is recorded out of chronological sequence in Matt and Mark. As such, when one reads *DLS* I.xxv (for the problems relating to Matt, Mark, and Luke) and *De Consensu Euangelistarum* II.lxxviii (problems relating to the four) one has a solution to all the problems. And, when these two works are read in conjunction, upon their principles, all the problems mentioned above can be eliminated in some way. Furthermore, while a reading of Augustine *De Consensu* II.lxxvii and lxxviii is unsatisfactory, and *DLS* on its own is incomplete, when *DLS* is read instead of II.lxxvii, and with II.lxxvii, the difficulties of when and where and of sequence can all find acceptable solutions. Neither Augustine nor Adomnán, nor both combined, is a wholly satisfactory solution; but no full explanation, on their terms, is possible.

Conclusion

This chapter has been an attempt to set out a piece of Hiberno-Latin exegesis and understand it within its own world. As such it should help us to appreciate the judgement of Adomnán's contemporaries that he was 'most learned in the science of the Scriptures' and to see his exegetical presuppositions and methods. He emerges as a most careful and accurate scholar, who, though fully part of the Latin tradition, can also be seen to stand apart from many in that tradition. By his time, the dominant characteristic of exegesis was the assemblage, excerption, and repetition of authorities. We see this in expert exegetes from before his time, like Isidore who acted as a funnel in the repetitive transmission of authorities. Adomnán's contemporaries, such as Julian of Toledo, created mechanical solutions to complex problems by excerpting and stringing together snippets of the Fathers, and those after him, for example Bede, made it a virtue that his authorities be visibly noted[50] and solved similar problems with an open reliance upon, and repetition of, Augustine's *De Consensu Euangelistarum*.[51] Adomnán conceals his authorities, neither slavishly following them, mistakes and all, nor challenging them. Rather, he provides materials that can be used in conjunction with the works of the illustrious authorities in the common work of exegesis. Perhaps the highest tribute we can pay Adomnán is to note that his work can stand alongside Augustine's, equalling it in exegetical skill and augmenting it in content.

In memoriam Dionysii Meehan, Benedicti discipuli et Adamnani interpretis, opusculum dedico[52]

[50] Cf. E. F. Sutcliffe, 'Quotations in the Venerable Bede's commentary on S. Mark', *Biblica* 7 (1926) 428–39.

[51] Cf. Ray, 'Augustine's *De Consensu Evangelistarum*', and also his 'What do we known about Bede's commentaries?', *Recherches de Théologie Ancienne et Médiévale* 49 (1982) 5–20 at 11.

[52] Denis Meehan died on 6 August 1994 in Valyermo Abbey, California. I wish to express my thanks to Dr Gervase Corcoran OSA (The Milltown Institute) for his help. The usual disclaimer applies.

7

The wisdom of the scribe and the fear of the Lord in the *Life of Columba*

Jennifer O'Reilly

THE *Life of Columba* contains vivid images of the saint as scribe. Some features of this composite portrait are depicted with circumstantial details so convincing that they have been regarded as true to life. However, the same stories which have provided modern historians with glimpses of contemporary book production and have set archaeologists discussing the likely form and location on Iona of Columba's writing-hut, disconcertingly show that Columba's pen, his inkhorn, the vellum on which he wrote, generated marvels and prophecies, and that from his writing-hut he commanded both demons and angels.[1] Pages written by the saint's own hand survived long immersions in water and his books continued to effect miracles and to be revered by his community as sacred objects and salvific relics in the lifetime of his biographer Adomnán, the ninth abbot of Iona (679–704). Such wonders are not presented as an editorial comment on historical episodes but are conveyed through the very narrative; the scribal equipment and activities which Adomnán describes are charged with an other-worldly significance whose precise meaning, it seems, is never spelled out.

A second point of difficulty in the interpretation of this material for the modern reader is that, although Adomnán repeatedly

[1] Sharpe, *Adomnán*, 284–8, nn. 125, 127; O'Neill, 'Columba the scribe'. See Richter, 'The personnel of learning in early medieval Ireland' for Irish uses of terms *scriba*, *sapiens*.

depicts Columba as a scribe, he does not explicitly portray him as a scholar or name a single text he authored or any non-biblical work he read. This seems an enigmatic image of the founding-father of Iona, particularly in view of Adomnán's own impressive learning and the range of texts which modern scholarship suggests must have been available to him in the island monastery. It also appears to contradict other testimony, including that of the early praise poem, *Amra Choluimb Chille*, that Columba was a pillar of learning, a great teacher and interpreter of the Law, a scriptural exegete and a reader of Basil and Cassian, who had also studied computistics and Greek grammar.[2] Is Adomnán's image of Columba to be explained as the evocation of some different kind of hagiographic stereotype? The radical renunciation of earthly property and preoccupations by the eremitical desert fathers, for example, had certainly involved an ambivalent attitude towards the written word, the pursuit of learning and even the possession of books, which was personified in the image of the unlearned holy man. Athanasius described St Antony as one in whom memory of the Scriptures took the place of books: 'Neither from writings nor from pagan wisdom nor for some craft was Antony acclaimed but from religion alone.'[3] If, however, Adomnán's silence on Columba's achievements as a scholar is simply seen as part of an attempt to show the saint continuing the traditions of the desert at the Ocean's edge, then the question of why Adomnán shows Columba producing books in a coenobitic monastery only becomes more rather than less puzzling.

The *Life of St Martin* had formed a very early link between the desert tradition and monasticism in the north. His biographer, Sulpicius Severus, says that Martin could expound the Scriptures with words of wisdom but was a man untrained in letters. Sulpicius had been concerned to show that St Martin, though living in a monastery in Gaul and having pastoral responsibilities, had not only equalled but excelled the spiritual merits of the

[2] Clancy and Márkus, *Iona. The Earliest Poetry*, 104–15.

[3] *Vita Antonii*, 93, *PG* 26.974: *Nequaquam enim scriptis suis, non gentili sapientia, non aliqua arte*. Adapted in Evagrius of Antioch's version, *quem nec librorum disseminatorium oratio luculenta, nec mundane sapientiae disputatio*. For this tradition of unlearned wisdom, see Burton-Christie, *The Word in the Desert*, 54–62; Cameron, *Christianity and the Rhetoric of Empire*, 112–13.

desert anchorites and that the stark austerities of monastic life at Tours recalled the heroic desert tradition and its biblical models. It is in this ascetic context that Sulpicius says, approvingly, of Martin's monastery, 'No art was practiced there, except that of transcribers, and even this was consigned to the brethren of younger years, while the elders spent their time in prayer.'[4] The implication is that the copying of certain texts was a practical necessity for the monastic community, but not one which could be allowed to distract those advanced in the spiritual life. Adomnán, on the contrary, shows that Columba transcribed texts while he was abbot and until the day he died, and that he commended his successor to continue the tradition of writing. The influence of the *Life of Antony* and the *Life of St Martin* on the *Life of Columba* has long been recognised but, clearly, cannot account for Adomnán's particular use of the scribal image. Before simply assuming the influence of some further hagiographic source to explain this apparently discrepant feature, it may be useful to recall what theological and other concerns informed the earlier image of the unlearned holy man and to ask whether Adomnán's overall portrait of Columba is compatible with these concerns.

Learned writers in Late Antiquity used the image of the unlearned holy man, together with accounts of miraculous manifestations or signs of his wisdom, as a sophisticated rhetorical device in distinguishing between the nature of a transcendent Christian knowledge, derived from divine revelation, and the limitations of knowledge derived from human learning and demonstrated through reason and eloquence alone. The hagiographic image did not, therefore, embody a general argument for rejecting human learning, but provided a model for understanding the inspired word of God. In the Preface to *De Doctrina Christiana* St Augustine acknowledged that, in exceptional cases, learning was directly given by God and he specifically cited the example of the holy and perfect Egyptian monk Antony who, though lacking any knowledge of the alphabet, is reported to have memorised the divine Scriptures by listening to them being read, and to have understood them by thoughtful meditation. But Augustine warned against the gross presumption that such

[4] *Vita Martinii*, 10; translation from *NPNF* 2nd series, vol. XI, 9. See also Rousseau, *Ascetics, Authority and the Church*, 138, 147.

miraculous enlightenment might be granted to oneself, that one could know the alphabet without learning it. For most people, he argued, understanding the divine word expressed in Scripture involved learning its language, just as children learn their native language and other tongues by listening and by learning from a human teacher. As the teacher who teaches the actual alphabet has the intention of enabling others to read too, so Augustine's highly influential work was intended as a guide to learning how to read the language of Scripture.[5] *De Doctrina Christiana* is not a handbook of the rhetorical rules he had learned and taught in pagan schools, and neither does it simply give examples of his own scriptural interpretation; rather, it provides rules on discovering what we need to learn, and the process of presenting what we have learnt both about things and about signs in Scripture, about its literal text and its spiritual meaning for an initiated Christian audience.[6] The rules encompass an encyclopaedic range of human learning.

Thomas O'Loughlin has shown that Adomnán's understanding of Augustine's interpretative rules is well demonstrated in his particular use of oral and non-biblical written sources in *De Locis Sanctis* to help elucidate problematic passages in the literal text of Scripture.[7] At first sight, this thought-world may seem remote from the collection of diverse 'prophetic revelations ... divine miracles ... appearances of angels and certain manifestations of heavenly brightness' which constitute the three books of the *Vita Columbae*. As *De Locis Sanctis* demonstrates, however, biblical learning could be expressed in genres other than scriptural commentaries. It has been suggested elsewhere that in the *Vita Columbae* Adomnán is also concerned with the exegesis of Scripture, but with the interpretation of its underlying meaning rather than the preliminary clarification of its literal text. Moreover, his two works are complementary in other ways. As *De Locis Sanctis* ostensibly describes a literal pilgrimage to the Holy Land and the earthly Jerusalem, so in the *Vita Columbae*, features

[5] *De Doctrina Christiana*, pp. 5, 9. For discussion and recent bibliography, see Markus, *Signs and Meanings. World and Text in Ancient Christianity*, 71–124.

[6] *De Doctrina Christiana*, I.1.4.

[7] O'Loughlin, 'The exegetical purpose of Adomnán's *De Locis Sanctis*', 37–53 and above, pp. 139f.

of the monastic interior pilgrimage towards the heavenly Jerusalem are mirrored in a number of ways, such as the text's reminiscences of the Israelites' desert Exodus to the Holy Land,[8] and brief allusions to the island monastery of Iona in terms of the earthly paradise and of Jerusalem.[9]

Scriptural learning is also evident in Adomnán's use of the image of the scribe to expound the nature and stages of the monastic life. The objective of the present discussion is not primarily to pinpoint specific sources but to attempt to read the image and resolve some of its apparent paradoxes in the light of Iona's inheritance of patristic and monastic traditions of reading Scripture.[10] It will be asked what associations Adomnán's account of Columba's scribal activity might have held for a contemporary insular monastic audience familiar with the techniques of the spiritual interpretation of Scripture through constant practical experience of *lectio divina*, the liturgy and the monastic office, and whether these associations can help to identify broader themes in the book for the modern reader. This is not, of course, to claim that biblical, patristic and liturgical influences are the only ones at work, but to suggest that they underlie rather more than the book's known hagiographic borrowings and *topoi*.

Knowledge and wisdom

Underlying Adomnán's account of Columba's sanctity is a precept which had been widely disseminated through the biblical commentaries of Origen, their Latin translations by Jerome and Rufinus and the whole tradition of the spiritual interpretation of scripture which they influenced. In particular, the precept had been articulated for early western monasticism by John Cassian. In this exegetical tradition, the process of understanding the divine word expressed through the inspired text of Scripture could be

[8] *VC* i.1, 37; ii.2, 10, 42; iii.23.

[9] *VC* ii.28, iii.23. O'Reilly, 'Reading the Scriptures in the Life of Columba', 80–106. The comparison of literal and inner pilgrimage was a patristic *topos*.

[10] For discussion of source materials and models see Brüning, 'Adomnans *Vita Columbae* und ihre Ableitungen'; Picard, 'Structural patterns in early Hiberno-Latin hagiography', 67–82; Herbert, *Iona, Kells and Derry*, 134–50; Sharpe, *Adomnán*, 56–65.

served by human learning (and in most cases required lifelong study); the objectives of such scriptural learning and of ancillary studies, however, were not intellectual but practical. Commentators repeatedly stressed the impossibility of understanding the divine word without obeying it. The study of Scripture therefore required not only human learning but the moral and spiritual conversion of the reader. The carnal passions were to be driven out so that the 'eyes of the heart' might begin to gaze on the mysteries (*sacramenta*) of Scripture, as though a veil had been removed. Following his well-known demonstration in *Conlationes* xiv.8 of the multiple ways in which the literal text of Scripture may be spiritually interpreted, Cassian had stressed that to gaze with the pure eye of the soul on such profound and hidden mysteries 'can be gained by no learning of man's, nor condition of this world, only by purity of soul, by means of the illumination of the Holy Spirit'.[11]

In the *Vita Columbae* Adomnán is concerned to show that the task of discerning Scripture's underlying spiritual meaning for the present reader or listener is a quest not for knowledge but for divine wisdom, a process dependant on the inspiration of the Holy Spirit and inseparably bound up with purity of heart and holiness of life. Adomnán, like Cassian, recognises that instruction and formation in this way of salvation is most effectively given through the practical example of elders (*seniores*) in the monastic life and especially through one particular example of perfection.[12]

Accordingly, it is because of Columba's spiritual wisdom (*sapientia*), not because of his superior knowledge or *scientia*, that he is presented as one pre-eminently fitted for the abbatial task of expounding the word of God to his community. But the lessons he has to teach do not arise from a biographical account of an inner conversion or stages on an arduous journey in the spiritual life. We are simply told in hallowed terms that, since boyhood, he 'had devoted himself to training in the Christian life, and to the study of wisdom; with God's help, he had kept his body chaste and his mind pure and shown himself, though placed on earth, fit for the life of heaven'.[13] There are no details of the

[11] *Conlationes* xiv.9; translation *NPNF*, 2nd series, XI, 439.
[12] *Conlationes* iv.20; translation *NPNF*, 2nd series, XI, 338.
[13] *VC* second preface; Sharpe, *Adomnán*, 105, n. 18.

syllabus of studies he pursued as a young deacon while studying the wisdom of sacred scripture (*sapientiam sacrae scripturae*) with the holy bishop Finnbar (Uinniau) in Ireland[14] or which he later taught his own monks. His learning is not questioned, but his role in exemplifying and teaching wisdom is shown by other means.

The idea of both the necessity and the limitations of books, even books of the Bible, often occurs in patristic and monastic discussion of learning spiritual wisdom. In a widely-known letter, *Epistula* 53, Jerome called Paulinus of Nola from his secular learning to the spiritual understanding of the books of Scripture, urging him 'to live among these books, to meditate upon them, to know nothing else, to seek nothing else. Does not such a life seem to you a foretaste of heaven here on earth?' Jerome, who had dedicated his own formidable learning and linguistic skills to the service of studying Scripture, had cautioned another correspondent, however, that although we come to recognise Christ, the light of believers, through the divine Scriptures, 'even if we were to know here everything that is written, we should know only partially and see darkly (cf. 1 Cor 13) ... And when we merit to be with Christ and when we are similar to the angels, all knowledge from books will cease'.[15]

Columba, who already merited while still in this life to speak with angels, is shown at heightened moments of illumination without books. Even though what was dark and difficult in the Scriptures might be divinely revealed to him on such occasions,[16] his experience is not conveyed to the reader in the form of scholarly scriptural commentary. The only example of Columba's direct exegesis – on the word 'Sabbath' – is conveyed by reported speech.[17] With considerable skill Adomnán resolves the difficulty of at once portraying Columba's exemplification of the wisdom which transcends books and his conduct of the abbatial task of teaching the word of God, which of necessity involved the written word. First, Adomnán often evokes and sometimes quotes

[14] *VC* ii.1.
[15] Jerome, *Ep*. liii.10, *Ep*. xxx.8: *Saint Jérôme Lettres*, iii.23; ii.34; translations *NPNF* 2nd series VI, 96–102.
[16] *VC* iii.18.
[17] *VC* iii.23.

scriptural texts whose underlying spiritual meaning according to exegesis is concealed in his very narrative. Certain episodes particularly invite a ruminative reading and reveal Columba expounding the Scriptures through his own life, death and post-humous miracles. Secondly, through using the image of the scribe and some of its particular associations in patristic and monastic traditions, Adomnán is able to show Columba as a teacher and a maker of books while avoiding any suggestion that Columba's wisdom is simply a superior grade of human learning.

The image of Columba as scribe differs in important respects from early medieval representations of the inspired biblical or saintly author. The Anglo-Saxon Whitby *Life of Gregory, ca* between 704 and 714, quotes from Gregory the Great's works of exegesis and gives the earliest version of the legend that the Holy Spirit in the form of a dove rested upon him while he was composing his *Homilies* on *Ezekiel*.[18] The legend influenced a number of early medieval depictions of Gregory writing or dictating to a scribe. Adomnán fully exploits exegesis on the dove to portray Columba as the vessel of the Holy Spirit but does not combine this with the scribal image to focus on the divine inspiration of a work of the saint's own authorship. The portrait of Columba as scribe also differs from the famous picture of Ezra in his well-appointed Late Antique study, which forms the frontispiece in the *Codex Amiatinus*, produced at Wearmouth-Jarrow before 716. The haloed figure of the Old Testament scribe, derived from an early tradition of Evangelist author portraits, is shown copying out the Hebrew Scriptures while seated in front of a bookcase containing all the books of the Latin Bible. The iconography is supplemented in the manuscript's opening quire by a series of inscribed diagrams showing patristic classifications of the books of Scripture and extracts from Jerome's *Epistula* 53 on their spiritual interpretation.[19] Bede's exegesis on Ezra stresses his sanctity, his exemplification of the wisdom of the scribe described in the Wisdom literature of the Old Testament, and the way in which he presents a figure of Christ himself. But he also describes the critical, editorial aspect of Ezra's work of transcribing

[18] *Vita Gregorii*, 24–7; *The Earliest Life of Gregory the Great*, 122, 120.

[19] All illustrations reproduced in Bruce-Mitford, 'The art of the Codex Amiatinus', pl. C, II, IX–XII.

Hebrew Scripture and his development of script, as part of the divinely inspired historical process of transmitting the divine word to all peoples.[20] For Bede and his contemporaries the portrait of the scribe Ezra in the *Codex Amiatinus* must have offered some comment on the scholarly and scribal contributions which Abbot Ceolfrith and his scriptorium made to the enterprise by producing this monumental Vulgate pandect and its two sister manuscripts. Notwithstanding the evidence of much earlier development of scripts and of critical approaches to the scriptural text in the Irish schools, however, and of Adomnán's own standing as a biblical scholar, there is no celebration of scholarly or calligraphic achievements in his pen portrait of the founding father of Iona as a scribe. What, then, does he show was the nature and purpose of Columba's scribal work and why were books in his handwriting so important?

Columba's books

Adomnán describes the saint copying out or supervising the copying out of texts. The only texts he specifies are psalters and a book of hymns for the week.[21] It is not known what form the *ymnorum liber septimaniorum* might have taken, but Jane Stevenson has argued that a cursus of hymns seems already to have been in use in sixth-century Ireland, probably modelled on the hymnody of southern Gaul, and in this connection she emphasises the importance of canticles and the influence of the monastic traditions of Lérins and of Cassian.[22] St Paul's recommendation of threefold praise in the early Church briefly hints at the range of spiritual functions it could serve: 'Let the word of Christ dwell in you abundantly: in all wisdom, teaching and

[20] Bede, *In Ezram et Neemian*, *CCSL* 119A, 307–10.

[21] *VC* i.23, ii.9, iii.23.

[22] Stevenson, 'Irish hymns, Venantius Fortunatus and Poitiers'. Jerome's second Psalm Preface, however, translates the original Hebrew title of the *Psalterium* as *volumen hymnorum*. Isidore of Seville noted that in the Hebrew title, *Sepher Thelim, quod interpretatur volumen hymnorum,* the original metrical nature of the psalms is made evident: *Biblia Sacra Iuxta Vulgatam Versionem* I, 768; Isidore, *Etymologiae* VI.15: *San Isidoro de Seville. Etimologias* I, 570. For early Irish use of Jerome's prefaces, see McNamara, 'Psalter text and psalter study in the early Irish church', 221, 254.

admonishing one another in psalms, hymns and spiritual canticles, singing in grace in your hearts to God' (Col 3:16; cf. Eph 5:19).

Even unglossed copies of the Psalm text could carry allusions to interpretative traditions through prefaces, and through the headings and numbering of the psalms which were regarded as part of the text. The earliest and one of the most widely attested of the various series of Latin *tituli psalmorum* is the 'St Columba series', so named by Pierre Salmon because its first extant appearance is in the *Cathach* (Dublin, Royal Irish Academy MS 12 R 33), a psalter of sixth- or early seventh-century date, which was traditionally ascribed to the hand of St Columba. The *tituli* in the rubrics of the *Cathach* provide a spiritual interpretation of each psalm's meaning and preserve a very early and Christological tradition of patristic psalm exegesis.[23] While Adomnán does not say which particular canticles, prefaces, headings and collects, if any, were contained in Columba's psalters, it is clear that the term *psalterium* could designate very much more than a copy of a book from the Old Testament.

In the long tradition stemming from the exegesis of Origen and the practice of the desert fathers, the Psalter was seen to embrace the whole of divinely inspired Scripture; spiritually interpreted, the words of the psalmist can not only apply to Christ but offer the words of Christ to his Church and to the individual soul in all the variety of its needs, and also articulate the soul's own prayer and compunction. Athanasius' pastoral letter to Marcellinus summarises this interpretative tradition, emphasising the uniqueness of the Psalms which contain the pronouncements of the patriarchs, prophets and evangelists: other books of Scripture offer past models of behaviour for emulation, but the listener or reader recognises in the Psalms his own words, 'And the one who hears is deeply moved, as though he himself were speaking, and is affected by the words of the songs, as if they were his own songs':

[23] McNamara, 'Psalter text and psalter study', 266–8, notes that the *Cathach*'s revision of the Gallicanum against the Irish family of Hebraicum texts 'indicates the existence of a critical textual approach to the Psalter text in Irish schools' already in the sixth century or the early seventh century at the latest. For psalm headings 'of St Columba', see Salmon, *Les 'Tituli Psalmorum' des manuscrits latins*, 45–74.

> He who chants (the Psalms) will be especially confident in speaking what is written as if it is his own and about him. For the Psalms comprehend the one who observes the commandment as well as the one who transgresses, and the action of each ... these words become like a mirror to the person singing them, so that he might perceive himself and the emotions of his soul ... he who hears the one reading receives the song that is recited as being about him and either, when he is convicted by his conscience, being pierced, he will repent, or hearing of the hope that resides in God, and of the succour available to believers – how this kind of grace exists for him – he exults and begins to give thanks to God.[24]

Praying the psalms was therefore intimately bound up with the inner journey of the spiritual life, with acquiring self-knowledge and trying to discern the divine will. Contemporary concerns and situations called to mind particular psalm texts, as is witnessed in insular hagiography, for example in *VC* i.30, 37 and iii.23. Modern scholarly interest in the Antiochene elements in Hiberno-Latin psalm commentary has sometimes tended to overshadow the continuing influence of this tradition for seventh-century insular monastic culture, which was mediated partly through Augustine's *Ennarationes in psalmos* and Cassiodorus' *Expositio Psalmorum*, but particularly through the work of Cassian. He details the arrangement of the nocturnal and daily psalms of the office in the *Institutiones* ii–iii, but in the *Conlationes* is concerned with the constant, interior, prayerful appropriation of the Psalms by the individual monk. In *Conlationes* x, Abba Isaac describes how the truly pure and humble 'will take in to himself all the thoughts of the Psalms and will begin to sing them in such a way that he will utter them with the deepest emotion of the heart not as if they were the composition of the Psalmist, but rather as if they were his own utterances'; he will recognise that the words of the Psalms 'are fulfilled and carried out daily in his own case'.

[24] *Ep. ad Marcellinum*, *PG* 28.11–46; translation from Gregg, *Athanasius: The Life of Antony and the Letter to Marcellinus*, 109–11; cf. Rondeau, 'L'épître à Marcellinus sur les psaumes'. For Cassian on the importance of psalmody to mystical prayer, see translation and discussion of *Conlationes* x.11 in Bouyer, *A History of Spirituality*, I, 507–8. On the spiritual interpretation of the psalms, see Torjesen, 'Origen's interpretation of the psalms'; Rondeau, *Les commentaires patristiques du psautier*; Ward, *Bede and the Psalter*.

Meditated upon in this way, the Psalms are not simply committed to memory but become implanted within the individual's very being and their meaning is revealed not by theoretical exposition but by daily practical experience. Like Athanasius, Cassian presents the Psalms as a mirror in which the soul can see and affectively understand itself and learn to enter into a more perfect recollection of God.

What is the significance of Columba copying out the Psalms? A primary association of Columba's scribal work is with the ceaseless offering of prayer and praise from the psalms and canticles constituting the monastic hours or office, in which the monastic life most especially aspires to the heavenly life of the angels (cf. Ps 118:62, 164; Ps 137:1). This is not to say that his writing is presented only as the task of producing service books for the liturgy and the office, which established members of the community are likely to have sung from memory. Copying out the Psalter could itself be regarded as singing the Lord's praises and as part of the meditative process of memorising and internalising the divine word through constantly hearing, reading and chanting Scripture. The method of prayerful meditation described by Cassian, whereby those praying the Psalms 'become like their authors and anticipate their meaning rather than follow it', would find concrete expression in the practice of writing out the Psalms. Columba's writing is categorised in Adomnán's Second Preface, together with prayer, reading, work, unwearying fasts and vigils, as one of the spiritual disciplines of the monastic life which, together with the office, occupied him by day and night, even the night of his death. Columba is distinguished from the various hagiographic models of sanctity he recalls – St Antony, St Martin and St Benedict – by his particular identification with *writing* as a holy task.

Adomnán's accounts of the many books written by Columba which later survived immersion in water, are not presented as haphazard wonder tales but as part of his demonstration of the saint's closeness to God and consequent power over 'contrary elements', even beyond death. The stories are localised in Ireland, but the details of perishable vellum manuscripts and leather satchels also transmute elements of a patristic store of images about books and their containers. The contrast of the transitory medium of manuscripts, the skin of dead animals (*membranas animalium mortuorum*), and the enduring nature of their contents, for example, had provided Jerome with a favourite conceit. The word *scrinium*, meaning a chest or coffer for storing letters and books, was also used by early Christian writers to denote a treasure chest or shrine enclosing secret and precious things, including books, and could refer to sacred books themselves, which contained the treasury of the Scriptures.[25] The image was to be embodied in the custom of covering or enshrining sacred books in precious metalwork. Adomnán does not describe a literal enshrinement of books and even displaces the image. A book of hymns, written in the hand of Saint Columba and salvaged from a river after many weeks, was unharmed by the water which had rotted its skin satchel; in contrast, the book within the satchel was of extraordinary whiteness and clarity, as clean and dry as if it had remained in a *scrinium*.[26]

Similarly, a page described simply as 'written by the holy fingers of St Columba', was recovered from a bag of books after being submerged in the River Boyne for three weeks; though protected only by a skin satchel, it emerged as dry and undamaged as though it had been kept *in scriniolo*, whereas the pages of other unidentified books in the satchel had rotted. The telling of the story leaves the inescapable conclusion that what distinguished this page from those which perished was not the medium on which it was written, the text it contained, or its calligraphy, but the holiness of the copyist. Columba's copying out of texts does not simply function as a metaphor of his exemplary interpretation of their life-giving meaning. Adomnán insists that the story of the salvaged book in *VC* ii.9 is based on the testimony of trustworthy eye-witnesses and he records his own presence at the ending of a drought on Iona, miraculously effected through the ceremonial carrying of books in Columba's handwriting (*libris stilo ipsius discriptis*) around the ploughland and reading from them at a spot where Columba had spoken with angels.[27] The books were clearly regarded as powerful relics of the saint and signs of his continuing presence with the community and were placed on the altar with psalms and fasting and invocation of his name in order

[25] *Saint Jerome sur Jonas*, *SC*, 4–3. 55 n. 3; Carruthers, *The Book of Memory*, 39–41 for *scrinium*.

[26] *VC* ii.9.

[27] *VC* ii.44.

to secure a favourable wind for the shipping of building materials to the island monastery. Adomnán's accounts of these posthumous miracles reveal a spiritual reality perceived to be sacramentally present in the earthly books produced by Columba's holy hand.[28] Similarly, the physical properties of a knife were miraculously changed when it was blessed with the sign of the cross Columba made with his pen while he was copying out a book. The knife was found to be incapable of wounding or killing and this quality was transferred to all the iron tools in the monastery which the monks overlaid with molten metal from the knife, 'because the efficacy of that blessing of the saint continued'.[29]

The tegorium

In evaluating the evidence in *Vita Columbae* for the monastic topography of Iona, Aidan MacDonald has noted the symbolic rather than archaeological significance of Adomnán's references to the hut where Columba wrote.[30] From the sparse information that it was in a raised-up place, supported on beams and that its door probably faced eastward, it is not possible to reconstruct the hut or its location if, indeed, Adomnán has in mind an actual building. In all six chapters where the hut or cabin is mentioned (*VC* i.25, 35; ii.16; iii.15, 22, 23), Adomnán uses the word *tegori(ol)um*, and the possible significance of his repeated use of this term in *De Locis Sanctis* will be discussed elsewhere. In the *Vita Columbae* he describes the writing hut, not in terms of a scriptorium or a contemplative retreat from abbatial business, but as the very hub of that activity and of Iona's spheres of influence. Adomnán pictures Columba working there with the door open, fully aware of the comings and goings in the monastery. He is variously seen writing or reading and with one or two

[28] For discussion of the post-Augustinian development of a sacramental vision in which carnal signs were seen to mediate between this world and the next, see Straw, *Gregory the Great*, 47–65 and Markus, *Gregory the Great and his World*, 47–50.

[29] *VC* ii.29. For further comment on these two sets of miracles, see above, Clancy, pp. 14–19, and Márkus, pp. 118–19.

[30] MacDonald, 'Adomnán's monastery of Iona', 42. Jerome uses the same term, *tuguriolum*, in the *Vita S. Hilarionis*, 9 to describe the anchorite's hut of sedge and reeds.

monks in attendance or studying with him, but he is also shown prophesying distant events outside the monastic life, receiving a visitor from outside the island enclosure and pronouncing blessings 'according to the custom' on tools and equipment and those engaged in the daily work of the monastery, such as milking the cows.[31] It is from the spiritual vantage-point of his elevated writing-hut that Columba has prophetic insights concerning his monks in Durrow as on Iona, which prompt him to chastise, exhort or sustain them according to their needs. While writing in the hut he routs a demon, invokes the help of angels, and receives a heavenly vision announcing his coming death and resurrection.[32] The active and contemplative aspects of the coenobitic life and of the abbatial vocation are inseparably combined in Adomnán's extended scribal image, which has various sources of inspiration but surely no equal in its scale and coherence.[33]

The *tegorium* was also the setting for the scene where Columba handed on his abbatial office to his successor, through the image of handing on his scribal task.[34] Columba was working on a copy of the psalms. He announced: 'Here, at the end of the page, I must stop. Let Baíthéne write what follows.' Adomnán comments: 'And the verse that follows, "Come my sons, hear me; I will teach you the fear of the Lord" (Ps 33:12), is fittingly adapted to the successor [Baíthéne], the father of spiritual sons.' This psalm verse had very early been interpreted as Christ's invitation to the faithful to learn from him 'the fear of the Lord' which is the way

[31] *VC* i.25, 35; ii.16, 29.

[32] *VC* ii.16; iii.15, 22.

[33] In contrast, the contemporary biographer of St Cuthbert says of Cuthbert's sojourn in the island monastery of Lindisfarne, 'He dwelt there according to Scripture, following the contemplative amid the active life, and he arranged our rule of life which we composed then for the first time and which we observe even to this day along with the Rule of Benedict'. The *Vita Columbae* and the *Vita Cuthberti* share certain themes and both draw on the *Lives* of Antony, Martin and Benedict (see Thacker, 'Lindisfarne and the origins of the cult of St Cuthbert', 112–15). But whereas Columba departs from their example in his frequent association with books and writing, Cuthbert, like Antony, is served by memory instead of books: *Vita sancti Cuthberti auctore anonymo*, III.1, IV.1: *Two Lives of St Cuthbert*, 94–6, 110–12.

[34] *VC* iii.23.

to eternal life, and so the text was applied in patristic and monastic literature to the role of the pastor or abbot who shares in Christ's work of teaching.[35] Cassian had frequently used the term 'the fear of the Lord' to describe the whole monastic way of compunction and longing for the heavenly life in which the monk is guided by the traditions of the elders and by the abbot in learning to understand and obey the divine word, as discerned in the spiritual interpretation of Scripture. In the Prologue to the *Rule of St Benedict*, the divine voice is heard through the words of Ps 33:12, summoning the faithful to the task of learning 'the fear of the Lord'. At the end of Columba's exemplary abbacy the task of teaching the fear of the Lord is not complete, however. It is concerned not simply with securing initial conversion to the monastic life, but with prompting a *continuing* process of inner conversion throughout this life, leading to a deepening understanding of what the term 'the fear of the Lord' can mean. The process cannot be seen at work in Columba himself, who was a son of promise from before his birth and already a figure of sanctity when first presented to the reader, but is evident in Adomnán's account of Columba's spiritual sons.

Learning the spiritual alphabet

Scribal work is already highlighted at an earlier stage of Baíthéne's monastic career. 'One day, Baíthéne went to Columba and said, "I have need of one of the brothers, to run through and emend with me the psalter that I have written."' Columba foretold that only a single letter 'i' would be found missing and so it proved to be.[36] Jean-Michel Picard sees this episode as primarily a borrowing from the *Life of Apollonius* of Tyana by Philostratus. Apollonius, a Pythagorean philosopher, marvelled when a brahman was able to foretell that a *delta* was missing from an epistle he had not seen. Picard suggests that Adomnán gave a Christian resonance to the story by changing the missing letter to an 'i' (alluding to the *iota* in Matt 5:18), so that an even greater power of prescience is attributed to Columba, *iota* or 'i' being the smallest letter of

[35] O'Reilly, 'Reading the Scriptures', 103–4.
[36] *VC* i.23.

the alphabet.[37] The episode may also be read as a demonstration of Baíthéne's high degree of scribal accuracy and as an instance of the scholarly practice of emending a transcript against its exemplar, which Adomnán earnestly commends to all future copyists of his own work.[38] But other readings are possible in the light of monastic uses of the scribal image. Adomnán does not directly use the metaphor of the spiritual alphabet which is featured in a number of Irish works, but its *context* in the work of Cassian and other early writers offers a key to understanding the function of the scribal image in the *Life of Columba* and even the format in which Adomnán tells the story.[39]

Cassian in his *Institutes*, for example, had likened the initial stages instructing monks to learn the true humility, obedience and mortification of carnal desires necessary to continue in the monastic life, to the process of teaching them 'the alphabet, as it were, and first syllables in the direction of perfection'. He describes the ideal response of learners of this alphabet when summoned from their cells to prayer or work: 'one who is practising the writer's art, although he may have just begun to form a letter, does not venture to finish it, but runs out with the utmost speed, at the very moment when the sound of the knocking reaches his ears, without even waiting to finish the letter he has begun; leaving the lines of the letter incomplete he ... hastens with the utmost earnestness and zeal to attain the virtue of obedience'.[40] The scene, which became something of a topos, shows the monk has learned

[37] Picard, 'Tailoring the sources: the Irish hagiographer at work', 261–2. I am grateful to Prof. Picard for a copy of his paper. Brian McNeil notes a relevant example among the accretion of parallels from legends about heroes, gods and holy men from other religions to the life of Jesus in early apocryphal literature, 'Jesus and the alphabet', and n. 29 below.

[38] *VC* iii.23.

[39] Ó Néill, 'The date and authorship of *Apgitir Chrábaid*'; Márkus, 'What were Patrick's alphabets?' has suggested the likely influence of Cassian's *Institutiones* in Tirechán's use of the alphabet as an image of a basic outline of Christian faith. See n. 40 below.

[40] *Institutiones* iv.9, 12, *NPNF* XI, 221–2. In the Life of Cainnech of Aghaboe the saint left the letter 'O' half-formed when he obeyed the summons of the monastic bell: O'Neil, 'Columba the scribe', 73. In *VC* ii.13, Adomnán avoids the obvious and St Cainnech's instant obedience is expressed in his running to the church with only one shoe on when he was summoned by Columba to pray.

an early lesson in the fundamental monastic virtue of surrendering his own will. The next chapter stresses that no-one should venture to say that anything is his own: 'it is a great offence if there drops from the mouth of a monk such an expression as "my book", "my tablets", "my pen"'; the following chapter warns against pride in one's own labour, even if it benefits the whole community. Similarly, the Rule of St Benedict forbids any monk to presume to retain anything as his own, 'not a book, writing tablets or a stylus ... since monks may not have the free disposal of their own bodies and wills'. Any monk, furthermore, who 'feels that he is conferring something on the monastery' by his own skill, is to cease practising his craft until he has demonstrated his humility and is ordered to resume by the abbot.[41] The task of the teacher is to help the pupil know himself and discern impurities of motivation, particularly any false humility which may be concealed beneath his apparent progress in the spiritual alphabet.

In Cassian's *Conlationes,* Abbot Nesteros teaches a younger monk how to seek purity of heart and guard himself against the spiritual temptations which will beset him in the process of learning spiritual wisdom:

> the first practical step towards learning is to receive the regulations and opinions of all the Elders with an earnest heart, and with lips that are dumb; and diligently lay them up in your heart, and endeavour rather to perform than to teach them ... And so you should never venture to say anything in the conference of the Elders ... as some who are puffed up with vainglory pretend that they ask, in order really to show off the knowledge which they perfectly possess. For it is an impossibility for one, who takes to the pursuit of reading with the purpose of gaining the praise of men, to be rewarded with the gift of true knowledge.[42]

It is a fundamental lesson which may readily be taught through the example of writing, too. In the light of this tradition, certain details in Adomnán's telling of the story of Baíthéne in *VC* i.23 come into sharper focus. Columba does not commend Baíthéne's remarkable scribal achievement at all. Rather, on hearing his request for help in checking his text he reproves him:

[41] *Institutiones* iv.13; *Regula Sancti Benedicti* 33, 57: *SC* 182, pp. 562, 624.

[42] *Conlationes* xiv.9; *NPNF* XI, 439.

> Why do you impose this trouble upon us, without a cause? Since in this psalter of yours, of which you speak, neither will one letter be found superfluous, nor another to have been left out, except a vowel 'i', which alone is missing. (*Cur hanc super nos infers sine causa molestiam? Nam in tuo hoc de quo dicis quae sola deest psalterio nec una superflua repperietur litters nec alia deese excepta .i. uocali quae sola deest.*)

There is here the suspicion that Baíthéne was drawing attention to his psalter and to his own skill, disturbing the abbot and others and presuming to initiate action. It is not the description of a bad monk but of youthful vainglory.

A number of sayings preserved in the literature of the desert monastic tradition offer interesting comparisons with this episode. For example, a brother who proudly told an old man at Scetis that he had copied out the whole of the Old and New Testament with his own hand was admonished with the words, 'You have filled the cupboards with paper.' A brother who had eagerly asked an elderly scribe to copy a book for him then pointed out some scribal omissions and demanded they be corrected, but the old man refused, saying, 'Practice first that which is written, then come back and I will write the rest.'[43]

The literary genre of such sayings or *apophthegma* assumes that the audience is seeking spiritual wisdom. In order to make sense of each story the reader must ponder the unexpected and enigmatic reply of the older monk, which discloses the young monk's true interior disposition in addressing him. The concern

[43] Noted in Burton-Christie, *The Word in the Desert*, 115, 154; cf. 59–60 for the story of Abba Arsenius, who, on entering the desert life, had humbly recognised the need for a new kind of knowledge. To those who marvelled that a man of rank and learning should consult an old monk of lowly origin, Arsenius replied: 'I have indeed been taught Latin and Greek, but I do not know even the alphabet of this rustic' (*Apophthegmata Patrum, De abbate Arsenio* 6, *PG* 5.89A). There is a reversal of roles between a teacher of the alphabet and his pupil, demonstrating their different kinds of knowledge, in an apocryphal story told by Irenaeus, *Adversus Haereses* I.xx.1, cf. Grant, *Irenaeus of Lyons*, 84. In the version which was known early in Ireland through the Gospel of Thomas, the infant Jesus is taught the alphabet from Alpha to Omega and then berates his teacher for presuming to teach the letter Beta when he does not know the meaning of the letter Alpha, whose mystery Jesus expounds, opaquely (see James, *The Apocryphal New Testament*, 50–1; McNeil, 'Jesus and the alphabet').

of the two younger monks for completeness and perfection in the execution of the external letter of Scripture contrasts with the elementary stage they are shown to have reached in learning humility and spiritual wisdom. In both cases, an apparently testy response to apparently harmless youthful enthusiasm over a question of scribal skill offers the reader a veiled spiritual insight. Typically, such stories do not go on to detail the younger monks' reaction: the reaction takes place within the heart and the life of the reader.

Frequently, as in these examples, Scripture is not quoted but evoked. By presumptuously addressing their elders and receiving a 'word' from them, the two young monks unwittingly demonstrate the importance of the Mosaic command on which this literature is based: 'Ask thy father and he will show thee; thy elders and they will tell thee' (Deut 32:7). Less often, Scripture is quoted and the teaching point made directly. One of St Antony's cautionary 'sayings', for example, simply describes some monks who 'fell away after many labours and were obsessed with spiritual pride for they put their trust in their own works and being deceived they did not give due heed to the commandment, "Ask thy father and he will tell you"'.[44] Adomnán's technique in his story of the scribe Baíthéne in *VC* i.23 has much more in common with the first two examples. The episode urges the need to pass beyond the literal text of Scripture, which Baíthéne transcribed almost perfectly, in order to seek its inner meaning. The image of writing Scripture therefore says something about how it should be read and lived.

Adomnán's approach may be further defined by comparison with that of Columbanus, who had also been influenced by Cassian and the traditions of desert monasticism and had dealt with some of the same themes discussed here concerning the humility and purity of heart necessary for the discernment and practice of God's word. In *Epistula* IV.6, Columbanus declares: 'none will be saved by his own right hand (cf. Job 40:9) ... except him who humbly uses his capacities, which are themselves gifts, with fear and trembling in the will of God.' In *Epistula* I.2 he

[44] Ward, *The Sayings of the Desert Fathers*, 7. In contrast Columba as a young deacon had ascribed his first miracle to his spiritual father, bishop Finbarr: *VC* ii.1.

explains that he is seeking the counsel of Gregory the Great, not from presumption but *illud canticum*, '*Interroga patrem tuum et annuntiabit tibi, maiores tuos et discent tibi*'(Deut 32:7). He quotes the same scriptural text in stressing a monk's constant need to 'ask his father' for spiritual counsel and teaching (*Regula Monachorum* ix, x; Sermon II.1). *Epistula* VI.1 warns the writer's own 'dear secretary', a young monk who asked for instruction beyond what he had already been given by his spiritual father, that 'the man to whom little is not enough will not benefit from more' (cf. Sermons I.3, III.4 and *Regularum Monachorum* viii).[45] This teaching appears in the form of precepts given in the context of *epistulae, instructiones* and monastic rules addressed to a variety of recipients, often supported with citations of scripture and patristic authority, and sometimes with specific application to current ecclesiastical problems and theological discussion. In the very different medium of the *Life of Columba*, the teachings of a living monastic tradition are renewed in the process of their being recognised by the reader in the saint's enigmatic deeds and sayings and in Adomnán's allusive scribal image.

The complete measure and the least letter

What are we to make of Columba's prophetic insight that there would not be one superfluous letter in Baíthéne's psalter and not one missing except a letter 'i'? The brief incident carries echoes of major exegetical themes. The complete measure and sufficiency of the divine word as a rule of life for the faithful, nothing more nor less, is strongly expressed in Moses' exhortation about the keeping of the law: 'The word which I have commanded you, you shall neither add to it, nor diminish it' (Deut 4:2). Columbanus cited this text in *Epistula* I.4 (*ca* 600), against those whose dating of Easter would, in his view, be adding to the divine instructions in Exodus 12:15 for the dating of the Passover. Such assertions of the inviolable integrity of Scripture had long featured in defences of orthodox belief against schismatics and heretics. Similarly,

[45] Walker, *Sancti Columbani Opera*. For the authenticity of *Ep.* VI and the sermons see Wright, 'Columbanus' *Epistulae*', 58–9 and Stancliffe, 'The thirteen sermons attributed to Columbanus', 93–202.

Eusebius in *The History of the Church*, v. 16, had quoted an early apologist who was anxious not to be accused of adding another paragraph or clause to the wording of the New Covenant, 'to which nothing can be added, from which nothing can be taken away, by anyone who has determined to live by the gospel itself'.[46] The concept was also expressed through the image of not adding or taking away even a single *letter* from Scripture. Eastern fathers directly paralleled the alphabet, complete in all its characters, with the truth of the gospel, complete in all the characters used to write it:

> Just as the body of the alphabet
> is complete in its members,
> And there is no character to take away,
> and none other to add,
> So also is the truth which is written
> in the holy gospel,
> in the characters of the alphabet,
> The complete measure, which is not susceptible of less or more.[47]

In these and other examples the complete measure and sufficiency of Scripture does not simply mean a canon of individual biblical books, but a particular way of reading Scripture *as a whole* enabling the reader to see the completeness of God's law as the way of perfection. Origen's sense of the divine mysteries contained by the sign of the literal text of Scripture was profoundly influential on Greek and Latin Psalm exegesis. In his commentary on Ps 1 he said that 'the wisdom of God has penetrated to all inspired Scripture even as far as the 'slightest letter'. Moreover, he explicitly identified that slightest letter with the Greek equivalent of 'i', the *iota*, citing as his authority Christ's reference to the *iota* in Matt 5:18, which is preserved in the Vulgate phrase, *iota unum aut unus apex* (familiar in the AV and Douai translations: 'one jot or one tittle shall not pass from the law, till all be fulfilled'). Origen several times used this image of the *iota* in stressing the unity and coherence of the whole of inspired Scripture, which is

[46] *Eusebius: The History of the Church*, 160; cf. 171 for the same argument used by Polycrates.

[47] Ephraem the Syrian, *Hymns against Heresies*, xxii:1, 78, translated in Griffith, 'The image maker in the poetry of Ephraem the Syrian', 259–60.

revealed if it is spiritually interpreted: in the holy Scriptures through which Christ speaks, 'there is not one superfluous jot or tittle'; there is 'no jot or tittle in the Scripture which will not receive its effect on those who know how to understand it'.[48]

The potency of the least of letters also arose from its numerological significance. *Iota* forms the tenth letter of the Greek alphabet and represents the number ten; in the Latin alphabet, the letter 'i' represents the number one. In the Pythagorean tradition of number symbolism the elemental relationships and ratios of musical and cosmic harmony were seen to lie in the first four numbers, whose aggregate is ten. Because counting, when it reaches ten, returns to begin again at one, which is the principle of all numbers, the number ten contains within itself all other numbers, proportions and harmonies.[49] Christian exegetes utilised such concepts as demonstrations of the all-embracing power of the divine Creator and the order and harmony both of his creation and of sacred Scripture. The number ten, a figure of perfection, was therefore likened to Jesus, in whom all things come together, and whose name in Greek begins with *iota*, meaning ten; in Latin, Iesus begins with the letter 'i', standing for the first number. Patristic and Insular exegetes found confirmation of these numerological concepts concealed not only in Christ's words concerning the *iota*, but within sacred Scripture's references to the decalogue and the *denarius* (Matt 20:2), to the numbers four, ten, their product and multiples. The number ten, composed of 1 + 2 + 3 + 4, in particular represented the ten commandments of the Old Testament law which, if spiritually interpreted and interiorised, could be seen to be filled with the four gospels.[50] This argues for the inspiration and harmony of the whole of sacred Scripture, both Old and New Testaments, in which Christ is revealed. Thus, alongside the notion that the complete alphabet represented the complete measure of Scripture, divinely inspired to its least letter, there had also developed the idea that the least letter could itself mysteriously express that wholeness and perfection. Such

[48] *Philocalia* ii.4; i.28: *SC* 302, 366–70; *The Philocalia of Origen*, 32, 28. Young, *Biblical Exegesis*, 21–4.

[49] Butler, *Number Symbolism*, 2–13.

[50] For example: Augustine, *De consensu evangelistiarum, CSEL* 43, II.4; *De Doctrina Christiana*, II.62–5; Cassiodorus, *Expositio Psalmorum, CCSL* 92, 62, 116.

numerological concepts help explain the weight of commentary on the letter *iota* in Matt 5:18.

Latin commentators similarly expounded the phrase *iota unum aut unus apex* which occurs in Christ's declaration in the Sermon on the Mount that he had come not to destroy but to fulfil the law and the prophets: 'Till heaven and earth pass away, one *iota* or one *apex* shall not pass of the law, till all be fulfilled' (*Donec transeat caelum et terra, iota unum, aut unus apex non praeteribit a lege, donec omnia fiant.* Matt 5:17–18). Augustine interpreted Christ's saying as 'a strong expression of perfection'. He explained that, since the *iota* is the smallest of all letters, being made by a single stroke, and the *apex* but a duct or serif at the top of even that, Christ by these words shows that the law is to be obeyed, down to its smallest commandment, not only in its moral requirements but in its spiritual interpretation.[51] Jerome too noted that from the figure of the letter, *iota*, Christ's words in Matt 5:18 show that even those things in the law which are considered to be of least importance are filled by 'spiritual sacraments' and that all things are brought together in the gospel.[52] Augustine expounded the next verses, Matt 5:19–20, to show that whoever obeys Christ in interpreting the law spiritually may enter the kingdom of heaven, but whoever obeys the command and also *teaches* it 'shall be called great in the kingdom of heaven'. The righteousness of such a person would be 'greater than that of the scribes and pharisees', who are often presented in the gospel as religious men skilled in copying, knowing and keeping the Law, but only in its literal letter and external observance.

The consequences of such limited understanding and practice of God's word by its professional interpreters are laid bare in Christ's indictment of those scribes and pharisees who thereby 'shut up the kingdom of heaven against men' (Matt 23:13–33); they are immediately contrasted with the prophets, wise men and

[51] *Quod autem ait: Iot unum vel unus apex non transit a lege, nihil potest aliud intelligi nisi nehemens expressio perfectionis, quando per litteras singulas demonstrata est, inter quas litteras iota minor est ceteris, quia uno ductu fit, apex autem etiam ipsius aliqua in summo particula.* Augustine, *De sermone domine in monte* I, 8, 20–9, 21: *CCSL* 35, 20–3.

[52] *Ex figura litterae ostenditur quod etiam quae minima putantur in lege, sacramentis spiritalibus plena sint et omnia recapitulentur in evangelio.* Jerome, *Commentariorum in Matheum* I.510–15: *CCSL* 77, 27.

scribes, his true disciples, whom Christ will send out into the world: *Ecco ego mitte ad vos prophetas, et sapientes, et scribas* (Matt 23:34). The scriptural contrasts of bad and good scribes were developed by the Fathers and their discussion of the least letter of the law in Matt 5:18 is closely in harmony with their exposition of Christ's words to his disciples commending the good scribe: 'Every scribe instructed in the kingdom of heaven is like a man that is a householder, who brings forth out of his treasure new things and old' (Matt 13:52). Bede identified the *scriba doctus in regno coelorum* not simply with scholars knowledgeable on both the Old Testament and the New, but with spiritual teachers, meaning those to whom the two testaments had been divinely revealed as harmonious parts of the unified expression of God's word, and who also practised the divine word and made it known to others by their example as well as their teaching. In *De Tabernaculo* and *De Templo* in particular Bede gave a close reading of two Old Testament texts, demonstrating that the gospels were already contained and figured within the Law, every part of which was important because, properly interpreted, it had an immediate application to living the spiritual life. He also repeatedly used the patristic interpretation of Christ's words in Matt 5:18 in commentaries on a variety of other scriptural texts. He observed that the number ten which denotes the Law (i.e. the ten commandments), also contains another 'sacrament' or heavenly mystery because both in Hebrew (*ioth*) and in Greek (*iota*), the tenth letter of the alphabet is the first letter of the name Iesus. He likened the letter *iota* to the observance of the Law which, when spiritually interpreted, contains all the fullness of faith and good works, hence 'the Law, grasped in a spiritual sense, should not lose one *iota* or one *apex* until the end of all things'.[53]

As is well known, Hiberno-Latin writers were drawn to the kind of information often used by Jerome, which Isidore of Seville had compiled in Book I.3, 4 of his *Etymologiae*, such as the Hebrew, Greek and Latin equivalents for certain names and terms, and the fact that Greek and Hebrew letters, and some Latin letters, have a numerical significance. Hiberno-Latin works

[53] Bede, *De Tabernaculo* III.13 and *De Templo* II, 18, 6, *CCSL* 119A 135, 200; *Libri quatuor in principium Genesis* IV, 547–55, 1678–92, *CCSL* 118A; *Homiliae evangelii* I. 14, *CCSL* 122, 139.

sometimes give the numerical equivalents of Greek letters or render the *nomina sacra* in Greek characters and occasionally cite bilingual psalters and gospel texts or give short texts in Greek, as in the Lord's Prayer at the end of the Schaffhausen manuscript of the *Vita Columbae*.[54] The Grecism *iota*, retained in the Latin text of Matt 5:18, was a spur rather than a bar to insular interest in developing its exegesis. The probably seventh-century Hiberno-Latin *Expositio IV Evangeliorum* succinctly comments on this verse:

> Iota unum, *nomen litterae, quae uno ducto: fit deca littera, id est, decem verba Legis, apud Graecos litterae, quod nos unum diximus.*
>
> Unus apex, *unum punctum, ad litteram; ad sensum autem, minima mandata Legis. Donec omnia fiant, quia quae lege minima fuerunt, plena mysteriis fiunt; iota vetus Lex, apex Nova.*[55]

Moreover, Augustine's *De sermone Domini in monte* and Jerome's commentary on Matthew's gospel were both well known to early Irish commentators. An unpublished eighth-century commentary on Matthew in Munich Clm 6233, ff. 87r–v, for example, expounds Matt 5:18 by dovetailing the comments of Augustine and Jerome on the immediate text (outlined above), with close verbal parallels, but also briefly expands the patristic description of the *iota*, made with a single stroke, and its *apex*: the stroke of the *iota* figures the Old Testament containing the Decalogue, and the *apex*, which has four letters in its name, signifies the four gospels.[56]

Commenting on Matt 5:18, the unpublished eighth-century compilation of early Hiberno-Latin exegesis known as the 'Irish Reference Bible', first quotes Jerome on the text. It notes the position of the *iota* as the tenth letter in both the Greek and Hebrew alphabets and its meaning as the number one in Latin

[54] Bischoff, 'Turning-points in the history of Latin exegesis in the Early Irish Church', 85–6. Nordenfalk, *Celtic and Anglo-Saxon Painting*, 32, pl. 1 for the Lord's Prayer in Greek written in Latin characters, in the earliest painted Hiberno-Saxon manuscript, Durham, Cathedral Library MS A.II. 10, fol. 3v.

[55] *PL* 30.545.

[56] See nn. 51 and 52 above. I am grateful to Dr Seán Connolly for kind permission to use his transcript.

and the significance of the visual form of the letter.[57] Such comments may be regarded as examples of Hiberno-Latin pseudo-philological interests, or as an idiosyncratic reading of meaning into the letter. When read alongside the patristic tradition, however, this material can be recognised as a distinctive and condensed expression of a long-established exegesis on the scribal image in Matt 5:17–20. It is a key text within the Sermon on the Mount, which drew the particular interest of Hiberno-Latin exegetes. Matt 5:18 offered an enigmatic summary of Christ's parallels and antitheses between the old law and the new, the literal letter and its spiritual meaning, external observance and interior obedience, and the words *iota* and *apex* appear in other contexts in Hiberno-Latin works in listings of highly allusive biblical pairs and opposites. At the end of the preface to Matthew's gospel (devoted to the harmony of Scripture), the 'Irish Reference Bible' had already elaborated Augustine's description of the two pen-strokes which form the letter: the *iota* refers to the Old Testament, the Law of the ten commandments and the righteousness of the scribes, while the letter's *apex* signifies the fulness of the spiritual sense, the New Testament, the precepts of the Sermon on the Mount, and the righteousness of the apostles, manifested in fasting, almsgiving and prayer. The whole letter therefore refers to the totality of Scripture and to the need for its spiritual interpretation as a guide to the spiritual life which is to go beyond 'the righteousness of the scribes' (cf. Matt 5:20). The biblical paradox of great things being contained in little is graphically expressed here in the use of the visual form of the written letter to carry the exegesis. The idea of seeing and obeying the 'fulness of the spiritual sense' of Scripture, even in its least commandment, is here figured in its least letter.

The psalter as primer

The familiarity of such exegetical traditions within insular monastic culture enabled Adomnán to use those traditions

[57] Preserved in the early ninth-century manuscript, Paris, B.N. lat. 11561, fol. 149v–150, 137v.; on the 'Irish Reference Bible', see Kelly, 'Catalogue of Early Medieval Hiberno-Latin Biblical Commentaries I', 552.

allusively. In the context not of a biblical commentary but of a brief apophthegmatic episode set in his own monastery on Iona, Adomnán cites neither Matt 5:18 nor the Greek letter *iota* in *VC* i.23. Through Columba's cryptic prophecy of the letter missing from Baíthéne's scribal work, however, he evokes both the smallest letter in the Latin alphabet and the idea of the sufficiency and measure of Scripture: neither will one letter be found superfluous nor another to have been left out, except a vowel 'i' (which, in the Schaffhausen manuscript of the *Vita Columbae*, written on Iona probably within the lifetime of Adomnán, appears as a minuscule 'i', not a capital 'I', as in the Andersons' edition).[58] The incident depicts Columba as spiritual teacher and demonstrates his discernment of the true state of Baíthéne's progress in learning. An interpretation which ignores the note of censure in Columba's response to Baíthéne's almost perfect copy of the literal text of Scripture and reads the episode simply as a wonder tale of Columba's arbitrary prophetic power, might regard the information that the text Baíthéne had copied was a psalter as an incidental detail. Of all the books of Scripture, however, the psalter was particularly appropriate to the metaphor of learning the complete spiritual alphabet, as it was in practice used as a primer to teach monks literacy. It has been noted, for instance, that the Gallican text of Pss 30, 31 and part of 32 inscribed on the waxed wooden writing tablets of *ca* 600 or earlier, found at Springmount Bog, Co. Antrim, is written in an accomplished script, suggesting it was an exemplar for a student to copy.[59] In the late seventh century, Tirechan said that he himself had seen a psalter which St Patrick had written for an ordinand. It is possible that Tirechan's repeated references to Patrick writing alphabets (*abgitoria, elementa*) when establishing new churches and priests

[58] Bernhard Bischoff observed, 'The most noticeable stylistic peculiarity of almost all Insular scripts, whether half-uncial or minuscule, is the triangular terminals of the ascenders, a decorative element that is repeated on the shafts of *i* and other letters. These triangular tips were written either with a short turn of the pen against the direction of the writing or by the easier method of adding a separate, angular stroke to the shaft.' *Latin Palaeography*, 86. The minuscule *i*, therefore, though undotted, is made up of two parts or strokes.

[59] Martin McNamara, 'Tradition and creativity in early Irish psalter study', 350.

may mean he wrote psalters or particular psalm texts for them as a guide to learning the spiritual life.[60]

The psalter opens with the image of the *beatus vir* who meditates on the law of the Lord day and night (Ps 1:2), an image often cited as a model of the monastic life. Ps 118's fervently expressed desire to know and to practise God's commandments was believed to articulate the longing of the exiles in Babylon for their return to Jerusalem, seat of God's law, and hence acted as a figure of the Christian spiritual life, journeying from earthly exile to the heavenly Jerusalem, and especially of the monastic life *in via*. The psalter itself was seen as encompassing the law so that the reading, copying out and chanting of the psalms meant constant meditation on the divine law and the interpretation of its continuing spiritual meaning. Moreover, both the alphabet metaphor and the motif of missing letters are specifically associated with the psalms in patristic tradition, and precisely within the context of discussion on learning wisdom in the spiritual life.

In the same commentary on Ps 1 in which Origen, citing Matt 5:18, proclaimed that the wisdom of God penetrates the whole range of Scripture, even to its least letter, the *iota*, he also observed that the canon of the Hebrew Bible has twenty-two books, 'the same in number as the letters of the Hebrew alphabet. For as the twenty-two letters of the alphabet may be regarded as an introduction to the wisdom and the divine doctrines given to men in those characters, so the twenty-two inspired books are an alphabet of the wisdom of God and an introduction to the knowledge of realities'.[61] He noted that certain books and sections within Scripture have twenty-two divisions; in some cases, the

[60] *Et scripsit illi librum psalmorum, quem viti.* Bieler, *Patrician Texts*, II.5; cf. 6.1, 33.1, 37.3, 47.2. Stevenson, 'Literacy in Ireland', 19–22 for Tirechán's account of St Patrick as a scribe and writer, concerned with Christian education, and for the suggestion that his description of Patrick writing out alphabets implies 'some form of elementary Christian knowledge, such as creed, or the Paternoster, or the Ten Commandments'; cf. G. Márkus,'What were Patrick's alphabets?'; McNamara, 'Psalter text and psalter study', 206, n. 7.

[61] Preserved in the *Philocalia of Origen*, ii.4, iii and cited by Eusebius, *The History of the Church*, vi.25. Josephus had earlier noted that no Jew had presumed to add to or take away from or alter the twenty-two books of Hebrew Scripture, which were regarded as the decrees of God.

twenty-two Hebrew letters are used successively to form the initial letter of the opening word of a section. In particular, Origen interpreted the alphabetical, twenty-two part structure of Ps 118 to refer to the spiritual education of the believer which encompasses the whole range of letters, from beginning to end. The learning of wisdom through this spiritual alphabet is envisaged not as a simple progression from the moral or active life in the beginning to the contemplative life at the end, but as learning both to discern the divine will expressed through the whole range of inspired Scripture and to practise its commands at every stage of the interior journey marked by the psalm's twenty-two alphabetical divisions. In Origen's extant works the individual Hebrew letters are not given a specific interpretation, but their totality stands for the way of perfection. His commentary formed the most important element in the fifth-century Palestinian compilation of Greek commentaries on Ps 118 and was extremely influential on Latin commentaries.[62]

Jerome, in the well-known Vulgate preface, the *Prologus Galeatus*, also related the twenty-two elements or characters of the Hebrew alphabet to the total of twenty-two books of the Bible (Old Testament) 'by which, as by the alphabet of the doctrine of God, a righteous man is instructed in tender infancy'. The alphabetical image is used again in his explanation of Ps 118, which incorporates this numerological image of universality and completeness of divine revelation in its very structure. Significantly, the psalm forms a long meditation on the divine commandments or law. In *Epistula* 30 Jerome explains that Ps 118 is divided into twenty-two sections, each of eight verses, each section introduced by one of the twenty-two letters of the Hebrew alphabet which he refers to as *aleph*, *beth*, etc.[63] Each of the twenty-two letters has a meaning, by which its appropriate section of psalm verses may be understood. Jerome says that it is necessary, therefore, to understand the meaning of the individual Hebrew letters (which

[62] *La chaîne palestiniènne sur le psaume 118*, I, 96–159.

[63] Jerome, *Ep. xxx Ad Paulam*: *Lettres* ii, 31–5. There were other substantial Latin commentaries on Ps 118 which emphasised its twenty-two sections. Hilary referred to the numerical position of the Hebrew letters, but Ambrose interpreted the meaning of each letter: *Hilaire de Poitiers: Commentaire sur le psaume 118*; *Sant' Ambrogio: Opere esegetiche* VIII, ii.

he supplies), in order to understand the divine commandments, just as one could not read and make sense of the words in his present epistle without first understanding the letters which make up the words. He immediately takes the image of how the skills of literacy are acquired in graduated stages and applies it to the priority of deeds in learning the elements of the spiritual life: 'so in the sacred Scriptures we cannot know the higher things unless we start with morals'. He quotes the experience of the psalmist who knew that it was only after he had practised the Lord's word that he had begun to have knowledge of its mysteries: 'By [obeying] thy commandments I have had understanding' (Ps 118:104). Conversely, it is necessary to meditate on the divine law day and night to discern how to obey the divine will. The individual interpretations of all twenty-two Hebrew letters in Ps 118 in Jerome's *Epistula* 30 are paralleled in the Latin Epitome of Theodore of Mopsuestia's Psalm commentary (which was transmitted through works of Irish provenance); in the Hiberno-Latin Gloss on the Psalms in an eighth-century manuscript, Vatican, Palatinus Latinus 68; and in the Psalter of Charlemagne, Paris B.N. lat. 13159. The Gloss's editor suggests it was compiled *ca* 700, probably within the *paruchia Columbae* and possibly on Iona.[64]

Cassiodorus' *Expositio psalmorum* was used by Adomnán in *De Locis Sanctis*.[65] It presents the psalter as providing instruction in the seven liberal arts necessary to an understanding of Scripture's literal text, and as an education in its spiritual interpretation (and therefore its application to the spiritual life). Jerome's *Epistula* 30 is closely cited by Cassiodorus in his own extensive treatment of Ps 118 and the six other psalms which employ an alphabetical structure 'teaching us that the sacred use of letters unfolds for us mysteries of heavenly matters'.[66] Citing

[64] McNamara, *Glossa in Psalmos*, 72–4; MacNamara, 'Psalter text and psalter study', 270, for use of the Hebrew letters or their Latinised names in other Hiberno-Latin psalm texts and commentaries. The use of a Latinised abecedarian form in two hymns ascribed to Columba in the *Liber Hymnorum* is well known; the preface to the *Altus prosator* in the *Leabhar Breac* notes its Hebrew alphabetic form and that Hebrew letters have a meaning.

[65] O'Loughlin, 'The Latin version of the Scriptures in Iona', 23–5; O'Reilly, 'Reading the Scriptures', 87.

[66] *Cassiodorus. Expositio Psalmorum*: Walsh, *Cassiodorus: Explanations of the Psalms*, i.246–7; iii.174. All translations quoted here are from this work.

Athanasius' letter to Marcellinus, he regards the book of psalms as signifying the whole treasury of the Scriptures. It embraces 'both Old and New Testaments in such a unique way that you can truly say that a spiritual library is built up in this book'.[67] The psalter is associated with the daily, life-long offering of praise in the psalms of the monastic office, which can represent the offering of the monastic life itself.

Cassiodorus explains that the alphabetical psalms are of two types, complete and incomplete, and that this is significant. The first type (Pss 110, 111, 118), using every letter in the Hebrew alphabet successively to introduce the various verses or groups of verses of the psalm, denotes the just or the righteous who sing the Lord's praises through 'the perfect devotion of their meritorious deeds'. Psalms in the second group (Pss 24, 33, 36, 144) only use some letters of the Hebrew alphabet in their structure: 'this incomplete alphabet denotes those who cannot sing the Lord's praises with the fullest purity of good works'.[68] He does not suggest that some *psalms* are better or holier than others but that the symbolism of these Hebrew letters can, if read properly, open up spiritual insights, just as the headings and the numbers of the psalms can.

Cassiodorus mentions that he decided to inscribe the Hebrew letters clearly in ink in the text of the Psalter where appropriate.[69] He is not concerned with speculating on the historical reason why some psalms use the abecedarian form incompletely, but regards their given form as an integral part of the divine word which, if read properly, continues to speak to the faithful. It is an aspect of the belief in the complete measure or sufficiency of inspired Scripture, nothing more or less, as a guide to the spiritual life.

In the *Expositio psalmorum* he repeatedly insists: 'Since all the Hebrew letters have their meaning, it is perhaps right to believe that an alphabet short of a particular letter does not embrace its

[67] Ps 150:6, Walsh, *Cassiodorus* iii.465–6.

[68] Walsh, *Cassiodorus* i.246–7, 325.

[69] The earliest extant (abbreviated) copy of Cassiodorus' *Expositio Psalmorum* is Insular, Durham Cathedral MS B II 30 (Northumbria, *ca* 750); apart from the first psalm, the opening of Ps 118 is alone distinguished with a decorated initial. Hebrew letters in Latinised form appear in the margin: Bailey, *The Durham Cassiodorus*, 4–5, 22.

meaning either.' Ps 36, which omits just one of the Hebrew letters, is therefore said to be symbolically 'attributable to those deficient in some degree in the perfection of holy men'.[70] Similarly, 'When a psalm unfolds with all the Hebrew letters, it denotes the just who through the Lord's grace are shown to lack no virtue; but when it does not bear the signs of all the characters, it seems to point to those in the Lord's Church not revealed as perfect in all good works ... In the case of this psalm (Ps 144), a single letter is missing from the alphabet, so it seems not to indicate the higher category.' It is like the words of Christ to the man who lived a praiseworthy life: 'One thing is wanting' (Mark 10:21). Cassiodorus uses the two types of alphabetical psalm, therefore, to distinguish not the good and the bad monk, but degrees of holiness within the community. The spiritual life will only be perfected in heaven; in this sense, 'the incomplete alphabet points to the Church which is still developing here on earth whereas the full alphabet denotes the Jerusalem to come'.[71]

Cassiodorus ascribes to Hilary the comment, 'We know that children and the uninstructed are taught by letters to seek the precepts of wisdom. In the same way, psalms of this [alphabetical] type are put before boys and learners so that their first lessons may be imparted by the letters acting, so to say, as teachers.' Their purpose is 'for the instruction of those who are novices and amenable to teaching in Christ's school'.[72] Ps 111 is one of those 'interlaced with the letters of the entire [Hebrew] alphabet as though with golden guiding-lines' and, through its progression, describes the blessed man whose deeds are rewarded: 'this alphabet ... undoubtedly points the way to the perfection of wisdom. Through it understanding of divine affairs is acknowledged'.[73] The image implies a progression in learning from the novice's performance of good works to the understanding of the higher mysteries of the divine commandments, but this is not to be misunderstood as a transition from a probationary period of active life to some higher contemplative state. Cassiodorus reveals that those truly advanced in the study of divine wisdom are

[70] Walsh, *Cassiodorus* i.357.
[71] *Ibid.*, iii.422–3.
[72] *Ibid.*, iii.125. The quotation is untraced, but see Hilary's tractate on Ps 118:1, *CSEL* 22, 355.
[73] Walsh, *Cassiodorus* iii.131, 137.

precisely those who excel in the humble and apparently elementary deeds of the monastic life. The good works of the monastic life predispose the monk to seek the mysteries of scripture, which in turn bears fruit in action and greater purity of heart and the desire for further understanding of the divine word. Whereas Jerome's *Epistula* 30 on Ps 118 had focused on verse 104, 'By thy commandments [i.e. by performing them] I have had understanding', Cassiodorus highlights the complementary verse 73: 'Give me understanding and I will learn [to carry out] thy commandments.' The verse begins with the tenth Hebrew letter, *ioth*. Cassiodorus comments, 'If we sought to draw together the arguments about this verse, we would disgorge the length of whole books.'[74] Ps 118's use of the complete alphabetical range of letters signifies its teaching on discerning and performing all the divine commandments.

Baíthéne's formation

Examples of scribal and alphabetical metaphors used by the Fathers to describe the process of learning how to discern and practise the divine word have here been cited from Jerome, Augustine, Cassian and Cassiodorus, major authors well-known to Irish commentators; some reference to Origen has indicated the greater antiquity and wider familiarity of these metaphors and traditions. Insular scholars not only knew these traditions but understood them and adapted them in their own exegesis. In the different literary genre of the *Vita Columbae*, the metaphors come to life. They are not didactically expounded or converted into parables, but their truth is concealed in brief narratives which, on initial reading, may seem inconsequential or puzzling or even depict Columba in an unfavourable light. The reader's gradual recognition of oblique hints of scriptural and patristic themes is itself an act of interpreting the literal text to reveal an underlying sense. To move from examples of the various strands within the patristic traditions illustrated here to a re-reading of Adomnán's text is to recognise more fully that, in omitting a letter from his psalter, Baíthéne falls short of monastic perfection. Columba's teaching is, through the story, renewed for his latter-day spiritual

[74] Walsh, *Cassiodorus* ii.205–6.

sons. The crucial test is whether such a reading of *VC* i.23 helps make sense of other episodes concerning Baíthéne and other monks learning the spiritual life, and of Adomnán's other uses of the scribal image.

In the immediately preceding story, Baíthéne is corrected by Columba for quoting certain passages of holy Scripture in support of a penitent whom Columba did not want to set foot on Iona.[75] We are not told what the scriptural texts were nor, apparently, given any justification for Columba's rejection of Baíthéne's plea for showing mercy. Modern commentators who regard Columba's behaviour as often irascible and peremptory, may warm to the attitude of Baíthéne in this episode. However, Adomnán's wording reveals Columba's superior spiritual discernment of Scripture enabling him to understand the divine commands. He knows that the man in question had committed 'fratricide, the sin of Cain' and an unheard of sin (*inaudium in mundo*) which is identified as incest with his own mother. St Paul had declared that he who committed this sin, 'such fornication as is unheard of even among the heathen', should be cast out of the Christian community (1 Cor 5:1; 6:18). Gildas had quoted Paul's words in explaining why the Britons, inured in sin, were divinely punished by the coming of the Saxon invaders, and Bede quoted this much-used text to explain why an Anglo-Saxon king who married his stepmother was subjected to 'the scourge of divine chastisement and correction' before proper fear of God drove him to repentance.[76] Although on another occasion Columba does show mercy and compassion to a genuine penitent (*VC* i.30), and applies to him the consolation of Ps 50:19, he discerns that the sinner in *VC* i.22, despite his protestations, is not truly repentant and should not, therefore, be allowed to violate the Christian community, here represented by the monastic sanctuary of the island of Iona. In the introductory chapter, Adomnán had already quoted 1 Cor 6:17 to explain that Columba's prophetic insight came from his closeness to the mind of God: 'he who clings to the Lord is one spirit'.[77] Baíthéne is shown to be still learning the wisdom of spiritual discernment which is prepared,

[75] *VC* i.22.

[76] *De Excidio Britonum* 21.2: *Gildas. The Ruin of Britain*, 24; *HE* ii.5–6.

[77] *VC* i.1.

when necessary, to denounce, reprove and exhort in making known the divine will.

There is no systematic chronological account of his spiritual progress, but Baíthéne is shown perfecting obedience and becoming more like his spiritual father Columba (*Iona*, Jonah, in Hebrew) in an encounter with a *cetus mirae et immensae magnitudinis* which evokes aspects of the Book of Jonah.[78] Baíthéne is seen acting with growing discernment and spiritual authority as an elder, while humbly acknowledging the power of Columba in *VC* i.37. His guidance was sought by other monks (cf. Deut 32:7), and he interpreted their experiences and offered them spiritual 'consolation' in the tradition of interpreting the monastic life as a recapitulation of the Exodus journey to the Promised Land. When Baíthéne was in charge of a church on the island of Eth (Tiree), Columba praised him for defending it by fasts and prayers from the assaults of demons who were devastating the island with disease.[79] From the wording of Adomnán's preceding account of Columba's own defence of Iona, it is clear that Baíthéne too had 'taken to himself the armour of the apostle Paul' and had learned to apply his understanding of the account of spiritual warfare in Eph 6:10–18. Columba, with the help of angels, entirely succeeded in driving the demons from Iona; Baíthéne lost just one man from his community.

Such episodes give a series of insights into how Baíthéne, who was Columba's kinsman, his *alumnus* and one of the original community, learned more of the spiritual life and the interpretation of Scripture and grew closer to Columba. Eventually he acquired a reputation as 'a wise and holy man' and was to be acclaimed as a 'worthy and fitting successor' to Columba (as Adomnán dramatically tells us at the very beginning of the book).[80] Baíthéne is three times quite specifically identified as a scribe and the story of his missing out a letter when copying a psalter is an important part of the process by which he came to succeed Columba.

[78] Layzer, 'The other dove: Jonah and Colum Cille', forthcoming. For Adomnán's use of the Columba-Iona (Jonah) etymology in the context of patristic and Insular exegesis, see O'Reilly, 'Exegesis and the Book of Kells', 315–26.

[79] *VC* iii.8.

[80] *VC* i.2.

Several related exegetical themes come together in the scribal image in *VC* i.23, most notably the role of the spiritual father in monastic formation, the teaching and learning of the spiritual alphabet, the significance of letters missing from the psalter and the importance of the smallest of all letters. In the alphabetical psalms the Hebrew letter equivalent to the Greek *iota* is rendered *ioth* or *iod*. Jerome in *Epistula* 30.5 explains that it means 'the beginning' (*principium*). Cassiodorus says that in Ps 33 the letter *iod* announces the verse 'Fear the Lord, all ye his saints: for there is nothing wanting to them that fear him' (verse 10). Cassiodorus comments that the psalmist, enjoining 'fear of the Lord' on all, however saintly they may be, shows in his next words exactly what this means: those rich in worldly goods, power and bodily health may still lack something: 'the only man short of nothing is he who is enriched with fear of the Lord'.[81] Adomnán quotes the last line of this verse as the last words Columba wrote when copying out the psalter on the night of his death: 'But they that seek the Lord shall not want for anything that is good' (Ps 33:11). Adomnán uses the Old Latin version, *Inquirentes autem dominum non deficient omni bono*. The use of *deficient*, rather than the Vulgate's *minuentur*, heightens his application of the text to Columba: 'The last verse that he wrote thus aptly fits the predecessor, who will never lack eternal things' (*cui numquam bona deficient aeterna*). Columba calls on Baíthéne to write out the next verse of the psalter, 'Come, my sons, hear me; I will teach you the fear of the Lord' (Ps 33:12). Adomnán quotes this verse too and comments that it was 'appropriate for Baíthéne his successor, a father and teacher of spiritual sons, who, as his predecessor enjoined, followed him not only as a teacher but also as a scribe'. (*Successori uero sequens patri spiritalium doctori filiorum, 'Venite filii audite me'; timorem domini docebo uos, congruenter conuenit, qui sicut decessor commendauit non solum ei docendo sed etiam scribendo successit.*)[82] Thus Baíthéne, whose imperfect understanding of the wisdom of the scribe had once been manifested in his omission of the smallest letter from the psalter he was copying, was now called on to continue copying out a psalter begun by the holy hand of Columba himself. He

[81] Walsh, *Cassiodorus* i.329.
[82] *VC* iii.23; Sharpe, *Adomnán*, 228.

had in the meantime learned from Columba more of that wisdom which is the proper 'fear of the Lord' and which, as a wise scribe himself, he was now to teach under Columba's posthumous guidance.

The vision on Hinba (*Vita Columbae* iii.18)

The same monastic traditions which help explain the thematic function of this remarkable scene in Adomnán's account of Columba's last hours, directly illumine the cluster of episodes leading up to the final chapter. Adomnán shows that Columba, while still on earth, spoke with angels: 'The grace of the Holy Spirit was poured out upon him abundantly and in an incomparable manner ... He saw, openly revealed, many of the secret things that have been hidden since the world began. Also everything that in the sacred scriptures is dark and most difficult became plain, and was shown more clearly than the day to the eyes of his purest heart'; very many mysteries were revealed to him 'both of past ages and of ages still to come, mysteries unknown to other men; and also a number of interpretations of the sacred books'.[83] Adomnán's description here evokes the Wisdom theme of the Pauline epistles: 'We speak wisdom among the perfect, yet not the wisdom of the world ... We speak the wisdom of God in a mystery, a wisdom which is hidden, which God ordained before the world'; such wisdom is revealed only by the Holy Spirit (1 Cor 2:6–7, 10); it is 'the mystery which was kept secret from eternity which is now made manifest' (Rom 16:25–26).

After this prolonged and ecstatic contemplative experience on the island of Hinba, the saint regretted the absence of his *alumnus* Baíthéne, 'who', comments Adomnán, 'if he had chanced to be present during those three days, would have written down from the mouth of the blessed man very many mysteries, both of past ages and of ages still to come, unknown to other men; and also a number of interpretations of the sacred books'.[84] Baíthéne is said to have been detained on the island of Eigg by contrary winds until these three days and nights had come to an end. As, on other occasions, Columba could command the winds and protect

[83] *VC* iii.18.
[84] *Ibid.*

his monks from peril at sea, it seems unlikely that we are here just being given an unusually bad coastal weather report. Adomnán draws attention to the absence of the scribe Baíthéne, yet the explanation he offers is unsatisfactory and prompts the reader to look further. The question '*Ubi sapiens? Ubi scriba?*' had been memorably asked by St Paul in 1 Cor 1:20 (quoting Isa 33:18), not in order to ascertain the physical whereabouts of a particular scribe, but to show that the manifestation of the wisdom of God goes beyond the understanding of human wisdom which the scribe represents. Paul explains that his teaching, therefore, is not based on 'the persuasive words of human wisdom', but on showing the power of God (1 Cor 1:18; 2:6). He reiterates that 'the deep things of God', which God has prepared for them that love him, are beyond human imagining and wisdom, are only revealed by the Holy Spirit and can be received only by 'the perfect' or 'the spiritual man' who has the mind of Christ (1 Cor 2:9–16).

The whole Pauline passage is central to the exegetical tradition stemming from Origen's spiritual interpretation of Scripture whereby Christ, the divine wisdom, is revealed not to 'the carnal', but to 'the spiritual man', by the gift of the Holy Spirit. The Pauline concept of 'the spiritual man' was particularly applied to St John, as in Jerome's *Epistula* 53.4, but is also embodied in the Lives of other saints, notably the *Vita Antonii*, 77–80, and Gregory's account of St Benedict in *Dialogii* ii.16, which substantially quotes 1 Cor 2:9–12, 6:17. The image of scribe could carry negative connotations, suggesting worldly wisdom, as in Paul's quotation from Isa 33:18 in 1 Cor 1:20, and in the gospels' frequent depiction of the scribes' and pharisees' merely literal understanding of the law. Both Antony and Benedict are appropriately and pointedly depicted, not as scribes but as wisely unlearned (cf. 1 Cor 1:19–31). It has been suggested here that Adomnán's portrait of Columba as scribe is by no means incompatible with this Pauline Wisdom theology, but draws on different aspects of the scribal image. It adapts patristic and monastic uses of the figure of the scribe to convey the process of learning the elements of the Christian life, in which human learning can have an important role. The tradition, however, influenced by the Wisdom literature of the Old Testament, pictured the wise scribe copying out in his heart and meditating on the divine commandments in order to practise them, and it constantly adverted to the limitations of human learning and reason in the search for divine wisdom (Prov. 3:1–7). Adomnán's powerful evocation of Columba's heightened experience of divine wisdom in the scene on the island of Hinba sets aside the role of the scribe. Though the reader has watched Baíthéne learning his scribal *elementa* and knows that he is to be Columba's worthy successor on Iona both as teacher and scribe, it is now made evident that Baíthéne is unable, in this life, to share the fulness of Columba's experience of the divine. The saint himself is shown without pen or books as the mysteries of Scripture are revealed 'to the eyes of his purest heart'. He exemplifies the spiritual man who has the mind of Christ and is joined to the Lord in spirit (1 Cor 2:16, 6:17).

At the opening of his earlier work, *De Locis Sanctis,* Adomnán, abbot of Iona, had presented himself as a scribe, writing down on tablets the eye-witness testimony dictated to him by Arculf. Whether one views Arculf as a historical figure or a literary device, he is clearly depicted as having been on a literal pilgrimage to the earthly Jerusalem. His visual, aural, tactile experiences of the Holy Places at the centre of the earth are recorded by Adomnán and then written up on parchment, supplemented with additional information from works of reference. Human learning, reason and sensory experience are used by Adomnán in the important task of explicating passages in the literal text of Scripture concerning the Holy Places which Christ and his patriarchs, prophets and apostles had hallowed by their physical presence.[85] In the *Vita Columbae* this is by no means discounted, but the images of scribe and pilgrim take on a different role. Adomnán shows that, at the ends of the earth, Columba's life itself offered a guide to the inner spiritual pilgrimage and its destination and fulfilment in the life of the heavenly Jerusalem. His monastic life on Iona is described as his pilgrimage in Britain, his death as a crossing over from this pilgrimage to the heavenly country, already anticipated in life, particularly in the vision on the island of Hinba, a vision he mediated to his spiritual sons.[86] The mysteries revealed to him on Hinba through manifestations of divine power

[85] *DLS*, 35; O'Loughlin, 'The exegetical purpose of Adomnán's *De Locis Sanctis*', 37–53 and above, pp. 139f.

[86] *VC* iii.22, 23; iii.18–21.

transcended the kind of knowledge which could be dictated to a scribe, even to a future abbot of Iona. Instead Adomnán uses the image of 'immeasurable brightness' lighting up the night. He shows that already, while in the darkness of this life, the saint shared in the eternal day of the heavenly life. Columba's wisdom – his wordless understanding of the divine word and heavenly mysteries – is the result neither of his learning nor even of his superior spiritual merits but is divinely given to him. He is filled with the Holy Spirit and beams of brightness from the house he is in can be seen at night, escaping through chinks in the door and through the key-holes. It is granted to Columba to reveal to others in this life some insight into the *heavenly* perfection of the pursuit of wisdom.

Teaching the fear of the Lord

The three stories which immediately follow the vision scene on Hinba (*VC* iii.19–21), each repeating the apparition of light, do not simply multiply marvels through anecdote. By deft pen portraits Adomnán compares three of Columba's spiritual sons who chance upon the vision, and Columba's response to each. The monk Virgno was praying in the church while others slept one night. When Columba unexpectedly entered the church accompanied by the radiance of heavenly light, Virgno could not endure the brightness 'just as none can look with direct and undazzled eyes upon the summer midday sun'.[87]

The well-known image of St John as the evangelist who alone could contemplate the light of the divine with sublime and steady gaze, just as the eagle, alone of all creatures, can look directly at the rays of the sun, had been used by St Augustine in his influential depiction of John as a figure of the contemplative life. The opening sentence of his homilies on John's gospel quotes 1 Cor 2:14, 'the natural man perceives not the things which are of the Spirit of God', and recognises that there must be many such natural or carnal men among Augustine's listeners who cannot raise themselves to the spiritual understanding of John's sublime gospel opening in which Wisdom is revealed. He distinguishes them from others who may understand when it is explained to them and a

[87] *VC* iii.19.

third category who may understand even before it is explained. Three levels of understanding the mysteries of Scripture had been directly related to the Pauline Wisdom texts by Origen. Augustine presents John as one who contemplated divine Wisdom and was able to receive that which 'eye has not seen, nor ear heard, neither has ascended into the heart of man' (1 Cor 2:9) because although a man, John 'had begun to be an angel. For all saints are angels, since they are messengers of God'. The first homily concludes with the image of John illuminated and filled by the divine light; Augustine urges those slow of heart who cannot yet receive that light, because of their sins, to strive to become pure in order to see the wisdom which is God: 'Blessed are the pure in heart, for they shall see God' (Matt 5:8).[88]

Like St John, the beloved disciple, Columba already shares in the life of angels, as Book iii of *Vita Columbae* repeatedly shows, and he is therefore able to contemplate the divine light and to illumine others, according to their purity of heart which determines their capacity to receive spiritual enlightenment. His response to Virgno, however, seems surprising. He commends him, but not for catching a glimpse of the light: 'You have been well-pleasing, little son ... in the sight of God, this last night, in lowering your eyes to the ground through dread of his brightness. For if you had not done so, your eyes would have been blinded by seeing that inestimable light.' The remaining two stories are even less edifying on an initial reading for they apparently portray Columba as arbitrary and severe. The second monk, Colcu, also prayed one night while others slept, and also caught sight of the apparition of light in the church and was also afraid yet, unlike Virgno, he was chastised by Columba next day: 'Henceforth take great care, my son, not to attempt like a spy to observe heavenly light that has not been granted to you.'[89] On a third occasion he very sternly reprimanded Berchán, who had tried to see the heavenly vision.[90] The attempt to interpret this group of enigmatic stories requires that their genre be identified.

[88] *Tractatus in Iohannem*, xv.1, i.1, 4, 18–19: *CCSL* 36.150, 1–11. Adomnán had earlier alluded to the image of St John and light in describing the first miracle of Columba (cf. John 2:1–11), which is set at *VC* ii.1 to 'illumine like a lantern the opening of this book'.

[89] *VC* iii.20.

[90] *VC* iii.21.

Adomnán is doing something new with traditional elements, both in terms of content and of literary format. To some extent he is taking features characteristic of the *Apophthegmata Patrum* and re-locating them in the coenobitic monastery of Iona. In addition to formal literary works devoted to the Life of a particular saint, most importantly the *Life of Antony*, the desert monastic tradition was preserved in a great gallery of spiritual exempla of the words and deeds of holy anchorites preserved by their disciples at different times and places and variously collected and arranged, without thematic structure. They feature brief incidents and epiphanies in the lives of the abbas and particularly their short, pithy sayings which often discern the innermost promptings of those who came to seek 'a word' from the holy man. Sometimes this took the form of a precept or command and the divine voice of Scripture was heard quite distinctly through the word of the holy man, but often it was given by an enigmatic verbal image or icon of holiness, or through a short story without any obvious scriptural citation or formal explanation of its meaning: only in pondering the word might the abba's listeners (and subsequent readers of the story) come to recognise its scriptural echoes and understand its relevance to the conduct of the spiritual life.

Something of this desert tradition was transmitted to the West through Latin translations and intermediaries such as the *Verba Seniorum,* works of hagiography, the *Historia monachorum* and particularly the *Institutes* and *Conferences* of Cassian.[91] At the end of his 'little rule for beginners', St Benedict famously directed that for anyone 'hastening on to the perfection of monastic life, there are the teachings of the holy Fathers'. In addition to Scripture, 'the truest of guides', he specifically commended the *Conferences* of the Fathers, their *Institutes* and their *Lives* and the rule of Basil.[92] But in the process of transmission, the desert fathers material was often adapted to different contexts and literary forms. John Cassian's influential presentation of the sanctity and spiritual insights of the heroic anchorites of the Egyptian desert, for example, is directed to his readers in a coenobitic monastery in Gaul. He dwells on the importance of

[91] For this tradition see Burton-Christie, *The Word in the Desert*, 76–103.

[92] *Regula*, §73.

having a guide or elder in the spiritual life and presents his material with a single authorial voice in the form of twenty-four sustained *conlationes*, rather than short sayings, elicited from fifteen desert fathers. He arranges the material thematically and frequently cites or quotes Scripture.

Conlationes xi is of particular interest in the study of the closing chapters of the *Vita Columbae*. When the aged and holy abba Chaeremon is prevailed upon by Cassian to lay aside his silence, he discourses on Perfection at some length. Scripture promises that 'all they that fear the Lord shall be blessed' (Ps 127:1) but also warns that they differ in their capacity to be blessed, 'as star differs from star in glory' (1 Cor 15:41–2). The holy abba then describes different kinds of fear which reveal different stages of spiritual capacity and growth. He established 'that Perfect love casts out fear ... he who fears is not yet perfect in love' (1 John 4:18) but shows that fear can at least bring us to 'the first beginning of blessedness' and the necessary realisation that we are unprofitable servants. We must, however, mount from this servile fear of punishment, and from the mercenary hope of reward, to that filial love of God which loves him because he first loved us.[93]

The importance of these ideas in monastic history has somewhat obscured the climax of his discourse. Cassian's companion Germanus is puzzled by Chaeremon's account because it seems at variance with a number of passages in Scripture which show fear of the Lord in a very positive light, most notably in the injunction, 'Fear the Lord, all you his saints, for they that fear him lack nothing' (Ps 33:10). Chaeremon then shows how this and other such texts on the fear of the Lord are perfectly reconcilable to his theme. He interprets the poetic parallelism of Isa 23:6, 'Wisdom and knowledge are the riches of salvation: the fear of the Lord is his treasure', to mean that the saving wisdom and knowledge of God can only be preserved by 'the fear of the Lord', which here means the fear only of falling short in love of God. He contrasts this kind of fear with the fear of his first quotation, the fear of punishment which prevents a person from being made perfect in love (1 John 4:18). Immediately, he alludes to further texts in the exegetical chain on *timor Dei* to underline

[93] *Conlationes* xi. 12, 7; *NPNF* 2nd series, XI, 420–1, 417.

the distinction between the fear in which nothing is lacking (Ps 33:10) and that imperfect but necessary fear of the Lord 'which is called the beginning of wisdom' (Ps 110:10; cf. Prov 1:7, 9:10). Finally he shows that the fear of the Lord in which nothing is lacking is among the sevenfold gifts of the Holy Spirit which Isaiah prophesied would fill Christ himself at the Incarnation. First among them the prophet lists 'the spirit of wisdom and understanding' but in the last place 'he adds as something special these words: "And the Spirit of the fear of the Lord shall fill him"' (Isa 11:2, 3). This kind of fear, then, which is not servile but is part of unfailing love, belongs to the pattern of perfection offered in Christ.[94]

Adomnán shows Columba to have been so filled with the wisdom which is the perfect fear of the Lord that all temporal preoccupations were driven out; he was already, therefore, living the heavenly life and mediating Christ's pattern of perfection to others. It is worth re-reading the account of his own vision in *VC* iii.18 before re-considering the three stories which follow. On Hinba the holy man (*sanctus vir; beatus vir*) is shown keeping watch in the night, alone and fasting, in a house that was barred to temporal distractions on an island temporarily out of the reach of his community. The narrative details are eloquent. This is the setting for the description of how 'the grace of the Holy Spirit was poured out upon him abundantly and in an incomparable manner and continued marvellously for the space of three days and as many nights', to the sound of 'spiritual songs unheard before'. Divine mysteries were revealed to him, 'things that have been hidden since the world began ... many mysteries, both of past ages and of ages still to come, mysteries unknown to other men' (cf. 1 Cor 2:7, 10; Rom 16:25–26).

The narrative details of Columba's experiences on the island of Hinba recall the contemplative experiences of the apostle and evangelist, St John. He too received his Apocalyptic vision of the heavenly Jerusalem and of past and future ages to the sound of a 'new canticle' while on an island (Rev 1:9, 14:3), and was believed to have fasted for three days before receiving the inspired revelation of the divine mysteries which was to form the Prologue of his gospel: 'In the beginning was the Word.' Moreover, the

[94] *Conlationes* xi.11–13; *NPNF* 2nd series, XI, 420–2.

heavenly light on which Columba, like St John, was able to gaze, is shown to have been unbearable to the still earth-bound figures in the three stories which follow. Columba's words on their different responses to the light reveal their three different spiritual capacities, but the teaching conveyed through the three episodes may also be understood at various levels by Adomnán's readers. St Paul had urged the faithful to graduate from being taught 'the first elements (*elementa*) of the words of God' and to 'go on to things more perfect' (cf. Heb 5:12, 6:1, 1 Cor 2:6), to strive for perfection in their understanding of Scripture, that is, for the divine wisdom which is Christ. Quoting Paul, Origen had also acknowledged the necessity of a graded threefold approach in teaching wisdom. He argued that even the person who does not understand the text can see that the revelations granted to St John in his gospel opening contain 'a hidden depth of ineffable mysteries'; textual analysis alone is inadequate to expounding the sublimity of such Scriptural passages. Understanding requires the grace granted to the apostle who said: 'But we have the mind of Christ that we might understand the gracious gifts bestowed on us by God and we impart it in words not taught by human wisdom but by the Spirit' (1 Cor 2:16, 12–13). Citing the wisdom of Solomon (Prov 22:20–21), Origen urged a threefold approach in teaching Scripture, suited to the capacity of its various recipients. Just as the human being consists of body, soul and spirit, so the faithful might be variously edified by Scripture at three different levels, rising from a fleshly or literal understanding, to the spiritual understanding of those who approach St Paul's description of the perfect (1 Cor 2:10–16). It was to such a person that the apostle said, 'we impart a wisdom which is not of this world ... a secret and hidden wisdom of God which God decreed before the ages for our glorification' (1 Cor 2:6–7; cf. 14–15). Origen then applied this approach to a story in which three teachers are sent to three different categories of people. The first group receives the moral exhortation of 'the mere light'; those 'whose souls have left the realm of bodily concerns and base thoughts' receive teaching from 'outside the letter' and, finally, the teacher described as the disciple of the Spirit addresses 'men who have turned grey with insight' (that is, the wise, who are not necessarily the old, cf. Wisd 4:8). He 'teaches them no longer through the written letter but through living words'.[95] There are obvious narrative differences between this and the three stories Adomnán tells after the vision on Hinba, in which a single teacher, Columba, encounters three individuals and gives no didactic explanation of their differing experiences. But Origen's exposition, much mediated in exegesis, has interesting echoes in *VC* iii.18–21, if these chapters are read as a sequence.

In the three stories following Columba's vision of divine wisdom the saint does not teach through reasoned argument or exegesis but through the manifestation of God's power. The three episodes enact a number of themes concerning the fear of the Lord and the learning of wisdom, familiar in the patristic and monastic tradition. Some of these themes Cassian had treated in the very different literary medium of the long discourse of abba Chaeremon in *Conlationes* xi, which was structured around the resolution of apparently incompatible scriptural texts to show that the fear of the Lord can, in its different aspects, describe both the lowest and the highest stages of the spiritual life and so can, for an informed audience, describe in shorthand the entire process of learning spiritual wisdom.

In a completely different literary format Cassian's contemporary, Augustine, used both the image of light and the same text from Isa 11:1–3 describing the seven gifts of the Holy Spirit, to set out the seven stages of wisdom in *De doctrina christiana* II.16–23. He reversed the order of gifts to demonstrate how 'the fear of the Lord is the beginning of wisdom': 'it is first necessary to be moved by fear of God towards learning his will'; this fear will inspire reflection on mortality and, therefore, amendment to a life of holiness. The third stage – knowledge – concerns reading Scripture in such a way as to realise it is about loving God and one's neighbour. At the fourth stage, a man turns from the transient to love of the eternal; when 'he beholds this light (as far as he is able to), shining as it does even into remote places, and realizes because of the weakness of his vision he cannot bear its brilliance, he is at the fifth stage ... and purifies his mind'. After perfecting love of his neighbour, 'he rises to the sixth stage, in which he now purifies the eye by which God may actually be

[95] *De Principiis* IV, ii.3–4 (*Philocalia* i.10–11); *Origen on First Principles*, 274–6 and Froelich, *Biblical Interpretation in the Early Church*, 57–8.

seen – to the extent that he may be seen by those who, to the best of their ability, die to this world'. The vision of that light, though now more steady and tolerable, 'is none the less said to be seen still obscurely and through a mirror' because we are still in this world though citizens of heaven (cf. 1 Cor 13:12). Finally, with a heart now purified 'such a son ascends to wisdom'.[96] Augustine returns to dwell at great length on the third stage of the pursuit of wisdom, which is the subject of his book, namely, the knowledge of Scripture, facilitating its spiritual interpretation, that those who fear God and seek to understand his word should attain.

These major works by Augustine and Cassian illustrate how the same important theological theme and its associated scriptural texts and images could be handled with different points of emphasis and in very different literary genres. Adomnán's creative renewal in an insular idiom of patristic and monastic traditions on teaching the fear of the Lord has gone unrecognised. In the brief but carefully crafted account of the 'sayings' of Columba in the triad of vision stories immediately following his own three-day vision on Hinba, there are no scriptural quotations but every circumstantial detail of *tempus*, *locus* and *persona* is of weight. On a re-reading of *VC* iii.19, the first thing said about Virgno now leaps out of the text: he was fired with the love of God (*in dei amore feruens*). He prayed at night and in winter, concealed within the exedra of the church, behind the half-opened door where, presumably, his solitary vigil would not draw attention to his devotion. His overwhelming reaction to the vision of heavenly glory was fear, even terror, 'so that his strength failed him utterly'. Realising his unworthiness in the divine presence, he responded not with cowardly flight but with awed humility and lowered his eyes. It is a brilliant little vignette describing someone who already understands and practises something of that fear of the Lord which is not only a proper sense of awe but also an aspect of the love of God; Virgno is warmly commended by his spiritual father in the words, '*Bene O filiole*'. The second monk, Colcu, has a different experience of the divine light, his fear is of a different order, and he is shown at a less advanced stage of the spiritual life, as will be discussed below.

[96] *De Doctrina Christiana*, 62–6.

Read in the light of the monastic tradition on 'the fear of the Lord' and the pursuit of wisdom, the third story suggests an explanation for Columba's apparently disproportionate reaction to a lad peering through a key-hole.[97] Again, Adomnán's narrative details are crucial. Berchán, a young *alumnus* who was studying sacred learning (*sapientia*) with Columba and was avid for advanced tuition, came to the saint's lodging nightly, but had so failed to grasp the most elementary lessons in the learning of wisdom that he wilfully disobeyed his spiritual father one night in order to spy on him, 'supposing that within the house some heavenly vision was being manifested to the saint'. Berchán found he could not bear to look upon the heavenly brightness, even through the key-hole, and fled from the light, but, as Columba pointed out next day, he had remained quite unaware of his sinful presumption in not having a proper awe and dread of divine power and punishment. In other words, Adomnán is showing through the story that the youth lacked that necessary initial fear of the Lord which precipitates penance and amendment of life. Columba discerned that Berchán would be unable, therefore, to pursue his study of wisdom but would leave the monastery of Iona for a life of dissipation in Ireland and would not be brought to a tearful penance until the time of his death. The story describes one who went through life without learning that basic fear of the Lord which is the beginning of wisdom. Adomnán makes it clear Berchán was only saved at the last because he was the saint's *alumnus* and because Columba interceded that he might obtain God's mercy. In contrast, Virgno, Columba's 'well-pleasing little son', went on to become the fourth abbot of Iona (d. 623), the next but one after Baíthéne. Each in his turn would take up the abbatial role of teaching 'the fear of the Lord'.

Adomnán presents his three vision stories as case histories and particularly insists that the first had come to him by the priestly testimony of Virgno's nephew. In his shaping and grouping of the three stories, however, it is possible that Adomnán is building upon Cassianic traditions particularly associated with Columba or which had been treated in other literary forms by Irish scholars. The influence of Old Testament Wisdom literature and of Cassian's *Conlationes* is discernible in the early Irish *Alphabet of*

[97] *VC* iii.21.

Devotion (*Apgitir Chrábaid*), which has been dated *ca* 600.[98] It opens its teaching on the spiritual life with precepts on the initial necessity of fear of God, 'For he who will not have fear of God will not have love of God.' It closes by affirming that 'Wisdom without learning is better than learning without wisdom' and with a description of the pure in whom desire for God has replaced all worldly desire: such a person is a vessel of the Holy Spirit. The intervening sections on learning the spiritual life include the image of light: 'As a lantern raises its light in a dark house, so truth rises in the midst of faith in a person's heart.' This is immediately followed by one of the work's triads: 'Three persons come to the Christian life. One of them is in it, another is beside it, another is far away from it.' This has suggestive parallels with *Vita Columbae* iii.19–21, though is devoid of the narrative details of Adomnán's triad of stories about visions in which the viewing-point of each of the three figures is related to their various spiritual states and progress in learning wisdom, and their subsequent fates are described in terms of their nearness to the Christian life exemplified by Columba at Iona. The *Alphabet of Devotion* says of the good which the first of the three figures heard and saw: 'he has loved it and has thus believed it and has fulfilled it.' The second figure in the descending hierarchy has denied the world with his lips but not in his heart, thus he is 'overkeen at fasting and prayer' but 'he has not declared war against greed and meanness. One of his hands is towards heaven and one towards earth'.[99] This may prompt a more careful reading of what Adomnán actually says about his second example and helps make sense of Columba's chastisement of Colcu despite the fact that, like Virgno, he had prayed at night while others slept.

Adomnán says that Colcu had 'chanced to come to the door of the church' and 'stood there in prayer for a little time'. When Colcu fleetingly saw the apparition of light coming from inside the church, he failed to realise its source and significance and, much afraid, returned to his dwelling. This contrasts with the

[98] Ó Néill, 'The date and authorship of *Apgitir Chrábaid*'; Ó Corráin, 'The historical and cultural background of the Book of Kells', 3–14.

[99] This suggestion is based on translations of the vernacular text: 'The Alphabet of Devotion' in Clancy and Márkus, *Iona*, 200–7, quoted here, and Hull, '*Apgitir Chrábaid*: The Alphabet of Piety'.

setting of the first vision deep within the church. Virgno remained humbly in the recesses of the light-filled church when he recognised the divine presence and was therefore associated with his spiritual master in this powerful image of the vessel or tabernacle of the Holy Spirit (1 Cor 3:16–17). In the twelve brief printed lines of the Latin text of *VC* iii.20 Adomnán explicitly draws attention to the fact that he has already mentioned at the beginning of his work this same Colcu 'son of Aid Draigniche, of the descendants of Fechre'. His background and subsequent history, told in *VC* i.17, complement the picture of him in *VC* iii.20 standing, as it were, between heaven and earth at the church door, zealous in prayer but denying the world with his lips only. In *VC* iii.20 Columba discerned Colcu was not worthy to observe the heavenly light. In *VC* i.17 Columba discerned he was of spiritually flawed ancestry. He did not remain on Iona with Columba, who foretold that he would for many years be the *primarius* of a church in Ireland. Richard Sharpe has commented that Adomnán generally uses the word *primarius* in a secular context and suggests that Colcu was not in holy orders but was the proprietor of a private church, which would sharpen the contrast with Virgno's future as abbot of Iona.[100] Unlike Finten in *VC* i.2 and some other non-Ionan church leaders who had had contact with Iona, Colcu is not honoured with any word of spiritual commendation from Columba or Adomnán (cf. Wisd 3:16–17). The point of Columba's apparently bizarre prophecy about the event which would signal Colcu's eventual death – the sight of his butler or steward swinging a pitcher by its neck at a feast for his friends – may simply be Colcu's status and his presence at the feast, suggesting he had not fully denied the world. Encapsulated in the story of Colcu's vision in *VC* iii.20 and its reference out to *VC* i.17, is the kind of spiritual profile given, by very different means, to the second figure in the *Alphabet of Devotion*'s account of the three people who come to the Christian life. Similarly, something of the spiritual state of Adomnán's third figure, Berchán, may be recognised in the *Alphabet*'s third figure, who does not practise Christian habits all his life: 'He reckons it will be easier to practise them some other season.'[101]

[100] Sharpe, *Adomnán*, 278–9, n. 103.
[101] Clancy and Márkus, 204.

Read in the context of the traditions outlined here, the three stories which follow Columba's contemplative vision on Hinba (*VC* iii.18–21) illumine each other and cumulatively reveal a coherent exposition of monastic teaching on sacred wisdom and the various stages of 'the fear of the Lord', which leads the reader to the final revelation of its meaning in the tableau in Columba's writing-hut (*VC* iii.23). The scene enshrines the text of Ps 33:11–12, 'Come my sons, hear me; I will teach you the fear of the Lord', as a highly charged summary of the continuing abbatial teaching task passed on by Columba to Baíthéne and, by implication, to Virgno. By describing aspects of how they learned from Columba the fear of the Lord which is the beginning of wisdom, and by showing Columba's continuing exemplification of that fear of the Lord which is the perfect love of God, Adomnán placed himself in the Ionan abbatial teaching tradition.

To the end, Adomnán shows Columba teaching monastic obedience in its least command. Columba's remark, 'Here, at the bottom of the page, I must stop', appropriately announces the end of his earthly life, but its exact position within the detailed timetable of that last day is of interest. Cassian's ideal novice, learning the spiritual alphabet along with his scribal task, had left off writing in the middle of forming a letter when summoned to prayer; Columba left off writing Ps 33 halfway through and, 'at the end of the page, the saint entered the church for the vesper office'. Shortly after, Adomnán stresses that the aged Columba obeyed the bell for the monastic office at midnight with alacrity: 'he rose in haste and went to the church and, running, entered in advance of the others' and knelt in prayer. His haste was prompted not by fear of death and punishment, but by joyful longing to be with God. Those monks nearing the church doorway briefly glimpsed the great light filling the church about the saint; the others then came running up in the darkness, bringing lights into the church, in time to witness Columba's entry into eternal life. In the Prologue to the *Rule of St Benedict,* Christ's invitation to the monastic life, voiced by the spiritual father through the words of Ps 33:12, 'Come my sons, listen to me; I will teach you the fear of the Lord', is immediately followed by the exhortation, 'Run while you have the light of life, that the darkness of death may not overtake you' (cf. John 12:35).[102]

St Benedict's biographer, Gregory the Great, never depicted him in the act of writing, but in the chapter preceding the saint's death, he did report that Benedict wrote a Rule for monks: 'If anyone wishes to know his character and life more precisely, he may find in the ordinances of that Rule a complete account of the abbot's practice; for the holy man cannot have taught otherwise than as he lived.'[103] Adomnán shows that with the wisdom of the scribe, Columba taught his spiritual sons the fear of the Lord through the monastic rule he offered in his own life and manner of death.

[102] *Regula*, Prol.; and cf. O'Reilly, 'Reading the Scriptures', 94–106 for fuller discussion of the final chapter, *VC* iii.23.

[103] Gregory, *Dialogi* ii.36.

PART III

The Columban legacy

8

Iona: archaeological investigations, 1875–1996[1]

Jerry O'Sullivan

Whatever withdraws us from the power of our senses; whatever makes the past, the distant or the future predominate over the present, advances us in the dignity of thinking beings. Far from me and my friends be such frigid philosophy as may conduct us, indifferent and unmoved, over any ground which has been dignified by wisdom, bravery or virtue. That man is little to be envied whose patriotism would not gain force on the plain of Marathon, or whose piety would not grow warmer among the ruins of Iona.

DR Johnson's famous eulogy on the ruins of Iona[2] is far better known than the opinion of James Boswell, his worldly travelling companion. On the same evening in 1773, Boswell could

[1] This chapter began life as a consultancy report to the Iona Cathedral Trust for AOC (Scotland) Ltd, but was subsequently presented at *Spes Scotorum* (June 1997), the Columban centenary conference of the Scottish Catholic History Association. It was prepared for publication with the aid of research grants from Historic Scotland and the Russell Trust, and with the support of colleagues at the Archaeology Department in the University of Glasgow, and has also appeared in the *Journal for Church Archaeology* (No. 2, 1998). The illustrations were produced on the MapInfo GIS programme by Dr Michael Givens and Stuart Jeffreys. Special thanks are due to Professor Charles Thomas for access to the archive of his own fieldwork on Iona, and to Dr Ian Fisher for information on archive material in the National Monuments Record for Scotland.

[2] *Johnson's Journey to the Western Isles*, 134.

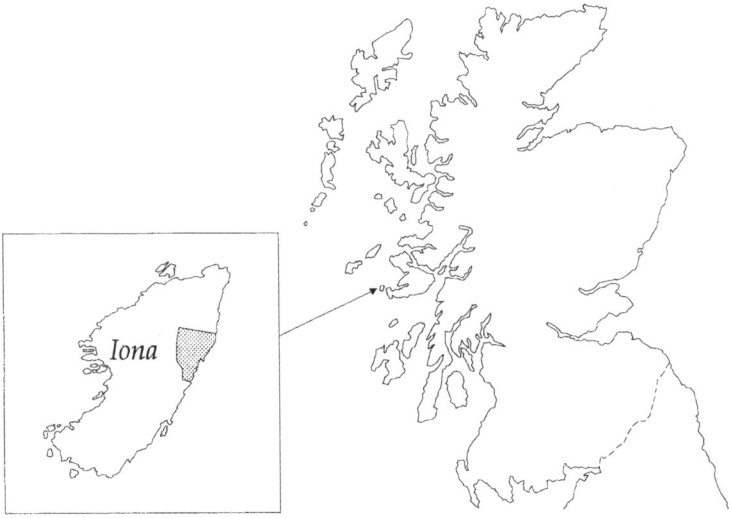

FIGURE 5. *Location map of Iona*

confide to his journal that he was disappointed by the Abbey.[3] The ground was mired with cow dung, and nettles stood high as his hat. He had not derived much pleasure, still less inspiration, from his visit to Iona's famous ecclesiastical ruins. This chapter echoes Boswell's complaint by offering a sceptical review of archaeological work on Iona over the last 120 years or so, and asks why numerous excavations have revealed so little about the primary monastic settlement.

Iona has been the scene of an extraordinary level of archaeological activity. Most of this work has taken place within the modern precinct of the Benedictine Abbey, the most likely site of the Columban settlement. Scores of trenches have been opened here by a dozen different investigators; others have investigated elsewhere in the ecclesiastical environs. (This chapter is not concerned with the excavated later prehistoric settlement at Dùn Chùl Bhuirg.)[4] Reviews of this work are available in the encyclopaedic *Inventory* compiled by Ian Fisher for the Royal Commission on the Ancient and Historical Monuments of

[3] *Boswell's Journal of a Tour to the Hebrides*, 330–8.
[4] Ritchie and Lane, 'Dun Cul Bhuirg'.

FIGURE 6. *A view of the Abbey from the north-west, looking across the sound to Mull; part of the earthwork is visible in the middle foreground* (from RCAHMS 1982, 31)

Scotland,[5] in Anna Ritchie's more up-to-date though briefer *Iona*,[6] and in a recent paper by Finbarr McCormick.[7] But no summary has explicitly stated the full extent and piecemeal nature of successive excavations, or the significance of this for the long-term curation of Iona as an early church site of international importance. This is a problem to which all fieldworkers on Iona have been party, including the present writer, and which may offer lessons for the care of other medieval church sites with extensive standing and buried remains.

The landscape of Iona is dominated by rocky outcrops and low hills, with peaty hollows or miniature glens between. There are pockets of good grazing, as well as larger tracts of light arable soil derived from wind-blown sand on the northern and western machairs, but the premium location for human settlement is the raised beach terrace which forms much of the more sheltered eastern shore of the island. This is where the present village stands – largely a planned re-settlement of the early nineteenth century

[5] RCAHMS, *Argyll* iv.
[6] Ritchie, *Iona*.
[7] McCormick, 'Iona: the archaeology of an early monastery'.

– and where most of the other houses on Iona can now be found. It is traversed by the island's only substantial stream (*Sruth a' Mhuilinn*: the mill stream) and has a prospect of the narrow sound dividing Iona from its much larger neighbour, the island of Mull. This has also been the area favoured by ecclesiastical settlement in all periods. Any prospect of the raised beach terrace is dominated by the restored Benedictine Abbey. This is the most conspicuous element in a constellation of minor churches, cemeteries and high crosses, with the ruined Augustinian Nunnery lying farther to the south.

Contained on one side by the sea and on the other by a low, inland cliff, this pleasing jigsaw of manicured lawns and postcard ruins is a core place in the Columban story. Because it is so self-contained a scene, it is easy to succumb to the illusion that it offers direct and intimate contact with the primary period of monastic settlement. William Skene thought so, and attempted to map sixth/seventh-century events onto the nineteenth-century landscape of the island, using evidence from Adomnán's *Vita Sancti Columbae*.[8] Indeed, it is very easy to imagine the island itself as a green and passive blank inscribed with clearly legible evidence of the Columban world. Yet on closer acquaintance, this proves not to be the case. The ciphers that have come down to us from that world – whether from documentary sources, excavated evidence, or the monumental landscape of the island – are not written in bold legible strokes, but in passages of confusing erasure and superinscription.

Adomnán's consecrated island

For the archaeologist as well as the historian, any reading of the landscape of Iona is mediated from the outset by Adomnán's *Vita*. The seventh-century life of St Columba is often cited as a rich source of information on the early monastery. A formula which is commonly repeated was first set out in the 1850s by Adomnán's earliest modern editor, Dr William Reeves:

> He had frequent opportunities for conversing with those who had seen St Columba, and he was now writing on the very spot where his great predecessor had indited his last words, and surrounded by

[8] Skene, 'Notes on the history'.

objects every one of which was fresh with the impress of some interesting association.[9]

Subsequent commentators have gleaned some interesting glosses on terms used in the *Vita* and, indeed, Adomnán does offer tantalising glimpses of the fabric of monastic life in the sixth and seventh centuries, with its fishing nets and deer traps, salt stores and harvest labour, book satchels, hand bells and ink horns.[10] But these are glimpses only. What the *Vita* certainly does not offer is a topographic history of early monastic Iona. Close reading can derive no detailed descriptions of the church and burial ground, the monks' houses and farm buildings, or the monastic enclosure and surrounding fields which comprised the main physical features of the primary foundation. On the contrary, Adomnán's account of Iona dedicates the island as a consecrated place, resplendent with Divine favour. The images which most often appear in the *Vita* – Columba's writing cell, preparation of the guest house and the passage of white-robed monks to their church – are repeated motifs which refer to an archetypal monasticism of literacy, community and liturgy, rather than to a particular place and history.

Monumental signposts

If the principal written source offers only uncertain, even mythologised knowledge about the Columban scene within the island landscape, perhaps it is to be hoped that the physical monuments might offer more reliable signposts. After all, even amongst farm meadows and mown lawns, each cross and ruined church on Iona has occupied its rooted and particular place for centuries. This may be true, yet these monuments – like Adomnán's *Vita* – refer to the primary decades of the monastic period in an indirect way only. Just as Adomnán presents the island as a consecrated place, the accretion of later monuments presents Iona more specifically as a ritual place. This can be seen in two main trajectories: one is the amplification of the primary monastic site by its satellite churches and cemeteries; the other is

[9] Reeves, *Saint Adamnan, Abbot of Hy*, 3.
[10] See discussions in MacDonald, 'Aspects of the monastery and monastic life', and 'Adomnán's monastery of Iona', or Sharpe, *Adomnán of Iona*.

the specific focus of several monuments around the tiny chapel known as St Columba's Shrine.

John Blair was writing about early minster churches when he observed that some were

> merely the nuclei of diffuse constellations, or even extended lines of churches and other related monuments. Groups of this kind might include holy wells, cemeteries and other older ritual sites, as well as chapels of specialised function such as hermitages or retreat houses ... In topographical, ritual and sometimes legal terms, an important minster extended far out beyond its vallum into the territory around.[11]

This is a description which transfers readily to several early Irish monastic sites which are amplified by multiple churches of different size and status (e.g. Glendalough, Inishmurray or Clonmacnoise), but it seems especially relevant to Iona. Here, remnants of a small church and cemetery enclosure at *Cladh an Disirt* lie beyond the Abbey to the north, and there are other outlying churches and burial grounds to the south at St Mary's Chapel, Oran's Chapel, St Ronan's church and the Nunnery. In addition, there are ancient burial grounds – with no known or surviving church – at *Cladh nan Druineach* and *Port nam Mairtir* to the south, and possibly at *Cill mo Neachdain* and *Cill mo Ghobhannan*, within the north-west angle of the vallum, as well as at *Cill Chainnech*, at the site of the present (early nineteenth-century) parish church. Perhaps these were not all ancient cemeteries, and some of the minor churches are undoubtedly later medieval in date, but the overall impression is that a constellation of sacred spaces had already formed beyond the primary monastic area by the end of the early medieval period.

In contrast to this constellation of outlying sites, there is a group of monuments which seems to focus very clearly on the heart of Iona's ritual landscape: the tiny church – probably a mortuary chapel – known as St Columba's Shrine. Adjacent to this are the three high crosses – named for St John, St Matthew and St Martin – which now stand before the Benedictine Abbey; the Abbey church itself can be included in this monumental group, embracing the mortuary chapel at its west front; so can the stone-lined well which stands before the church, and the paved roadway

[11] Blair, 'Anglo-Saxon minsters: a topographical review', 257.

– the so-called *Sràid nam Marbh* – which leads directly to this nucleus, via the supposedly royal cemetery at *Reilig Odhrain*. Individually, these features span a wide period of time, but their final grouping indicates a long-established and clear focus on the site now occupied by the mortuary chapel. Again, there are clear parallels with some other major Irish monastic sites – Clonmacnoise, Inchcleraun, St Mullins or Inishmurray – where Peter Harbison proposes that major churches were built in the vicinity of founders' tomb-shrines which had become the object of long pilgrim journeys.[12] In this context, *Sràid nam Marbh* may have been the processional route not only of funerals, but also of pilgrims, perhaps coming to harbour at *Port nam Mairtir*. Even the remains of the so-called Columban prayer-cell on the rock outcrop of *Tòrr an Aba*[13] may have been a public monument of this sort, embellished with masses of beach pebbles and a secondary cross to offer early pilgrims an appropriate visitor experience.

Already in the seventh-century *Vita* Adomnán could present Columba's grave as a sacred spot, and Iona as an island where kings were consecrated and angels came in hosts. This literary amplification of Iona's reputation is paralleled in the physical amplification of the primary monastery by its outlying churches and burial grounds, but also by the clear monumental focus at its centre. But does this point to a primary core in the area of St Columba's Shrine? Some commentators have thought so, and believe that this grouping must represent *prima facie* evidence for the site of the original monastic foundation.[14] Others are less sure of this and have argued that the primary foundation was in the area now occupied by *Reilig Odhráin*,[15] or even in the present-day meadowland north of the Abbey.[16]

Whatever the answer, these monuments represent not only gradual accretions, but active reorganisation of Iona's ecclesiastical landscape for ritual consumption by patrons, clerics, penitents and other pilgrims. Richard Bradley's *Altering the Earth*[17] is a

[12] Harbison, *Pilgrimage in Ireland*, 147–50.
[13] Fowler and Fowler, 'Excavations on Torr an Aba'.
[14] RCAHMS, *Argyll* iv, 31–48.
[15] Barber, 'Excavations on Iona, 1979'.
[16] Skene, 'Notes on the history'.
[17] Bradley, *Altering the Earth*.

meditation on much earlier prehistoric monuments, but has some relevance for Iona where it considers monuments as mnemonic devices – not memorials which refer directly to past persons and events – but physical cues which guide and structure human actions, especially ritual action, within a particular scene. Although monuments are mnemonic devices, they may also impose new patterns on old ground. Thus, like the *Vita* of Adomnán, it is possible that the surviving landscape of ecclesiastical monuments narrates a mythologised scene, and offers no clear signposts to the location and character of the earliest settlement.

Antiquarians, architects and archaeologists

Archaeology made its entry to this mythologised scene armed with dogged pragmatism, and implicitly promising concise empirical knowledge. By peeling back the smooth green turf, the smooth but unreliable surface of things, concrete evidence of the Columban scene would be brought to light, bagged, photographed, described, labelled, and confidently fixed in place and time.

The shadow of the monuments: 1870–1940

The first field investigations made a very modest beginning and were all ancillary to programmes of architectural conservation work. These created the circumstances for some significant chance discoveries: a hoard of tenth-century Saxon coins was uncovered at the Abbey during drainage works in 1950; and at the Nunnery, four silver spoons were found during conservation works in 1922.[18] But scarcely any systematic archaeological work was undertaken in this period. The recorded excavations which did occur were simply minor, local incisions into the less glamourous zone of stratified sediments and midden debris beneath the lawns. This appears surprising at first, as Iona was already acknowledged to be an internationally important site. The explanation is simple enough. In these early years, a higher priority was the transformation of the medieval ruins – by consolidation or even facsimile – into a grand monumental presence on the island.

[18] Stevenson, 'A hoard of Anglo-Saxon coins found at Iona Abbey'; Curle, 'A note on four silver spoons'.

Alexander Smith 1875

A major programme of consolidation works was directed in the 1870s by R. Rowand Anderson, and the Abbey church was restored in 1902–10. Details of buried drains, paving and wall remnants were recorded at the Abbey by Anderson and his successors, especially P. MacGregor Chalmers and the antiquary Sir Henry Dryden.[19] However, the first consciously archaeological approach to stratified remains was recorded by J. Alexander Smith in 1875. Quantities of earth were being removed from amongst the ruins, but some middens were left *in situ* for his inspection. Smith adopted a systematic approach, sieving through these in regular spits, and published a full record of the faunal remains, in particular. The results were promptly published in the *Proceedings of the Society of Antiquaries of Scotland*.[20]

E. W. Lovegrove 1946; Stewart Cruden 1949–50

Thereafter, despite some published commentaries on the ecclesiastical architecture,[21] the archaeological record is silent until the 1940s. Again, a major programme of architectural works was in hand, directed now by Ian Lindsay, which was to extend from 1938–65. Lindsay himself probably trenched speculatively throughout the Abbey. There is little record of this in his notebooks or sketch plans, though his correspondence refers to a fruitless investigation within the Chapter House.[22] In the summer of 1946, E. W. Lovegrove, an amateur archaeologist, was encouraged to trench about between the east range of the Abbey and the neighbouring Michael Chapel. His annotated field sketches and the typescript of a short report record an irregular cutting which exposed areas of paving and medieval lintelled

[19] Anderson, *National Art Survey of Scotland*; National Monuments Record of Scotland [NMRS] MS 28: Manuscript collections of Sir Henry Dryden.

[20] Smith, 'Notes on medieval kitchen middens'.

[21] McGibbon and Ross, *The Ecclesiastical Architecture of Scotland*, vol. 3, 47–75.

[22] Scottish Development Department [SDD] SC 22042/8. Correspondence from I. G. Lindsay to J. S. Richardson, regarding the Chapter House, April 1947.

drains.[23] Stewart Cruden's excavations – *ca* 1950 – are likely to have been conducted at several sites, over a number of seasons.[24] Unfortunately, the surviving record is negligible. A few photographs record a group of trenches extending westward from St Columba's Shrine to a point beyond St John's Cross; and annotated sketches of these depict a well-laid pavement beneath layers of redeposited soil, rubble and midden material. An annotated plan of the Abbey shows the locations of these and other trenches at two locations in the east range.[25]

Research excavations for the Russell Trust: 1956–76

Priorities were to change in the following decades, when Iona's archaeological potential was at last accorded a higher degree of recognition. An extensive programme of research excavations was undertaken for the first time by Professor Charles Thomas from 1956–63. The benefactor of this work was Sir David Russell. His aim was that 'organised excavation should begin to sort out the many traditions and traces of former occupants and, to this end he provided, by means of a Trust, for a long term campaign'.[26] Indeed it was to become a very long campaign: from the mid-1950s to the mid-1970s, Professor Thomas and his successors opened numerous trial trenches throughout the area of the Abbey precinct and the surrounding meadows.

Charles Thomas 1956–63

The most important feature investigated by Professor Thomas was the early monastic vallum ditch. His interpretation of 'the

[23] NMRS AGD/23/400 I. G. Lindsay, Sketch plan. Excavations in 1944; NMRS AGD/23/239.1 I. G. Lindsay, Sketch plan. Excavations carried out by E. W. Lovegrove in June 1946; SDD SC 22042/6 Report by E. W. Lovegrove to the Iona Cathedral Trustees (= unpublished typescript) 1946.

[24] Personal communication from Dr Ian Fisher.

[25] NMRS (uncatalogued): S. Cruden, Sketches in plan and section of excavations west of the Abbey, in the vicinity of St John's Cross, 1949. Dyeline plan of the Abbey subscribed 'Orphoot, Whiting & Lindsay Architects, Edinburgh, June 1946', annotated and signed 'S H Cruden. M.O.W. 122 George Sq Edinburgh 2' (from the personal archive of Professor Charles Thomas). SDD SC 22042/14. Memoir from S. H. Cruden, describing a single green-glazed late medieval strap handle, from an investigation in the East Range, August 1950.

[26] Thomas, 'Excavations on Iona, 1956 and 1957'.

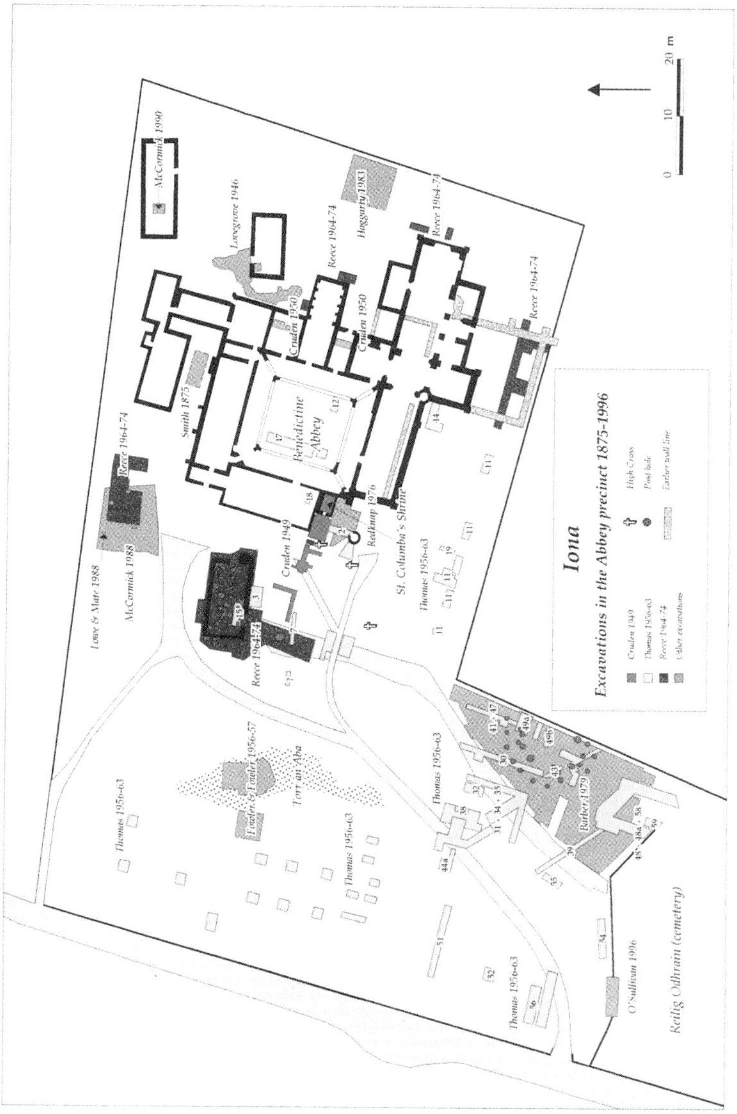

FIGURE 7. *A plan of excavations at the Abbey (1875–1996)*

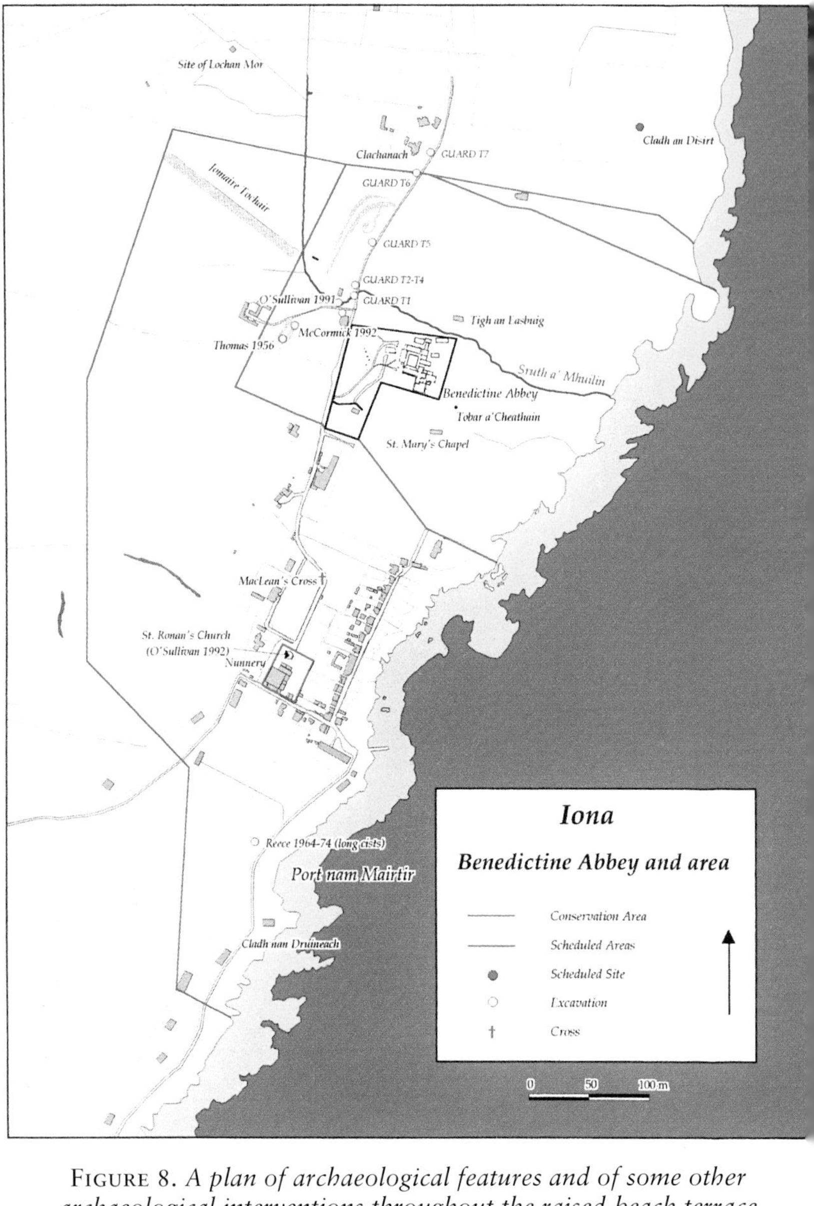

FIGURE 8. *A plan of archaeological features and of some other archaeological interventions throughout the raised-beach terrace which forms the setting for Iona's ecclesiastical monuments* (based on the Ordnance Survey map; Crown copyright)

wandering layout of the Iona vallum' was based on the assumption that there was only one earthwork, forming a single circuit.[27] This view has been superseded by information from geophysical surveys and aerial photographs, supplemented by further excavations, and it is now generally accepted that the traces of earthworks lying about the Abbey are complex and possibly multi-period.[28] The identification of a feature representing sleeper-beam construction (Trenches 37, 40) is also potentially important. An alternative interpretation of this feature is that it may represent a Yeavering-type (Style IV) plank-walled structure.[29] This type of construction is unprecedented in the archaeological record of early medieval Irish ecclesiastical sites. In the same area (Trench 40a), an extensive spread of iron slag was recorded. It is not certain, however, whether this was actually an industrial deposit, or highly concreted minerals which had naturally precipitated in the compact sands and gravels of the raised beach zone. Within the cloister (Trench 12), excavations failed to establish the history of a stone structure pre-dating the Abbey church, but did identify a mass-burial, or re-burial, of skeletal remains against its outer walls.[30] At the opposite, or west side of the cloister (Trench 17), a trench was opened to investigate an observation by Skene that there were surviving foundations of early medieval cells in that area; these proved to be no more than later medieval lintelled drains.[31]

Elizabeth Burley and Peter Fowler 1956–7

Investigation of the rock outcrop known as *Tòrr an Aba* also formed part of the programme of research which was funded by the Russell Trust.[32] Here, a small rock platform was occupied by low stone wall butts forming a square structure with a scooped or hollow interior. The walls are thought to have supported a light wooden superstructure. Within this, several large granite slabs were tentatively interpreted as the furnishings of an ascetic's prayer cell. The evidence of Adomnán's *Vita* is cited – with

[27] *Ibid.*

[28] RCAHMS, *Argyll* iv, 32; Reece, *Excavations on Iona, 1964–74*, 1–35; Barber, 'Excavations on Iona, 1979', 362–3.

[29] Hope-Taylor, *Yeavering*, 36–9; RCAHMS, *Argyll* iv, 40.

[30] Thomas, 'Iona', 10.

[31] Skene, 'Notes on the history', 340; Burley and Fowler, 'Iona', 14.

[32] Fowler and Fowler, 'Excavations on Torr an Aba'.

guarded enthusiasm – to suggest that this may have been Columba's own prayer cell. A later cross base was erected on the summit, surrounded by quantities of beach pebbles within the wall remnants: evidently the site was venerated after the structure became defunct.

Richard Reece 1964–74

Throughout the 1960s and 1970s, the research excavations funded by the Russell Trust were continued by Richard Reece.[33] Now, however, practical considerations had begun to reassert themselves within the archaeological programme. Thus, some areas were excavated in advance of construction work, or as an adjunct to the programme of architectural recording which had been initiated by the Royal Commission on the Ancient and Historic Monuments of Scotland. Excavation in Trench VIb, at the east wall of the Chapter House, recorded deeply stratified sands, gravels and ash spreads ascribed to the early medieval period. In Trench VId, a considerable depth of sediments was recorded, comprised of building debris, soils, gravels and ash spreads. Finally, south of the Abbey church, Trench VIe was opened to investigate mortared foundations which had been first exposed during conservation work in 1900. Again, excavations here found that deeply stratified sediments of early medieval or pre-Benedictine date survived over a wide area east of the Abbey.

Excavation in Area III recorded areas of cobbled paving, a stone-filled drain or sump and stratified dumps of sand, gravel and ash, interpreted as the surface debris of a yard or 'working area'. Finds in this area included imported Mediterranean pot sherds, a small bronze bell and a clay mould which was probably used to produce a decorative glass stud. Excavation in Area V investigated the building formerly known as the Old Guest House, west of the Abbey. Here, a concentration of post-holes formed the earliest phase and was interpreted as evidence for a succession of at least two or three timber buildings. The 'Guest House' itself is considered to have been built in the later medieval period and was probably used as the 'free-standing bakehouse and brewhouse of the Benedictine Abbey'.

[33] Reece, 'Recent work on Iona'; Reece, *Excavations on Iona, 1964–74*.

Far beyond the Abbey precinct, to the south, numerous medieval burials were crammed into the sandy rock crevices of the shoreline at *Port nam Mairtir*, some within roughly formed 'long cists'. The assemblage was dominated by women's remains. Two skeletons were radiocarbon dated with results in the mid-first and early second millennia AD.

Mark Redknap 1976

This excavation at the west front of the Abbey church was the final episode in the long programme of research excavations which had been begun by Charles Thomas in the 1950s.[34] The aim of this work was to examine the structure known as St Columba's Shrine as well as the adjacent well, previously described as the base of a round tower. Excavation recorded a number of early features in a buried topsoil layer, including post-holes and linear cuts, but could establish no clear date for these. The Shrine itself was found to be relatively early and was evidently once a free-standing chapel, pre-dating the Abbey church. A later group of features consisted of rough paving cut by several graves of medieval date. (This paving was compared by the excavator to the paved surface of the nearby medieval roadway.) These features, in turn, were sealed by further areas of later medieval paving which were found to be contemporary with the well-shaft. There was no evidence that the well was formed from the foundations of a round tower of early Irish type.

State-sponsored rescue excavations: 1979–91

In some ways, Iona offers a kind of localised history of field archaeology in these islands. Thus, the 1970s saw the end of privately sponsored research work, and the emergence in its place of state-sponsored rescue archaeology. Not only the circumstances, but the practice of excavation was changing rapidly: excavation techniques had become more exacting and refined; the full range of natural or palaeoenvironmental sciences was gradually being brought into play; and the level of detail recorded generally exceeded that of earlier investigations.

[34] Redknap, 'Excavation at Iona Abbey, 1976'.

John Barber 1979

Excavations at *Reilig Odhráin* by John Barber in 1979 were undertaken for the Central Excavation Unit (Scottish Development Department/Historic Buildings and Monuments Directorate).[35] The ancient royal burial ground had become too congested to bear continuing use by the local community. In response, complete excavation of a single large cutting to the north of *Reilig Odhráin* would allow the cemetery to be extended in that direction. Though the site was chosen in response to practical needs rather than research considerations, this was one of the most successful excavations on Iona to date. The larger area of excavation was a key factor, but also the wide scientific capabilities which were then being developed at the Central Excavation Unit, assisted by more rigorous techniques of sampling and excavation.

Some worked Mesolithic flint testified to the presence of man on this raised beach terrace from the earliest period of human settlement in Scotland. Other prehistoric features included a series of shallow ditches, possibly field enclosures or drains, but two later ditches could be attributed to the early medieval period. The deep, water-logged fills of the main vallum ditch included quantities of well-preserved wood and leather, as well as abundant faunal remains. Artefacts from elsewhere in the excavated area included medieval and possibly early medieval pot sherds, miscellaneous iron objects and industrial debris representing metal and glass working. Other early medieval features, though somewhat later than the vallum ditch, were the numerous pits and stake-holes thought to represent wooden structures. Remains of a stone-built industrial feature, possibly a corn-drying kiln, were attributed to the later medieval period.

Alison Haggarty 1983

In 1983 a cutting for the buried plant-room of a new heating system was machine-excavated on a small site immediately east of the Abbey.[36] Alison Haggarty recorded a deep sequence of dumped soils and midden deposits extending to *ca* 2.5 m below the present ground surface. Finds included miscellaneous animal bones and several iron objects, as well as a large assemblage of

[35] Barber, 'Excavations on Iona, 1979'.
[36] Haggarty, 'Iona: some results from recent work'.

medieval pottery which was described by Alan Lane and Ewan Campbell.[37]

Ian Mate and Chris Lowe 1988; Finbarr McCormick 1988

Following test-pitting by Chris Lowe and Ian Mate, Finbarr McCormick opened a large cutting north-west of the Abbey.[38] A thick layer of man-made topsoil overlay cobbled paving remnants and a lintelled drain. The drain is likely to have carried fresh water to the reredorter at the north side of the Abbey complex. Finds included fifteenth-century pottery, several metal objects and quantities of animal bone. Other excavations were undertaken beyond the precinct area and included a section cut across the vallum bank. This has proved to be an important trench, as a radiocarbon-dated sample of the peaty topsoil beneath the bank indicated a construction date – not in the sixth century, as expected – but which pre-dated the Columban period by some 400 or 500 hundred years.

McCormick 1990

Prior to erecting the reconstructed St John's Cross in a permanent display in the Infirmary, a small part of the floor area in this building was excavated in 1990 for the Central Excavation Unit.[39] No structures were identified, but finds included medieval pot sherds and crucible fragments representing early metal-working.

O'Sullivan 1991

Finally, excavations on the bank of *Sruth a' Mhuilinn* brought the period of state-sponsored rescue work to a close in 1991.[40] The mill stream was to be culverted where it traversed the western sector of the monastic earthworks. In advance of this, excavation recorded a man-made, sub-rectangular pool cut into the gravels of the stream bed, as well as an adjacent group of large post-pits. These features are most likely to represent the site of an early horizontal water mill (though this example may have been Early Modern rather than medieval).

[37] *Ibid.*, 208–12.
[38] Lowe, 'Recent fieldwork on Iona'; F. McCormick, 'Excavations on Iona in 1988'.
[39] McCormick, 'Early Christian metalworking on Iona'.
[40] O'Sullivan, 'Excavations on the mill stream, Iona'.

Developer-funded mitigations

The early 1990s saw the introduction of new Scottish Office policies which place a firm emphasis on avoidance of archaeological features, preferring preservation *in situ* to the large-scale rescue excavations which would formerly have been enacted. Thus, current protective measures combine with the conservation ethos fostered by the Iona Cathedral Trust to ensure that the ecclesiastical environs are exempt from development works on any significant scale. (A site for the Iona Cathedral Trust's new workshop and visitor centre was found on Mull, for instance, within view of Iona, rather than on the island itself.) Nonetheless, intermittent archaeological activity on the island is generated by the work of private utility companies, or by the Trust's own ongoing maintenance and restoration work.

O'Sullivan 1992; 1996

Archaeological excavation in St Ronan's – the ruined medieval parish church – was undertaken by AOC (Scotland) Ltd in advance of building refurbishment by the Iona Cathedral Trust.[41] An earlier and smaller church was found to underlie the walls of the standing medieval ruin. This was pre-dated by oriented graves, possibly of early medieval date. Numerous later graves were ascribed to the post-Reformation or Early Modern period. Analysis of the skeletal remains confirmed that the church cemetery had been exclusively for women's burials.

Finally, there have since been several other, minor archaeological interventions in recent years, chiefly in the form of watching briefs or trial trenching. Notably, a minor excavation in *Reilig Odhráin* in 1996 recorded a remnant of the medieval cemetery enclosure described in 1540 as 'a fair kirkyard biggit about with stone and lime'.[42]

Geophysical surveys

Non-intrusive work has also yielded useful results. Resistivity survey guided Richard Reece's programme of earthwork investigations in the 1970s, but far more extensive geophysical survey

[41] O'Sullivan, 'Excavation of a women's cemetery and early church'.
[42] O'Sullivan, 'Reilig Odhrain, Iona'; *Monro's Western Isles*, 62.

results were subsequently published by the Royal Commission.[43] This form of investigation was especially successful in the area to the south of the Abbey where a complex of plough-truncated earthworks was identified.

A second major episode of resistivity surveys was commissioned by the Iona Cathedral Trust to investigate the area of the modern precincts at both the Abbey and the Nunnery and conducted by Geophysical Surveys of Bradford in 1995.[44] At the Nunnery, a broad, curvilinear magnetic anomaly appears to respect the north-east corner of the convent buildings and may have been a track or road. In the same area, a rectilinear group of high resistance anomalies may represent buried wall-butts. At the Abbey, numerous geophysical anomalies could be identified with known features (walls, paths or service structures) and clear linear traces to the south and east of the claustral buildings are probably buried drains. A group of weakly-defined, rectilinear anomalies within the north-west angle of the present boundary wall suggests buried wall remnants, but these are likely to be relatively recent garden beds.

What results?

This brief review can do no more than offer a glimpse of the number and variety of archaeological investigations on Iona to date. As each new ground-breaking venture has reduced the total sum of a finite archaeological resource, it is worth asking whether this high level of activity has yielded a corresponding harvest of information. The answer is that successive archaeological investigations have yet to produce a coherent narrative of the island's earliest ecclesiastical settlement. There are several reasons for this. Some are inherent in the character of the archaeological remains; others relate to the management of the buildings. These problems have been compounded, however, by the way in which the stratified remains have been sought by successive archaeological investigators.

[43] N. Balaam, 'The vallum', 14. RCAHMS, *Argyll* iv, 32.

[44] Geophysical Surveys of Bradford. *Geophysical Surveys on Iona: the Abbey & Nunnery Precincts* (unpublished survey report to AOC (Scotland) Ltd for the Iona Cathedral Trust, 1995).

The formation and management of an archaeological resource

Iona's ecclesiastical settlements developed over the span of a thousand years. This alone will have taken a toll on the accumulating archaeological remains. Limited excavations at some larger early Irish church sites – such as Moville or Armagh[45] – indicate that the use of any particular area does not remain constant throughout the early medieval period: burial grounds are replaced by workshops, industrial areas by other buildings, and so forth. Added to this mundane pattern of scouring and superinscription is the exceptional factor of Iona's importance as a pilgrim site: thus, its development as an ecclesiastical settlement has been amplified by its development as an arena for controlled public access and ritual. And beyond the period of its early medieval *floruit*, Iona was subject to a whole new period of transformation and reorganisation by the Benedictine community. There is ample evidence that the establishment of other later medieval abbeys and priories in Scotland was characterised by energetic programmes of landscaping or site preparation and, on Iona too, some evidence for this can be found in the archaeological record.[46] Furthermore, the environs of the Abbey would certainly have been subject to intensive cultivation in this period, and the deep, man-made topsoil within the precinct has been attributed to Benedictine gardeners.[47] This soil was produced not only by adding manure, midden materials, lime and seaweed, but by deeply milling the existing Columban or early medieval strata.

This sort of re-working and reorganisation has continued throughout the modern period, despite Iona's remote island location. The physical fabric of many Scottish abbeys and priories suffered badly after the Reformation, as the ruins were commonly quarried for stone and the sites taken into other forms of land use. In contrast, Iona's medieval ruins have been cherished; but, ironically, this has been the cause of an invasive modern history. Major programmes of conservation, landscaping or reconstruction

[45] Ivens, 'Moville Abbey, Newtonards, Co. Down'; Brown and Harper, 'Excavations on Cathedral Hill, Armagh, 1968'.

[46] Haggarty, 'Iona: some results from recent work'; Reece, *Excavations on Iona, 1964–74*, 55–62.

[47] McCormick, 'Excavations on Iona in 1988'.

works were undertaken in the 1750s, the 1870s, the early 1900s, the 1930–60s and again in the 1990s. In terms of the conservation and enjoyment of the ecclesiastical buildings, these must be regarded as positive, and sometimes creative interventions. But from a narrower point of view, these works have drastically depleted the buried archaeological resource. During the earlier works, in particular, unrecorded quantities of stratified material were removed from amongst the later medieval ruins; and beyond the buildings themselves, all phases of restoration have included landscaping works on some scale.

Keyhole investigations

The same difficulties are often found to occur on extensive archaeological sites with standing medieval buildings. Iona, however, has suffered a form of depletion which relates directly to the conduct of archaeological work itself. The prevailing approach, in every decade, has favoured dispersed trial trenches and test-pits, or small excavations limited by the extent of associated development works. Remains of primary settlement evidence are notoriously elusive on early medieval sites in these islands, both secular and ecclesiastical. On early Hiberno-Scottish church sites, domestic and industrial activities are most likely to be represented by dispersed, amorphous spreads of ash, slag or burnt bone, while structures will most likely be represented by the truncated negative features – pits and wall-slots or slight foundation trenches – representing earth-fast timber buildings. Features of this sort are not susceptible to discovery and interpretation via keyhole incisions, especially on a large, complex site. It is irrelevant here whether such cuttings are research-driven or in response to a rescue/development need. What is important is that this approach simply has not worked. Indeed, Richard Reece made a frank observation about one of his own cuttings – which exposed a complex stratigraphy of early medieval sediments but failed to derive a significant interpretation – when he admitted that 'the information extracted in a small trench was not commensurate with the information which was destroyed'.[48]

[48] Reece, *Excavations on Iona, 1964–74*, 56.

Burials, buildings and boundaries

Burials, buildings and boundaries are central strands in the investigation of any early church site, and can supply examples in the present case which illustrate the difficulty of deriving a coherent overall narrative from Iona's piecemeal archaeological record.

Burials: the women's cemetery

Reilig Odhráin is the only cemetery on Iona which is still in use. It is uncertain whether this was the primary burial ground of the monastic community or, alternatively, was first amongst a series of secondary or satellite cemeteries. Human remains or possible grave cuts have been recorded at several sites within the Abbey precinct, but larger groups of burials are recorded at only two sites. The first is the group of skeletal remains excavated from the sandy crevices of the shoreline at *Port nam Mairtir*; the second is from St Ronan's, the ruinous medieval parish church.[49] Here, the standing ruins were found to overlie remains of an earlier and smaller church. Both the ruined church and its environs were used for women's burials only in the post-medieval period, and there is a strong likelihood that this perpetuated a much older tradition of segregation by sex. This must be considered a key question in understanding the social and ritual history of Iona's earliest monastic settlement, but it is unanswered in the archaeological record, for a variety of practical and strategic reasons.

Though the later burials survived very well, the earliest burials had almost entirely vanished within the acidic conditions of the raised beach gravels, so that neither radiocarbon dates nor a full palaeopathologist's report could be obtained for these. Further, these earliest burials were pretty badly damaged by the construction of the tiny early medieval church over them; in fact, the walls of this building had been intruded into the earlier graves. Prior to excavation the earlier church was itself completely unknown, as its walls had been levelled and robbed for the construction of the later medieval parish church. In the post-Reformation period, this latter building itself became ruinous

[49] Reece and Wells, 'Martyr's Bay'; O'Sullivan, 'Excavation of a women's cemetery and early church'.

and was incorporated into the surrounding cemetery, so that the stratigraphic record of its interior is dominated by later, post-medieval burials. Thus, the archaeological resource was simultaneously depleted and enlarged in a variety of ways by ongoing use of the site.

Successive conservation works also played a role here. The later building had been consolidated in the 1870s and again in the 1920s. When the excavation was completed, it would be re-floored and re-roofed once again, to house a display of medieval sculpture fragments. Thus, the uppermost burials had probably been truncated by some unrecorded episode of earlier conservation work in which sediments were removed from within the church to level its floor area. But the aim of the present work was also to reduce the floor area, as the excavation was conducted to a specific architectural brief. Thus, although the re-development of the church supplied the circumstances for a significant new excavation, these same circumstances set firm limits to the scale of the investigation. Only as much of the internal deposits were removed as was considered necessary for consolidation and re-flooring; and when the fieldwork programme pressed on to record the earlier church and underlying graves, this could only be done within a narrow sample trench. Thus, the earliest levels were partly exposed but remained substantially unexcavated. Furthermore, nothing beyond the building was excavated, so that no information was recorded on the extent of this cemetery, whether it was enclosed or, critically, how it came to be incorporated within the precinct of the Nunnery.

The published excavation report – as is often the case – dwells on the positive aspects of the project, rather than on these shortcomings. In retrospect, however, it might have been better in the long term simply to note the presence of the early building and withdraw, without making a deep keyhole incision in the earlier strata.

Buildings: magna domus *or farmyard pen?*

The stratified remains of early medieval buildings are elusive in all but the most favourable circumstances. The earliest community on Iona did not build in stone. Stone churches on Hiberno-Scottish ecclesiastical sites would not have appeared until at least the eighth century and the earliest domestic and farm buildings on the island would also have been of timber. Adomnán's *Vita* cites building work with withies, and with larger timbers of pine and oak.[50] Excavation in the waterlogged vallum ditch recovered numerous worked wood fragments, including several structural timbers.[51] But these are the sole glimpses to date of a landscape of early medieval buildings which is otherwise represented only by the post-holes recorded throughout the area of the Abbey precinct. Only one group of these post-holes suggests the ground-plan of an early building. This is the double arc of pits – tentatively dated to the seventh or eighth century – recorded by John Barber's excavation north of *Reilig Odhráin*.[52] With a projected diameter of *ca* 20 m, this would be at least twice the size of any archaeologically excavated round-house of the period in Ireland. Opinion is divided as to whether this immense structure was the communal house of Columba's monks – i.e. the *magna domus* described by Adomnán – or simply a large livestock pen, built with especially stout timbers to resist the energetic rooting and scratching of pigs.[53] More to the point, this single putative example represents the only ground-plan of a timbered structure to be derived from the scores of trenches which have been excavated throughout Iona's ecclesiastical environs.

Boundaries: monastic vallum or prehistoric settlement enclosure?

The monastic vallum was noted by numerous early visitors to Iona as some sort of artificial landscape feature, but O. G. S. Crawford was the first field archaeologist to describe the scale and form of the surviving earthwork, and to appreciate its possible relationship with the primary monastic site.[54] Some years later, Charles Thomas made the first exploratory cuttings across the projected line of the earthwork where it had been levelled beneath the lawns and meadows about the Abbey. The results were puzzling. Those sectors which could be identified from trial

[50] *VC* ii.3, ii.45.

[51] Barber, 'Excavations on Iona, 1979'.

[52] *Ibid.*

[53] MacDonald, 'Aspects of the monastery and monastic life', 284–9; 'Adomnan's monastery of Iona', 34–8; McCormick, 'Iona: the archaeology of an early monastery', 53.

[54] Crawford, 'Iona'.

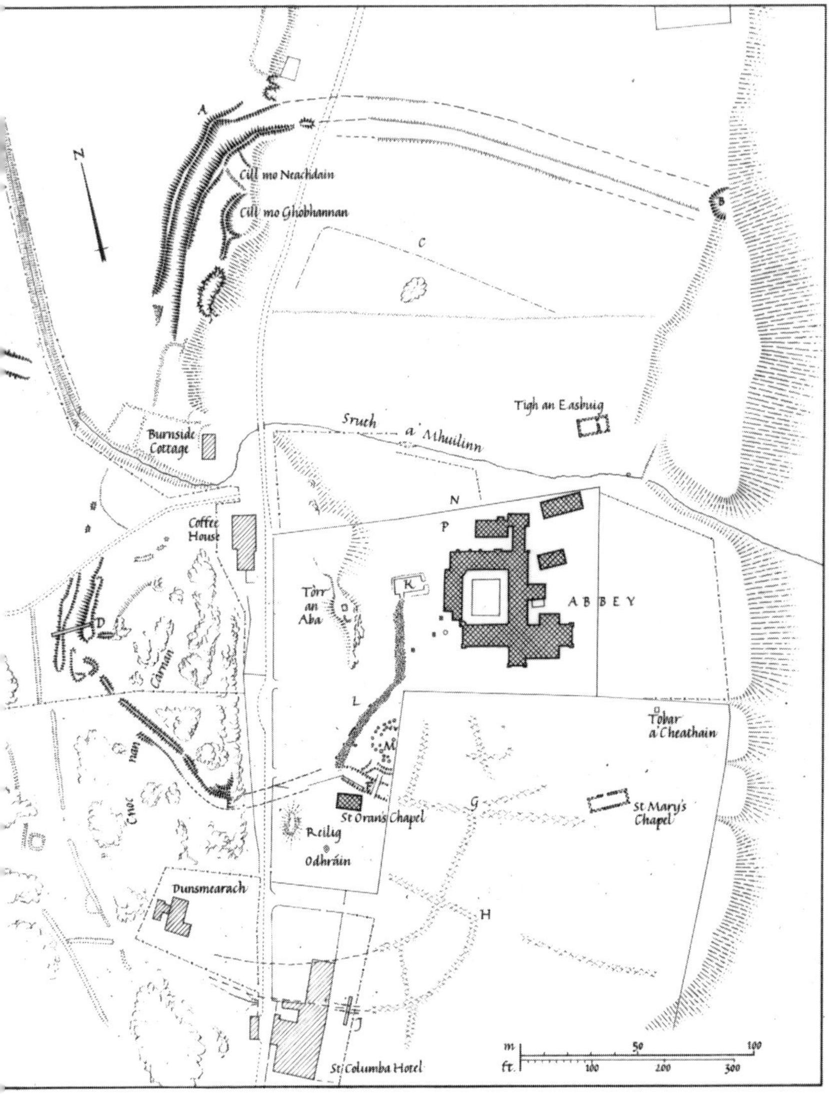

FIGURE 9. *The extent of the early monastic earthworks, based on evidence from air photos, geophysics and upstanding remains* (from RCAHMS 1982, 32)

trenching did not add up to elements of a regular overall plan; this is reflected in the meandering earthwork reconstruction which was published by Professor Thomas in *The Early Christian Archaeology of North Britain*.[55] In fact, several factors were at work to thwart a successful reconstruction. The search for a single vallum was a flawed enterprise in any case as it is now known that the earthworks were complex and perhaps multi-period. This could not be recognised by earlier excavators, partly because the earthworks had been erased by ongoing use and reorganisation of the site over several periods; but also because the limited information available from trial trenches alone would never be adequate for a reconstruction. The interpretation offered by Ian Fisher and his team from the Royal Commission on the Ancient and Historic Monuments of Scotland is undoubtedly closer to the mark.[56] Here, aerial reconnaissance and electrical resistivity survey were brought into play. But although this reconstruction is generally accepted as the definitive plan on present knowledge, it is not the only one. An alternative reconstruction by John Barber favours the view that the ancient cemetery of *Reilig Odhráin* occupies the site of the primary monastic enclosure, which was subsequently expanded to encompass the area now occupied by the Benedictine Abbey.[57]

A more far-reaching element of doubt was added by Finbarr McCormick's excavation of a section trench through the western sector of the vallum in 1988.[58] A sample of the peaty topsoil beneath the bank returned a radiocarbon date in the first or second century AD, indicating that the vallum – the one feature which had hitherto been attributed to the primary Columban period by all parties – might actually be a much older earthwork than supposed. Again, the problem here is one of scale. The riddle of Iona's earthworks will never be entirely resolved by piecemeal and opportunistic excavation, but only by a concerted programme of excavations conducted within a comprehensive research design.

[55] Thomas, *Early Christian Archaeology*, 30.
[56] RCAHMS, *Argyll* iv, 32.
[57] Barber, 'Excavations on Iona, 1979'.
[58] McCormick, 'Excavations on Iona in 1988'.

Conclusions

Iona is beguiling, but also challenging. No other early ecclesiastical site – indeed no other site of any period in these islands – has been the subject of so much archaeological fieldwork. Despite this, extensive excavations have yet to produce a coherent archaeological narrative of early ecclesiastical settlement on the island. Though we have become attached to the idea that the island landscape offers intimate access to the Columban scene, the main narratives of this scene – either Adomnán's *Vita* or the monumental tableau of churches, cemeteries, crosses and earthworks – refer only indirectly to this world and may even offer misleading signposts. Archaeology claims the special privilege of access to concrete evidence which can be fixed in time and place. But a long and complex settlement history has produced an uneven archaeological resource; and the surviving remains have been further depleted by successive conservation works. The excavation strategies which have been applied to this resource have not always been appropriate or successful. Often, excavations have not been carried out in the context of any overall research strategy, but in direct response, instead, to the requirements of ongoing development works. Even in those cases where research was the primary or sole objective, too many small cuttings have resulted in a piecemeal record with little potential for overall integration or synthesis.

There have, of course, been many important individual discoveries, and some of these point to the potential of further work. Mark Redknap's excavation of an area adjacent to St Columba's Shrine in 1976 discovered that, despite successive conservation and reconstruction works, undisturbed layers of complex medieval stratigraphy do survive in the immediate vicinity of the Abbey; and excavations by Richard Reece and Alison Haggarty in the 1980s have demonstrated the existence of extensive and deeply stratified early medieval sediments in areas east of the Abbey. John Barber's investigations north of *Reilig Odhráin* attest to the value of open area excavations on a large scale (in contrast to the numerous keyhole excavations of earlier fieldworkers), and also demonstrate the existence of well preserved organic artefacts and environmental materials. At the Nunnery, despite the largely unrecorded removal of stratified deposits during early conservation works, the recent excavation of St Ronan's church has indicated that an unsuspected horizon of earlier ecclesiastical monuments may be represented by buried features and this area should certainly be regarded as having a high archaeological potential.

A future programme of work might explore some of the outlying cemeteries and their associated churches. This would help to characterise and date the elaboration of a ritual landscape of sacred spaces on Iona. Closer to the Abbey, the development of public spaces for medieval pilgrims is a fascinating subject which would certainly reward further excavation, especially at the west front of the Abbey church, in the area around St Columba's Shrine. Finally, although it has been asserted throughout that trial trenching is generally an unrewarding tactic, a programme of keyhole excavations – guided by the existing information from geophysics and air photos – could be invaluable in characterising and dating the development of the earthwork complex, and would certainly recover quantities of palaeoenvironmental materials from secure contexts.

New investigations are strictly regulated, however, by existing Scottish Office policy, and are scrutinised both for the quality of their research designs, as well as for their provision of adequate resources for post-excavation analyses and publication. The area around the Abbey which is defined as a Scheduled Ancient Monument has recently been extended to include the adjacent meadows, so that the whole of the area of likely early monastic settlement is now protected against any form of ground-breaking work. An even larger area is designated a Conservation Area, and almost every part of the island which was not originally endowed on the Iona Cathedral Trust is now owned instead by the National Trust for Scotland.

Yet despite this overarching legislative embrace, concessions are still made every year to the minor ground-breaking works associated with ongoing maintenance and development. Thus, last year's *Discovery & Excavation in Scotland 1996*[59] records

[59] A gazetteer of archaeological excavation and survey work is published annually under this title by the Council for Scottish Archaeology, a non-statutory organisation based at the Royal Museum of Scotland, in Edinburgh.

local interventions by several field units, including the Scottish Urban Archaeological Trust (SUAT), Glasgow University Archaeological Research Division (GUARD), AOC (Scotland) Ltd and Headland Archaeology Ltd. This continuing archaeological presence on Iona has a positive side: it represents the will of the authorities to impose monitoring or site preparation on all ground-breaking works within archaeologically sensitive areas. But perhaps it is time at last to be more creative, and insist on design solutions in maintenance and development work which do not require that each year, another small portion of the island's archaeological fabric is quarried away.

9

Celebrating Columba on Iona, 1897 and 1997

E. Mairi MacArthur

> They simply took the boat to Iona, held a special service in the ruined Cathedral and got back to Oban in time to catch the train.[1]

THE gentleman of the press who reported for *The Scots Pictorial* on the Columban commemoration of 9 June 1897 appeared to adopt a mildly irreverent tone. There was little of the colour of a mediaeval pilgrimage, he mused, as the participating clergy 'wore no scallop-shells and carried no staffs except those of their umbrellas'. He did admit that, as a solidly Presbyterian undertaking, it had never been officially called a 'pilgrimage'. Yet those who journeyed to the sacred isle for the worthy purpose of celebrating a chief founder of their church should, he felt, have as much right to title themselves 'pilgrims' as had 'any devotee who ever walked on unboiled peas'.

The article was, regrettably, anonymous. For I should like to have acknowledged by name this correspondent with the cheerful turn of phrase who has left us such a lively first-hand account from a century ago. Reading on, moreover, it becomes clear that he found the simplicity and sincerity of the event impressive.

Following a decision by the General Assemby of the Church of Scotland in 1896 to mark the following year by 'A thanksgiving for the introduction of the Gospel into our land', a committee was formed.[2] The eighth Duke of Argyll, then owner of Iona and

[1] *The Scots Pictorial*, 19 June 1897, pp. 303–6, opening paragraph.
[2] *The S. Columba Commemoration, Iona* (Edinburgh and London, 1897), 3.

all its historic sites, willingly granted permission to hold a day of memorial services. A temporary roof was constructed for the ruined choir of the Cathedral church, its windows glazed and a pulpit, harmonium and benches installed. Details of the day, including the entire texts of psalms, prayers and sermon from the noon service, are recorded in a little booklet *The S. Columba Commemoration, Iona* published by William Blackwood on the initiative of the church committee.

A copy of this booklet in my possession is inscribed 'from the Minister of Iona' to Mr Donald McNiven, a relative of my grandmother, from Fidden on the Ross of Mull side of Iona parish. He will have been among the many local people who came together that June morning to worship, first of all, in their own language:

> The islanders observed the day as a holiday and turned out in Sunday attire to participate in the celebration. They were present in strong force at the Gaelic service and many of them remained afterwards to show their interest in the English portion.[3]

The Gaelic service was conducted by the parish minister, the Revd Archibald MacMillan. Donald Macfarlan, minister of Morven, rose to lead the praise by giving out the line and visitors waiting outside listened to 'the singing of the psalms after the good old style'. The *Scots Pictorial* reporter later noted that the sound of the *Te Deum* at the following service, sung by a special choir and accompanied by the harmonium, contrasted strangely with 'the long notes of the Gaelic singing' heard an hour before. Yet he was sure that both would have been appreciated by Columba, a Gaelic-speaker and a musician.

The communion service at noon, conducted in English, involved ministers from Campbeltown, Tiree and Tobermory in addition to some of the most eminent clergymen in the land. White beards of biblical proportions feature in the dignified official photograph taken outside the nave. Included in the group of around twenty are the Very Revd Dr James MacGregor of St Cuthbert's and the Revd Dr Robert Blair of St John's, both in Edinburgh, the Revd Dr R. H. Story, principal of Glasgow University and the Revd Dr McAdam Muir of St Mungo's Cathedral. Lord

[3] *The Oban Times*, 12 June 1897.

Balfour of Burleigh, whose steam yacht brought a special party, can also be identified.

By the middle of the day up to 300 people had crowded into the choir where Benedictine monks once chanted the psalter. Some may have remained, and others joined in, for a second Gaelic service in the afternoon and an evening one in English.

Meanwhile, at the House of Retreat erected in Iona village three years earlier by the Bishop of Argyll and the Isles, a small gathering of Episcopal churchmen kept their own day of prayer and remembrance.[4] And on 15 June the Roman Catholic church in Scotland paid its tribute to Columba when over 600 pilgrims came by special steamer to attend mass on Iona. They were led by Archibishop Angus MacDonald of St Andrews and Edinburgh and Bishop George Smith of Argyll and the Isles while their large flock included 'a great many humble people from the Western Isles'.[5]

The three denominations evidently kept a careful distance one from the other – a fact to which *The Oban Times* devoted an editorial, regretting that there had not been a combined celebration to honour one whom no church could claim as their own. Indeed, it surmised rather grandiosely, 'a chance for the Millennium' had been missed.[6] The eighth Duke was only too well aware of the competition for access to Iona's sacred sites by the different churches and, indeed, found this wearisome. There was increasing public demand too for another chance to worship within Iona Cathedral.

His decision, in 1899, to hand over the ruins to a new trust linked to the Church of Scotland was thus galvanised by the Columban anniversary two years earlier.[7] A declared purpose of the transfer was to restore the Cathedral church and make it available for ecumenical worship. Within a decade this had been achieved and the local congregation regularly used the building for weekly services. My grandparents were the first to be married there, in 1909.

As far as Iona was concerned, 9 June 1897 was akin to a special sort of Sunday, a day set aside for worship. Other keynotes appear

[4] *Cowley Evangelist*, 1896–7, 157.

[5] *The Oban Times*, 19 June 1897.

[6] *The Oban Times*, 19 June 1897, editorial.

[7] Correspondence quoted in Frances Balfour, *Lady Victoria Campbell, A Memoir*, 280–5.

to have been simplicity of style, the involvement of the local community and the equal place granted to Gaelic and English. The three religious commemorations were contained within two single days, less than one week apart.

The columns of *The Oban Times* make clear that over the rest of the year there were many other events, large and small, to claim the attention of the islanders. A telegraph service began in the new post office; a notice outside, astutely aimed at summer trade, read: 'Wire your friends from the Holy Isle.' Queen Victoria's Diamond Jubilee was enthusiastically celebrated, with picnic and prizes for the children and a bonfire on Dùn I. A cairn was erected there in her honour. In August the crops looked good and in December the gales blew hard, isolating the island for several days. Eventually, the year ended with 'a day which will be long remembered on Iona', when pipes, dance, song, story and much good cheer accompanied the wedding of Angus MacPhail, postmaster, to Marion MacArthur.[8]

Nothing else from 1897 relating directly to Columba can now be gleaned, save for one publication from The Iona Press. Between 1887 and 1893 this small printing venture had turned out about a dozen booklets of prayer, poetry or local lore including one entitled *The Great Hymn 'Altus' of S. Columba Abbot of Iona.* By 1897 William Muir, one of the Press founders,was living in London but his sister Hannah had remained on Iona to run a souvenir shop. On her initiative, presumably, a second edition of their *Altus* was prepared that year. The Latin words of this hymn, composed by an Iona monk, were placed alongside an English translation by Muir. And the pages were ornately and beautifully illuminated, after the style of an early psalter, by Beatrice Ann Waldram, then in her early twenties. She was to become a well-known potter in London and had been taught by Lewis F. Day, a prominent member of the Arts and Crafts movement of the late nineteenth century.[9]

William Muir, an enthusiast for the illustrated poetry of William Blake, undoubtedly moved in artistic circles and he must have provided the link between the young London artist and Iona. The 1897 *Altus* was a particularly fine memento, purchased

[8] *The Oban Times*, 18 December 1897.

[9] Private correspondence from Ian Waldram, great-nephew of B. Waldram

perhaps by our man from the *Scots Pictorial.* Before the steamer bore them all off, he recorded, they had time 'to spend a shilling or two upon the harmless necessary souvenir in the shape of books or pebbles'.

To attempt a comparison with 1997, I turn to a file bulging with cuttings, leaflets and programmes spanning almost the entire year.[10] There was music and drama, poetry and prose, conferences, lectures and religious celebrations of every hue. Harps and doves made regular appearances.

Exhibitions were held as far afield as Stornoway and Pittenweem,[11] while the shinty-hurling international between Scotland and Ireland was battled out under the banner of Columba '97.[12] The saint's name was also given to a postage stamp, a new tartan and a shiny railway train.[13] In a Highland schools' painting competition he was seen receiving a pasta necklace from a little girl and meeting Councillor Brude to ask for more children's facilities.[14] And in a pageant beside the River Ness Columba again banished the famous monster, a green and silver creation that danced in the sunlight to the delight of the crowd.[15]

There was, of course, much of interest and merit among the whimsy. The visit by Mary Robinson, then President of Ireland, made a particularly positive impact.[16] Members of the island's community council had an opportunity to meet her at the opening of the new Saint Columba Exhibition centre across the Sound of Iona in Fionnphort. Overall, however, very little out of the whole

[10] See, for example, 'St Columba 97 Programme of Events May–December 1997', published by Argyll and The Isles Tourist Board, Oban.

[11] 'Colum Cille and the Saints of the Western Isles', Museum nan Eilean, Stornoway, see *West Highland Free Press*, 13 June 1997; 'Celtic Airts', part of Pittenweem Arts Festival, see *Artwork* no. 86, June/July 1997.

[12] *The Oban Times*, 20 November 1997.

[13] Royal Mail Mint Stamps, set of four 'St Augustine and St Columba', issued 11 March 1997; St Columba's tartan designed by Rosslyn Jones, Mull, see *The Oban Times*, 30 January 1997; train named 'Saint Columba' at Oban, see *The Oban Times*, 11 December 1997.

[14] Organised under auspices of Columba '97 Inverness Committee, exhibited Old High Church Halls, Inverness 24 May–7 June 1997.

[15] Organised under auspices of Columba '97 Inverness Committee, held 7 June 1997.

[16] Official visit to Iona, Stornoway, Skye, Glasgow 8–10 June 1997.

year's programme of events on or off the island was initiated by, or fully involved, the local population.

On Sunday 8 June 1997 the morning service on BBC Radio Scotland, and the evening television programme *Songs of Praise* on BBC1, were both broadcast from Iona Cathedral to the nation. The local minister played no part, no native faces were to be seen in the congregation and there was not one word in Gaelic, the language used continuously by the population – both religious and secular – for nearly fourteen centuries. The day looked hectic and complicated, with television crews and helicopters, pilgrims on foot and coracles by sea. The most straightforward facts were mangled in the television commentary: for example, the abbey was *not* all in ruins 'until rebuilt by the Iona Community under George MacLeod from 1938'.

A Gaelic programme *Lorgan Dhè*, broadcast on STV and Grampian on 6 July, made the same error. What was even more baffling, local place-names were ignored and replaced by cavalier translations from recent English equivalents. Thus *Port a' Churaich* [bay of the coracle], for example, became '*Bagh Chaluim Chille*'. Watching it was a curiously alienating experience.

The sincerity of those who participated in those broadcasts should not be decried. But I know I am not alone in feeling that the contents somehow lacked *gravitas*, and did not adequately reflect the cultural heritage they were intended to honour. It is admittedly true that in two central areas of monastic life – spiritual and linguistic – things have changed greatly from the time of Columba or indeed from a century ago. Regular church-going by the local population, and the daily use of Gaelic, both declined sharply on Iona – but only within the last two or three decades, a period well within living memory. The casual onlooker last year might have been forgiven for thinking that they had never been. That stands in stark contrast to 1897.

Lastly, no programme took a thoughtful, informed look at the island itself, at the physical landscape in which Columba and his successors moved. My own research into Iona's social and economic history has been able to mine a rich seam of documentary, archaeological and oral sources.[17] There is no lack of

[17] MacArthur, *Iona. The Living Memory of a Crofting Community*; *eadem*, *Columba's Island. Iona from Past to Present*; *eadem*, *Iona*.

material to shed light on the long and varied settlement pattern, over twenty centuries at least, of this attractive green dot in the Hebridean sea.

Thus, no commentator in 1997 drew the most obvious parallel between the world of Columba and that of today. From the early Christian settlement on Iona onwards, and up through the Benedictine period, monks managed the land, drew a living from soil and sea and gave hospitality to those arriving on their shores. As 1997 unfolded, the folk of Iona continued to work their crofts and farms, to run local services and prepared to receive the usual intake of summer visitors. It is what they have done for generations.

The islanders have long had to live with sloppy journalism and with the effective appropriation of the island's religious history and image by others. It does seem ironic that the Columban commemorations of 1997 simply seemed to reinforce, rather than reverse, those trends. Yet, a rare native voice heard on one of the special radio programmes[18] did come through with a quiet, but strong, last word – a reminder that when Oxford was a swamp and Edinburgh a rock, Iona was already famous. And that it always will be.

Islands are not easy places in which to live. The enduring fame of this one has not protected its dwellers, in every age, from their share of hardship, suffering and great peril. When, in some future century, a celebration of Columba comes around once again, let us profoundly hope that people will have continued to find ways of making the saint's island home of Iona also theirs.

[18] *Voyage to Iona*, series of four programmes broadcast 1–7 June 1997 by Radio Religion BBC Scotland.

10

Between faith and folklore: twentieth-century interpretations and images of Columba

Donald E. Meek

LATE twentieth-century society is currently much concerned with the celebration of 'Celtic' saints and saintliness, particularly within the context of the 1400th anniversary of the death of Columba. Popular interest in the saints is, of course, something that is far older than 1997, and has not been generated merely by modern *fin de siècle* nostalgia, though latter-day, so-called 'post-modern', mania has undoubtedly played its part. Not least because of the happy chronological accident that the centennial celebration of Columba's festival day falls at the end of each century, and has coincided with pre-millennial awareness as we approach the year 2000, an efflorescence of 'saint seeking' has occurred in Scotland.

In some Christian traditions, notably Roman Catholicism, the saints have been invoked, celebrated and commemorated at a variety of popular levels across the centuries. This has led to the reshaping of saintly profiles to meet a broad range of needs, including changing fashions within both faith and community. In trying to assess the saints and give them a place in their modern worldviews, contemporary seekers maintain the tradition of popular pliability, and approach the subject in different ways, depending on what they want to get out of the saint. At the risk of oversimplifying, it can be said that what a Roman Catholic seeker expects to find in a 'saint' may be quite different from what a Protestant seeker may wish to find; but it is unlikely that there can be a single Roman Catholic approach or a single

Protestant one. Nowadays, there may be many 'saint seekers' who have only the vaguest connection with Christianity in any form. Their reasons for seeking the saints may be quite diverse, in many cases unashamedly secular rather than devotedly sacred. As a result, the quest for the saints may be motivated by factors ranging from general curiosity to a special concern for the local economy or the environment. It is important to recognise the diversity of approaches within contemporary 'saint seeking', since the preconceived expectation will almost inevitably lead to a degree of reconstruction of the (rediscovered) saints. The saints, however, are no strangers to reconstruction. Their profiles have been rearranged by politicians, clerics and special pleaders since the earliest days. Columba himself has hovered between faith and folklore, between preaching and propaganda, between saint and symbol, across the years. This chapter will consider some of the perceptions of Columba that have emerged, and continue to emerge, in various popular (rather than academic) domains in the closing years of the present millennium.

The Columba of folklore

Columba's place in Gaelic folklore was fairly well attested at the beginning of the present century, and has been maintained to some extent throughout it, but it would be wrong to suppose that a 'Columba consciousness' is pervasive in the Highlands and Islands. The gradual attrition of the Gaelic communities has affected the saints as well as the sinners. Columba's memory has been preserved in these communities and beyond partly because of the folklore-collecting ventures of the second half of the nineteenth century, especially the work of Alexander Carmichael. These ventures came off the presses at the very beginning of this century. Carmichael's *Carmina Gadelica* began to be published in 1900, and ensured that the twentieth century would be well supplied with a store of popular belief which has enjoyed some degree of artificial revival in the last twenty-five years.[1] Other

[1] *Carmina Gadelica*, collected by Alexander Carmichael, 6 vols (Edinburgh, 1900–71). The first two volumes, which are of particular relevance to Columba, were published in 1900. Numerous anthologies based on those earlier editions of the Carmina continue to be produced.

late nineteenth- and early twentieth-century collectors, notably Duncan MacGregor Campbell and Kenneth MacLeod, also recorded fragments of lore relating to Columba.[2] Such sayings and fragments indicate that, during the centuries, Columba became a figure of invocation, in proverbs and rhymes. These have been particularly well preserved in the Roman Catholic communities of the Hebrides, though the saint is also remembered in the Protestant islands.

Columba's role as a spiritual warrior, efficacious in prayer and triumphant in worsting the Devil, is well attested in traditional Gaelic lore,[3] but he is most frequently portrayed as a protector of the weak and as a facilitator of the regular tasks of life. His festival day (officially 9th June, but falling on the second Thursday of June, according to Gaelic tradition) has long been regarded as an auspicious day for undertaking new ventures:

Diardaoin, Là Chaluim Chille chaoimh,
Là chur chaorach air seilbh;
Là deilbh 's a chur bà air laogh.[4]

('Thursday is gentle St Columba's Day; the day to send sheep to pasture, the day to lay warp, and to give a calf a foster-mother.')

For Hebrideans at the beginning of the twentieth century, Columba was generally a benign and beneficent figure. This aspect of his character was summarised and perpetuated in the regular application of the Gaelic adjective *caomh* ('gentle') in neat alliteration with his Gaelic name, as the above saying bears witness. The regularity of the epithet might suggest that there was once a darker side to Columba which needed to be placated. The Hebridean designation, tinged with cultural romanticism, is echoed in the verse of a modern Gaelic poet, George Campbell Hay (1915–84). Expressing his deep affection for his 'homeland' of Kintyre, Hay imagines the days when Columba visited its harbours:

Is domhain a chaidh freumh do sheanchais,
luingeas Lochlainn, airm is trod,

[2] Meek, *Campbell Collection.*
[3] *Ibid.*, 124 (no. 675), 163 (no. 868).
[4] *Ibid.*, 80 (no. 419).

Clanna Lir air Sruth na Maoile,
Calum Cille caomh 'nad phort.[5]

('Deep went the root of your story, ships of Lochlann, arms and strife, the Children of Lir on the Mull Race [i.e. the stretch of water between Ireland and the Mull of Kintyre], gentle Calum Cille in your port.')

Hay, who appears to have regarded Columba as a legendary figure on a par with the mythological Children of Lir, places him in the context of the traditional Gaelic cultural links between Ireland and Scotland. The image of the saint as 'bond and bridge' across the North Channel was to reappear in potent and productive guise later in the century.

The generally kind Hebridean portrait of the saint stands in contrast to the manner in which he has been remembered in Donegal, where he looms large as a somewhat sinister figure.[6] Only occasionally does a less attractive dimension of Columba's character surface in the Hebrides, notably in Tiree tradition. There he is still remembered for his powers of cursing, commemorated in local *dindshenchas* ('the lore of famous places'). The rock *Mallachdag* ('The Little Cursed One') in Gott Bay is said to have been at the receiving end of the saint's wrath because its seaweed failed to provide adequate mooring for his coracle. When he returned to the bay, at the end of his visit to the island, he found that his little ship had drifted out to sea. As a result of the saint's curse, the rock failed to produce or attract any more seaweed.[7] Later maritime enterprise evidently forgot the saint's unhappy encounters with boats, and his name was used benevolently on at least three vessels of the MacBrayne (later Caledonian MacBrayne) fleet. Despite the application of his name, these ships were not entirely saintly in maintaining their schedules. Yet Columba, it would seem, missed not only his own boat but also the opportunity to become the patron saint of the ferry-frustrated passengers of the Hebrides.

[5] Hay, *Fuaran Sléibh*, 16.

[6] For an overview of Columba in Irish tradition, see Ó hÓgáin, *Myth, Legend and Romance*, 92–6. Ó hÓgáin comments (p. 95) that he was 'popularly regarded as having been a short-tempered saint'.

[7] The story is very well attested in Tiree lore. The Tiree tale seems to contain a picture of Columba which is closer to Donegal tradition.

The Columba of ecclesiology

In Hebridean folklore, Columba's memory was preserved mainly in prayers and sayings relating to daily work on the crofts. In the churches, both Scottish and Highland, he has been remembered rather more as the exemplar of orthodoxy, defined from the position of the church or denomination concerned. In particular, Columba has had a long and seemingly paradoxical link with Presbyterianism. Within Scottish Protestantism more generally, the commemoration of saints has varied depending on the extent to which each form of Protestantism has (or has not) disavowed its pre-Reformation past. Although most forms of Protestantism would be uneasy with the invocation of the saints, many Protestant churches and individuals have maintained a lively interest in the saints, and Columba in particular has bucked the Protestant trend. This is largely because he was understood by medieval historians and propagandists to be a priest and presbyter, rather than a bishop, within the ecclesiastical structure, and thus failed to make a niche for himself within the episcopal ecclesiology of pre-Reformation Scotland.[8] Following the Reformation, however, as the reformers struggled to find an appropriate cultural and spiritual lineage for their new movement, Columba's support was gladly enlisted.[9] He remains something of a saintly comforter in times of disruption and anomie.[10] Even today, Columba may be vaguely regarded by denominational apologists as a Puritan of Puritans, a Knox of Knoxes, a Calvin of Calvinists, belonging to that consoling stream called 'Pre-Reformation Protestantism'. From time to time in the present century, he has

[8] The approaches of medieval and post-Reformation historians to Columba and the Columban Church are splendidly covered in Ferguson, *The Identity of the Scottish Nation,* 98–119.

[9] Cf. the espousal of Columba by David Calderwood: Ferguson, *The Identity of the Scottish Nation*, 112.

[10] Following the Disruption of 1843, the Free Church minister, Revd Thomas McLauchlan, helped to elaborate the view that Columba and his followers stood in sharp contrast to the 'Roman' missionaries in England: 'Thus did these men represent the ambitious, grasping spirit of their system, covetous of place and power; while the humble missionaries of Iona and Lindisfarne represented the spirit of their own system, covetous of exalting Christ, but crucifying self'; cited in Sharpe, *Adomnán*, 97.

been given at least a kindly and admiring pat on the head by evangelical Presbyterians, particularly within the Free Church of Scotland.[11]

The wistful 'backward look' of Scottish Protestantism finds expression in ecclesiastical nomenclature. A considerable number of Protestant (often Presbyterian) church buildings have been dignified with the names of saints; in this respect, Columba is probably more popular in Scottish Protestant practice than in Scottish Catholic tradition. This simple act of Presbyterian *pietas* may contribute to the reshaping of the profile of the saint. Since his name is used on church buildings belonging to the Church of Scotland (in Glasgow) and the Free Church of Scotland (in Edinburgh), it may be tacitly assumed by those who enter the hallowed portals that the saint thus commemorated had all the qualities and ideals which the denomination itself aspires to have.

Such wishful thinking (which skips over such minor problems as the mass, relics, penance, etc.) is sometimes assisted by the well-meaning but misguided efforts of those romantic historians who manage to see 'the legacy of Columba' in every aspect of Highland ecclesiastical practice. The austerity of the conservative Presbyterian Churches, the Reformed tradition of unaccompanied psalm-singing and the rejection of certain aspects of secular culture, may somehow be seen as deriving strength and even validation from the earlier example of Columba.[12] The forces and processes which created the much more recent religious

[11] The Revd J. Douglas MacMillan, formerly Professor of Church History at the Free Church of Scotland College, Edinburgh, wrote of Columba: 'The teaching of this zealous missionary who, with his disciples, had crossed over the Irish sea, was warmly evangelical and under his labours the North and West of Scotland became the cradle of a robust, literate Church which in its best days sent many Christian scholars and preachers out across Europe.' See Campbell, *Gleanings of Highland Harvest*, 130.

[12] Bradley, *Columba: Pilgrim and Penitent*, 98–101. One of the curious aspects of the quest for Columban influence is the manner in which Presbyterians leap backwards across the Middle Ages, ignoring the Catholic centuries, while those who are more inclined to espouse modern 'Celtic Christianity' and emphasise its pervasiveness omit the inconveniences of Highland church history in the eighteenth and especially the (evangelical and fissiparous) nineteenth century. Austerity and asceticism are not features which belong solely to the Columban Church.

complexion of the Highlands are forgotten, and Columba becomes an ecclesiastical father figure who transcends not only time, but also modern denominational divisions and theological disputes.

The Columba of culture and heritage

The 'Celtic' saints are purposefully reconstructed by churches and wishful thinkers, but they are also big business nowadays for the heritage industry. Heritage centres – all too often potent reminders of the retreat of Gaelic culture into the glitzy, non-Gaelic world of the cellophane package and the perfume flask – are increasingly popular in the Highlands and Islands. Because 'heritage' is itself a contemporary buzz-word, and also because the pervasive Christian ethos of the earlier and later Middle Ages is hard to avoid in any quest for 'heritage', Christianity in various forms, real and imagined, is finding its way back into the mind of the people at large, sometimes packaged and marketed (like a neatly wrapped bar of soap) as a version of the more neutral and less offensive commodity called 'spirituality'. In such centres, which sometimes allow push-button access to colourful interpretations of what was once 'culture', the local saint may be enjoying a timely resurrection. Such resurrection is occasionally achieved by recreating him on video; from the mists of modernity the video-saint beckons. His new electronic *vita* is generally low on fact, but high on graphic art and design, incorporating much mist, swirling low in Highland glens; his voice is deep and resonant, beckoning the New Age believer and the Old Age sceptic. Fillan, a saint associated with southern Perthshire, has been recreated in this way in Breadalbane Heritage Centre in Killin. I am not aware that Columba has yet become a video-saint, but a centre devoted to him is now established in Fionnphort in the Ross of Mull. In such a context, saints like Fillan and Columba represent local awareness of a phase of history which is both prestigious and potentially beneficial in the present day.[13]

To visit the saint in his heritage centre is to support the cause, but what is the cause? Those with a less appreciative view of

[13] For further comments on the modern Highland heritage industry, see Meek, 'Gaelic: a future for the heritage'.

cultural tourism may hear a version of the Reformation jingle singing in their ears – 'As soon as the coin from the sporran springs, the till of cultural tourism rings', or words to that effect. The use of the saints to enhance the local economy may indeed be an indication of the secularisation of spirituality, but there is no reason why a properly researched and well constructed heritage centre should not be able to enrich culture and economy, and also project a reliable image of what can be known about the saint from historical sources. Columba, of course, has a more secure basis in hard fact than many Scottish saints; the date of his arrival in Iona is fairly well established, and the evidence of Adomnán's *Life* of the saint can be supplemented with material drawn carefully from other historical sources. However, to use the name of a saint like Ninian, Kentigern or even Fillan, for example, and to reconstruct his personality on a hair-breadth of fact, is fraught with danger, though such historical insecurity is not something that most people will worry about, provided that the requirements of economic regeneration and accompanying romantic reconstruction are served.

It is certainly clear that the most common use of Columba and other saints in the contemporary Gaelic context is to encourage economic and cultural renaissance. Columba's role as a potent symbol, capable of igniting new initiatives of this kind, is most singularly demonstrated in *Iomairt Chaluim Chille* ('The Columba Initiative'), which seeks to provide closer links between Gaelic-related enterprises in Ireland and Scotland. Here Columba's name alone is serving the wider cause of 'cultural connectionalism', by creating a bridge which reclaims the relationship between the Gaelic components of Scotland and Ireland. He himself, as a Donegal man resident in Iona, linked the two Gaidhealtachds, and operated on both sides of the North Channel throughout his active career. This important aspect of the saint's life was emphasised by the President of Ireland, Mrs Mary Robinson, when she visited Sabhal Mòr Ostaig, the Gaelic College in Skye, on 9 June 1997, Columba's festival day, and also the day when *Iomairt Chaluim Chille* was publicly unveiled. She had been in Iona and Lewis prior to her arrival in Skye. Her sensitive and moving address had the theme of Gaelic culture at its heart, and opened with an appealing picture of Columba, uniting the two Gàidhealtachds:

> As prince, poet and priest he symbolises many of the links between these islands and between Scotland and Ireland. Of noble birth, he was regarded as a person of authority who could adjudicate in the political disputes between Ireland and the growing kingdom of Dal Riata. . . .
>
> As a poet he's representative of a society which took the role of the poet seriously. Of the stories which are told about him, two of the most famous concern literary disputes. His exile from Ireland, it is claimed, was a result of his defeat in the dispute about copying a manuscript. Later, at the legendary convention of Drumcath [*sic*] in 575 he ensured the privileged position of the bardic order in Gaelic society, an order which was to retain its power and influence for a thousand years.
>
> As an exile for Christ he founded Iona, which was to become a great monastic settlement, the centre of the Celtic church in these islands and a beacon of learning in Europe, and yesterday in Iona I had a sense of what had been founded there and how relevant it is to our modern world. These three strands of politics, learning and religion embodied in Columba are intimately linked.[14]

The power of the late medieval legend of Columba is graphically illustrated by these words. He is perceived by President Robinson as the pan-Gaelic protector of culture in a neat trinity of concerns. We may wonder whether the saint, on his own, actually guaranteed the special position of the poets. To what extent there was a single 'Celtic church in these islands' may also be disputed by some scholars, but the foundational role of Columba in Iona is not in doubt. The President duly emphasises the spiritual dimension of the saint, and alludes to 'how relevant it is to our modern world'. Yet, as reconstructed by modern enterprise managers and image-makers, Columba is very much a secular saint. *Iomairt Chaluim Chille*, while using Calum Cille's saintly name, is about developing primarily secular links between Scotland and Ireland.

One wonders how the saint himself would have regarded the ethos which has produced the range of fund-raising ventures now found in the Highlands and Islands, notably in the monetarist (and non-monastic) cells of local enterprise. Columba is given his place in the matrix. He is a name worth having at the masthead, to bring blessing on such ventures, but it is open to question

[14] Robinson, *Signatures on our own Frequency*, 11–12.

whether, for the promoters of Highland enterprise generally, he represents more than a name. His person, thus construed, may appear to contain more in the way of economic *élan* than of spiritual power, but in *Iomairt Chaluim Chille* he is identified with modern Gaelic culture in a context which will respect much more than his name.

The Columba of 'Celtic Christianity'

In the present day, the Gaelic cultural dimension of Columba, and any awareness that he belonged to a particular cultural group whose language continues to be used in Scotland, are preserved much more evidently in the plans and purposes of heritage-related enterprises. In such a context, however, the saint is in danger of being secularised. By contrast, when the saint enters the realm of modern spirituality, especially that of 'Celtic Christianity', he tends to lose most, if not all, of his innately Gaelic cultural qualities. Along with other 'Celtic' saints, he falls victim to the dreams and designs of those who wish to remake the Gaelic west in their own essentially Anglocentric image. The majority of writers on 'Celtic Christianity' are English, with little or no knowledge of Celtic languages.[15]

'Celtic Christianity', with its textual roots in Carmichael's *Carmina*, has had a long incubation period. In its most modern (post-1980) forms, it covers a wide spectrum of thought and expression. It has a scholarly following which conducts academic research into the manner in which culture has shaped the expression of the Christian faith in the British Isles in the so-called Dark Ages, but most scholars who are active in the analysis of the early Christian experience of the British Isles would not regard themselves as part of the modern movement. Indeed, they would find it very difficult to agree with many, if not all, of the presuppositions which undergird the modern bandwagon which regularly fills the bookshelves with dubious and misleading products. Even when an academic thread runs through some of these products, that thread is often overlaid by a colourful and

[15] Meek, 'Modern Celtic Christianity'. See also my forthcoming book, *The Quest for Celtic Christianity*, for a detailed assessment of the modern movement.

beguiling tapestry, designed to appeal to the pains and aches of modernity. 'Celtic Christianity', in its popular package, is thus shamelessly promoted as a potent panacea, capable of meeting every ailment from environmental degradation to political realignment.[16] The particular emphases of the movement have varied with time, but most are based on false dichotomies (such as bureaucratic versus 'simple' ecclesiastical structures, rural versus urban lifestyles, transcendence versus immanence).[17] None of these dichotomies would have been issues of any significance to so-called 'Celtic' Christians.

The 'Celtic' saints have been reinterpreted to suit the modern trends of 'Celtic Christianity'. They are often seen to be approachable and near at hand, in contrast to other European saints, who are cold and stand-offish in their shrines; they are environmentally friendly folk, always ready to show kindness to human or animal.[18] Columba has not been immune to plastic surgery of this kind, and regularly changes shape to appeal to the current fad. Thus, to take but one example, Columba's concern for a sick crane which has flown from his own homeland in the north of Ireland and lands, weak and tired, in Iona – an incident famously described in Adomnán's *Life* of the saint[19] – is regularly interpreted by modern romanticisers as an indication of his environmental kindness.[20] In fact, as Adomnán makes abundantly clear, Columba's concern is not for the bird as such, but for a creature which represents his native region. In Adomnán's portrait, as Columba moves beyond the circles of kin and culture, he becomes an altogether more aggressive figure.[21] Thus, by his very word, he slays a boar in

[16] Political messages relating to the current movement towards devolution in Wales and Scotland seem to be evident in the latest effusions; see, for example, Ellis and Seaton, *New Celts*.

[17] Cf. Fraser, *Celebrating Saints: Augustine, Columba, Ninian*, 17–23.

[18] Cf. de Waal, *The Celtic Way of Prayer*, 143.

[19] *VC* i.48.

[20] Simpson, *Exploring Celtic Spirituality*, 70.

[21] Columba exhorts the brother who is to attend to the crane, 'I commend it to you thus earnestly, for this reason, that it comes from the district of our fathers (*quia de nostrae paternitatis regione est oriunda*).' (*VC* i.48; Anderson, *Adomnán*, 86–7.)

Skye – an incident which (for some reason) scarcely figures in the frame of modern Christian Celtophiles.[22]

Again, Columba is frequently portrayed as a Christian druid, taking on the offices of the pre-Christian druids of the early Gaelic world.[23] Such an interpretation panders to the tastes of those who wish to argue that Celtic Christianity, unlike modern Christianity, was tolerant of pagan belief and practice. The more evidently biblical and confrontationally Christian dimensions of the saint are often played down when making a pitch for the attention of modern neo-paganism.

Columba's persona undergoes reconstruction not only in the context of popular perceptions of modern problems, but also in the services of worthy causes. He has been associated (inevitably) with the Iona Community since its inception in 1938, and has given good service as a figurehead and validator of its aspirations. He has been a focal point in the ecumenism which lies at the heart of the movement; his arrival in Iona in 563, like his death in the island in 597, has been the occasion for great ecumenical gatherings.[24] If we can accept the argument recently put forward by Dr Ian Bradley, Columba has much in common with the founder of the Iona Community, Lord George MacLeod of Fuinary.[25] What MacLeod and Columba do not have in common, of course, is the Gaelic language and the deeply Gaelic profile of the latter. Gaelic culture does not seem to be central to the modern Iona Community.

Columba in the post-modern 'Dark Ages'

Columba is at the heart of the modern Iona Community, but he tends to live on the edge of the indigenous Gaelic community. In the former, he loses his Gaelic identity, but he retains it in the

[22] Anderson, *Adomnán*, 130–3. See Gilbert Márkus, above, pp. 115f. for further discussion of these incidents.

[23] According to Fraser, *Celebrating Saints*, 12, 'Druidism, its lore kept secret and never set out in writing, seems to have been fairly easily assimilated.' For the alleged debt of Columba to the druids, cf. Marsden, *Sea-Road of the Saints*, 109.

[24] Meek, 'Modern Celtic Christianity: the contemporary "revival" and its roots', 21–4.

[25] Bradley, *Columba Pilgrim and Penitent*, 120–1.

latter, though his sanctity is sometimes sacrificed on the altar of economic expediency. Contradictions and conflicts of interest abound, but Columba is not alone in having to endure such slings and arrows. The 'Celtic' saints generally occupy a curiously peripheral, but at times very central, place within the structures of post-modern Christian belief. They are pulled from the periphery to the centre, or sometimes pushed out to the margins, as required, or even dropped off the edge of the popular record. Five centuries after the Reformation, even the most thoroughly reformed of Protestants still maintain an awareness of some of the saints, and are not averse to remembering them on special occasions. The most secular of people, too, trusting their lives utterly to Mammon, occasionally feel the need to slip their futures, their enterprises, and even their chequebooks, into the hands of the saints. For this reason, the saints' claims to distinction have been modified skilfully in the course of the centuries. This is reflected in the endurance of their legends, and the very fact that their names exist at all. In the twentieth century, the saints have continued to be recreated, not so much to press the case for a monastic cause, but more to meet the needs of a whole variety of causes which, in some cases, might make the real Columba rattle in his reliquary. The profiles of the saints in the earlier texts (themselves created to meet the need of a cause) have been split, rather like a light spectrum, and the separate 'colours' have become not partial emanations of saintly effulgence, but the full orbs of their individual beings. Can we put the lights back into the real spectrum, so to speak, and should we even try to do so?

The temper of modern society suggests that anyone who tries to reverse the 'Humpty Dumpty' trends of modernism and post-modernism, so that Columba and other saints are 'put together again', is facing an up-wall struggle. Powerful forces – ecclesiastical partisanship, economic determinism, local pride, national and even nationalist aspirations, to name but a few – are ranged against the academic who calls attention to the problems inherent in discovering the identity and reality of any saint. Personal and public involvement with, and perspectives on, saints may also militate against any attempt to set the record straight.[26] Most

[26] Cf. the correspondence re. Ninian triggered by Thomas Owen Clancy's letter in *The Scotsman*, 8 January 1997.

people who invoke the saints will not be concerned so much about the profile of the saints in the past; their main concern will be with the power and efficacy of the saints in the present. Saints are public property, and are in every sense 'popular' figures; they do not belong to scholars exclusively, and scholars cannot dictate the outlines of the saints' profiles.

The difficulty goes back to the origins of the saints; in the saints' ends were their beginnings. Consequently, with the best will in the world, we cannot rediscover the full historical reality of any saint. Hindsight has been too thoroughly spiritualised, and has become the main driving-force of saintly business. When people looked back, then as now, they believed that these ordinary men and women had many remarkable achievements to their credit, and they attached special honour to them. It was thought that God had used them greatly, and it was believed that human beings could benefit from their qualities. From all of this, an industry came into existence, issuing in saintly biographies, cults, statues, place-names, invocations, and the use of saints' names in a range of circumstances, to bring blessing, to add validity, and to secure the cause.[27] The patterns of retrospective reconstruction of saints' lives, which the scholar may use to illustrate the problem of being 'sure' about the saints, have a momentum which defies any attempt to set out 'the truth' about saints, even if that 'truth' is that we cannot know 'the truth'! What we see in the closing years of the late twentieth century is, to a great extent, the largely secular version of this centuries-old process.

Yet it could be argued that it is not fair to the saints, or to ourselves, to allow what remains of their 'real' profiles to be shaped out of existence because of the exigencies of economics or political opportunism, local or national. In the sentimental, weepy-sleepy years of the late twentieth century, we need to recover the cutting edge of our reason, and apply that to the evidence. Even if the earliest sources are biased, it is worth using these sources to check, and, where necessary, to correct contemporary, modernist biases. We need to begin our attempt to 'recover' the saints by drilling through the various layers of (mis)interpretation which have been deposited on top of the

[27] Brown, *The Cult of the Saints*; Clancy, above, pp. 1–5.

'historical' saints, so that we may hope to arrive at the earliest level of interpretation.

Recovering the saints

Perhaps the first priority in any modern agenda to recover the 'Celtic' saints in general, and Columba in particular, is to restore them to their positions in terms of the religious tenor of early medieval society. This point has special relevance to Protestant revampers of the saints. There is need to clear the ecclesiastical cupboards of denominational skeletons, and return to a broader view of the saints. 'Celtic' saints were, in reality, part of the European mainstream; they were not, in fact, completely different from saints elsewhere in Europe. They belonged to the pre-Reformation period, and shared the Catholic faith of East and West. 'Celtic' saints, including Columba, adhered broadly to the same theology as those in the East, and practised the same kinds of rituals. They celebrated the mass and exacted penance, and their successors believed in the power of their relics. Many of them, of course, were never formally canonised by the Roman Catholic Church, but here too they are typical of a wider pattern. Columba himself is an extra-canonical saint whose 'sanctity' has been recognised by tradition, like most of the other early European saints.[28]

It follows that we must be wary of making the 'Celtic' saints role-models for contemporary ecclesiastical developments, or even secular initiatives, simply because we suppose that their particular 'outfit' was different from the mainstream (as we perceive it). Sometimes people think that the so-called 'Celtic Church' somehow stood in contrast to the Roman Church, and that it anticipated all the virtues of the Reformation. Occasionally such a perception, with Columba at its heart, becomes a weapon in a journalistic jihad against the Pope.[29] Sadly for those who rejoice

[28] For discussion of canonisation, see Attwater, *The Penguin Dictionary of Saints*, 9–10.

[29] For a recent (and by no means isolated) example of this perception, with the accompanying notion of outright opposition between the Roman Church and the Celtic Church, see John Macleod, 'Pope not Spiritual Heir to Columba', *The Herald*, 17 December 1996; Thomas Owen Clancy offers a measured response, *ibid.*, 28 December 1996.

in turning missives into missiles, their perspective is not upheld by the historical record. There were certainly matters of divergence between the so-called 'Celtic tradition' and the practice of the wider 'church universal', but these were gradually ironed out. The main difference lay in the dating of the celebration of Easter, but the so-called 'Celtic' churches gradually came into conformity with the rest of Christendom.[30] We are thus not at liberty to re-interpret our 'Celtic' saints – not even Columba! – as forerunners of modern distinctions; they were not proto-Presbyterians, proto-Free Kirkers, proto-Baptists or proto-Brethren. They were part of the universal Catholic church of their time.

In short, if we are going to be honest with ourselves and with the verdict of history, we have to accept the 'Celtic' saints, including Columba, as they are presented to us in our earliest sources, with all their faults – a phrase that can apply to both the saints and the sources. They were a motley crew, with good and bad among them. Protestants cannot dismiss them simply because they lived before the Reformation, nor can they, with a clear conscience, remake the saints to suit their own agendas. This last point applies equally to Roman Catholics, and to any who try to subvert the saints. Failure to consult the earliest sources, to assess their messages and to heed the warnings of scholars, will ensure that the saints will find their place in a parallel universe which owes more to the human imagination than to a healthy sense of history.

The relevance of Columba for today

Columba is adaptable. He has shown a capacity to be relevant to the needs of many phases of history. Adomnán, his first Latin biographer whose work survives, obviously constructed his *Vita Columbae* in such a way as to make the exemplary nature of the saint's life clear to all who read his work. The purpose of Adomnán's portrait of Columba was in large measure commemorative, but he also raised the flag for Iona, and, in the bygoing, intended that others might be made in the mould of the saint. Of course, that mould was determined by Adomnán, and

[30] Sharpe, *Adomnán*, 36–9, 48–9, 76–7, discusses this issue with particular reference to Iona.

by the various strands of fact and folklore to which he had access and which he chose to use. The academic (always the sleepless spoiler of dreams) might say that we will learn more about Adomnán than about Columba by reading his account of the saint. Nowadays, modernity follows a similar course, bringing its own range of preconceptions to the saint and remaking him in its own image. The crucial difference is that Adomnán was some thirteen hundred years closer to Columba.

Adomnán's interpretation contains a timeless Christian message which has lost none of its potential relevance for those who wish to be so inspired. But is his perspective attractive in the present day? Is it in order to recover such a perspective that the average Islander, Highlander, Lowlander, Scot (or whoever) will remember, or reflect on, Columba? Sadly, one must respond in the negative. The picture of Columba that most average people have (if they have any at all) will seldom go beyond the saint's name, and perhaps a few generalities picked up from a passing acquaintance with lore and legend. This meagre mixture will be well garnished with generous helpings of public commemoration and personal preference. Such a recipe for 'making your own saint' guarantees the exclusion of inconvenient ingredients. The sharp-edged saintliness of the saint, as portrayed by Adomnán, is therefore unlikely to be a palatable pill for many in our modern day. His flesh-subduing austerity – not a prominent theme in modern 'Celtic Christianity' – stands in sharp contrast to the narcissism of contemporary popular philosophy. The 'Celtic' saints of modernity are all too often recognisable as the 'cushion saints' of the middle-class comfort-zone.

The earliest records of the saint will therefore remain a challenge to popular (mis)understanding. It is only by taking these sources as our primary founts of knowledge that we will have any hope of encountering reality. But is reality what we want to discover in any saint? Is that what our ancestors wanted? It is hard to escape the conclusion that, since at least the first centenary of his death, Columba has been the flexible friend of a wide variety of seekers and, of course, finders who have not hesitated to use his good offices for their own earthly purposes. His great quality is his perennial availability. He exists to be of occasional service; otherwise he is forgotten by the world, and lives quietly in his heavenly Hinba. The relevance of Columba at the end of the twentieth century, some might say, comes into focus only when he 'clicks' with the latest good cause or the latest aspiration of contemporary society, in its sacred or secular aspects. The process will doubtless continue into the next century. Columba, it seems, is eternally fated to be summoned periodically from his heavenly Hinba to sail the perilous ocean of popular belief which lies between Iona and the edge of the world, between faith and folklore.[31]

[31] I am very grateful to Dr Thomas Owen Clancy and Dr Dauvit Broun for their helpful comments on the first draft of this chapter.

Abbreviations

Aberdeen Breviary	*Breviarium Aberdonense* (Bannatyne, Maitland and Spalding Clubs, 1854).
AClon	*The Annals of Clonmacnoise, being Annals of Ireland from the Earliest Period to A.D. 1408, translated into English A.D. 1627 by Conell Mageoghagan*, ed. Denis Murphy (Dublin, 1896).
AI	*Annals of Innisfallen*, ed. S. Mac Airt (Dublin, 1951).
Alexander, *Place-Names*	W. M. Alexander, *The Place-Names of Aberdeenshire* (Spalding Club, 1952).
Anderson, *Adomnán*	*Adomnán's Life of Columba*, ed. A. O. and M. O. Anderson (revd edn, Oxford, 1991).
APS	*The Acts of the Parliaments of Scotland*, ed. T. Thomson and C. Innes (Edinburgh, 1814–75).
AT	*The Annals of Tigernach*, ed. and trans. Whitley Stokes, 2 vols (Felinfach, 1993).
Atlas	P. G. B. McNeill and H. L. MacQueen, edd., *Atlas of Scottish History to 1707* (Edinburgh, 1996).
AU	*The Annals of Ulster (to AD 1131)*, ed. S. Mac Airt and G. Mac Niocaill (Dublin, 1983).
Bede, *HE*	*Bede's Ecclesiastical History*, ed. B. Colgrave and R. A. B. Mynors (Oxford, 1969).
CA	Kuno Meyer, *Cáin Adomnáin* (Oxford, 1905).
CA Rent.	*Rental Book of the Cistercian Abbey of Cupar Angus* (Grampian Club, 1879–80).

Camb. Reg.	*Registrum Monasterii S. Marie de Cambuskenneth* (Grampian Club, 1872).
CCH	*Collectio Canonum Hibernensis* = H. Wasserschleben, *Die irische Kanonensammlung* (Leipzig, 1885).
CCSL	*Corpus Christianorum, Series Latina* (Turnhout, 1954– continuing)
CGSH	P. Ó Riain, ed., *Corpus Genealogiarum Sanctorum Hiberniae* (Dublin, 1985).
CMCS	*Cambrian* [formerly *Cambridge*] *Medieval Celtic Studies.*
Conlationes	*Jean Cassien: Conferences*, 3 vols, ed. Jean-Claude Guy, SC 42, 54, 64 (Paris, 1955–9).
Cowan, *Medieval Parishes*	I. B. Cowan, *Parishes of Medieval Scotland*, Scottish Record Society, vol. 93 (Edinburgh, 1967).
CS	*Chronicum Scotorum. A Chronicle of Irish Affairs from the Earliest Times to A.D. 1135, with a supplement, containing the events from 1141 to 1150*, ed. and trans. William M. Hennessy (Rolls Series, London, 1866).
CSCO	Corpus Scriptorum Christianorum Orientalium.
CSEL	*Corpus Scriptorum Ecclesiasticorum Latinorum* (Vienna, 1892– continuing).
CSSR ii	A. I. Dunlop, ed., *Calendar of Scottish Supplications to Rome 1423–28* (Scottish History Society, 1956).
CSSR iii	A. I. Dunlop and I. B. Cowan, edd., *Calendar of Scottish Supplications to Rome 1428–32* (Scottish History Society, 1970).
De Doctrina Christiana	*Augustine: De Doctrina Christiana*, ed. and trans. R. P. H. Green (Oxford, 1995).
DLS	*Adomnán: De Locis Sanctis*, ed. Denis Meehan, *Scriptores Latini Hiberniae* vol. 3 (Dublin, 1958).
Dunf. Reg.	*Registrum de Dunfermelyn* (Bannatyne Club, 1842).

Dunk. Rent.	*Rentale Dunkeldense* (Scottish History Society, 1915).
ECMS	J. Romilly Allen and J. Anderson, *The Early Christian Monuments of Scotland* (Edinburgh, 1903; repr. in 2 vols with new preface and introduction by Isabel Henderson, Balgavies, Angus, 1993).
ER	*The Exchequer Rolls of Scotland*, ed. J. Stuart *et al.* (Edinburgh, 1878–1908).
ES	A. O. Anderson, *Early Sources of Scottish History*, 2 vols (Edinburgh, 1922).
FAI	*Fragmentary Annals of Ireland*, ed. and trans. J. Radner (Dublin, 1978).
Forbes, *Kalendars*	A. P. Forbes, *Kalendars of Scottish Saints* (Edinburgh, 1872).
GCS	*Die griechischen christlichen Schriftsteller der ersten drei Jahrhunderte* (Leipzig, later Berlin, 1897– continuing).
Geog. Coll.	*Geographical Collections relating to Scotland made by Walter Macfarlane* (Scottish History Society, 1906–8).
Glas. Reg.	*Registrum Episcopatus Glasguensis*, 2 vols. (Bannatyne and Maitland Clubs, 1843).
Hymns against Heresies	*Des heiligen Ephraem des Syrers Hymnen contra Haereses*, ed. E. Beck (CSCO 169 and 170, 1957).
Institutiones	*Jean Cassien: Institutiones cenobitiques*, ed. Jean-Claude Guy (SC 109, Paris, 1965).
Isidore, *Etymologiae*	*Isidori Hispalensis Episcopi Etymologiarvm sive Originvm*, ed. W. M. Lindsay, 2 vols (Oxford, 1911).
JRSAI	*Journal of the Royal Society of Antiquaries of Ireland.*
JTS	*Journal of Theological Studies.*

Lapidge and Sharpe	*Bibliography of Celtic-Latin Literature, 400–1200* (Dublin, 1985).
MacKinlay, *Dedications*	J. M. MacKinlay, *Ancient Church Dedications in Scotland: Non-scriptural* (Edinburgh, 1914).
Melr. Lib.	*Liber Sancte Marie de Melros* (Bannatyne Club, 1837).
Moray Reg.	*Registrum Episcopatus Moraviensis* (Bannatyne Club, 1837).
NMRS	National Monuments Record of Scotland.
NPNF	The Nicene and Post-Nicene Fathers series.
OPS	*Origines Parochiales Scotiae*, 2 vols (Bannatyne Club, 1851–5).
OSA	*Old Statistical Account.*
PG	J.-P. Migne, ed., *Patrologiae cursus completus ... series Graeca*, 161 vols (Paris).
PL	J.-P. Migne, ed., *Patrologiæ cursus completus ... series Latina*, 221 vols (Paris).
RCAHMS	The Royal Commission on the Ancient and Historical Monuments of Scotland.
Reeves, *Adamnan*	*Adamnan Life of Columba*, ed. W. Reeves (Dublin, 1857).
Regula	*Sancti Benedicti Regula*: SC 182.
RIA, *Dictionary*	Royal Irish Academy, *Dictionary of the Irish Language* (Compact Edition, Dublin, 1983).
RMS	*Registrum Magni Sigilli*, ed. J. M. Thomson *et al.* (Edinburgh, 1882–1914).
RRS i	*Regesta Regum Scottorum* vol. i, *Acts of Malcolm IV*, ed. G. W. S. Barrow (Edinburgh, 1960).
RRS ii	*Regesta Regum Scottorum* vol. ii, *Acts of William I*, ed. G. W. S. Barrow, with the collaboration of W. W. Scott (Edinburgh, 1971).
SC	Sources Chrétiennes.

Scotichronicon i	*Scotichronicon by Walter Bower in Latin and English*, gen. ed. D. E. R. Watt, 9 vols (Aberdeen/ Edinburgh, 1987–98) i (1993), edd. John and Winifred MacQueen.
Scotichronicon ii	*Scotichronicon by Walter Bower in Latin and English*, gen. ed. D. E. R. Watt, 9 vols (Aberdeen/ Edinburgh, 1987–98) ii (1989), edd. John and Winifred MacQueen.
Scotichronicon vii	*Scotichronicon by Walter Bower in Latin and English*, gen. ed. D. E. R. Watt, 9 vols (Aberdeen/ Edinburgh, 1987–98) vii (1996) edd. A. B. Scott and D. E. R. Watt, with Ulrike Morét and Norman F. Shead.
Sharpe, *Adomnán*	R. Sharpe, *Adomnán of Iona: Life of Columba* (Harmondsworth, 1995).
SRO	Scottish Record Office.
SSD	Scottish Development Department (former Ancient Monuments; now Historic Scotland).
St A Lib.	*Liber Cartarum Prioratus Sancti Andree in Scotia* (Bannatyne Club, 1841).
VC	Adomnán, *Vita Columbae.* (For edition and translation see Anderson, *Adomnán*; for translation see also Sharpe, *Adomnán.*)
Vita Martinii	*Sulpice Severe, Vie de saint Martin*, ed., J. Fontaine (Sources Chrétiennes 133, Paris, 1967). 3 vols (Paris, 1857–65).
ZCP	*Zeitschrift für celtische Philologie.*

The following abbreviations of pre-1975 counties are used:

ABD	Aberdeenshire
ANG	Angus
ARG	Argyll
BNF	Banff
BWK	Berwickshire
ELO	East Lothian
FIF	Fife
INV	Inverness-shire
LAN	Lanarkshire
MLO	Midlothian
PEB	Peeblesshire
PER	Perthshire
WIG	Wigtownshire
WLO	West Lothian

Bibliography

Abou-El-Haj, Barbara, *The Medieval Cult of Saints: Formations and Transformations* (Cambridge, 1994).

The Acts of the Parliaments of Scotland, ed. T. Thomson and C. Innes (Edinburgh, 1814–75).

Adomnán's Life of Columba, ed. A. O. and M. O. Anderson (revd edn, Oxford, 1991).

Airlie, Stuart, 'The view from Maastricht' in Crawford, ed., *Scotland in Dark Age Europe*, 36–41.

Aland, K., *Synopsis Quattuor Evangeliorum* (13th revd edn, Stuttgart, 1985).

Alcock, L., and Alcock, E. A., 'Reconnaisance excavations on early historic fortifications and other royal sites in Scotland 1974–84: 5', *PSAS* 122 (1992) 215–87.

Alexander, W. M., *The Place-Names of Aberdeenshire* (Spalding Club, 1952).

Allen, J. Romilly, and Anderson, J., *The Early Christian Monuments of Scotland* (Edinburgh 1903; repr. in 2 vols with new preface and introduction by Isabel Henderson, Balgavies, Angus, 1993).

Anderson, A. O., *Early Sources of Scottish History*, 2 vols (Edinburgh, 1922).

——, 'Ninian and the Southern Picts', *SHR* 27 (1948) 25–47.

Anderson, Joseph, 'The architecturally shaped shrines and other reliquaries of the early Celtic church in Scotland and Ireland', *PSAS* 44 (1909–10) 259–81.

——, *Scotland in Early Christian Times* (Edinburgh, 1881).

Anderson, M. O., *Kings and Kingship in Early Scotland* (2nd edn, Edinburgh, 1980).

——, 'Columba and other Irish saints in Scotland', in J. L. McCracken, ed., *Historical Studies V* (London, 1965), 26–36.

ANDERSON, M. O., 'Dalriada and the creation of the kingdom of the Scots', in D. Whitelock *et al.*, edd., *Ireland and Early Medieval Europe* (Cambridge, 1982), 106–32.

——, 'Lothian and the early Scottish kings', *Scottish Historical Review* 39 (1960) 98–112.

——, 'Picts: the name and the people', in A. Small, ed., *The Picts: a New Look at Old Problems* (Dundee, 1987), 7–14.

——, 'The Scottish materials in the Paris manuscript, Bib. Nat., Latin 4126', *SHR* 28 (1949) 31–42.

ANDERSON, R. R. *et al.* edd., *National Art Survey of Scotland: examples of Scottish architecture from the twelfth to the seventeenth century* (Edinburgh, 1921–33).

Annales Cambriae, ed. John Williams Ab Ithel (Rolls Series, London, 1860).

The Annals of Clonmacnoise, being Annals of Ireland from the Earliest Period to A.D. 1408, translated into English A.D. 1627 by Conell Mageoghagan, ed. Denis Murphy (Dublin, 1896).

The Annals of Tigernach, ed. and trans. Whitley Stokes, 2 vols (Felinfach, 1993), a facsimile reprint of *Revue Celtique* 16 (1895) 374–419; 17 (1896) 6–33, 119–263, 337–420; 18 (1897) 9–59, 150–97, 263–303, 374–90.

The Annals of Ulster (to AD 1131), ed. S. Mac Airt and G. Mac Niocaill (Dublin, 1983).

ATTWATER, DONALD, *The Penguin Dictionary of Saints* (Harmondsworth, 1983).

BAILEY, RICHARD, *The Durham Cassiodorus* (Jarrow Lecture, 1978).

BALAAM, N., 'The vallum', in Reece, *Excavations on Iona, 1964–74*, 5–14.

BALFOUR, FRANCES, *Lady Victoria Campbell, A Memoir* (London, 1911).

BANNERMAN, J., *Studies in the History of Dalriada* (Edinburgh, 1974).

——, '*Comarba Coluim Chille* and the relics of Columba', *IR* 44 (1993) 14–47.

——, 'Notes on the Scottish entries in the early Irish annals', *Scottish Gaelic Studies* 11 pt 2 (1968) 149–70 (republished in *Studies in the History of Dalriada*, 9–26).

——, 'The Scots of Dalriada', in G. Menzies, ed., *Who are the Scots?* (London, 1971).

BARBER, J., 'Excavations on Iona, 1979', *PSAS* 111 (1981) 282–380.

BARR, A., *A Diagram of Synoptic Relationships* (Edinburgh, 1987).

BARROW, G. W. S., *The Kingdom of the Scots* (London, 1973).

——, 'Badenoch and Strathspey, 1130–1312. 2: the church', *Northern Scotland* 9 (1989) 1–16.

——, 'Macbeth and other mormaers of Moray', in L. Maclean, ed., *The Hub of the Highlands*, Inverness Field Club Centenary Volume (Inverness, 1975), 109–22.

Bede's Ecclesiastical History, ed. B. Colgrave and R. A. B. Mynors (Oxford, 1969).

Betha Adamnáin: The Irish Life of Adamnán, ed. M. Herbert and P. Ó Riain, Irish Texts Society, vol. 54 (Dublin, 1988).

Betha Colaim Chille: Life of Columcille compiled by Manus O'Donnell in 1532, ed. A. O'Kelleher and G. Schoepperle (Urbana, 1918).

Biblia Sacra Iuxta Vulgatam Versionem I, ed. B. Fischer, J. Gribmont, H. F. D. Sparks, W. Thiele (Stuttgart, 1983).

BIELER, LUDWIG, *The Irish Penitientials* (Dublin, 1975).

——, *The Patrician Texts in the Book of Armagh* (Dublin, 1979).

BINCHY, D. A., *Críth Gablach* (Dublin, 1979).

BINNS, A., 'Pre-Reformation dedications to St Oswald in England and Scotland: a gazetteer', in C. Stancliffe and E. Cambridge, edd., *Oswald: Northumbrian King to European Saint* (Stamford, 1995) 241–71.

BISCHOFF, BERNHARD, *Latin Palaeography. Antiquity and the Middle Ages*, tr. Dáibhí Ó Cróinín and David Ganz (Cambridge, 1990).

——, 'Wendepunkte in der Geschichte der lateinischen Exegese im Frühmittelalter', *Sacris Erudiri* 6 (1954) = *Mittelalterliche Studien* i (Stuttgart, 1966) 205–73.

——, 'Turning-points in the history of Latin exegesis in the Early Irish Church A.D. 650–800' in M. McNamara, ed., *Biblical Studies. The Medieval Irish Contribution* (Dublin, 1976), 73–164.

BLAIR, J., 'Anglo-Saxon minsters: a topographical review', in Blair and Sharpe, edd., *Pastoral Care before the Parish*, 226–66.

——, and Sharpe, R., edd., *Pastoral Care before the Parish* (Leicester, 1992).

The Book of Rules of Tyconius, ed. F. C. Burkitt (Cambridge, 1894).

BORSJE, JACQUELINE, *From Chaos to Enemy: Encounters with Monsters in Early Irish Texts* (Turnhout, 1996)

BORSJE, JACQUELINE, 'The Monster in the River Ness in *Vita Sancti Columbae*: a Study of a Miracle', *Peritia* 8 (1994) 27–34.

Boswell's Journal of a Tour to the Hebrides with Samuel Johnson, LL.D, 1773 edd. F. Pottle and C. Bennett (London, 1963).

BOURKE, CORMAC, ed., *Studies in the Cult of St Columba* (Dublin, 1997).

——, '*Insignia Columbae* II', in Bourke, ed., *Studies in the Cult of St Columba*, 162–83.

BOUYER, LOUIS, *A History of Spirituality*, I (London, 1968).

BOWEN, E. G., *Saints, Seaways and Settlements in the Celtic Lands* (Cardiff, 1969).

BOYLE, A., 'The Edinburgh synchronisms of Irish kings', *Celtica* 9 (1971) 169–79.

BRADLEY, IAN, *Columba: Pilgrim and Penitent* (Glasgow, 1996)

BRADLEY, J., 'Moynagh Lough: an insular workshop of the second quarter of the eighth century', in R. M. Spearman and J. Higgitt, edd., *The Age of Migrating Ideas. Early Medieval Art in Northern Britain and Ireland* (Edinburgh, 1993), 74–81.

BRADLEY, R., *Altering the Earth* (Society of Antiquaries of Scotland Rhind Lecture Series. Edinburgh, 1996).

Breviarium Aberdonense, ed. William Blew (Bannatyne, Maitland and Spalding Clubs, 1854).

BROOKE, D., *Wild Men and Holy Places: St Ninian and the Medieval Realm of Galloway* (Edinburgh, 1994).

BROUN, DAUVIT, 'Defining Scotland and the Scots before the wars of independence', in D. Broun, R. Finlay, and M. Lynch, edd., *Image and Identity: the Making and Remaking of Scotland through the Ages* (Edinburgh, 1998), 4–17.

——, 'The origin of Scottish identity in its European context', in Crawford, ed., *Scotland in Dark Age Europe*, 21–31.

——, 'The origin of Scottish identity', in C. Bjørn, A. Grant, and K. J. Stringer, edd., *Nations, Nationalism and Patriotism in the European Past* (Copenhagen, 1994), 35–55.

——, 'The seven kingdoms in *De situ Albanie*: a record of Pictish political geography or imaginary map of ancient Alba?', in E. J. Cowan and R. Andrew McDonald, edd., *Alba: Medieval Celtic Scotland* (East Linton, forthcoming.)

Brown, C. G. and Harper, A. E. T., 'Excavations on Cathedral Hill, Armagh, 1968', *Ulster Journal of Archaeology* 47 (1984) 109–61.

Brown, P. H., *Scotland before 1700 from Contemporary Documents* (Edinburgh, 1893).

Brown, Peter, *Society and the Holy in Late Antiquity* (Berkeley, 1982).

——, *The Cult of the Saints: its Rise and Function in Latin Christianity* (Chicago, 1981).

——, *The Rise of Western Christendom* (Oxford, 1996).

Brown, R. E., *The Gospel According to John*, 2 vols (London, 1967–70).

Bruce-Mitford, R. L. S., 'The art of the Codex Amiatinus (Jarrow Lecture, 1967)', *Journal of the Archaeological Association*, 3rd ser., 32 (1969) 1–25.

Brüning, G., 'Adomnans *Vita Columbae* und ihre Ableitungen', *ZCP* 11 (1917) 213–304.

Bullough, D. A., 'Columba, Adomnán and the achievement of Iona', *SHR* 43 (1964) 111–130, and 44 (1965) 17–33.

Burley, E. and Fowler, P. J., 'Iona', *Discovery and Excavation in Scotland* (1958) 14.

Burton-Christie, Douglas, *The Word in the Desert* (Oxford, 1993).

Butler, Christopher, *Number Symbolism* (London, 1970).

Bynum, Caroline Walker, *Fragmentation and Redemption: Essays on Gender and the Human Body in Medieval Religion* (New York, 1991).

——, *The Resurrection of the Body in Western Christendom, 200–1336* (New York, 1995).

Byrne, M. E., 'Féilire Adamnáin', *Ériu* 1 (1904) 225–8.

Cameron, Averil, *Christianity and the Rhetoric of Empire. The Development of Christian Discourse* (Berkeley, 1991).

Campbell, Murdoch, *Gleanings of Highland Harvest*, with biography and historical background by J. Douglas MacMillan (Tain, 1989).

Carmina Gadelica, collected by Alexander Carmichael, 6 vols (Edinburgh, 1900–71).

Carney, J., '*A maccucáin, sruth in tíag*', *Celtica* 15 (1983) 25–41.

——, *The Poems of Blathmac*, Irish Texts Society, vol. 47 (Dublin, 1964).

CARRUTHERS, MARY, *The Book of Memory. A Study of Memory in Medieval Culture* (Cambridge, 1990).

Cassiodorus. Expositio Psalmorum, ed. M. Adriaen *CCSL* 97 and 98.

CHADWICK, H. M., *Early Scotland* (Cambridge, 1949).

CHADWICK, OWEN, 'The evidence of dedications in the early history of the Welsh Church', in N. Chadwick *et al.*, edd., *Studies in Early British History* (Cambridge, 1954) 173–88.

Chronicum Scotorum. A Chronicle of Irish Affairs from the Earliest Times to A.D. 1135, with a supplement, containing the events from 1141 to 1150, ed. and trans. William M. Hennessy (Rolls Series: London, 1866).

CLANCY, T. O., 'Annat in Scotland and the origins of the parish', *Innes Review* 46 (1995) 91–115.

——, 'Iona, Scotland, and the *céli Dé*', in Crawford, ed., *Scotland in Dark Age Britain*, 111–30.

——, 'Personal, political, pastoral: Adomnán's multiple agenda in the *Life of Saint Columba*', in E. J. Cowan and D. Gifford, edd., *The Polar Twins: Scottish History and Scottish Literature* (Edinburgh, 1999).

——, 'Scottish saints and national identities in the early middle ages' in R. Sharpe and A. Thacker, edd., *Local Saints and Local Churches* (forthcoming).

——, 'Philosopher-king: Nechtan, king of Picts (d. 732)' (forthcoming)

——, ed., *The Triumph Tree: Scotland's Earliest Poetry, 550–1350* (Edinburgh, 1998).

——, and Márkus, G., *Iona: The Earliest Poetry of a Celtic Monastery* (Edinburgh, 1995).

COGITOSUS, *Vita Brigitae*, in *PL* 72, cols 775–90.

CONNOLLY, SEAN, 'Cogitosus's *Life of St Brigit*', *JRSAI* 117 (1987) 5-27.

CORBISHLY, T., 'The chronology of New Testament times', in Orchard *et al.*, edd., *A Catholic Commentary*, 847–50.

COWAN, E. J., 'The Scottish Chronicle in the Poppleton Manuscript', *IR* 32 (1981) 3–21.

COWAN, I. B., *Parishes of Medieval Scotland*, Scottish Record Society vol. 93 (Edinburgh, 1967).

COWAN, I. B., and EASSON, D. E., *Medieval Religious Houses: Scotland* (2nd edn, London, 1976).

CRAWFORD, B. E., ed., *Scotland in Dark Age Britain* (St Andrews, 1996).

——, ed., *Scotland in Dark Age Europe* (St Andrews, 1994).

CRAWFORD, O. G. S., 'Iona', *Antiquity* 7 (1933) 453–67.

——, 'Western seaways', in L. H. Dudley Buxton, ed., *Custom is King* (London, 1936).

CRICK, JULIA C., *The Historia Regum Britannie of Geoffrey of Monmouth*, iii: *Summary Catalogue of the Manuscripts* (Woodbridge, 1989).

CURLE, A. O., 'A note on four silver spoons and a fillet of gold found in the Nunnery at Iona; and on a finger ring, part of a fillet, and a fragment of wire, all gold, found in St. Ronan's Chapel, the Nunnery, Iona', *PSAS* 58 (1923–4) 102–11.

CURTI, C., 'Eusebius of Caesarea', in A. di Berardino, ed., *Encyclopaedia of the Early Church*, trans. A. Walford, 2 vols (Cambridge, 1992) i, 299–301.

De Locis Sanctis, ed. Denis Meehan, *Scriptores Latini Hiberniae* vol. 3 (Dublin, 1958).

DE WAAL, ESTHER, *The Celtic Way of Prayer: The Recovery of the Religious Imagination* (London, 1996).

DOHERTY, CHARLES, 'The basilica in early Ireland', *Peritia* 3 (1984) 303–15.

——, 'The use of relics in early Ireland', in P. Ní Chatháin and S. Tranter, edd., *Irland und Europa: die Kirche im Frühmittelalter* (Stuttgart, 1984), 89–101.

DOVE, G. W., 'Saints, Dedications and Cults in Mediaeval Fife' (unpublished M.Phil. dissertation, University of St Andrews, 1988).

DOWNS, ROGER M., and STEA, DAVID, *Maps in Mind: reflections on cognitive mapping* (New York, 1977).

DRISCOLL, STEPHEN T., 'Power and authority in early historic Scotland: Pictish symbol stones and other documents', in J. Gledhill, B. Bender and M. T. Larson, edd., *State and Society: the Emergence and Development of Social Hierarchy and Political Centralization* (London, 1988), 215–36.

——, 'The archaeology of state formation in Scotland', in W. S. Hanson and E. A. Slater, edd., *Scottish Archaeology: New Perceptions* (Aberdeen, 1991), 81–111.

DUMVILLE, DAVID N., *Saint Patrick: AD 493–1993* (Woodbridge, 1993).

——, *The Churches of North Britain in the First Viking-Age*, Fifth Whithorn Lecture, 14 September, 1996 (Whithorn, 1997).

——, 'Britain and Ireland in *Táin Bó Fraích*', *Études Celtiques* 32 (1996) 175–87.

——, 'Latin and Irish in the *Annals of Ulster*, A.D. 431–1050' in D. Whitelock *et al.*, edd., *Ireland in Early Medieval Europe* (Cambridge, 1982), 320–41.

DUNCAN, A. A. M., *Scotland: The Making of the Kingdom* (Edinburgh, 1975; revd edn, Edinburgh, 1978).

DUNLOP, A. I., 'Bagimond's Roll', *Scottish Historical Society Misc VI* (1939), 3–77.

——, and COWAN, I. B., edd., *Calendar of Scottish Supplications to Rome 1428–32* (Scottish History Society, 1970).

——, ed., *Calendar of Scottish Supplications to Rome 1423–28* (Scottish History Society, 1956).

The Earliest Life of Gregory the Great, ed. and trans. Bertram Colgrave (Cambridge, 1968).

EELES, FRANCIS C., 'The Monymusk reliquary or brecbennoch of St Columba', *PSAS* 68 (1933–4) 433–8.

ELLIS, ROGER, and SEATON, CHRIS, *New Celts* (Eastbourne, 1998).

ENRIGHT, MICHAEL, *Iona, Tara, Soissons: The Origin of the Royal Anointing Ritual* (Berlin, 1985).

EPHRAEM THE SYRIAN, *Des heiligen Ephraem des Syrers Hymnen contra Haereses*, ed. E. Beck (CSCO 169 and 170, 1957).

ETCHINGHAM, COLMÁN, *Viking Raids on Irish Church Settlements in the Ninth Century* (Maynooth, 1996).

Eusebius: The History of the Church, tr. G. A. Williamson, revd and ed. Andrew Louth (Harmondsworth, 1989).

The Exchequer Rolls of Scotland, ed. J. Stuart *et al.*, 23 vols (Edinburgh, 1878–1908).

FERGUSON, WILLIAM, *The Identity of the Scottish Nation. An Historic Quest* (Edinburgh, 1998).

FINLAY, IAN, *Columba* (London, 1979).

FORBES, A. P., *Kalendars of Scottish Saints* (Edinburgh, 1872).

FORSYTH, KATHERINE, 'The inscriptions on the Dupplin Cross', in Cormac Bourke, ed., *From the Isles of the North: Medieval Art in Ireland and Britain, Proceedings of the Third International Conference on Insular Art, Belfast, April 1994* (Belfast, 1995), 237–44.

FOSTER, SALLY M., *Picts, Gaels, and Scots* (London, 1996).

FOTHERINGHAM, J. K., 'Astronomical evidence for the date of the Crucifixion', *JTS* 12 (1911) 120–7.

——, 'The evidence of astronomy and technical chronology for the date of the crucifixion', *JTS* 35 (1934) 146–62.

FOWLER, E., and FOWLER, P. J., 'Excavations on Torr an Aba, Iona, Argyll', *PSAS* 118 (1988) 181–201.

Fragmentary Annals of Ireland, ed. and trans. J. Radner (Dublin, 1978).

FRASER, IAN M., *Celebrating Saints: Augustine, Columba, Ninian*, Wild Goose Reflections vol. 3 (Glasgow, 1997).

FRASER, W., *The Chiefs of Grant*, 3 vols (Edinburgh 1883).

FROELICH, K., trans., *Biblical Interpretation in the Early Church* (Philadelphia, 1984).

GEARY, PATRICK J., *Furta Sacra: Thefts of Relics in the Central Middle Ages* (2nd edn, Princeton, N.J., 1990).

——, *Living with the Dead in the Middle Ages* (London, 1994).

Geographical Collections relating to Scotland made by Walter Macfarlane, edd. Sir Arthur Mitchell and James T. Clark, 3 vols (Scottish History Society, 1906–8).

GEOPHYSICAL SURVEYS OF BRADFORD. *Geophysical Surveys on Iona: the Abbey & Nunnery Precincts* (unpublished survey report to AOC (Scotland) Ltd for the Iona Cathedral Trust, 1995)

Gildas. The Ruin of Britain and other Works, ed. M. Winterbottom (Chichester, 1978).

GOULD, PETER, and WHITE, RODNEY, *Mental Maps* (Harmondsworth, 1974).

GRABOWSKI, KATHRYN, and DUMVILLE, D. N., *Chronicles and Annals of Mediaeval Ireland and Wales: the Clonmacnoise-group Texts* (Woodbridge, 1984).

GRANT, R. M., *Irenaeus of Lyons* (London, 1997).

GREGG, R., *Athanasius: The Life of Antony and the Letter to Marcellinus* (London, 1980).

GREGORY THE GREAT, *Dialogi*, ed. U. Moricca (Instituto Storico Italiano, Rome, 1924).

GRIFFITH, S. H., 'The image maker in the poetry of Ephraem the Syrian', *Studia Patristica* 25 (1993) 258–69.

HAGGARTY, A. M., 'Iona: some results from recent work', *PSAS* 118 (1988) 203–13.

HALL, M. A., HENDERSON, I., and TAYLOR, S., 'A sculptured fragment from Pittensorn Farm, Gellyburn, Perthshire', *Tayside and Fife Archaeological Journal* 4 (1998) 129–44.

HARBISON, P., *Pilgrimage in Ireland* (London, 1991).

HAY, GEORGE CAMPBELL, *Fuaran Sléibh* (Glasgow, 1947).

HERBERT, MÁIRE, *Iona, Kells, and Derry: The History and Hagiography of the Monastic* Familia *of Columba* (Oxford, 1988, repr. Blackrock, 1996).

——, 'Hagiography', in K. McCone and Katharine Simms, edd., *Progress in Medieval Irish Studies* (Maynooth, 1996) 79–90.

——, 'The preface to the *Amra Coluim Cille*', in D. Ó Corráin, L. Breatnach and K. McCone, edd., *Sages, Saints and Storytellers: Celtic Studies in Honour of Professor James Carney* (Maynooth, 1989), 67–75.

Hilaire de Poitiers: Commentaire sur le psaume 118, ed. Marc Milhau, 2 vols. *SC* 344, 347 (Paris, 1988).

HILL, PETER, *Whithorn and St Ninian: The Excavation of a Monastic Town, 1984–91* (Stroud, 1997).

HOOD, A. B. E., *St Patrick: His Writings and Muirchu's Life* (Chichester, 1978).

HOPE-TAYLOR, B., *Yeavering: an Anglo-British centre of early Northumbria* (London, 1977).

HOWLETT, DAVID, *Caledonian Craftsmanship: the Scottish Latin Tradition* (Blackrock, forthcoming).

HUCK, A., and GREEVEN, H., *Synopse der drei ersten Evangelien* (13th revd edn, Tübingen, 1981).

HUDSON, BENJAMIN T., *Kings of Celtic Scotland* (Westport, Connecticut, 1994).

——, *The Prophecy of Berchan* (Westport, Connecticut, 1996).

——, '*Elech* and the Scots in Strathclyde', *Scottish Gaelic Studies* 15 (1988) 145–9.

HUDSON, BENJAMIN T., 'Kings and Church in early Scotland', *SHR* 73 (1994) 145–70.

——, 'The conquest of the Picts in early Scottish literature', *Scotia* 15 (1991) 13–25.

——, 'The language of the Scottish Chronicle and its European context', *Scottish Gaelic Studies* 18 (1998) 57–73.

HUGHES, KATHLEEN, *Early Christian Ireland: Introduction to the Sources* (London, 1972).

——, *The Church in Early Irish Society* (London, 1966).

——, review of Bowen, *Settlement of the Celtic Saints in Wales*, in *Irish Historical Studies* 10 (1956–7) 239.

HULL, VERNAM, '*Apgitir Chrábaid*: The Alphabet of Piety', *Celtica* 8 (1968) 44–89.

INNES, THOMAS, *Critical Essay on the Ancient Inhabitants of the Northern Parts of Britain or Scotland*, 2 vols (London, 1729).

Isidori Hispalensis Episcopi Etymologiarvm sive Originvm, ed. W. M. Lindsay, 2 vols (Oxford, 1911).

IVENS, R. J., 'Moville Abbey, Newtonards, Co. Down: excavations in 1981', *Ulster Journal of Archaeology* 47 (1984) 71–108.

JACKSON, KENNETH. H., *The Gaelic Notes in the Book of Deer* (Cambridge, 1972).

——, *A Celtic Miscellany* (revd edn, Harmondsworth, 1971).

——, *The Gododdin: The Oldest Scottish Poem* (Edinburgh, 1969).

——, 'Edinburgh and the Anglian occupation of Lothian', in *The Anglo-Saxons. Studies Presented to Bruce Dickins*, ed. P. Clemoes (London, 1959), 35–42.

——, 'The *Duan Albanach*', *SHR* 36 (1957) 125–37.

JAMES, M. R., trans., *The Apocryphal New Testament* (Oxford, 1924).

JENNINGS, ANDREW, 'An Historical Study of the Gael and Norse in Western Scotland from c.795 to c.1000' (unpublished Ph.D. dissertation, University of Edinburgh, 1994).

JEREMIAS, JOACHIM, *The Eucharistic Words of Jesus*, trans. of the 3rd edn of *Die Abendmahlsworte Jesu* (Göttingen, 1960, revd 1964), trans. N. Perrin (London, 1966).

JERVISE, A., *Land of the Lindsays* (2nd edn, Edinburgh, 1882).

Johannis de Fordun Chronica Gentis Scotorum, ed. W. F. Skene, Historians of Scotland vol. i (Edinburgh, 1871).

John of Fordun's Chronicle of the Scottish Nation, trans. Felix J. H. Skene, ed. and annotated W. F. Skene, Historians of Scotland vol. iv (Edinburgh, 1872).

Johnson's Journey to the Western Isles of Scotland, ed. R. Chapman (London, 1924).

JONES, A., 'St Matthew', in Orchard *et al.*, edd., *A Catholic Commentary*, 851–904

JOYCE, P. W., *Irish Names of Places*, 3 vols, vol. i (Dublin, 1869, repr. with new intro., Dublin, 1995).

KELLEHER, JOHN V., 'Early Irish history and pseudo-history', *Studia Hibernica* 3 (1963) 113–27.

KELLY, JOSEPH F., 'A catalogue of early medieval Hiberno-Latin biblical commentaries', (I) *Traditio* 44 (1988) 537–71; (II) *Traditio* 45 (1989–90) 393–434.

KENNEY, JAMES F., *The Sources for the Early History of Ireland: Ecclesiastical* (New York, 1929).

KINSELLA, T., *New Oxford Book of Irish Verse* (Oxford, 1986).

La châine palestiniènne sur le psaume 118, 2 vols, ed. M. Harl *SC* 189, 190 (Paris, 1972).

LANE, A., and CAMPBELL, E., 'The Pottery', in Haggarty, 'Iona: some results from recent work', 208–12.

LANG, M. B., *Whittingehame* (Edinburgh, 1929).

LAPIDGE, MICHAEL, ed., *Columbanus. Studies on the Latin Writings* (Woodbridge, 1997).

——, and SHARPE, RICHARD, *A Bibliography of Celtic-Latin Literature, 400–1200* (Dublin, 1985).

LAYZER, VARESE, 'The other dove: Jonah and Colum Cille', in Proceedings of the Hagiography Conference, University College Cork, 9–13 April, 1997 (forthcoming).

Lebor Bretnach, ed. A. G. Van Hamel (Dublin, [1932]).

Lebor na hUidre, edd. R. I. Best and Osborn Bergin (Dublin, 1929).

LEONARD, W., 'St John', in Orchard *et al.*, edd., *A Catholic Commentary*, 971–1017.

Liber Cartarum Prioratus Sancti Andree in Scotia, ed. Thomas Thomson (Bannatyne Club, 1841).

Liber Sancte Marie de Melros, ed. Cosmo Innes, 2 vols (Bannatyne Club, 1837).

Liber Vitae Ecclesiae Dunelmensis: A Collotype Facsimile of the Original Manuscript, with Introductory Essay and Notes, ed. A. H. Thompson (Surtees Society, 1923).

LIDDELL, A. A., *Pitlochry: Heritage of a Highland District* (Pitlochry, 1993).

The Life of Bishop Wilfrid by Eddius Stephanus, ed. B. Colgrave (Cambridge, 1927).

LORIMER, D., 'Human skeletal remains', in O'Sullivan, 'Excavation of a women's cemetery and early church', 327–65.

LOWE, C. E., 'Recent fieldwork on Iona', *Central Excavation Unit Annual Report 1988* (Scottish Development Department/Historic Buildings and Monuments: Edinburgh, 1988) 30.

LUCAS, A. T., 'The social role of relics and reliquaries in ancient Ireland', *JRSAI* 116 (1986) 5–37.

MACARTHUR, E. MAIRI, *Columba's Island. Iona from Past to Present* (Edinburgh, 1995).

——, *Iona* (Colin Baxter Island Guides, 1997).

——, *Iona. The Living Memory of a Crofting Community 1750–1914* (Edinburgh, 1990).

MCCORMICK, F., 'Excavations on Iona in 1988', *Ulster Journal of Archaeology* 56 (1993) 78–108.

——, 'Early Christian metalworking on Iona: excavations under the "Infirmary" in 1990', *PSAS* 122 (1992) 207–14.

——, 'Iona: the archaeology of an early monastery', in Bourke, ed., *Studies in the Cult of Saint Columba*, 45–68.

MACDONALD, A. D. S., 'Adomnan's monastery of Iona', in Bourke, ed., *Studies in the Cult of Saint Columba*, 24–44 .

——, 'Aspects of the monastery and monastic life in Adomnan's Life of Saint Columba', *Peritia* 3 (1984) 271–302.

——, 'Gaelic *Cill* (*Kil(l)-*) in Scottish Place-Names', *Bulletin of the Ulster Place-name Society*, series 2, vol. 2 (1979) 9–19.

MACGIBBON, D., and ROSS, T., *The Ecclesiastical Architecture of Scotland*, vol. 3 (Edinburgh, 1896–7).

MAC GIOLLA EASPAIG, D., 'Early ecclesiastical settlement names of County Galway' in G. Moran *et al.* edd., *Galway: History and Society* (Dublin, 1996), 795–815.

MCINTYRE, J. P., 'Optional priestly celibacy', *Studia Canonica* 29 (1995) 103–53.

MACKAY, W., 'Saints associated with the valley of the Ness', *Transactions of the Gaelic Society of Inverness* 27 (1908–11) 145–62.

——, *Urquhart and Glenmoriston* (Inverness, 1893).

MACKINLAY, J. M., *Ancient Church Dedications in Scotland: Non-scriptural* (Edinburgh, 1914).

MACKINLAY, J. M., *Folklore of Scottish Lochs and Springs* (Glasgow, 1893).

MACLEAN, D., 'Knapdale dedications to a Leinster saint', *Scottish Studies* 27 (1983) 49–65.

MCNAMARA, MARTIN, 'Psalter text and psalter study in the early Irish church (A.D. 600–1200)', *PRIA* 73 C (Dublin, 1973), 201–72.

——, 'Tradition and creativity in early Irish psalter study', in P. Ní Chatháin and M. Richter, edd. *Irland und Europa: die Kirche im Frühmittelalter* (Stuttgart, 1984), 338–89.

——, *Glossa in Psalmos. The Hiberno-Latin Gloss on Psalms of Codex Palatinus Latinus 68* (Ps 39.11–151.7), *Studi e Testi* 310 (Vatican, 1986).

MCNEIL, BRIAN, 'Jesus and the alphabet', *JTS* ns 27 (1976) 126–28.

MCNEILL, P. G. B., and MACQUEEN, H. L., edd., *Atlas of Scottish History to 1707* (Edinburgh, 1996).

MAC NIOCAILL, G., *The Medieval Irish Annals* (Dublin, 1975).

MACQUARRIE, ALAN, *The Saints of Scotland: Essays in Scottish Church History AD 450–1093* (Edinburgh, 1997).

——, 'Early Christian religious houses in Scotland', in Blair and Sharpe, edd., *Pastoral Care before the Parish* (Leicester, 1992), 110–33.

——, '*Vita Sancti Servani:* The Life of St Serf', *IR* 44 (1993) 122–52.

MACQUEEN, JOHN, *St Nynia* (revd edn, Edinburgh, 1990).

MCROBERTS, DAVID, 'A catalogue of Scottish medieval liturgical books and fragments', *IR* 3 (1952) 49–63.

MÁRKUS, GILBERT, 'What were Patrick's alphabets?', *CMCS* 31 (1996) 1–15.

——, *Adomnán's 'Law of the Innocents'* (Glasgow, 1997).

MARKUS, R. A., *Gregory the Great and his World* (Cambridge, 1997).

——, *Signs and Meanings. World and Text in Ancient Christianity* (Liverpool, 1996).

MARSDEN, JOHN, *Sea-Road of the Saints: Celtic Holy Men in the Hebrides* (Edinburgh, 1995).

The Martyrology of Donegal, edd. J. H. Todd and W. Reeves (Dublin, 1864).

The Martyrology of Gorman, ed. W. Stokes, The Henry Bradshaw Society, vol. 9 (London, 1895).

The Martyrology of Tallaght, edd. R. I. Best and H. J. Lawlor, Henry Bradshaw Society, vol. 68 (London, 1931).

MEEK, DONALD E., 'Gaelic: a future for the heritage', *Aberdeen University Review*, LVII, no. 197 (Spring, 1997) 13–18.

——, 'Modern Celtic Christianity', in Terence Brown, ed., *Celticism*, special issue of *Studia Imagologica: Amsterdam Studies on Cultural Identity*, 8 (Amsterdam and Atlanta, 1996), 143–57.

——, 'Modern Celtic Christianity: the contemporary "revival" and its roots', *Scottish Bulletin of Evangelical Theology* 10 (1992) 6–31.

——, 'Surveying the Saints: reflections on recent writings on "Celtic Christianity"', *Scottish Bulletin of Evangelical Theology* 15 (1997) 50–60.

——, ed., *The Campbell Collection of Gaelic Proverbs and Proverbial Sayings* (Inverness, 1978).

——, *The Quest for Celtic Christianity* (forthcoming).

MELIA, DAN, 'Law and the shamanic saint', in Patrick K. Ford, ed., *Celtic Folklore and Christianity: Studies in Memory of William W. Heist* (California, 1983), 113–28.

METCALFE, W. M., *Pinkerton's Lives of the Scottish Saints* (Paisley, 1889).

MEYER, KUNO, 'Mitteilungen aus irischen Handschriften', *ZCP* 12 (1918) 290–7.

——, *Cáin Adomnáin* (Oxford, 1905).

MILLER, MOLLY, 'Matriliny by treaty: the Pictish foundation-legend', in D. Whitelock *et al.*, edd., *Ireland in Early Mediaeval Europe* (Cambridge, 1982), 133–61.

——, 'The last century of Pictish succession', *Scottish Studies* 23 (1979) 39–67.

Monro's Western Isles of Scotland and Genealogy of the Clans 1549, ed. R.W. Munro (Edinburgh, 1961).

Monumenta Germaniae Historiae: Poetae Latini Aevi Carolini, ed. Ernst Dümmler, vol. 2 (Hanover, 1884).

MURPHY, GERARD, *Early Irish Lyrics* (Oxford, 1956).

NEIRYNCK, F., 'Synoptic problem', in R. E. Brown, J. A. Fitzmyer, and R. E. Murphy, edd., *The New Jerome Biblical Commentary* (London, 1989), 587–95.

NÍ CHATHÁIN, PRÓINSÉAS, and RICHTER, MICHAEL, edd., *Irland und Europa im früheren Mittelalter: Bildung und Literatur* (Stuttgart, 1996).

NÍ DHONNCHADHA, MÁIRÍN, 'The guarantor list of *Cáin Adomnáin*, 697', *Peritia* 1 (1982) 178–215.

——, 'The *Lex Innocentium*: Adomnán's Law for women, clerics and children, 697 AD', in Mary O'Dowd and Sabine Wichert, edd., *Chattel, Servant or Citizen: Women's Status in Church, State and Society* (Belfast, 1996), 58–69.

——, *Cáin Adomnáin* (forthcoming).

NICHOLSON, M. FORTHOMME, 'Celtic theology: Pelagius', in James P. Mackey, ed., *An Introduction to Celtic Christianity* (Edinburgh, 1989).

NICOLAISEN, W. F. H., *Scottish Place-Names* (London, 1976).

——, *Scottish Place-Names* (second impr. with additional information, London, 1979).

NORDENFALK, CARL, *Celtic and Anglo-Saxon Painting* (London, 1977).

Ó CORRÁIN, D., 'Nationality and kingship in pre-Norman Ireland', in T. W. Moody, ed., *Nationality and the Pursuit of National Independence* (Belfast, 1974), 1–36.

Ó CORRÁIN, D., 'The historical and cultural background of the Book of Kells' in F. O'Mahony, ed., *The Book of Kells* (Aldershot, 1994), 1–32.

Ó FLOINN, RAGHNALL, '*Insigniae Columbae* I', in Bourke, ed., *Studies in the Cult of St Columba*, 136–61.

Ó HÓGÁIN, DÁITHÍ, *Myth, Legend and Romance: An Encyclopaedia of the Irish Folk Tradition* (London, 1990).

Ó MURAÍLE, N., 'The Columban onomastic legacy', in Bourke, ed. *Studies in the Cult of St Columba*, 193–228.

Ó NÉILL, PÁDRAIG P., 'The date and authorship of *Apgitir Chrábaid*: some internal evidence', in P. Ní Chatháin and M. Richter, edd. *Irland und die Christenheit: Bibelstudien und Mission* (Stuttgart, 1987), 203–15.

Ó RIAIN, P., 'A misunderstood annal: a hitherto unnoted *cáin*', *Celtica* 21 (1990) 561–6.

Ó RIAIN, P., ed., *Corpus Genealogiarum Sanctorum Hiberniae* (Dublin, 1985).

O'FLYNN, J. A., 'St Mark', in Orchard *et al.*, edd., *A Catholic Commentary*, 905–34.

O'LOUGHLIN, T., 'Adam's burial at Hebron: some aspects of its significance in the Latin tradition', *Proceedings of the Irish Biblical Association* 15 (1992) 66–88.

——, 'Adomnán the illustrious', *IR* 46 (1995) 1–14.

——, 'Adomnán's *De locis sanctis*: a textual emendation and an additional source identification', *Ériu* 48 (1997) 37–40.

——, 'Biblical contradictions in the *Periphyseon* and the development of Eriugena's method', in G. Van Riel, C. Steel, and J. McEvoy, edd., *Iohannes Scottus Eriugena: The Bible and Hermeneutics* (Leuven, 1996), 103–26.

——, 'Julian of Toledo's Antikeimenon and the development of Latin exegesis', *Proceedings of the Irish Biblical Association* 16 (1993) 80–98.

——, 'Living in the Ocean', in Bourke, ed., *Studies in the Cult of Saint Columba*, 11–23.

——, 'The view from Iona: Adomnán's mental maps', *Peritia* 10 (1996) 98–122.

——, 'The controversy over Methuselah's death: proto-chronology and the origins of the Western concept of inerrancy', *Recherches de Théologie ancienne et médiévale* 62 (1995) 182–225.

——, 'The exegetical purpose of Adomnán's *De Locis Sanctis*', *CMCS* 24 (1992) 37–53.

——, 'The Latin version of the scriptures in use on Iona in the late seventh century: the evidence from Adomnán's *De Locis Sanctis*', *Peritia* 8 (1994) 18–26.

——, 'The library of Iona in the late-seventh century: the evidence from Adomnán's *De locis sanctis*', *Ériu* 45 (1994) 33–52.

——, 'Tyconius' use of the canonical gospels', *Revue Bénédictine* 106 (1996) 229–33.

——, 'Why Adomnán needs Arculf: the case of an expert witness', *Journal of Medieval Latin* 7 (1997) 127–46.

O'NEILL, TIMOTHY, 'Columba the scribe', in Bourke, ed., *Studies in the Cult of Saint Columba*, 69–79.

O'Rahilly, T. F., ed., *Measgra Dánta* (Cork, 1927).

——, *Early Irish History and Mythology* (Dublin, 1946).

O'Reilly, Jennifer, 'Exegesis and the Book of Kells: the Lucan genealogy' in Thomas Finan and Vincent Twomey, edd., *Scriptural Interpretation in the Fathers* (Dublin, 1995), 315–55.

——, 'Reading the Scriptures in the Life of Columba', in Bourke, ed., *Studies in the Cult of St Columba*, 80–106.

O'Sullivan, J., 'Excavation of a women's cemetery and early church at St. Ronan's medieval parish church, Iona', *PSAS* 124 (1994) 227–65.

——, 'Excavations on the mill stream, Iona', *PSAS* (1994) 491–508.

——, 'Reilig Odhrain, Iona', *Discovery & Excavation in Scotland* (1996) 35.

Orchard, Bernard, *et al.*, edd., *A Catholic Commentary on Holy Scripture* (London, 1953).

Origen on First Principles, trans. G. W. Butterworth (London, 1936).

Origines Parochiales Scotiae. The Antiquities, Ecclesiastical and Territorial, of the Parishes of Scotland, ed. Cosmo Innes and James B. Brichan, 2 vols in 3 (Bannatyne Club, 1851–5).

Peck, E. H., *Avonside Explored: A Guide to Tomintoul and Glenlivet* (revd edn, Tomintoul, 1989).

Penna, A., 'Il *De consensu euangelistarum* ed i Canoni Eusebiani', *Biblica* 36 (1955) 1–19.

The Philocalia of Origen, trans. G. Lewis (Edinburgh, 1911).

Picard, Jean-Michel, 'Structural patterns in early Hiberno-Latin hagiography', *Peritia* 4 (1985) 67–82.

——, 'Tailoring the sources: the Irish hagiographer at work' in Ní Chatháin and Richter, edd., *Irland und Europa im früheren Mittelalter: Bildung und Literatur*, 261–74

Plummer, Charles, *Bethada Náem nÉrenn: Lives of Irish Saints*, 2 vols (Oxford, 1922).

——, *Miscellanea Hagiographica Hibernica: vitae adhuc ineditae sanctorum Mac Creiche Neile Cranat* (Brussels, 1925).

Portalié, E., *A Guide to the Thought of St. Augustine* (Chicago, 1960; original French, 1902).

Preece, Isobel, programme notes to the Capella Nova CD, *Columba, Most Holy of Saints* (Gaudeamus, 1992).

PURSER, JOHN, *Scotland's Music: A History of the Traditional and Classical Music of Scotland from Earliest Times to the Present Day* (Edinburgh, 1992).

RAY, R. D., 'Augustine's *De Consensu Evangelistarum* and the historical education of the Venerable Bede', *Studia Patristica* 16 (1985) 557–63.

——, 'What do we known about Bede's commentaries?', *Recherches de Théologie Ancienne et Médiévale* 49 (1982) 5–20.

RCAHMS, *Argyll: An Inventory of the Monuments, Vol 4, Iona* (Edinburgh, 1982).

REDFORD, M., 'Commemorations of Saints of the Celtic Church in Scotland' (unpublished M.Litt. dissertation, University of Edinburgh, 1988)

REDKNAP, M., 'Excavation at Iona Abbey, 1976', *PSAS* 108 (1976–7) 228–53.

REECE, R., and WELLS, C., 'Martyr's Bay', in Reece, *Excavations on Iona, 1964–74*, 63–85.

——, 'Recent work on Iona', *Scottish Archaeological Forum* 5 (1973) 36–46.

——, *Excavations on Iona, 1964–74* (Institute of Archaeology Occasional Paper No. 5. University of London, 1981).

REEVES, W., ed., *Saint Adamnan, Abbot of Hy, Life of St. Columba, Founder of Hy*, Historians of Scotland 6 (Edinburgh, 1874; partial reprint, Felinfach, 1988).

Regesta Regum Scottorum vol. i, *Acts of Malcolm IV*, ed. G. W. S. Barrow (Edinburgh, 1960).

Regesta Regum Scottorum vol.ii, *Acts of William I*, ed. G. W. S. Barrow, with the collaboration of W. W. Scott (Edinburgh, 1971).

Registrum de Dunfermelyn, ed. Cosmo Innes (Bannatyne Club, 1842).

Registrum Episcopatus Glasguensis, ed. Cosmo Innes, 2 vols (Bannatyne and Maitland Clubs, 1843).

Registrum Episcopatus Moraviensis, ed. Cosmo Innes (Bannatyne Club, 1837).

Registrum Magni Sigilli, ed. J. M. Thomson *et al.* (Edinburgh, 1882–1914).

Registrum Monasterii S. Marie de Cambuskenneth, ed. Sir William Fraser (Grampian Club, 1872).

Rental Book of the Cistercian Abbey of Cupar Angus, ed. Charles Rogers, 2 vols (Grampian Club, 1879–80).

Rentale Dunkeldense, ed. F. C. Eeles (Scottish History Society, 1915).

RICHTER, MICHAEL, 'The European dimension of Irish history in the eleventh and twelfth centuries', *Peritia* 4 (1985) 328–45.

——, 'The personnel of learning in early medieval Ireland', in Ní Chatháin and Richter, edd., *Irland und Europa im früheren Mittelalter: Bildung und Literatur*, 275–308.

RITCHIE, A., *Iona* (London, 1997).

RITCHIE, J. N. G., and LANE, A., 'Dun Cul Bhuirg, Iona, Argyll', *PSAS* 110 (1978–80) 209–29.

ROBINSON, MARY, *Signatures on our own Frequency, Oraid Sabhal Mòr Ostaig 1997* (Ostaig, 1998).

ROLLASON, D. W., 'Lists of saints' resting places', *Anglo-Saxon England* 7 (1978) 61–93.

RONDEAU, MARIE-JOSEPHE, *Les commentaires patristiques du psautier III-Ve siècles*, ii (Rome, 1985).

——, 'L'épître a Marcellinus sur les psaumes', *Vigiliae Christianae* 22 (1968) 17–197.

ROSS, ANNE, *Pagan Celtic Britain* (London, 1967; repr. London, 1993).

ROUSSEAU, PHILIP, *Ascetics, Authority and the Church in the Age of Jerome and Cassian* (Oxford, 1978).

ROYAL IRISH ACADEMY, *Dictionary of the Irish Language* (Compact Edition, Dublin, 1983).

RYAN, JOHN, 'The *Cáin Adomnáin*', in R. Thurneysen, N. Power, *et al.*, *Studies in Early Irish Law* (Dublin, 1936) 269–76.

The S. Columba Commemoration, Iona (Edinburgh and London, 1897)

Saint Jérôme Lettres, ed. and trans. Jerome Labourt, 8 vols (Paris, 1949–63).

SALMON, PIERRE, *Les 'Tituli Psalmorum' des manuscrits latins, Collectanea Biblica Latine* 12 (Vatican, 1959).

San Isidoro de Seville. Etimologias, I, ed. J. O. Reta (Madrid, 1982).

SANDERS, J. N., '"Those whom Jesus loved" (Jn xi.5)', *New Testament Studies* 1 (1954) 29–41.

Sant' Ambrogio: Opere esegetiche VIII, ii, ed. L. F. Pizzolato (Milan/Rome, 1987).

Scotichronicon by Walter Bower in Latin and English, gen. ed. D. E. R. Watt, 9 vols (Aberdeen/Edinburgh, 1987–98) i (1993), edd. John and Winifred MacQueen; ii (1989), edd. John and Winifred MacQueen; vii (1996) edd. A. B. Scott and D. E. R. Watt, with Ulrike Morét and Norman F. Shead.

SELLAR, W. D. H., 'Sueno's Stone and its interpreters', in W. D. H. Sellar, ed., *Moray, Province and People* (Edinburgh, 1993), 97–116.

——, 'Warlords, holy men and matrilineal succession', *IR* 36 (1985) 29–43.

Series Episcoporum Ecclesiae Catholicae Occidentalis Series VI, vol. i *Ecclesia Scoticana*, ed. D. E. R. Watt *et al.* (Stuttgart, 1991).

SHARPE, RICHARD, 'Hiberno-Latin *laicus*, Irish *láech* and the devil's men', *Ériu* 30 (1979) 75–92.

——, *Adomnán of Iona: Life of Columba* (Harmondsworth, 1995).

SIMPSON, RAY, *Exploring Celtic Spirituality: Historic Roots for our Future* (London, 1995).

SINCLAIR, SIR JOHN, ed., *The Statistical Account of Scotland*, 12 vols (Edinburgh, 1791–9), repr. with general intro. by Donald J. Withrington and additional introductory material by Ian R. Grant, 20 vols (Wakefield, 1983).

SKENE, W. F., *Celtic Scotland: A History of Ancient Alban*, 3 vols (Edinburgh, 1876–80).

——, *Chronicles of the Picts, Chronicles of the Scots, and other early memorials of Scottish History* (Edinburgh, 1867).

——, 'Notes on the history and probable situation of the earlier establishments at Iona', *PSAS* 11 (1874–6) 330–49.

SMITH, J. A., 'Notes on medieval kitchen middens recently discovered in the monastery and the nunnery on the Island of Iona', *PSAS* 12 (1876–7) 103–17.

SMYTH, A. P., *Warlords and Holy Men: Scotland 80–1000* (London, 1984).

STACEY, ROBIN CHAPMAN, *The Road to Judgment: from Custom to Court in Medieval Ireland and Wales* (Philadelphia, 1994).

STANCLIFFE, C., 'Early "Irish" biblical exegesis', *Studia Patristica* XII (1975) 361–70.

——, 'The thirteen sermons attributed to Columbanus and the question of their authorship', in Lapidge, ed., *Columbanus. Studies on the Latin Writings*, 93–202.

Stancliffe, C., and Cambridge, E., edd., *Oswald: Northumbrian King to European Saint* (Stamford, 1995).

Stevenson, D., 'The travels of Richard James in Scotland c.1615', *Northern Scotland* 7 (1986) 13–18.

Stevenson, Jane, 'Irish hymns, Venantius Fortunatus and Poitiers', in Jean-Michel Picard, ed. *Aquitaine and Ireland in the Middle Ages* (Dublin, 1995), 81–110.

——, 'Literacy in Ireland: the evidence of the Patrick dossier in the Book of Armagh', in Rosamond McKitterick, ed., *The Uses of Literacy in Early Medieval Europe* (Cambridge, 1990), 11–35.

Stevenson, R. B. K., 'A hoard of Anglo-Saxon coins found at Iona Abbey', *PSAS* 85 (1950–1) 170–75.

Stokes, Whitley, *Félire Óengusso: The Martyrology of Oengus the Culdee* (London, 1905, repr. Dublin, 1984).

——, *Lives of the Saints from the Book of Lismore* (Oxford, 1890, repr. Felinfach, 1995).

——, 'The Bodleian *Amra Choluimb Chille*', *Revue Celtique* 20 (1899) 31–55, 132–83, 248–89, 400–37.

Stone, J., *Illustrated Maps of Scotland, from Blaeu's Atlas Novus of the Seventeenth Century* (London, 1991).

Straw, Carole, *Gregory the Great: Perfection in Imperfection* (Berkeley, 1988).

Sutcliffe, E. F., 'Quotations in the Venerable Bede's commentary on S. Mark', *Biblica* 7 (1926) 428–39.

Taylor, S., 'Columba East of Drumalban', in L. Breatnach, C. Etchingham, C. Swift, edd., *Columba and his Churches* (forthcoming).

——, 'Place-names and the early Church in Eastern Scotland', in Crawford, ed., *Scotland in Dark Age Britain*, 93–110.

——, 'Settlement-Names in Fife' (unpublished Ph.D. dissertation, University of Edinburgh, 1995).

Thacker, Alan, 'Lindisfarne and the origins of the cult of St Cuthbert', in G. Bonner, D. Rollason and C. Stancliffe, edd., *St Cuthbert, his Cult and his Community to AD 1200* (Woodbridge, 1989), 103–22.

Thomas, C., 'Excavations on Iona, 1956 and 1957', *The Coracle* 31 (1957) 10–14.

——, 'Iona', *Discovery and Excavation in Scotland* (1957) 10.

THOMAS, C., *The Early Christian Archaeology of North Britain* (Oxford, 1971).

THURNEYSEN, R., 'Synchronismen der irischen Könige', *ZCP* 19 (1931–2) 81–99.

TODD, J. M., 'St Bega: cult, fact and legend', *Transactions of the Cumberland & Westmorland Antiquarian & Archaeological Society* 80 (1980) 25–35.

TORJESEN, KAREN, 'Origen's interpretation of the psalms', *Studia Patristica* XVII. 2 (1982) 944–58.

Two Lives of St Cuthbert, ed. and trans. Bertram Colgrave (Cambridge, 1940).

VAN DAM, RAYMOND, *Saints and their Miracles in Late Antique Gaul* (Princeton, 1993).

VEITCH, KENNETH, 'The Columban Church in northern Britain AD 664–717: a re-assessment', *PSAS* 127 (1998) 1–43.

Vita Sancti Columbae, Auctore Adamnano, Monasterii Hiensis Abbate. The Life of Columba, founder of Hy; written by Adamnan, ninth abbot of that monastery, ed. William Reeves (Dublin, 1857).

VITZ, E. B., 'From the oral to the written in medieval and renaissance saints' Lives', in R. Blumenfeld-Kosinski and T. Szell, edd., *Images of Sainthood in Medieval Europe* (London, 1991), 97–114.

WAINWRIGHT, F. T., 'The Picts and the problem', in F. T. Wainwright, ed., *The Problem of the Picts* (Perth, 1955), 1–53.

WALKER, G. S. M., *Sancti Columbani Opera* (Dublin, 1957).

WALLACE-HADRILL, M., *Early Germanic Kingship in England and on the Continent* (Oxford, 1971).

WALSH, MAURA, and Ó CRÓINÍN, DÁIBHÍ, *Cummian's Letter* De Controversia Paschali *and the* De Ratione Conputandi, Pontifical Institute of Medieval Studies, Studies and Texts 86 (Toronto, 1988).

WALSH, P. G., *Cassiodorus: Explanations of the Psalms, Ancient Christian Writers* 51–3 (New York, 1990–1).

WARD, BENEDICTA, *The Sayings of the Desert Fathers. The Alphabetical Collection* (Oxford, 1975).

——, *Bede and the Psalter* (Jarrow Lecture, 1991).

WATSON, W. J., *Scottish Poetry from the Book of the Dean of Lismore* (Edinburgh, 1937).

WATSON, W. J., *The Celtic Place-Names of Scotland* (Edinburgh, 1926).

——, 'The place-names of Breadalbane', *Transactions of the Gaelic Society of Inverness* 34 (1927–8) 248–79.

WILLIAMS, M., 'Non-Celtic Place-names of the Scottish Border Counties' (unpublished Ph.D. dissertation, University of Edinburgh, 1943).

WOODS, ISOBEL, '"Our Awin Scottis Use": chant usage in medieval Scotland', *Journal of the Royal Musical Association* 112 (1987) 21–37.

WORMALD, P., 'The emergence of the *regnum Scottorum*: a Carolingian hegemony?', in Crawford, ed., *Scotland in Dark Age Britain*, 131–60.

WRIGHT, NEIL, 'Columbanus's *Epistulae*', in Lapidge, ed., *Columbanus. Studies on the Latin Writings*, 29–92.

YOUNG, FRANCES, *Biblical Exegesis and the Formation of Christian Culture* (Cambridge, 1997).

Index